Breaking Night

Breaking Night

A Memoir of Forgiveness, Survival, and My Journey from Homeless to Harvard

LIZ MURRAY

hachette
BOOKS

NEW YORK   BOSTON

Hachette Books
Hachette Book Group
1290 Avenue of the Americas
New York, NY 10104

www.HachetteBookGroup.com

Printed in the United States of America

RRD-C

Originally published in hardcover by Hyperion.
First Hachette Books hardcover edition: February 2015

20 19 18 17 16 15 14 13 12 11 10

Hachette Books is a division of Hachette Book Group, Inc.
The Hachette Books name and logo are trademarks of Hachette Book Group, Inc.

The Hachette Speakers Bureau provides a wide range of authors for speaking events. To find out more,
go to www.hachettespeakersbureau.com or call (866) 376-6591.

The publisher is not responsible for websites (or their content) that are not owned by the publisher.

Book Design by Karen Minster

Library of Congress Cataloging-in-Publication Data has been applied for.

ISBN 978-0-7868-6891-9

This book is dedicated to three people
whose love made it possible.

TO EDWIN FERMIN, for the years behind us, for the years ahead of us, side-by-side. Thank you for taking care of my father when we needed you. Thank you for sharing your dreams with me and for being my family. Thank you for being my no-matter-what. When I look at all the good in my life, inside all of it, I see you.

TO ARTHUR FLICK, for the fishing trips, the motorcycle rides, the camping and each one of our adventures that I will always cherish. Thank you for being my Guardian Angel and my heart's compass. You were right, Arthur, you do get to choose your family.

TO ROBIN DIANE LYNN—a Trusting, Powerful and Giving woman. Robin, you are a beautiful soul and the embodiment of contribution. This world was blessed to have you in it. Because of you, so many of us are blessed still. Thank you for showing me what it looks like to stand in a commitment, come what may.

"Don't let what you cannot do interfere with what you can do."
—COACH JOHN WOODEN

* ✦ *

Those who wish to sing always find a song.
—SWEDISH PROVERB

"Breaking Night"

URBAN SLANG FOR:
staying up through the night,
until the sun rises.

Breaking Night

Prologue

I HAVE JUST ONE PICTURE LEFT OF MY MOTHER. IT'S 4×7, BLACK-and-white, and creased in different places. In it, she is seated slightly hunched, elbows touching knees, arms carrying the weight of her back. I know very little about her life when it was taken; my only clue is written in orange marker on the back. It reads: *Me in front of Mike's on 6th St. 1971.* Counting backward, I know that she was seventeen when it was taken, a year older than I am now. I know that Sixth Street is in Greenwich Village, though I have no idea who Mike is.

The picture tells me that she was a stern-looking teenager. Her lips are pressed together in thought, offering a grimace for the camera. Framing her face, her hair dangles in beautiful wisps of black, smokelike curls. And her eyes, my favorite part, shine like two dark marbles, their movements frozen in time forever.

I've studied each feature, committing them to memory for my trips to the mirror, where I let my own wavy hair tumble down. I stand and trace similarities with the tip of my finger through the curve of each line in my face, starting with our eyes. Each pair offers the same small, rounded shape, only instead of my mother's brown, I have Grandma's rich yellow-green. Next, I measure the outline of our lips; thin, curvy, and identical in every way. Although we share some features, I know I'm not as pretty as she was at my age.

In my years with nowhere to live, behind the locked bathroom doors in different friends' apartments, I've secretly played this game in the mirror throughout all hours of the night. Tucked in by their parents, my friends sleep while images of my mother's graceful movements dance throughout my mind. I spend these hours in front of their bathroom mirrors, my bare feet cooled by gridded tiles, palms pressed on the sink's edge to support my weight.

I stand there fantasizing until the first blue hints of dawn strain through the frosted bathroom glass and birds announce themselves, chirping their morning songs. If I'm at Jamie's house, this is just the time to slip onto the couch before her mother's alarm beeps her awake, sending her to the bathroom. If I'm at Bobby's, the grinding noise of the garbage truck tells me it's time to sneak back to the foldout cot.

I travel quietly across their waking apartments to my resting spot. I never get too comfortable with my accommodations, because I'm not sure if I will sleep in the same place tomorrow.

Lying on my back, I run my fingertips over my face in the dark, and I envision my mother. The symmetry of our lives has become clearer to me lately. She was homeless at sixteen too. Ma also dropped out of school. Like me, Ma made daily decisions between hallway or park, subway or rooftop. The Bronx, for Ma, also meant wandering through dangerous streets, through neighborhoods with lampposts littered with flyers of police sketches and sirens blaring at all hours of the night.

I wonder if, like me, Ma spent most days afraid of what would happen to her. I'm afraid all the time lately. I wonder where I will sleep tomorrow—at another friend's apartment, on the train, or in some stairwell?

Tracing my fingertips over my forehead, down to my lips, I long to feel my mother's warm body embracing me again. The thought sends tears streaming from my eyes. I turn to my side, wiping my tears away, covering myself with my borrowed blanket.

I push the feeling of needing her far out of my mind. I push it beyond these walls lined with Bobby's family portraits; past the drunken Latino men just outside, slamming down winning hands of dominoes, seated atop milk crates on Fordham Road; away from the orange blinking lights of the bodegas and over the rooftops of this Bronx neighborhood. I force my thoughts to fade until the details of her face blur. I need to push them away if I am ever to get some sleep. I need sleep; it will be only a few more hours before I'm outside on the street again, with nowhere to go.

Ma, 6th Street, Greenwich Village, 1971

CHAPTER 1

University Avenue

THE FIRST TIME DADDY FOUND OUT ABOUT ME, IT WAS FROM BEHIND glass during a routine visit to prison, when Ma lifted her shirt, teary-eyed, exposing her pregnant belly for emphasis. My sister, Lisa, then just over one year old, sat propped against Ma's hip.

Reflecting on this time in her life, Ma would later explain, "It wasn't supposed to turn out that way, pumpkin. It wasn't like me and Daddy planned for this."

Even though she'd been on her own and in trouble with drugs since age thirteen, Ma insisted, "Daddy and me were gonna turn around. Somewhere down the line, we were gonna be like other people. Daddy was gonna get a real job. I was gonna be a court stenographer. I had dreams."

Ma used coke, shooting dissolved white dust into her veins; it traveled through her body much like lightning, igniting her, giving the *feel*, however fleeting, of something forward-moving, day in and day out.

"A lift," she called it.

She started using as a teenager; her own home had been a place of anger, violence, and abuse.

"Grandma was just nuts, Lizzy. Pop would come home drunk and beat the crap out of us, with anything—extension cords, sticks, whatever. She would just go clean the kitchen, humming, like nothing was happening. Then just act like Mary-friggin-Poppins five minutes later, when we were all busted up."

The oldest of four children, Ma often spoke of the guilt she harbored for finally leaving the abuse—and her siblings—behind. She went out on the streets when she was just thirteen.

"I couldn't stay there, not even for Lori or Johnny. At least they had mercy on Jimmy and took him away. Man, you bet your ass I had to get out of there. Being under a *bridge* was better, and *safer*, than being there."

I had to know what it was Ma did under bridges.

"Well, I dunno, pumpkin, me and my friends all hung out and talked . . . about life. About our lousy parents. About how we were better off. We talked . . . and I guess we got high, and after that, it didn't matter where we were."

Ma started out small, smoking grass and sniffing glue. During the years of her adolescence, moving between friends' couches and earning her living through teen prostitution and odd jobs like bike messengering, she moved on to speed and heroin.

"The Village was a wild place, Lizzy. I had these thick, tall leather boots. And I didn't care if I was skinny as hell; I wore short shorts and a cape down my back. Yeah, that's right, a cape. I was cool, too. *Jivin', man*. That's how we used to talk. Pumpkin, you should have seen me."

By the time Ma met Daddy, coke had become a popular seventies trend, alongside hip-huggers, muttonchops, and disco music. Ma described Daddy at the time they first hooked up as "dark, handsome, and smart as hell."

"He just got things, ya know? When most of the guys I hung around didn't know their ass from their elbow, your father had something about him. I guess you could say he was *sharp*."

Daddy came from a middle-class, Irish Catholic family in the suburbs. His father was a shipping boat captain and a violent alcoholic. His mother was a hardworking and willful woman who refused to put up with what she called "foolishness" from men.

"All you need to know about your grandfather, Lizzy, is that he was a nasty, violent drunk who liked to bully people," Daddy once told me, "and your grandmother didn't tolerate it. She didn't care how unpopular divorce was back then, she got herself one." Unfortunately for Daddy, when his parents' marriage ended, his father left him, and he never came back.

"He was a real piece of work, Lizzy. It's probably better he wasn't around, things weren't easy and he only would have made them worse."

People who knew Daddy when he was growing up describe him as a lonely child and a "hurt soul" who never seemed to get over his father's abandonment and his resulting status as "latchkey kid." His mother took on a demanding full-time job to make ends meet and she worked long hours while Daddy was mostly alone, searching for an outlet, someone or something to connect with. Most nights, he spent evenings by himself, or in the homes of friends, where he became a fixture in other people's families. Back at his house, he and Grandma grew distant, and things were mostly serious and silent between them.

"Your grandmother wasn't the talkative type," he told me one day, "which was very Irish Catholic of her. In our family, if you said the words 'I feel,' they better be followed with 'hungry' or 'cold.' Because we didn't get personal, that's just how it was."

But what Grandma lacked in warmth, she made up for in her tireless devotion to securing her son's future. Determined not to let Daddy suffer from the absence of his father, Grandma set out to give him the best education she could afford. She worked two bookkeeping jobs in order to put her only child through the best Catholic schools on Long Island. At Chaminade, a school with a reputation for being rigorous and elite, Daddy shared classes and a social life with a more well-to-do crowd than he'd ever known existed. Most of his classmates were given new cars as gifts on their sixteenth birthdays, while Daddy took two buses to school, his mother praying that the monthly tuition check wouldn't clear through the bank before her paycheck did.

The irony was, as much as this upper-class, private school setting was meant to position Daddy for a life of success, instead, it would put my father at odds with himself forever: in this environment he became both well-educated and a drug addict.

Throughout his late teen years, Daddy read the great American classics; vacationed in his classmates' beachfront summer homes, ignoring his mother's incessant phone calls; and as a pastime, popped amphetamines beneath the bleachers of the high school football field.

Though he'd always been quick to learn and absorbed much of his rigorous education, the drugs made it hard to concentrate in school, so he slacked on homework and dozed in class. In his last year, Daddy applied and was admitted to a college located right in the heart of New York City. When graduation rolled around, he just barely squeaked by. Manhattan was meant to be his real start in life, college his springboard. But it wasn't long before his high school setting recast itself around him, except now he was older and not in the suburbs of Baldwin, New York, but in the center of everything. In a few years' time, Daddy came to apply his aptitude more toward peddling drugs than his college work. Slowly, he rose to the top ranks of a small clique of drug pushers. Being the most educated member of the group, he was nicknamed "the professor," and was looked to for guidance. He was the one who drew blueprints for the group's schemes.

Daddy abandoned school when he was two years into a graduate degree in psychology, a time during which he also gained some experience in social work, earning slightly above minimum wage. But the upkeep involved maintaining two very separate lives—a legitimate attempt at the "straight life" versus the "high life"—required too much effort. His lucrative drug earnings had a gravity far too powerful; it simply outweighed what an average life seemed to offer. So he rented an East Village apartment and worked full-time in the drug trade, surrounded by odd, lower-Manhattan types with criminal records and gang affiliations—his "crew." It so happened that Ma was hitting the same scene, right around this same time, floating in the same offbeat crowd.

Years down the line, they connected at a mutual friend's loft apartment. Speed and coke were distributed as casually as soft drinks, and people discoed the night away surrounded by soft glowing lava lamps, the air perfumed by incense. They'd met a few times before, when Daddy'd dealt Ma speed or heroin. Coming from the streets, Ma's first impressions of Daddy were something like an encounter with a movie star.

"You just had to see the way your father worked the room," she'd tell me. "He called all the shots, commanded respect." When they hooked up, Ma was twenty-two and Daddy was thirty-four. Ma dressed for the seventies, in flower-child blouses and nearly invisible short-shorts. Daddy described her as radiant and wild-looking with long, wavy black hair and bright, piercing amber eyes. Daddy said he took one look at her and loved her innocence, yet also her toughness and her intensity. "She was unpredictable," he said. "You couldn't tell if she was calculating or totally naïve. It was like she could go either way."

They connected immediately, and in many ways became like any other new couple, passionate and eager to be with each other. But instead of taking in movies or hitting restaurants, shooting up was their common ground. They used getting high to find intimacy. Slowly, Ma and Daddy abandoned their crowds to be together, taking long walks down Manhattan streets, clasping hands, warming up to each other. They carried small baggies of cocaine and bottles of beer to Central Park, where they perched on hilltops to sprawl out in the moonlight and get high, anchored in each other's arms.

If my parents' lives had held different degrees of promise before they met, it didn't take long for their paths to run entirely parallel. The premature start of our family leveled them, when they began living together in early 1977. Lisa, my older sister, was born in February 1978, when Ma was twenty-three.

In Lisa's infancy, my parents initiated one of Daddy's more lucrative drug scams. The plot involved faking the existence of a doctor's office in order to legitimize the purchase of prescription painkillers that Daddy said were "strong enough to knock out a horse." Typically reserved for cancer patients on hospice, just one of the tiny pills had a street value of fifteen dollars. On his graduate student clientele alone, Daddy could use phony prescriptions to unload hundreds of these pills per week, earning Ma and Daddy thousands of dollars every month.

Daddy went through great pains to avoid getting caught. Patience and attention to detail would keep them out of jail, he insisted. "It had to be done *right*," he said. Meticulously, Daddy used the phone book along with maps of all five boroughs of New York City to carefully create a schedule of pharmacies they would hit systematically, week by week. The riskiest part of the scam, by far, was actually walking into the pharmacy to collect on a prescription, a task made riskier by the pharmacist's legal obligation to phone doctors and verify all "scripts" for pain pills as strong as these.

Daddy devised a way to intercept pharmacists' calls. The phone company at the time didn't verify doctors' credentials, so Daddy frequently ordered and abandoned new phone numbers under names he picked out of thin air, or sometimes he drew ideas from his former professors, Dr. Newman, Dr. Cohen, and Dr. Glasser. The pharmacists did indeed reach a doctor at the other end of their phone calls; a secretary even patched them through. But really it was only Ma and Daddy working together as a team. They worked long days, utilizing rent-by-the-week rooms in flophouses across New York City while friends cared for Lisa, who at that time was only a few months old.

The prescriptions themselves Daddy created with the help of his crew. He gave friends in a printing shop a cut of his profits in exchange for an ongoing supply of illegal, custom-made rubber stamps bearing the names of the phony doctors and a supply of legitimate-looking prescription pads. With the help of his connections, and for the cost of twenty-five dollars per pad, Daddy transformed blank prescriptions into gold, a stamp-by-stamp moneymaking machine. By design, Daddy said, his plan was "airtight" and would have con-tinued to work if not for Ma's slipup.

Though he did claim responsibility for at least half of the mistake, admit-ting, "We never should have been using from our own supply, that's a rookie move. Getting hooked on your own stash fogs your head, makes you des-perate."

But there was no way to tell whether it was Ma's addiction that made her desperate enough to ignore the obvious red flag, or if it was simply Ma's typical impatience. Daddy had been careful to warn Ma of the signs that a pharmacist was onto you: surely, if you dropped off a prescription for highly suspicious pain meds at a pharmacy one entire day prior, there could only be one reason for a pharmacist to instruct you to wait twenty additional minutes when you arrived—he was calling the police, and you should get out of there as fast as possible. Daddy had warned Ma of this scenario, made it perfectly clear.

But on the day of her arrest, Ma, who was known for being relentless and never backing down from something she wanted, would later explain, "I just couldn't not come back, Lizzy. There was a chance he was gonna give me the pills, ya know? I had to try." She was handcuffed in broad daylight and marched unceremoniously into a nearby police cruiser by an officer who had responded to the call hoping (correctly) that he would catch the criminals responsible for hitting countless pharmacies throughout the five boroughs. Unknowingly, Ma was already pregnant with me.

For over a year, the Feds had been compiling evidence that included a paper trail and a string of security camera footage that undeniably linked Ma and Daddy to nearly every pharmacy hit. If that wasn't enough, when the Feds kicked in the door to arrest Daddy, they found bags of cocaine and dozens of pills littered across the tabletop of their East Village apartment, along with luxury items like a closetful of mink furs, dozens of leather shoes, leather coats, gold jewelry, thousands of dollars in cash, and even a glass tank holding an enormous Burmese python.

Daddy, who had orchestrated and executed the majority of their illegal activities, was hit with numerous counts of fraud, including impersonating a doctor. On his day in court, for dramatic effect, the prosecution wheeled into the courthouse three shopping carts brimming with prescriptions, all of which bore Daddy's handwriting and fraudulent stamps. "Anything to say for yourself, Mr. Finnerty?" the judge asked. "No, Your Honor," he said. "I think that speaks for itself."

In all of this, they almost lost custody of Lisa permanently, but Ma maintained strict attendance in a parental reform program in the months between her arrest and her eventual sentencing. This, combined with a very pregnant belly on her day in court, solicited just enough leniency to get her set free.

Daddy wasn't so lucky. He received a three-year sentence. He was transported from holding to Passaic County Jail in Patterson, New Jersey, the day Ronald Reagan was elected president.

On the day Ma was to be sentenced, she brought with her two cartons of cigarettes and a roll of quarters, certain that she would do time. But in a move that surprised everyone in the courthouse, right down to Ma's lawyer, the judge looked her over with pity, then merely ordered probation and called the next case.

The bail money, one thousand dollars—the very last of my parents' earnings from their heyday—was released to her in a check on her way out the door.

Check in hand, Ma saw an opportunity to start over, and she took it. The bail went for cans of fresh paint, thick curtains, and wall-to-wall carpeting for every room in our three-bedroom Bronx apartment on University Avenue, in what would soon become one of the most crime-ridden areas in all of New York City.

I was born on the first day of autumn, at the end of a long heat wave that had the neighborhood kids forcing open the fire hydrants for relief, and had Ma lodging loud, buzzing fans in every window. On the afternoon of September 23, 1980, Daddy—in holding, but awaiting his sentence—received a phone call from Charlotte, my mother's mother, informing him that his daughter had been born, with drugs in her system but no birth defects. Ma hadn't been careful during either pregnancy, but both Lisa and I were lucky. I peed all over the nurse and was declared healthy at nine pounds, three ounces.

"She looks like you, Peter. Has your face."

From his cell later that night, Daddy named me Elizabeth. Because Daddy and Ma were never legally married and he wasn't there to verify paternity, I got Ma's last name, Murray.

A new crib in my own freshly decorated nursery awaited me at home. Ma never got over the look on her caseworker's face when she arrived to check on us. Lisa and I were dressed in brand-new clothing, the apartment was spotless, and the fridge was packed with food. Ma beamed proudly and received a glowing report. She was issued steady income from welfare to take care of us, and we started on our new beginning, as a family.

The next few years were mapped by Ma's solo visits to Daddy, and her efforts to gain assistance in her role as a newly sober, single parent. Once in a while, through the side door of nearby Tolentine Church, a nun passed Ma free bricks of American cheese and oversized tubs of salt-free peanut butter that came with loaves of uncut bread in long, brown paper bags. With packages filling her arms, Ma would stand still for the sister while she waved the sign of the cross over the three of us. Only then were we allowed to go, Lisa helping to push my stroller along.

These supplies, along with raisin packets and oatmeal, were what we had for breakfasts and snacks. Down at Met Food supermarket, pork hot dogs were only ninety-nine cents for a pack of eight. Dinners were these discount franks cut into thick slices, with warm scoops of boxed macaroni and cheese.

When it came to clothing, although we'd never met her, Daddy's mother helped us. On holidays she mailed packages from a place called Long Island, where Daddy said the streets were lined with beautiful houses. The boxes were reused from bulk purchases of paper towels or bottled water, but they carried treasure inside. Under layers of newspaper, we found bright clothing, small kitchen supplies, and freshly baked, sweet-smelling walnut brownies in decorative tins, which collected in a clumsy stack next to the "no-frills" cans in our kitchen cabinet. Polite little notes written in careful script—which Ma never bothered to read—came pinned to the opening cardboard flap, sometimes with a crisp five-dollar bill taped neatly inside.

Ma threw away the notes, but kept the money wrapped in a rubber band in a small red box on the dresser. Whenever the wad grew thick enough, she took us to McDonald's for Happy Meals. For herself, she picked up packs of Winston cigarettes, beer in tall, dark bottles, and Muenster cheese.

When I was three years old, Daddy fanned out his release papers beside me on the king-sized mattress in my parents' room. I stared up in wonder at the sound of a man's voice in the apartment; at the way Ma moved gingerly around him in the afternoon sunlight. His movements were quick and impatient, making it hard to focus on the features of his face.

"*I'm your fath-er,*" he enunciated loudly from under his newsboy cap, as though his sternness should impact my understanding.

Instead, I hid behind my mother's legs and cried softly in confusion. That night, I spent the evening alone in my own bed, rather than beside Ma. My parents, together for the first time in my life, were muddled voices rising and falling unpredictably through the thick door that separated our rooms.

In the months that followed, Ma grew more laid-back about keeping up with things. Chores were neglected; dirty dishes sat untouched for days in the kitchen sink. She took us to the park less often. I sat at home for hours waiting to be swept up in Ma's activities, and couldn't understand why they no longer included me. Feeling pushed out by these changes, I became determined to find my way back to her.

I learned that Ma and Daddy shared strange habits together, the full details of which were hidden from me. Ritualistically, they would spread spoons and other objects along the kitchen table in some kind of urgent preparation. Over the display, they communicated in quick, brief commands to each other. Water was needed—a small amount from the faucet—and so were shoelaces and belts. I was not supposed to bother them, but observing their busy hands from a distance was allowed. From the doorway, I often watched, trying to understand the meaning behind their activity. But each time Ma and Daddy were done setting the strange objects across the table, at the very last minute, one of them would close the kitchen door, blocking my view entirely.

This remained a mystery until one summer evening when I parked myself in my stroller (which I would use until it finally gave under my weight) in front of the kitchen. When the door was closed to me again, I didn't budge from where I sat, but remained and waited. I watched roaches weaving their way in and out of the door crack—a recent addition to the apartment since Ma had stopped cleaning regularly—while each minute dragged by. When Ma finally emerged, her face was tense, her lips pursed together.

Sensing that they had finished, I said something that would be retold to me in story form for years.

I raised my arms into the air, and gave a singsong, "Al-l-l do-ne."

Taken off guard, Ma paused, leaned in and asked disbelievingly, "What did you say, pumpkin?"

"Al-l-l done," I repeated, delighted at Ma's sudden interest.

She yelled for Daddy. "Peter, she knows! Look at her, she understands!"

He laughed a light laugh and went about his business. Ma remained there at my side, stroking my hair. "Pumpkin, what do you know?"

Thrilled to have found my place in their game, I made a habit of seating myself in front of the kitchen each time they retreated inside.

Eventually, they left the door open.

By the time I was almost five years old, we had become a functional, government-dependent family of four. The first of the month, the day Ma's stipend from welfare was due, held all the ritual and celebration of Christmas morning. Our collective anticipation of the money filled the apartment with a kind of electricity, guaranteeing that Ma and Daddy would be agreeable and upbeat for at least twenty-four hours each month. It was my parents' one consistency.

The government gave the few hundred dollars monthly to those who, for one reason or another, were unable to work for a living—although I often saw our able-bodied neighbors crowded beside the mailboxes, eagerly watching as they were stuffed with the thin, blue envelopes. Ma, who was legally blind due to a degenerative eye disease she'd had since birth, happened to be one of SSI's legitimate recipients. I know, because I went with her the day she interviewed to qualify.

The woman behind the desk told her that she was so blind that if she ever drove a car, she would "probably end the life of every living thing in her path."

Then she shook Ma's hand and congratulated her both for qualifying and for her ability to successfully cross the street.

"Sign right here. You can expect your checks on the first of every month."

And we did. In fact, there was nothing our family looked forward to more than Ma's check. The mailman's arrival had a domino effect, setting the whole day, and our treasured ritual, in motion. It was my job to lean my head out of my bedroom window, which faced the front, and to call out any sighting of the mailman to Ma and Daddy.

"Lizzy, let me know when you see *any* sign of him. Remember, look *left*."

If Ma could know a few minutes earlier that he was coming, she could grab her welfare ID out of the junk drawer, snatch her check from the mailbox, and be the first in line at the check-cashing store. The role I played in those days became an invaluable part of the routine.

Elbows jutting behind me, I would clutch the rusted window guard and extend my neck as far as possible into the sun, over and over again throughout the morning. The task gave me a sense of importance. When I saw the blue uniform appear over the hill—an urban Santa Claus pushing his matching cart—I could not wait to announce him. In the meantime, I'd listen to the sound of my parents waiting.

Ma in her oversize worry chair, picking out yellow stuffing.

"Damn. Damn. He's dragging his ass."

Daddy going over the details of their plans a hundred times, pacing, weaving circles in the air as though to somehow shorten the feel of his wait.

"Okay, Jeanie, we're going to stop off to buy coke, then we take care of the electric bill with Con Edison. Then we can get a half pound of bologna for the kids. And I need money for tokens."

The moment I spotted the mailman, I could tell them the very second I knew, or I could wait just a little longer. It was the difference between having their attention and giving it away—relinquishing the one moment when I was as significant as they were, as necessary as the mailman or even the money itself. But I could never hold back; the moment I saw him round the corner, I'd shout, "He's coming! I see him! He's coming!" Then we could all move on to the next stage of our day.

Behind the gaudy glass storefront of the check-cashing place, there was something for everyone. Children gravitated to the twenty-five-cent machines, a row of clear boxes on metal poles with toys jumbled inside. They waited impatiently for quarters to free the plastic spider on a ring, the man who expanded to ten times his size in water, or the wash-away tattoos of butterflies, comic book heroes, or pink and red hearts. Tacked up high near the register were lottery tickets for stray men with gambling ailments or hopeful women who allotted just a few of the family's dollars to the allure of a lucky break. Often these ladies dramatically waved the sign of the cross over themselves before scratching away with a loose dime or penny. But for many, even the smallest item was completely unaffordable until their turn in line.

Women made up that endless line; women clutching the monthly bills, women frowning, women with children. Their men (if present at all) stood off to the side, leaning coolly on the metal walls. Either they came in with the women but stood back, waiting for the check to be cashed, or they arrived beforehand, anticipating the routine, sure to shake down their wives or girlfriends for a portion. The women would fend them off to the best of their ability, giving up what they had to and making the most of what was left. Lisa and I became so used to the chaos that we hardly looked up at the adults clamoring with one another.

Lisa lingered by the quarter machines, captivated by the glittery stickers. I stayed close to our parents, who were different from the other adults in that they functioned as a team, having arrived in pursuit of a shared goal. I was a participant in their giddiness, eager to make their excitement my own.

If I could break the joy of check day down into small segments, then nothing topped the time Ma and I spent together in line. As she waited for her turn at the counter, again I was her helper. In these urgent moments, full of anticipation, Ma relied on me most. It was my moment to shine, and I always rose to the occasion.

"Eight more ahead of us, Ma. Seven. Don't worry, the cashier's moving fast."

Her smile as I delivered the progress report belonged to me. Calling out the numbers in a reassuring tone determined the amount of attention she paid me. I would have traded the rest of check day for ten more people in line ahead of us, because for this guaranteed amount of time, she wasn't going anywhere. I wouldn't have to worry about Ma's habit of leaving us in the middle of things.

Once, the four of us walked over to Loews Paradise Theater on the Grand Concourse to see a discounted showing of *Alice in Wonderland*. Daddy explained on the walk over that the Concourse used to be an area of luxury, a strip of elaborate architecture that attracted the wealthy. But all I could see as we walked were vast, dirty brick buildings with the occasional tarnished cherubs or gargoyles over doorways, chipped and cracked but still hanging on. We sat down in a nearly empty theater.

Ma didn't stay until the end. It's not that she didn't try; she got up once, twice, three times for a "smoke." Then she got up for a final time and didn't come back. When we returned home that evening, the record player was spinning a woman's sad, throaty singing. Ma was taking a pull off her cigarette and studying her own slender, naked body in the full-length mirror.

"Where were you guys?" she asked naturally, and I wondered if I might have imagined that she'd come with us at all.

But in the check line, she wasn't going anywhere. As much as she fidgeted, Ma wouldn't leave without the money. So I took the opportunity to hold her hand and to ask her questions about herself when she was my age.

"I don't know, Lizzy. I was bad when I was a kid. I stole things and cut school. How many more people in front of us, pumpkin?"

Each time I faced her, Ma motioned toward the cashier, urging me to keep an eye out. Holding her attention was tricky, a balancing act between slipping in questions and showing that I was on top of things. I always assured her that we were almost there; privately, I wished she'd have to wait as long as possible, longer than anyone else.

"I don't know, Lizzy. You're a nicer kid, you never cried when you were a baby. You just made this noise like *eh*, *eh*. It was the cutest thing, almost polite. Lisa would scream her head off and smash everything, rip up my magazines, but you never cried. I worried you were retarded, but they said you were all right. You were always a good kid. How many more people, pumpkin?"

Even if I was told and retold the same stories, I never tired of asking.

"What was my first word?"

"'Mommy.' You handed me your bottle and said 'Mommy,' like you were telling me to fill 'er up. You were a riot."

"How old was I?"

"Ten months."

"How long have we lived in our house?"

"Years."

"How many?"

"Lizzy, move over, my turn's coming."

At home, we split off into two rooms: the living room for us kids, and next to it, the kitchen for Ma and Daddy. Unlike most times, on that first day of the month, food was abundant. Lisa and I dined on Happy Meals in front of the black-and-white TV, to the sound of spoons clanking on the nearby table, chairs being pulled in—and those elongated moments of silence when we knew what they were concentrating on. Daddy had to do it for Ma because with her bad eyesight she could never find a vein.

At last, the four of us enjoyed the second-best part of the day. We sat together, all spread around the living room, facing the flickering TV. Outside, the ice cream truck rattled its loop of tinny music and children gathered, scrambled, gathered, and scrambled again in a game of tag.

The four of us together. French-fry grease on my fingertips. Lisa chewing on a cheeseburger. Ma and Daddy, twitching and shifting just behind us, euphoric.

"Between the cushions, Lizzy. Yes, I'm telling you, inside the sofa. Press your ear down hard enough, give it a few minutes, and you will hear the ocean."

"Really?"

"Yes, Lizzy. Don't make me say it twice. You know I don't like that. Either you want to hear it, or you don't."

"But I do!"

"Then put your ear down there, press hard, and *listen*."

"Okay."

Being my older sister, Lisa held an air of mystery; there was a power about her that gripped and awed me as a child. Some of her talents that most impressed me then—just to name a few—ranged from braiding hair to snapping her fingers to whistling the entire *Bewitched* theme song. She seemed regal in my eyes, holding herself high by professing authority over multiple matters of no particular consistency; declarations that I, in my youth, believed without question. Even if her claims seemed abstract, I figured that she possessed knowledge the way that math teachers command arithmetic: mysteriously and unquestionably so. My blind trust left me at the mercy of more than a few of her practical jokes.

"Okay, now put this other cushion on top of your head."

"Why?"

"You're aggravating me. Do you or don't you want to hear the ocean?"

Why not? I knew that you could hear the ocean inside the lowly seashells we brought home from trips to Orchard Beach with Ma, which were nowhere near the ocean, so why should a couch cushion be any less likely? And how was I to know what Lisa was going to do when she then upped and sat on my head? How could I have guessed she might blow one huge, hot fart all over me?

"Take that! Hear the ocean breeze now, Lizzy!" she shouted while I flailed wildly beneath her, my screams muffled under her weight.

Should that experience have better prepared me for the Halloween when Lisa and her friend from the first grade, Jesenia, "taste-tested" all of my candy "for safety," leaving behind only pennies and old-lady lozenges in my trick-or-treat bag? During the whole "inspection," I'd concealed a single stick of gum in my closed palm, truly believing that *I* was putting one over on *her.*

But as the younger sibling, I wasn't always the one shortchanged; once in a while it was the other way around. As second in line, I could approach most of life's curiosities with a kind of borrowed knowledge, thanks to my older sister. By watching Lisa deal with all kinds of issues in our household, I was able to maneuver similar situations with less difficulty.

This advantage helped me navigate life with our parents. Watching where Lisa made the wrong moves, I understood at least what *not* to do. I was able to figure out the exact behavior it took to gain my parents' approval and attention— something that could prove slippery in our home.

Saturday was furniture garbage day for the people who lived in Manhattan, which Daddy said automatically meant that they were "living well." Manhattan people threw things away that were still perfectly useable; you just needed to look hard to find the good stuff. Daddy had several regular spots where he knew to look. I had a collection going already in my room: three metal army men with only slightly chipped paint, their protruding muskets cracked in different, scarcely visible places; an old set of trick handcuffs I liked to clip on my belt loop with a plastic gun so that I could be just like a real cop; and a set of marbles in a worn, leather pouch stamped GLEASON's on the side.

Always, along with the gifts, came a triumphant story of the retrieval process; tales all about how Daddy dug through bags while bystanders gawked, turning their noses up at "perfectly good stuff." In his stories, Daddy was always the hero, underestimated by people who he managed, eventually, to dazzle with his ironic wit.

Once in a while, I'd go downtown with him. Standing there, it was hard to know how to feel when people stared and Daddy just turned his back to them and continued to dig unabashedly. I tried to see through their eyes what this man must look like, dressed in a dirty, buttoned-up flannel shirt tucked neatly into his equally filthy jeans, mumbling to himself, picking through Dumpsters— as though he had stubbornly dressed for some long-lost professional life from years ago. A serious man, dark-haired, with angular facial features that made him both handsome and stern-looking, with a young daughter, standing in the middle of garbage that everyone else walked wide circles around. I can remember feeling nakedly embarrassed, until Daddy stopped me in my tracks.

"What, you embarrassed, Lizzy?" he asked, briefly lifting his face from the rancid pile and removing his newsboy cap. "Who cares what people think?" He stared into my eyes, unblinking, leaning in. "If you know something's good for you, go right ahead and get it, and let them go blow it out of their asses. That's *their* hang-up."

Staring up at Daddy in all his defiance, I felt proud, like he was sharing a secret with me: how to forget what other people thought of you. I wanted to feel the way he did, but it was something I'd have to work at. When I tried hard enough, for those moments, I could manage it, standing there beside Daddy and sneering back at the people who stared. But only if I used his voice to tell myself, over and over, that it was *their hang-up.*

Daddy took a certain pride in his treasure hunting. He never stopped telling this one story about how he'd found a brand-new keyboard at the precise moment some guy called him a "garbage-digger." In the story, the guy had enough nerve to ask, after he saw how good it was, whether or not Daddy was keeping the keyboard for himself. Daddy enjoyed repeating his answer in an indignant tone: "Fat chance, buddy."

"Their loss, our gain," he would say when we delighted over our second-hand toys, hardly used, or when he presented Ma with a blouse with a loose stitch simply in need of sewing.

Sitting before us on the couch, he sang the indecipherable lyrics to an oldies song and fumbled with his bag while we waited in anticipation. Daddy had his own calculated way of doing things, such as opening a backpack or unbuttoning an eyeglass case. We weren't supposed to interrupt him; the exact motions were a routine he didn't like to break. If he missed a step, he became obviously flustered and had to start over again. Ma called his habits obsessive.

Lisa and I were impatient.

"What did you get, just tell us! I wanna know," Lisa demanded.

"Yeah, please Daddy," I said.

"Hold it a minute, guys."

He was stuck on a zipper. It wasn't caught, but he had a certain way of undoing it. He hummed and continued.

"Daaa, da dum, darlin', you're the one."

Ma, tired from a nap, looked at us and shrugged her shoulders.

Finally, he produced a pink plastic toy hair dryer for Lisa. The creases where the plastic had been welded together were dirty. Stickers substituted for buttons; the settings were marked by a color-coded HIGH, MEDIUM, and . . . the lowest setting had been ripped off; only a streak of white remained. Lisa dangled the dryer by its end and rolled her eyes.

"Thanks, Daddy," she said unenthusiastically.

"I thought you might like that," he commented, rummaging in his bag for what he'd brought me.

"Can we eat now?" Lisa asked.

"Just a minute," Ma replied with a raised finger.

Next, Daddy lifted up a white-and-blue toy monster truck with reflective windows and thick, grooved tires. Dirt had found its way into every crevice, darkening the white parts to gray, making the truck look truly road-worn.

Before it even left his hands, I knew just the way I would react to Daddy's gift. Most of my behavior toward my parents was deliberate; I carefully thought out choices about my actions and exact words. This way, I didn't leave things to chance. Instead, it was a skill I developed, knowing exactly how to get their attention. In this case, Daddy was giving me what he thought to be a "boy's toy," and I knew exactly how to respond. Years of listening carefully to Daddy's comments scorning "girly" things told me so.

Whenever Ma watched TV talk shows discussing women's issues like "feeling fat" or "standing up to your man," Daddy drifted through the living room and sent his voice into a high-pitched wail, impersonating the women using an agonized whine.

"Oh, the world is so foul to women. Let's have a pity party and never get over it. Oh!"

He reacted the same way to Lisa's habit of looking in the mirror. Lisa liked to sit curled in a corner and examine her reflection, trying out different smiles and facial expressions. She could spend a whole hour looking at herself.

In response to this, Daddy rolled his eyes way back, lifted his chin, and fanned his fingers out behind his head in the rough shape of a crown. He spoke in that same voice that I grew to interpret as the way he viewed anything "female." *"Will you just look at my face? Oh, well, I'll just look at it then."*

Daddy always followed up his own jokes with a roar of laughter that would make Lisa hide her mirror and fidget.

"Creep," I'd once heard her say angrily.

Early on, I decided that I would ridicule anything "girly" right along with Daddy, so he would forget I was a girl, too. I made sure never to let my voice sound meek. Dresses were an absolute joke—"girl crap" that I wasn't interested in anyway. I knew it was working when Daddy began to bring home these boys' toys for me, which, I noticed, made him smile and watch me far longer than he would Lisa.

I grabbed the toy truck (which I happened to sincerely like) roughly from him and exclaimed, "Wow! Thanks, Daddy!" I ran the wheels along the coffee table and made loud, throaty engine noises for him to hear.

Daddy smiled approval at me, reaching back into his bag.

"I saved the best for last," he said, turning to Ma, who looked up curiously at him from her seat at the living room table. She'd been adjusting the table fan onto all of us, but in the humidity, it only circulated hot air.

Her gift must be special, I thought as I watched Daddy unwrap it from a careful layering of newspaper sheets.

"Here we go," Daddy said, tonguing his cheek and holding up a thick glass jewelry box on the ends of his stiffened fingers, like a waiter presenting a delicate platter.

Ma let out a long, pleased sigh as she cupped the gift in her hands. Before, she'd seemed only mildly interested, but from her reaction, I could tell that she truly liked the box—although I couldn't help thinking that she had no jewelry to put inside it. While Ma stared at the box, Daddy narrated.

"You should have seen this woman look at me like I was nuts, going through her neighbors' bags. You know what I have to say to that."

He raised his middle finger into the air and made a sour face. "Screw you, that's what. *Nosy.*"

The jewelry box was a shallow, rounded work of carved glass. A thick, silver lid sat on the top, covered with intricate designs. The lid held a single silver rose in the corner, which bowed gracefully forward. When you twisted it, the softest music played while the rose moved in slow circles, as though dancing a sad ballet. It was beautiful. Instantly, I wanted it for myself.

"Daddy! Can *I* have it?" Lisa yelled, speaking my mind. Daddy ignored her.

"This is so nice, who could throw it away?" Ma asked.

"I don't know, but too bad for them. Picked it up on Astor Place, under those big loft buildings," Daddy said as he unlaced his sneakers with rough, quick jerks. He had a habit of double-, sometimes triple-knotting his laces.

"All right, can we eat now?" Lisa asked.

I was relieved that she brought it up; my stomach had begun to burn, but I was reluctant to interrupt. We hadn't eaten since that morning, when Lisa and I had rolled-up mayonnaise sandwiches. Most days, that's all we ever ate, eggs and mayonnaise sandwiches. Lisa and I hated them equally, but they got us through a lot of days when my empty stomach cramped and burned, and all we would have had otherwise was water. It was five days after check day by now, so the money was completely gone and the food in the fridge mostly eaten. I'd been looking forward to some dinner.

"Just a minute," Daddy answered. "Just wait a *minute*, let me get settled."

While Lisa sat watching TV, Ma and Daddy busied themselves in their bedroom. Off to the side, I watched them from the edge of the doorway that provided the only separation between my room and theirs.

Ma sifted through their stack of records in the closet. Since she was with Daddy, she wasn't going to play Judy Collins; she was in a good mood, so it would be something light. Together they worked a two-man assembly line with some mysterious purpose. Daddy sat on the edge of the bed, sorting through something that looked like dirt, which he pinched between his fingertips and, carefully, spread on a *New Yorker* magazine taken from the squeaky nightstand drawer that was on his lap. Ma then rolled the gathered bits into an onionskin paper and licked the ends before twisting them tight. Ma raised her lighter, sparking it several times before it fired up, her eyes directed at the cigarette. She took three labored pulls and passed it to Daddy. I'd never seen Daddy smoke a cigarette before.

"What are you guys doing?" I asked, unable to help myself. I questioned them about everything from "Why are you making cigarettes if Ma has some ready-made ones right on her dresser," to "How come they don't smell like cigarettes?"

Their nervous laughter told me I was being lied to.

"Liz, enough," Daddy managed, through his giggling with Ma. I got the feeling that I had said something naïve, and the thought embarrassed me. I could feel myself begin to blush.

"Enough for now," he said.

Strange smoke filled the air and I tugged my shirt collar over my nose to avoid inhaling the foreign smell. They were in their own world, and not one of my attempts could penetrate it. I stood, seeking Ma's eyes in the hope that she'd let me in on their secret, but she didn't look at me. On the bed, the *New Yorker* sat open to a typed page sprinkled with their cigarette filler.

"Are we ever going to eat anything?" Lisa bellowed when the credits from her show began to roll across our small television screen.

"Sure, honey," Ma replied smoothly. Unsteadily, she rose to enter the kitchen, moving her legs in large strides, like an astronaut venturing onto the moon's surface. The awkwardness of her movements went unnoticed by anyone but me.

Soon Lisa and I sat at the living room table to a dinner of scrambled eggs and ice water. The fight began as soon as Ma set down our plates in front of us.

"Why do we have to eat eggs *again*?" Lisa complained. "I want chicken."

"We don't have chicken," Ma answered flatly before walking back over to Daddy to take another puff.

"Well, I want *real* food. I don't want any more eggs; we eat eggs every single day, eggs and franks. I want chicken."

Daddy could hardly get over his laughter to speak. "Think of it as a small chicken," he said.

"Screw you!" Lisa snapped.

"It tastes good," I said, hoping to make things better.

Lisa whispered across the table, "*Liar*. You hate this crap as much as I do."

Lisa detested my urge to be agreeable, regarding it as the threat to her ongoing campaign of demanding better from our parents.

I stuck my tongue out at her and dumped globs of ketchup on my eggs to drown out the bad taste. Lisa was right; I did hate eggs. On television, a picture of Donald Trump shaking hands with a city official flickered and crackled into static. I ate hurriedly, hoping to get rid of the hot mush by forcing down large mouthfuls. I ran my truck around and around my plate, making sound effects that shot wet bits of egg onto the table and onto Lisa.

Back and forth, I watched her argue a losing battle. If there was nothing but eggs, then we had to eat them. It seemed simple to me. At least if Lisa was quiet, we could all get along. But I was also grateful that she was demanding, because it gave me a chance to be agreeable. I would be the easy-going daughter. I didn't need to look into mirrors; I wasn't vain or girly. I liked trucks, and I ate my eggs.

Lisa went on until she'd worked herself up into tears. When she was sure of the dead end before her, she screamed, "I hate you!" at both of them. But, from the smoke-filled bedroom, which was heavy now with slow guitar music and a man's singing, neither of them responded.

Lisa always seemed to be pulling her standards from some higher place, apparent only to herself. If I had to guess now where her resistance to being shortchanged came from, I'd say it had something to do with the year before I was born.

When she was pregnant with me, Ma had what she called a nervous breakdown. With Daddy in prison, Ma had trouble managing her mental health while caring for Lisa at the same time, and Lisa was placed with a foster family for nearly eight months.

The couple who cared for Lisa were wealthy and could not conceive children of their own, so they treated Lisa as a permanent fixture in their family. They lavished so much attention and care on her that when Ma got well and came to get Lisa, she protested by locking herself in the closet and refusing to leave. Ma had to pry Lisa out of the house and drag her back to University Avenue, both of them in tears—which, it seemed, Lisa never got over. From then on, Ma said Lisa was tough to please. It appeared she had developed a sharp sense of what was owed to her, and she was quick to put her foot down whenever she was presented with less—which was nearly all the time.

Lisa screamed a final "I hate you" from the table, folding her arms over her chest, staring back at the TV. "And, *I'm* not poor—*my* daddy's Donald Trump!" she shouted.

"Well then, go ask Daddy Trump for some chicken, why don't you?" Daddy said. Ma buried her laughter as Daddy howled at his own joke openly, clapping his palm over his knee.

Abruptly, Lisa clanked her plate into mine, which tipped, scooting my eggs into a pile. She stomped off and slammed her door, hard. The noise faded into the blare of pop music from her distorted speakers. Ma and Daddy had taken over the living room, two tired bodies sprawled over the cushions, limp as cooked noodles.

"I ate *all* my eggs," I said, but no one was listening.

Grandma, my mother's mother, lived in Riverdale, across the street from Van Cortlandt Park, in a sixties-style old-age home where she smoked, prayed, and made pay-phone calls to our apartment daily. Apart from us four, she was the only family we really connected with. Daddy's mom sometimes sent gifts from Long Island, but by falling into drugs, he'd become the black sheep of his middle-class family. My whole life, they never once visited; they never came to see how we lived in the Bronx. Although Ma had run away from home at the age of thirteen, she and her mother reconciled later in life. By the time Lisa and I were born, Grandma would visit once a week, on Saturdays, when she boarded the number 9 bus using her senior citizens' half-fare card to travel to University Avenue.

Before her visits, Ma sped across the apartment tucking sheets into the corners of beds and gathering plates into the sink and running hot water over them. She swept dust into a pile under the couch and sprayed air freshener over our heads minutes before Grandma was due to arrive.

From the couch, Lisa shooed Ma away each time the vacuuming blocked her view of *Video Music Box*, a show that appeared in snowy grains on our TV only if Lisa turned the UHF dial around and around.

On one hot summer afternoon, Grandma was expected to arrive at twelve sharp, but Ma—as always—waited until the last minute to do anything. The mist from the aerosol spray was settling over me in cold drizzles when Grandma arrived, dressed too warmly for the weather. She was wheezing heavily from her brief walk up the two flights of stairs, and the strong reek of cigarettes kicked up from her sweater when we hugged. Her hair was a tight bun of gray and silver. Her eyes were crisp and green, and her skin was wrinkled and tough-looking, with faded brown blotches of age. Lisa didn't look up from the TV. For her, Grandma had to lean in to get a hug. I threw my arms around Grandma's waist and asked how her bus ride—a pivotal part of her week— had gone. Her answers were always brief and delivered with a complacent smile.

"Everything was simply wonderful, dear. I'm just glad to have been given another day from our Lord to come see my beautiful girls."

Grandma was deeply religious. In her tan pleather purse—which she held in the crook of her right arm wherever she went, even to the bathroom (a habit she attributed to "those filthy crooks at the home")—Grandma carried a Bible—the King James edition—hair clips, Lipton tea bags, and two packs of Pall Mall cigarettes, her "smokes."

Usually, no one cared to have a conversation with Grandma but me. Ma said she was so lonely living in the home that she would talk anyone's ear off who'd listen, her sole focus being religious education. Ma also insisted that I would eventually lose interest, just like everyone else had, when I realized Grandma "wasn't all there."

"She's not working with a full deck," Ma would say. "I figure she couldn't help the things she put me through. You'll understand what I mean one day, Lizzy."

But I couldn't imagine. Grandma was unlike other adults. She would indulge my every question, no matter how many I asked. My curiosities ranged from how rainbows were made to who looked more like Ma when she was little, Lisa or me. And Grandma came ready to offer answers to absolutely everything, drawing all reasoning from her pious know-how, assuring me that all mysteries of the world were God's doing. From the doorway, Ma watched, commenting that we were a match made in heaven.

Grandma set up station in our kitchen, offering tea and scripture to any takers. I liked the sweet taste of the tea after Grandma stirred in two sugars and some milk, which ribboned through the smoke curling from one of Ma's cigarettes. I sat, my knees drawn to my chest, nightgown pulled over my legs, sipping the warm drink, and listened to her describe how sins kept the wicked from heaven.

"Don't curse, Lizzy. God doesn't favor a foul mouth. Clean the house for your poor mother once in a while. God sees and hears all, and He never forgets. He knows when you don't do right by others. Trust me, missy, there will be plenty of sinners who never enter the pearly gates of heaven into God's love. Be careful, God is our Lord, and He is all-powerful."

The only other thing Grandma made conversation about, unrelated to religion, was what I wanted to be when I grew up.

"A comedian. I want to tell jokes onstage," I declared, recalling the nights I'd watched men on TV, wearing suit jackets, delivering nervous anecdotes to invisible audiences, their confidence mounting with each explosion of laughter. I figured Grandma would be as impressed as I was at the idea. Instead, she looked at me with concern and set her glass down to raise her finger to the sky.

"Oh dear God, no, don't do that. Don't do that. Lizzy, no one will laugh. Sweetie, be a live-in maid. I became a live-in maid when I was sixteen years old. You'll love it. You go to stay with a nice family and if you take good care of their kids, you can eat for free and make a good, honest living that God would be proud of. Doesn't that sound nice? Be a live-in maid, Lizzy. Besides, it's good practice for when you have a husband, you'll see."

At my age, it was hard to understand what Grandma meant. I envisioned a wife and husband seated at a square table, in a large, square, white house. Their toddler, chubby and wailing, was waiting for me to serve him, along with the couple, whose faces were blank blurs. Grandma smiled reassuringly. I smiled back. Her vision of my future disheartened me so much that I decided that while I would outwardly agree to anything she said, secretly, I'd keep my true wishes private. I nodded and smiled, pretending to be as pleased with her advice as she was. Then I gave her an excuse about needing something from the living room and joined Lisa on the couch.

But Grandma didn't need me—or anyone, for that matter—to keep up a good conversation. If she was left alone in the kitchen for too long, she was just as happy to kneel on the floor and carry on a private dialogue with God Himself. Lisa lowered the volume on the television so we could eavesdrop from the next room on Grandma's passionate repetitions of "Hail Mary, full of grace, the Lord is with thee." She went on, over and over, clicking her rosary and murmuring until her speech was more rhythm than words. This meant that she'd made direct contact.

Lisa snapped the TV off completely when Grandma's praying got louder, her voice raised and deepened in a way I found frightening as she called out for guidance from above—her own sort of CB radio calling to the Lord. Grandma could lose hours in this trance, never moving, never opening her eyes while the sun set and darkened the room around her, the tea cooling in glass mugs on the table. The kitchen remained off-limits to the rest of us when Grandma was speaking to God.

"Lisa, shhh, I wanna hear." I believed she might truly be reaching heaven and strained to listen, through Grandma's responses, to what God's direct advice might sound like. Lisa twisted her lips into a smirk.

"You're so dumb," she chided. "Grandma's just crazy. Ma says she hears voices. She's not talking to God—she's nuts."

Many times, while Ma was busily cleaning in preparation for Grandma's arrival, she told us stories about how her childhood was ruined by her mother's mental illness. As a girl, Ma was forced to return home every day only minutes after school let out, many long blocks away from home. Grandma would synchronize Ma's watch to their living room clock, and if Ma was late, even by minutes, she received a fierce beating. Grandma used anything from extension cords to spiked heels; all blows were delivered to Ma's tender inner thighs until black-and-blue bruises colored her flesh from crotch to knee. In the middle of the night, Ma, her sister, Lori, and her brother Johnny were often shaken out of bed, pots and spoons thrust into their hands. They were instructed to bang hard, to make as much noise as possible, and to scream a phrase of Grandma's devising: "Its-a-bits-of-para-kitus, Its-a-bits-of-para-kitus" over and over, until the voices that tormented Grandma were drowned out by the clatter.

This is partly why, Ma said, she'd left home to live on the streets when she was very young and why she cried, listening to sad records in her darkened bedroom, remembering all the trouble she'd run into since.

"A childhood like that can really mess with you," Ma would say. "What'd she expect me to be after all that, Miss America?"

A firm regimen of medication and talking to God kept Grandma tame later in life. Without that, Ma swore, the devil in her was easily provoked.

"But you should know, it's not her fault," Ma once explained in a gentle voice that told me she loved Grandma. "It's hereditary. Her mother had it, and her mother's mother had it. And once in a while, pumpkin, I got a spell of it, but I was nothing like Grandma. With treatment, mine went away, one hundred percent. She's always half in la-la land. She can't help it."

The "treatment" Ma spoke about was two- or three-month stints in the psychiatric ward of North Central Bronx Hospital, after Daddy found her hallucinating and hearing voices. Before I was born, they tried a few types of medication before Ma was given Prolixin and Cogentin to keep her balanced. Daddy explained that more attacks were unlikely because this had happened years ago, and Ma had been all right since. Either way, I was convinced that Ma could never be anything less than one hundred percent herself, partly because the very thought of her being any different frightened me.

Inside the kitchen, Grandma laughed knowingly to herself, in some private joke.

"There she goes," Lisa said, rolling her eyes at me and spinning her finger in small circles beside her head. Until Lisa and Ma pointed it out, I'd never once connected Grandma's solo conversations with her insanity. I blushed at my gullibility.

"I know she isn't talking to God. What do you think, I'm retarded?" I snapped back.

In the summertime, Ma bridged some of the gaps in our income by feeding us through other government programs, like the free lunch offered throughout local public schools. Lisa and I often had to coax her out of bed to dress us and ready herself, so we were almost never on time. Having waited until the last minute, Ma would rush around the apartment frantically, feverishly scrambling to make the cut-off time.

"Just—sit—still! If you move around, it'll only be worse."

My head jerked and swayed with the tug of Ma's fine-toothed comb, which ripped fire like nails along my skull. "Owww, Ma!"

"We have only fifteen minutes, Lizzy. We need to go. I'm being as gentle as I can. If you sit still, it won't hurt," she insisted, tugging my hair to prove her point. I knew from experience that this was a complete lie. From the doorway, Lisa poked her tongue out at me; her hair was manageable. My cheeks burned with anger. As I went to return the gesture, the teeth of the comb snagged an enormous knot. Without hesitation, Ma dug furiously, snapping the stubborn pieces like dry grass. I winced my eyes shut and grabbed the corner of the mattress beneath me to wrestle with the pain.

"See. If you sit still, it's not so bad."

I would rub my throbbing scalp for the rest of the morning.

We were in danger of being given cold servings for the third time that week—or worse, there might be no food left at all. This was especially difficult when we were between SSI checks, and the free lunch was often our only full meal of the day.

July's intense sun broke the Bronx open, split it down the center, and exposed its contents. High temperatures drove our neighborhood's occupants out from their muggy, un-air-conditioned apartments to crowd the cracked sidewalks.

I waved hello to the old ladies who spent all day sharing gossip on lawn chairs, each claiming one full square of cement for themselves and their battery-operated radios.

"Hi, Mary." I smiled at the woman who gave me nickels to buy peanut chews whenever I saw her downstairs.

"Good morning, girls. Good morning, Jeanie." She waved back.

Old Puerto Rican men played dominoes in front of the corner store on planks of rotted wood suspended over cinder blocks. Ma always called them *dirty old men* and said that I should stay far away, because they think *dirty thoughts* and would do *dirty things* to little girls if given the chance. As we approached the men, I tried to keep my eyes on my shoes to show Ma that I was obedient. They called things out to her that I never understood. *"Mami, venga aquí, blanquita."* And they made whistling and sucking noises with their wet, beer-shiny lips.

We passed a few of Ma's friends sitting nearby, perched on stoops, eyes trained on their children, clutching overloaded keychains decorated with plastic Puerto Rican flags and smiling *coquí* frogs in straw hats. The plastic jumble of trinkets clinked with each disciplinary raise of the mothers' hands. Children circled sprinklers and teenagers claimed street corners.

The block thumped salsa as we crossed University onto 188th, Lisa and I tugging on Ma's arms, helping guide her through traffic while she squinted.

"Four more blocks, Ma, all right?"

Ma smiled absentmindedly. "Yep, okay pumpkin."

The cafeteria was filled with the distinct smell of fish. I sucked up disappointment, grabbed a yellow Styrofoam tray partitioned into four sections, and got in line. I hesitated over the pyramid of fish cakes glistening with grease.

"You got something better to eat at home?" the milk lady asked over the cafeteria chatter.

"No," I answered, hanging my head as I accepted the limp fish.

"Then come on, keep it movin'." I grabbed a pint of milk, the container slippery between my fingers, and tried not to let my Tater Tots roll off the tray as I went to sit on a bench connected to a long, crowded table.

Lisa stabbed holes into her fish cake, drawing the bright yellow cheese filling from its center. I was staring at a faded poster of children raising their sporks—a cheap plastic spoon combined with a fork—to demonstrate the importance of proper nutrition, when a lady with a clipboard began talking to Ma.

"So, how old are *your* children, ma'am?" she asked.

"Seven, and the smaller one is almost five." Ma squinted and smiled vaguely, but I could tell that the woman's face was too distant for Ma's bad eyes to see clearly. The woman wrote something down, humming a quick, "Mmm-hmm, really," as though Ma had said something interesting.

They talked for a while, the woman asking Ma a lot of personal questions about our family income from welfare, Ma's level of education, and whether or not she lived with our father. "Where is he? Does he work?" and so on. I pushed the Tater Tots around in my mouth, breaking them into bits with my one front tooth. Still cold in the center, they tasted like cardboard moistened by freezer ice.

"I see. So when do you plan on starting this one in school?" She pointed her finger at me. I slid closer to Ma. The clipboard woman spoke to her with the same voice adults used when they leaned down to tell me how big I was getting.

"This fall, down the block at P.S. 261," Ma replied.

"Mmm-hmm, really? Thank you, ma'am. Enjoy your lunch, children," she instructed us as she went on to the next parent.

"My baby's growing up," Ma said, ignoring the woman's intrusion and briefly hugging me to her side. "You start school in just two months."

I thought of the words *growing up*—grown up, I mouthed to myself. I looked at the adults in the cafeteria, searching for what *grown up* looked like, hoping to find some signs of what to expect for myself.

I watched the way the clipboard woman interviewed the new lady, making her nervous as she leaned in to take her information. I didn't like it when Ma smiled for her questions, just like when she was nice to the cold women who sat like royalty behind big wooden desks at welfare—the way Ma sounded like she was begging. I didn't like being afraid of Ma's caseworker and racing around the apartment to help clean for the in-home checkups, or having to be overly grateful to the moody cafeteria workers. It scared me that strangers had the power to give or take so much of what we depended on.

The cafeteria rules stated that food was for kids only, but at Ma's request, Lisa snuck her a piece of fish. Careful not to let the lunch ladies see, Ma stuffed it into her mouth and had me scan the room to ensure that she had not been seen. Watching her and Lisa, I thought of Ma's words, about the fact that I was growing up.

I stared over at doorways leading up to stairwells that held so much mystery for me in the summers I'd attended P.S. 33's free lunch program. I cherished the last few years when Lisa always went off to school in the morning, while I got to spend time alone with Ma. We'd wake up when we felt like it, and Ma would sit me down on the couch and if we had enough food, I'd get the rare treat of a peanut butter and jelly sandwich. We would watch the morning game shows; Ma would light up for Bob Barker and *The Price Is Right*. Ma said he was "one of the last real gentlemen around," and she always sat extra close to the TV, squinting when his face filled our screen, his white hair perfectly neat, his suit freshly pressed. Together, we would bet on the "showcase show-down," taking turns pretending to be contestants, winning boats, new living room sets, and glamorous trips around the world. I'd stand and clap extra loud for the contestants who won big. Ma sometimes vacuumed, humming smoothly while I was parked in front of the TV for hours, our apartment bright with the morning sun. It was a brief time when I felt that Ma belonged only to me.

And then some days Daddy brought me to the library, where he helped me pick out books that were mostly pictures. For himself, he'd choose thick ones with photographs of contemplative men in suit jackets on the back, which he stacked around the house and never returned. He was always applying for a library card in a new name. Some nights, I liked to take one of his books and bring it to my room, where I would try to read it the same way Daddy did— held directly under the light of my bedside lamp, searching for any words that might be familiar to me from nights when Ma read to me at my bedside. But the words were too big and they made me tired. So I'd just fall asleep beside the book, smelling the yellowed pages, relaxed by the feeling that I shared some-thing special with my father.

It worried me to think that I would be away in the mornings now, missing out on this. I got the feeling that something was slipping through my fingers, and that I was the only one who saw the loss of our special time as a bad thing.

I wondered what starting school would be like, and how it was supposed to help me become grown up. I wondered what *grown up* could mean, when there were different types of adults all around me. Though I wanted to, I didn't dare ask Ma to help me figure things out, because I knew it would only make her feel bad about herself and the scrounging we had to do to get by. Some things I was just going to have to figure out on my own.

Later that week, the evening newscaster—a white man in a suit who wore a triangle hat with colorful streamers dangling from the top—called the day, July Fourth, *a time to celebrate our independence.* Then he and the poofy-haired woman beside him waved good-bye under the rolling credits and blew simul-taneously into kazoos. The noise honked in our living room, becoming the second-loudest thing next to our window fan whirring behind me. I sat alone on the couch, motionless. Ma had promised me earlier, when it was still light outside, that she would take us downtown by the water so we could watch fireworks along with everyone else. I had run to get dressed and chosen my blue shorts and tie-dyed shirt to match the festivities. But I had stayed in my room too long. By the time I came out, Ma had left for the Aqueduct Bar without telling anyone—a new place she'd recently discovered and been running off to more and more lately.

Her trips there started on St. Patrick's Day, that past March. Ma and Daddy had taken us down to the parade spontaneously, after we'd seen it announced on TV.

Under a light sheet of rain, we watched from Eighty-sixth Street, just off the park, as men in kilts played eerie notes on bagpipes and beat drums so powerful I could feel them in my chest and legs. Lisa and I had our cheeks painted with four-leaf clovers, for luck, and Daddy let me fall asleep on his lap for the whole train ride home.

Ma didn't make it back to the apartment with us. Just as we were about to come off Fordham Road, she ran into an old friend who was headed into a bar, and she decided to catch up with us later. After all, what was St. Patty's Day without a drink, he'd insisted. Without bothering to wash the paint off my face, I'd set my blanket down on my windowsill to watch for Ma's return. I waited for hours, dozing off against the window, until she finally came home around three in the morning, smelling of liquor and walking in zigzags. Ma slept then like she did after her longer coke binges, without waking up once for the entire next day. After that, the bar became a regular thing. We could be in mid-conversation, or sitting down to dinner, it didn't matter; she would leave at any time.

Hours later that night of the fourth, still dressed in my tie-dyed shirt and blue shorts, I sat on the couch, turning the TV dial, flipping through the different televised celebrations. I decided then and there that Ma had snuck away because of me. It was because I'd developed this habit of asking her over and over if she *really* had to go to the Aqueduct, and what time *exactly* I could expect her back. Sometimes it was hard to help myself, and I even followed Ma to the door, holding her hand for as long as I possibly could. I made it so that our fingers touched down to the very tip before she exited. "See you soon, Ma, come back soon, okay? Okay?" I called down repeatedly, until I heard the hallway door click shut. I supposed that this had become too much for her to deal with. That must be why she'd felt a need to slip out secretly tonight. If only I'd been less difficult.

A couple more hours passed and the replay of the news ended. I stood up, readying myself for bed, walking out of the living room. Just as I did, Ma came through the door.

"Guess who's here," she sang. I heard two sparks from a lighter and thought she was lighting a cigarette. Then I heard a fluttering noise, like a small swarm of bees.

"Ma!"

"Look what I brought you, pumpkin. Go get your sister."

Ma stared at a sparkler that she held like a magic wand. The brightest light in the living room, it shot glowing, silvery threads all over her pinched fingers, around her bare arm. Flecks of light danced in her eyes.

"Ta-da!" she sang, raising the sparkler. Just then, I noticed the large plastic bag filled with fireworks hanging from her other arm.

We never made it downtown by the water that night, but we did sit on the stoop out front, surrounded by people from our building. We set off every last firework Ma had brought home. With the neighborhood kids, we made Jumping Jacks dance and spin. Firecrackers popped, ringing in our ears. Daddy was the safety supervisor for Lisa and me. With a glass bottle from the trash, which he cleaned off with newspaper, Daddy taught me how to send a bottle rocket soaring into space without hurting my fingers. Ma sat on the stoop and talked to Louisa from apartment 1A, whose daughters played with their own fireworks beside us.

"Here, Lizzy," Daddy said to me, his deep voice reassuring. "You've got to prop the stick into the bottle first. You don't want to get burned."

I crouched into a ball down by the cement to help Daddy light the fuse. Daddy wrapped himself over me, engulfing my small body, protecting me. I smelled his scent, the musk and sweat mixed with our freshly struck matches. His hands were enormous, cupping mine as he showed me how to position the small explosive. Together we backed off to watch it fly, screaming through the air, flashing radiant pink beams in the black night sky. With Lisa and I taking turns shooting bottle rockets, we finished the whole bag in under a half hour. I sent each one flashing into the dark with a round of applause, looking over my shoulder at Ma, who hooked her arm through Daddy's and was leaning on his shoulder, smiling.

That was the summer of 1985, just before school, and the last time I can remember the four of us being close, and happy. Before then, whatever went on in our household, I simply had nothing to compare to. I had no idea how different we could be from other people. All I knew was Ma was a real mother then, and my parents, together, tended to our needs. Or whatever they didn't tend to didn't matter because I had no clue that I needed anything more.

The fade of that summer withdrew not just its own warmth, but with it, the only family unity I'd ever known, and as a result my very last clear memory of stability, too. I guess you could say we'd lived in some kind of bubble before that, a little world made up of just the four of us. But in my eyes, we were just one of the many families living and struggling to make it on University Avenue. Things were sometimes tough, but we had each other, and in having that, we had it all.

That August, I made a habit of standing on one of the kitchen chairs to count the passing days off the free Met Food supermarket calendar tacked high up next to the fridge—something I'd learned watching my big sister. For two Augusts, I'd seen Lisa repeatedly squint at the dates framed neatly beside coupons for bargain poultry and ninety-nine-cent frozen burritos while she muttered complaints and groaned extravagantly over the start of school. To-morrow would be my first day to join her.

"You're in for it now," she said, digging through her extra school supplies to split with me. "No more bumming around here, that's for sure. You're going to have to work now, just like the rest of us."

I thought of all the times Lisa returned home and headed straight for her room to labor over homework, emerging hours later, droopy-eyed and ex-hausted, only to find that I'd been sitting on Ma's lap, watching TV most of the evening. Routinely, she'd strike up some petty fight with me shortly thereafter, demanding control over the TV or the couch, since she'd been working hard and I'd just been sitting around on my butt. Her helping me prepare for school felt, to me, like some form of revenge.

Lisa peeled open a pack of very old lined paper that she'd dug up from her closet and divided it in half.

"You'll need this," she said, passing one stack to me. "Don't put it in upside down or people will make fun of you. Kids tease about a lot of things, you'll see." My small hands worked to hook the whole stack at once into my three-ring binder, just the way I had seen Lisa do many times before. Ma circled the room frantically.

"Tomorrow, Lizzy. I can't believe it. It wasn't too long ago that you were in diapers. In diapers!" Ma's voice was panicked. I couldn't tell whether she realized that she was shouting.

Ma had just spent time in the kitchen with Daddy, getting high. Now, with her jaw tight, her lips pursed, and her eyes wild, I knew she would go on like this for a while, circling and ranting. I'd been pressing Ma the whole week to get me ready for school, but she wouldn't get out of bed. Luckily, check day had just come. And now that she'd shot up, Ma absolutely came to life. Whatever the reason, I was thrilled with her attention.

"Now look at you, starting school. I can't believe it, pumpkin." She lit a cigarette and sucked so hard that the tip glowed bright.

"You're going to love it, Lizzy. You'll do so well."

Her excitement became my excitement. I *would* love it.

"Wait, do you have a notebook?" she asked with sudden, manic concern.

It was eleven thirty at night. I'd found the used binder under Lisa's bed a few hours before. The paper she'd provided, which we'd rescued from the trash room downstairs last spring, was yellow with age.

"Yeah, Ma. It's right here." With great effort I held the thick notebook high for her to see, but she didn't look.

"Good, but did I give you a haircut?"

"A haircut? No. Do I need one?"

"Yes, pumpkin, the day before school everyone gets new things, they get their hair cut, they brush their teeth. Go sit on the floor by the coffee table, I'll get some scissors and take care of you right now. You probably don't need your whole head, just your bangs. That's all people really look at anyway."

She went to search the junk drawer. Her movements were impatient, unfinished, like her sentences, which usually stopped before any point was made.

"Lizzy, you just . . . It'll be good. Wait until you see . . ." Her energy felt frantic.

I could hear the contents of the junk drawer clanking from the kitchen as she stirred through them. Lisa had gone to bed, saying she needed sleep to get up early and warning that if I knew what was good for me, I would do the same.

Something about the way Ma moved made me nervous. Did she even know how to cut hair? And what about her eyesight? I didn't want my hair to look anything like hers, which was long and wavy, but also kinky and unkempt. The thought filled me with worry.

"Here we go!" she yelled, holding up a pair of rusted scissors. Daddy was still in the kitchen; I could hear him fidgeting and making small mumbling noises. There was nothing to do but go with it, so I did.

I had to stay perfectly still, with my chin held in place by Ma's fingertips while she made each cut, or I would interfere with her concentration. Ma made me close my eyes to avoid getting any hair in them. I held a piece of loose-leaf paper below my chin to catch what fell. I'd never had bangs before, but Ma didn't seem to realize this. She just took clumps of my longer hair and made the necessary cuts. The real panic didn't set in until I could feel the cool metal of the scissors slide along my forehead, over an inch above my eyebrows.

"Ma, are you sure that's not too short?" I asked.

"Pumpkin, it's okay, I just need to make it even. I almost had it before; I just need to try again. We're almost there. Just . . . sit . . . still."

On the ground beside me, my hair had fallen in scattered chunks. Ma tapped her foot impatiently. Every so often she'd hiss a curse.

"Shit!"

My heart raced and I tried not to ruin her concentration by flinching.

In small bits, Ma chopped away my bangs, until they were so short, only a cropped border remained, so stubbly that pieces of it stuck straight out from my head. When she rested the scissors on the coffee table, I touched my forehead, rubbing it frantically in search of hair, pinching the short stubble in disbelief. Tears welled up in my eyes.

"Ma-aaa," I whimpered. "You made it really short, Ma. Isn't this too short?"

She was already putting on her shoes to head out to the bar. From the way her face had dropped, I could tell her high had worn off. The alcohol was what she needed now, to calm her. She was out of my reach again.

"I know honey, it'll grow back. I just had to make it even. Those damn scissors are no good for cutting hair. I had to keep going back to fix it."

Lisa said that kids teased about a lot of things. Imagining what the kids in school would think when they saw me, I began to cry softly. Ma took me by the hand and walked me down the hall to the bathroom, which was just beside the front door. She stood behind me, both of us facing the mirror together. Her jacket was already on. Suddenly, her chin was down on my shoulder, her fingers stroked my forehead.

"It's just hair, pumpkin, it'll grow back. When I was little, my sister, Lori, cut my favorite doll's hair off. I was so angry. She told me it would grow back and I *believed* her. Can you imagine?"

I wiped tears from my cheeks and studied us together in the mirror. Ma's eyes couldn't stay in one place, and her hands on my shoulders had blood spots on them. Tiny pieces of hair were stuck to her fingers.

"At least yours grows back, Lizzy. It's really fine. School will be so much fun, you'll see."

With that, I watched her reflection plant a single kiss on my head, and she slipped out the front door. I could hear her stomping quickly down the battered marble steps. Then she was gone.

CHAPTER 2

Middle of Everything

"THEY DON'T LIKE RED. I'M TELLING YOU, IF YOU PUT RED IN YOUR hair, they'll leave. I swear, Lizzy, it's how I got rid of mine."

"Yeah right. . . . *Liar!*"

For apparently nothing more than to relieve her own boredom, Lisa would torment me in our parents' absence. When Ma and Daddy disappeared for a full day or when they'd stream in and out of the house, preoccupied with copping drugs, leaving us to ourselves for whole nights, she would dream up new and terrible things to do to me.

"Look, first, I'm going to have to braid your hair, Liz. But, not just any braids—stiff ones that point out in all directions."

"But why! I *know* you're lying. Why would it matter if my hair was braided?" While I believed almost everything Lisa told me, I had, by the time I reached the first grade, been fooled by more than one of her practical jokes, so my instincts were slowly growing sharper. This claim seemed too outrageous, I thought; surely she was up to something.

"All right, Lizzy," she said, turning to walk away from me. "I'm only trying to help you out here. Isn't that what you wanted? Well, I know what it takes, but if you don't want to get rid of your lice, I guess there's nothing I can do about it."

But I did want to get rid of my lice. They'd been crawling on my head for weeks. Chasing them with my fingernails, I'd dug burning furrows into my scalp, painful and sensitive to the touch. At night, I could feel them moving around, weaving their way through my hair, biting until I scratched deep to disperse the sensation. I awoke frequently to dreams of angry bugs eating at my scalp, laying eggs in my skin.

At first, it wasn't this bad. I'd barely noticed them at all. It took the building superintendent's daughter, Debbie, to come knocking on our door, telling

Ma to look out for lice in our hair, before I connected the persistent itching on my scalp with anything specific.

"All those creeps my father has down there," Debbie said. "I swear, half of them come right out of the gutter, Jeanie. Check your kids out; they've spent enough time hanging out in the basement with you to have caught 'em. I know. I just spent the whole damn afternoon scraping those nasty things off of my own scalp."

A memory of the super's place from the past weekend flashed back to me. I'd waited in the doorway that divided his apartment from his cellar, watching Ma pass Bob money in exchange for a small, foil package. It was midday; my vanilla ice cream was melting over my hand. People were asleep or just waking up all around me, spread out across the basement floor, over two dirty mattresses. Debbie was there; she'd gotten up to hug me and Ma, and stunk of beer. The place was littered with people, some snoring, some not fully dressed. Fly tape hung from the ceiling, covered with black, lifeless bugs: bare bulbs provided the only light.

Just before Ma took me out of there, a shirtless man had sat up and begun to rub sleep from his eyes. Without noticing me, he shook another sleeping person, a girl, and woke her. I stood there, shifting my weight from foot to foot, uncomfortably, while they kissed, empty beer bottles and overflowing ashtrays at their feet.

When Debbie left, Ma stepped into our living room to ask, lightly, if either of us had caught lice. I didn't know for sure, so I just said, "My head's itchy." Lisa said the same. We were promised a shampoo called Quell, and that was that. It had been roughly a month since then, with no Quell in sight. So this is why I reluctantly gave in to Lisa and allowed her to twist my hair in all directions while my face curled in pain.

"Now, pass me the barrettes." Each time another braid was finished, Lisa spun me around to note her progress, her face glowing, as if she took some private delight in the sight of me. I grew particularly suspicious when she flat-out laughed.

"Sorry! Sorry, Liz. It just looks funny. I can't help it. You would have laughed when I did this to my hair, too, believe me. You should have been there, it was such a mess. Don't worry, it's all part of the cure."

I believed Lisa just enough to let her go on, but her giggles made it difficult for me to contain my growing anger. Once I even pulled away when she looked too amused, only to have Lisa make me beg her to finish. After all, she seemed to be my only hope for a remedy. She agreed to continue grudgingly, and warned that I shouldn't be so doubtful of people's good intentions. I told myself to concentrate less on her and more on how good it would feel once this was all over.

She grabbed my hair into rigorous twists, sending the tiny bugs into a frenzy. I cringed and watched the clock drag its hands along. Earlier, Ma and Daddy had promised groceries, but they had stayed away for hours. Embarrassed over what they might say if they walked in and this turned out to be another one of Lisa's pranks, I hoped she would finish quickly.

After what felt like three hours, when my legs had grown sore from kneeling on the thin carpet and I'd fidgeted in every direction in search of comfort, Lisa finally lifted her hands away from my head.

"Okay . . . Done! Now, listen carefully to me, Lizzy. Next we need to find anything red that we can stick in your hair. They're terrified of red. Let's get something, and then you'll see how this works. But you have to move fast, or they'll catch on."

"Anything red?"

Lisa slid one of Daddy's garbage treasure-hunt finds, a red Barbie dress, over my largest braid at the very front of my head. The empty sleeves pointed outward, and the open collar presented a barrette-pinched puff of hair.

"Is that it? Is it working?"

"More! We need more. Hurry, they're all going to run to one side. That makes it harder. Go!"

With nothing useful in sight, I raced across the apartment and threw open my drawers, tossing trinkets and all kinds of junk around my room. I searched feverishly, but it seemed there was nothing red to be found—until I remembered Ma's dresser. With one wide sweep of my arm, I grabbed Ma's bouquet of red plastic roses from her green vase and crashed onto the bed, Lisa cheering me on at my side.

"Hurry, Lizzy! Put them anywhere there's room, fast!"

One by one, I ripped the heads from the stems' sockets and began working them into my hair, around the base of each braid. I tried my hardest to cover every last available spot. In the tight zigzags of my braids, they clung nicely. When I was done, my head sported a helmet of bright, red roses and a small red dress emerging from the front, like a unicorn's horn. I looked at Lisa for confirmation.

She explained that it would take at least twenty minutes for there to be any noticeable difference. The most important part now was to remain as still as possible. So I shut the bathroom door behind me and took a seat in the bathtub. I figured it might be good to send every last horrible bug streaming down the drain as soon as they began to retreat from this red they feared so much.

I decided to remove all of my clothing in case they tried to survive in some fold along my shirt or in one of my pockets. I stripped completely, crouched in the tub, and waited.

Time passed and nothing happened. Lisa knocked and asked to see how things were coming along, but I sent her away. The empty tub became icy under my feet. I began to shiver. Then, without warning, a bug dropped.

A small thrill ran through my body. I shook my head, and another dropped. Time passed, but that was all. The bugs wriggled, dwarfed in the white basin, just the way they did when they had recently caused me trouble in school.

As far back as last year, I'd felt different. The kindergarten teacher assigned us to walk with a buddy then, but I always cried when it was time to pair up because I didn't want anyone to be close enough to get a good look at my spiky bangs. I knew the kids couldn't help but stare. Soon I became the crybaby with the weird haircut. With all the name-calling, I'd kept to myself, and that had made me something of an outcast. Now, in the first grade, when I had told and retold myself I would be a perfectly "normal" kid, the lice had ruined everything all over again.

It happened during Mrs. McAdams's spelling test, when I was seated across from a boy named David at table three. Mrs. Reynolds, the teaching assistant, a heavy, turkey-necked woman with gray tufts of worn-out Velcro for hair, walked around the classroom to make sure we behaved during Mrs. McAdams's reading aloud of the week's spelling words.

Pencils scratching paper and Mrs. Reynolds's penny loafers dragging along the tiles were the only sounds. I spread my sloppy handwriting across the handout page, struggling to spell *Sunday*.

From her desk, Mrs. McAdams called out the next word, *time*. Just as I leaned in to give it a try, I caught a deep itch on my scalp. When I scratched, a tiny gray bug landed with a light click in the center of my worksheet. My heart raced with a sharp pang of fear that shook off my drowsiness. I quickly swatted the insect off my desk. My eyes darted in all directions in search of a witness, but no one had seen.

I would have been in the clear had the itch not persisted. Another scratch, and two more bugs came clicking down. I swatted again. One landed on the ground; the other shot across my desk and landed on David's side of the table that we shared. Mrs. McAdams called out another word, but I missed it. I was too busy pretending not to notice the bug struggling for firm footing right under David's nose as he looked up to Mrs. McAdams for further instruction.

My itch persisted and grew, demanding attention. It took all of my will not to scratch again. Suddenly, David raised his hand, bringing the test and the entire class to a dead halt.

"Mrs. Reynolds? There's a weird bug on my desk." The creature had stopped for a rest at the top of David's page, right where he'd spelled out *time* in neat little letters.

A girl beside him cried out, "Ewwww, that's disgusting! David, you're disgusting!"

"I didn't—it wasn't me. I don't know where it came from." The class broke into whispers. David turned bright red and folded his arms across his chest, holding in tears.

Mrs. Reynolds hurried over to investigate, mistakenly searching for food in all the desks. She was in the middle of delivering a quivery-pitched speech about how sneaking food into the classroom brought roaches, when I had to scratch my head and another bug fell, *click*, against my page. There was no hiding from the girl seated to the right of me the fact that that creature had fallen from my hair onto my nearly blank, white test sheet.

"Oh my God. They're coming from her *hair*," Tamieka called out.

Shrieks and noises of disgust exploded throughout the room.

Mrs. Reynolds's cold, bony hand took me by the wrist, through the whooping and hollering, out of the room, and down the hallway. As the secretary watched, she ordered me to sit in an office chair that had been dragged to the center of the room, away from everything else. She ripped two thick Popsicle sticks from a thin package, parted my hair with the tips, and immediately found the lice. But instead of backing away, she dug around and remarked on how my head was "infested," moving over to allow the secretary a look as she used the Popsicle sticks to shake loose a few more lice, which dropped onto the green tiles, both women watching.

Mrs. Reynolds dragged me back into the classroom and ordered me to remain in the doorway. She went to the teacher's cabinet and rummaged around in search of something.

Looking over at me, Tamieka whispered into another girl's ear. They giggled, pointed, and stared. Mrs. McAdams slammed her palm down hard on her desk and shouted for them to "be nice," inadvertently calling the rest of the class's attention to me. Just then, Mrs. Reynolds lifted a bottle of vinegar into the air and called through the silence, "I've got it. Let's go. Walk ahead of me—those suckers jump." The children roared behind us. But as much as I was humiliated, I was more worried about what the vinegar was for.

She took me to the front of the school building, where two teachers stood, sharing a cigarette. The street was busy; cars whizzed by and a train rumbled overhead. For a moment, I considered escape.

But hope for freedom vanished with Mrs. Reynolds's grip on my shoulder. She pushed me into a bent-over position, with my hands pressed against the rough brick wall. She rolled up her sleeves, readying herself.

"Now, this is a home remedy passed down in my family. Don't fret, it won't hurt you one bit. All you need to do is close your eyes. I'll take care of the rest."

Cold liquid splashed over my head, stinging the spots where I'd scratched. Mrs. Reynolds rubbed my scalp in harsh circles that tangled my hair. I inhaled deep whiffs of vinegar until I felt sick and woozy.

From where I stood, only the splashing of vinegar against cement and our four feet—my sneakers and Mrs. Reynolds's penny loafers—remained visible. Soon, a small crowd of new feet gathered nearby—the teachers on break.

There was no way I'd ever enter that classroom again. How could I look into their faces, much less reclaim my seat between David and Tamieka? I wished I would die from the fumes, and that Mrs. Reynolds would be blamed for killing me.

When Mrs. Reynolds finally allowed me to stand, she commented, "That's enough. You don't want anyone to mistake you for a salad, do ya, kid?" She let out a quick snort of laughter. Then, just as quickly as her smile had come, it was gone. "Let's go, you. Back to class."

✦ ✦ ✦

Crouching in the tub back at home, I watched the bugs float away, helpless in the stream of water I released from the faucet. My scalp throbbed in the grip of the tight braids. I thought of how Mrs. Reynolds's "home remedy" had done nothing, the way Lisa's "cure" seemed to be doing the same.

I stood to get a look at myself in the mirror. The image that stared back was startling. When my effort to evenly arrange the roses had failed, Lisa volunteered to help fix it. A perfect headdress of roses was spread all around my hair—a symmetrical sort of bouquet.

A single bug crawled on the hem of Barbie's dress, walking leisurely along the red cloth. Had Lisa lied? Or was there something she'd forgotten? I slipped my clothing back on, exited the bathroom, and called out for my sister.

"It's not working. What do I do?"

Lisa tried to muffle her laughter. Then, before I could think to do anything, our parents' voices sounded in the stairwell. Lisa quaked with laughter, holding her sides, savoring my horror. In that one awful moment, I realized that it had all been a joke at my expense. She'd completely tricked me, again.

Lisa grabbed my arms to prevent me from undoing her work. Her laughter followed me as I broke free and slammed the door to my room. I clamped my hand over the fake petals and tore every last one from my head.

I pulled the doll's dress off, ran over to the window, and threw it out angrily. The barrettes followed behind, falling noiselessly down to the street. In the next room, my parents rustled in with plastic bags. I slammed my body into my bedroom door to hold it shut. On the other side, Lisa used her weight to combat my resistance. With one hand, I unraveled the braids, while holding the door shut at the same time. Then I moved out of the way at just the right moment so that she fell through the door and flat on her face. I stood, looking down at the bright red roses spilled around my bare feet.

"What's going on?" Ma poked her head through the door. I burst into tears.

"What happened? Lisa, what did you do?"

"Nothing. I didn't do anything! Lizzy said she wanted me to do her hair. Now she's crying. I don't know why."

"Get out!" I screamed.

"Lisa, tell me—" Ma started.

"Get *out*! Idiot!" I snapped even louder.

Lisa picked herself up and left without another effort to torment me.

Crouching down, Ma opened her arms and engulfed me. I dissolved in her warmth.

"What's wrong with my baby? Tell Mommy what happened."

She combed her fingers through my hair and wiped my tears away with her thumbs. Ma kissed my cheeks and forehead, her eyes so sympathetic I thought she was going to cry, too. In her arms, my anger evaporated.

"Talk to me. Shhhh. Don't cry, pumpkin."

But the crying was what kept her close to me; there was no stopping it.

The world was filled with people who were repulsed by me. Only my mother knew that I deserved to be held. So I let her embrace me and demand over and over to know what was wrong, just so I could hear her voice, feel it vibrating in her chest and humming against my whole body, lulling me into a sense of safety. I buried my face against Ma's neck, trembling and gripping her shirt each time I suspected she might pull away.

I tried to be a good student. I really did. I wanted to be one of those kids who raised her hand in class, knew the answers, and handed in all my work. Like Michelle—during story time she was the best at reading out loud to the class. Or like Marco, who knew the right answers to math problems. I tried to be a good student like them; tried to get good grades. It just didn't work out that way. There was too much going on.

Maybe getting more sleep on school nights would have helped. But I wasn't getting sleep; no one made me. Nearly seven days a week, I bore witness to the endless traffic streaming through our apartment. Ma and Daddy flowed in and out of the house like tireless joggers, all night long. Their need for drugs had become more urgent and out-of-control than ever, and their habits played out in a routine that took up all the space in our apartment. If I wanted to, I could have taken out a calendar, pointed directly at a given day, and guessed ahead of time exactly what would happen, and when. They became that predictable.

Six or seven days into each month, Ma and Daddy blew the SSI check and ran us broke. Then, if there was no money because the check was spent—and it always was—Ma would shake down regulars at the bar for a few dollars, over at the Aqueduct or McGovern's. There was an assortment of older men from whom she'd get one dollar here, two dollars there, loose change from a broken five or ten spread out across the bar. Sometimes she'd beg for a couple of quarters to play the jukebox and instead she'd pocket them. Other times Ma took the men to the bathroom or out in a back alley, and after a few minutes alone with them she could earn even more.

Ma did this until she gathered just enough for a hit. The minimum was five dollars for a "nick's worth" of coke, though this was a cheap high, a junkie's high. Returning from the bars, Ma reported straight to Daddy: "Peter, I got five dollars. Petie, I got five." Then he'd quietly slip on his coat in their room, before trying to sneak away, in case Lisa was still awake.

Daddy knew he'd never hear the end of it if Lisa caught him leaving to buy drugs while we went hungry. There'd be no way to avoid the insults, curses, tears, and shouting.

"You can't spend the money! We need food! I'm starving, my stomach burns. We didn't eat dinner, and you're going to get high?" she'd scream.

Listening to Lisa fight Daddy and Ma, I knew she made perfect sense. There was no excuse for them to spend our last few dollars on drugs when the fridge contained only a jar of rotten mayonnaise and an old, watery head of lettuce. Lisa had every right to be angry.

But things weren't always so clear for me, not like they were for Lisa. Ma said she needed drugs to help her forget the bad memories that haunted her, the thoughts of her mom and dad that caused her to suffer all day long. And even though I wasn't sure what exactly in his past Daddy got high to forget, I knew it must be something very painful, because if Daddy didn't get high, then he would spend days collapsed on the couch in a withdrawal-induced depression. In that state, he became unrecognizable to me.

Lisa's request of our parents was simple—all she wanted was a hot meal and for them to do better by us. I wanted the same. Still, I couldn't help noticing that if we hadn't eaten a hot meal for the entire day, Ma and Daddy hadn't eaten a hot meal in two or three days, either. And when I needed a new winter coat, my eyes kept finding Daddy's sneakers, which were cracked and held together with duct tape. One way or another, Ma and Daddy were always making it clear that they simply couldn't give me what they didn't have.

They had no intention to hurt us. It wasn't as if they were running off during the daytime to be better parents to some other kids and then returning home at night to be awful to us. They simply did not have it in them to be the parents I wanted them to be. So how could I blame them?

I remember one time when Ma stole five dollars from me on my birthday. It had been a gift from my father's mother, mailed from Long Island. The crisp bill had arrived in the mail taped neatly inside a glittery card right above my grandmother's signature and her handwritten birthday wishes. I tucked the bill away in my dresser and planned a trip to the candy store. But that never happened. Instead, Ma waited for me to leave my room and then took the money to buy drugs.

When she returned home half an hour later with a nickel bag, I was furious with her. I demanded that she give me my money, and I shouted mean words at her that are hard for me to think about now. Ma said nothing back. She snatched up her works—syringe and cocaine—from the kitchen table and stormed to the bathroom. I trailed behind her, shouting harsh things. I assumed that she was running away from me to get high in privacy, but I was wrong. Instead, from the bathroom doorway, I saw Ma throw something into the toilet. Then I realized she was crying, and what she had flushed down the toilet was her coke. She'd thrown away the entire hit—despite her desperation.

She looked at me with tears in her eyes, "I'm not a monster, Lizzy," she said. "I can't stop. Forgive me, pumpkin?"

Then I was crying too; we both were. We ended up on the bathroom floor together, hugging each other, her syringe resting on the surface of the sink, directly in my view, my mother's arms riddled up and down with aging needle marks. In the softest voice, she kept asking me for that same simple thing: "Forgive me, Lizzy."

So I did.

She didn't mean to do it; she would have stopped if she could have. "It's okay, Ma, I forgive you," I assured her. I forgave her in that moment, and I forgave her again two months later when she went into the freezer and took the Thanksgiving turkey we'd gotten from the church and sold it to a neighbor so that she could buy another hit. Forgiving her didn't mean that I wasn't devastated. I was heartbroken and deeply hurt whenever they left us hungry. I just didn't blame Ma or Daddy for my hurt. I wasn't angry at them. If I hated anything at all, I hated drugs and addiction itself, but I did not hate my parents. I loved my parents, and I knew they loved me. I was sure of it.

At night, Ma would take breaks from shooting up to visit my bedside and tuck me in, sing to me, just one verse of "You Are My Sunshine." She'd smile at me, rubbing her fingers through my hair. She'd kiss my face and tell me her children were the best thing that ever happened to her. "You and Lisa are my angels, my babies," she'd say, and I knew I was loved. The smell of her Winston cigarettes and the faint, sour smell of coke always lingered—scents that lulled me to sleep.

One winter night, around four a.m. when Daddy was exhausted, he gave in to my demands for a walk around the neighborhood in the virgin snow. The early-morning hour and the new snow, which sparkled like a bed of bright diamonds beneath the glow of Bronx street lamps, insulated us, and made it seem as if the crunching underfoot was the only sound for miles. The more I pressed him, the more we walked. He told me stories of his psychology studies in college; he taught me things he'd learned there, insisting I would need them someday. "I love you, Lizzy," he told me. We walked for miles that night without seeing another soul in the empty, snow-covered streets, until it felt as if there really was no one else; as if Daddy belonged only to me and the world belonged only to us. And I knew I was loved.

Drugs were like a wrecking ball tearing through our family, and even though Lisa and I were impacted, I couldn't help but feel that Ma and Daddy were the ones who needed protecting. I felt like it was my job to keep them safe. There was just something so fragile about them; the way their addiction made them barrel out of the house in total disregard of their safety, at all hours of the night, despite the many news reports about neighborhood rapes, muggings, and cab drivers being shot for their earnings within a ten-block radius of our apartment building.

As though she were impervious to harm, and as though she weren't legally blind, Ma bounded up University Avenue, fearless, throughout the night, even though her vision made it tricky to navigate the darkened Bronx streets. Ma was blind enough to pass someone she knew on the sidewalk—even her family—without recognizing them. But she was familiar enough with shapes and movements to distinguish a moving vehicle from a parked one, or a person approaching her from one walking away, and even a green traffic light from a red one. Still, that did not stop her from encountering dangerous situations.

A handful of times, Ma was attacked in our neighborhood. These incidents horrified me and I pleaded with her to stay home, but nothing could stop Ma when she wanted to get high. One night she was robbed at knifepoint. More than likely, she had been unable to see her attackers targeting her, something an average-sighted person could have spotted. She came home with a black eye, a busted lip, and a story about how the mugger had gotten furious when he found nothing of value on Ma, and had taken it out on her face.

Another time, she came home making her typical single-minded dash from the front door to kitchen with her bag of coke, and it actually took a moment for me to notice the foot-long rip down the side of her jeans and her bloody leg. Ma told me she was hit by a car.

"Nothing serious, Lizzy. It wasn't going that fast, I got right up. Same thing happened when I was a bike messenger. I'm fine," she said, cutting her story short to ask Daddy for her syringe. Ma was either oblivious to the fact that these moments were brushes with death, or she didn't care. It was hard to tell. The only thing that was clear was that when Ma was bent on having something, she was willing to do anything for it.

Blind as she was, Ma had spent three weeks in the seventies working as a bike courier on the busy streets of Manhattan. Of course, they didn't normally hire the near-blind, but Ma needed cash and didn't tell her employer about her impairment. Instead, she borrowed a friend's mountain bike, and because they paid her by the package, she plowed into traffic at life-threatening speeds. Ma had given up on the job after her second accident, but only because her friend's bike was totaled and she had no replacement. That's just the way Ma was, unstoppable when she was determined to get something; unafraid and seemingly unaware of how fragile her life could be.

Daddy wasn't much better at taking care of himself. On drug runs, he would race up University Avenue through gang territories, the dangerous streets of Grand Avenue and 183rd. Once, he'd returned home badly injured, fresh blood spilled over his face, down onto his neck and shirt. A man had beaten Daddy's head into the cement just down the block, and it had taken him almost an hour to stagger home. But by the very next day, Daddy was out of the house again, copping drugs. Like Ma, his addiction was so strong that he gambled with his safety night after night, seeing only the destination ahead of him and not the hazards around him. That destination was the blue door on Grand Avenue, where he climbed the stairs to smooth out Ma's crinkled dollar bills, giving them over to the drug dealers in exchange for the packages of powder that ruled my parents' world.

Sleep on school nights was impossible. Somebody had to watch the windows and time how long they took to come back. Somebody had to keep them safe. If not me, then who? Thirty to forty minutes for a drug run was about the average time it took. Too much longer and that meant there was trouble. "9-1-1," I'd think to myself as I leaned out the window to watch Daddy trek the avenue, shrinking over the curve of University, on his way to another pickup. If he ran into any trouble, I had my plan set. We frequently lost our home phone to unpaid bills, but I could be down at the corner pay phone in moments.

But my responsibilities for the evening did not end there. As Ma and Daddy made their endless drug runs, I passed the hours alongside my parents, searching for other ways that I might be helpful. Ma and Daddy were willing to include me in their activities, and I was thrilled to be a part of them. One way I figured I could be most useful was to help Daddy sneak past Lisa, who was sure to protest if she caught him on his way out. Given that her room was right beside the front door, leaving the house undetected was always tricky for Daddy. That's where I stepped in.

In the corridor leading out of our apartment, I would be lookout, while he hung back. I felt daring, like a character from Daddy's favorite cop show, *Hill Street Blues*; like we were partners in crime.

"Let me know when," he'd whisper, dressed and ready to go, ducking behind the living room partition, waiting for my signal.

"Now." On his way out, Daddy always gave a nod of acknowledgment, something that sent a rush of happiness through me. We were a team. "Don't worry," I'd whisper down the hall behind him, "you're covered."

And how could I go to bed when Ma became giddy setting up their "works" while she waited for Daddy to return with the drugs? There was no way I could pass up these brief moments when she was talkative, a thrill emanating through her bright amber eyes. School could not have been a more distant notion when Ma and I spent our own special time together. We would sit in the living room, talking about her adolescence in the late sixties and early seventies in Greenwich Village.

"You should have seen me, Lizzy. I used to wear thigh-high leather boots with clog heels."

"Really?" I pretended she hadn't repeated these stories a hundred times, and instead acted as though each detail was new to me, feigning shock and curiosity.

"Yup, you bet. I had an Afro too. I've always had kinky hair; that's from my Italian side. Everyone did stuff like that, though. Your father had huge sideburns, *muttonchops*. Seriously!"

Ma talked to me like an old friend on those nights, sparing no detail about her street life, the drug scene, sex with her old boyfriends, and especially her hurt feelings about her childhood. I acted as if there were nothing surprising or vulgar about what Ma shared. Instead, I played it cool and tried to make Ma feel listened to, nodding agreement for things that I hardly understood at all. Ma never noticed. She only continued on, lost in her stories.

The fun part of the night would always come when Ma's past occurred to her as a positive thing, a sort of adventure. But I knew this was temporary, a side effect of her anticipation of shooting up. Later—on the other side of her high, when she was coming down and the drug had begun to lose its effect— the very same thoughts would depress her. I'd be there for the letdown, too. If I didn't listen when she needed to confide in someone, then who would? But first, there was this short, wonderful window of time while we waited. I frequently checked the windows for Daddy, as Ma told her stories, full of rare joy.

"Man, I was always trippin' then! Yeah, acid can really mess with you, Lizzy. Especially when you're at a concert. Don't you do acid, okay? It'll make you think all sorts of things that aren't real. It's funky like that."

Before Daddy's heavy footsteps sounded in the hallway, Ma laid out spoons to cradle the powder, in which she would later deposit a syringe's worth of warm water to dissolve it. Old plastic wonton soup bowls held the water. She placed them beside the shoelaces, which were used to draw up veins; they always used separate syringes to shoot up. Our conversation continued as she inspected each needle, holding it up to the pulsing fluorescent light before placing it back down on the black Formica surface of the kitchen table. My watching her set up their "works" was part of the routine.

"Yup, I used to get modeling offers all the time. Most of the agents wanted sex, though. Watch out for guys like that, they're everywhere. Just a sec"—she'd break away to squirt water out of a syringe to test it. "Yeah, I'm telling you, guys can be scumbags, but I had a lot of fun back then anyway." As she spoke I followed the dried, spattered blood spots along the wall behind her, from the times they missed veins. If it weren't for the absence of a sterilization process, the ritual might resemble a doctor's aide laying out tools for some minor surgery. Soon Daddy would return with the small foil package—the remedy for their ailment.

Every night was like this. While Ma and Daddy injected themselves with cocaine and ran in and out, like a tag team, I stayed close by and shared the night with them. While Lisa slept in her bed, I had them all to myself; I helped keep them safe. And even if they were high, they were still right there, within my reach.

Ma's and Daddy's reactions to the powder were always the same: eyes flung wide open, as though in perpetual shock; small, involuntary twitches running over their faces like electrical surges. Ma was moved by some reflexive force to circle the room, sniffling, holding her fingers pinched shut, directing her speech to the ceiling. At this stage of her high, she never made eye contact.

Roughly twenty minutes later, when she began to come down from the pleasurable part of her habit, the broken version of Ma returned. Her shift in storytelling reflected the change.

"He promised—Pop *swore* he'd get us out of there. He was going to take us to Paris, Lizzy. You know, I was his favorite daughter, I knew it and Lori knew it. Everyone knew it. His favorite. You know, he broke my collarbone when I was a kid, tried to throw me out the window!" she shouted, eyes fixed on the living room ceiling. Ma's pain about her past broke my heart, everything her parents did to her I wished so badly I could take away. I wanted more than anything to take her pain away from her.

Behind her, Daddy twitched and fidgeted with his set of works, cleaning and re-cleaning them in super-slow motion—spilling things, tripping, fumbling, his mind warped from the effects of his high.

"It was the alcohol that made Pop that way, Lizzy. He was always sorry about that. He loved me. You think he loved me, don't you?" Ma asked, chugging on her forty-ounce beer. This was the part when she started crying.

Many times Ma pulled down the neck of her T-shirt to expose her uneven collarbones. One bone jutted out, disjoined from its twin after her collision with the wall when she was a toddler. The fear on her face, real each time, told me that she was there again, reliving her memories. She shot up to feel better, to escape, but somehow the drugs always returned her to the trouble, as though it might be happening to her all over again, right there in our living room.

"I love you, Ma. I'm right here with you," I'd assure her. "We all love you here, Ma."

"I know, Lizzy." But I could tell that my words never got through. Her sadness was just too thick; it drew her miles away from everything, from me.

While Ma spoke, I abandoned my needs—sleep, homework, television, and my toys, unused in my darkened bedroom. Her pain blanketed me in its urgency, so that it became difficult to realize that there was any distance— age-wise or responsibility-wise—between us.

So I learned to talk to her like a friend, even if I didn't really know what I was saying. I insisted, "He must have loved you; he was your daddy. I think the beer made him angry, Ma. If he could have stopped, he would have been a good daddy for you." If this provided any comfort for Ma, it was short-lived. It took her only a half hour to slip on her beige coat, filthy at its cuffs, so that she could return to the dark streets in search of the next hit, still wiping tears from her flushed face. Inside their bedroom, by the light of the street lamp streaking through our murky windows, Daddy fell into a catatonic slumber, deteriorated by the numerous highs he'd achieved this far into the night, but also jolted awake occasionally by the powder still surging through his system.

I went back to my place at the window, to make sure Ma made it up University Avenue. "9-1-1," I'd mumble to myself, "9-1-1," as she shrank down the avenue on her way back to the Aqueduct Bar so that she could set the whole routine in motion, all over again.

When she was out of my view, I counted half-hour chunks of time by the nightly sitcoms I enjoyed, *Cheers* and *The Honeymooners*. Television kept me company during all of the breaks in Ma and Daddy's cycles. I usually rounded off my nights with these shows, then infomercials, and finally morning news announcements, around five a.m. As I got ready to take myself to bed, a faint blue filled the morning sky. By this time, the bars had finally locked their doors, so the only people still out on the street were prostitutes, homeless people, and drug addicts—all as penniless as Ma, and fruitless targets for panhandling. So Ma came home to stay. Safe at last, she collapsed into bed beside Daddy, exhaustion finally overtaking the need to use. Indeed, exhaustion was one of the few things that ever did. When I knew for sure she was in bed, I could finally relax and we could all get some rest.

At dawn, the only noise in our apartment was the upbeat music of early-morning news and Ma's snoring. I readied myself for sleep, slipping into a long, blue nightgown sent from Long Island, Ma's and Daddy's bodies rising and falling as they drew breath, Ma still fully dressed, Daddy in his underwear. Snapping the television off, I settled into bed, knowing that if they didn't need drugs so much, Ma and Daddy would spend more time with Lisa and me. They would make things better, if they could.

✦ ✦ ✦

"Liz, get the hell out of bed!" Lisa had lost any patience for my truancy back when I was in kindergarten. By the time I was in first grade, she'd grown down-right hostile.

"The same crap every day, get out of bed!" She stripped the blankets off me, sending shivers up my body. Outside the window, children clamored to catch a bus. A woman in a blue raincoat directed them by blowing her whistle. I couldn't have gotten more than two hours' sleep.

Each day, by the force of some mysterious strength within her, Lisa rose without prompting to the screech of her alarm, ran water over her face, and took down one of two or three tired shirts from the hook outside her closet. Once dressed, she began our routine battle on her way out the door.

She started off gently, nudging my shoulder and calling out, "Lizzy, it's time to get up. . . . Liz, it's morning," smoothly and encouragingly. But it didn't take her long to learn that she needed a much firmer approach to get me conscious, let alone dressed.

Months passed with Lisa ripping the sheets off me dozens of times, expos-ing my legs and arms to the shocking cold of our rarely heated apartment. In defense, I would curl up in a ball and grip my pillow while she jerked at its free corners, fighting to loosen my grip. In those moments, I hated her more than the idea of going to school; more than the faces of the awful, taunting children I kept in mind throughout my entire struggle to stay home. And I especially resented the pleasure that I sensed she took from volunteering to take on the role of my disciplinary figure.

"I'm your older sister," she'd scream. "You have to listen to me. I'll dump cold water on your head if you don't *move your ass!*"

She meant it too. Lisa splashed a cup of ice cold water right on my head, and I was furious with her. But even being wet and cold couldn't get me out of bed on some days.

On those mornings after staying up with Ma and Daddy, it felt as though I'd just laid my head down for a moment before Lisa was standing over me, angry and frustrated. On this particular morning, grudgingly, I dressed in whatever clothing I had tossed aside the night before, tiptoeing around cautiously, so as not to wake Ma or Daddy. But Lisa didn't seem to notice they were sleeping. She shouted out the time of day every five minutes to warn me we'd be late if we didn't move it. Outside, the cold air hitting my face woke me a little; but the fluorescent lighting and noisy classrooms of P.S. 261 had an adverse effect. They made me sleepy, and this made my head feel fuzzy; and by then all my interest in learning was gone.

Each day, Mrs. McAdams dictated lessons on reading, which I could already somewhat do on my own. Ma had read enough of *Horton Hears a Who!* at my bedside so that I figured out how to read it on my own, which led to trying to read other things, like Lisa's third-grade English lessons and little bits of Daddy's true crime books that he left all over our apartment. This made it easy to ignore the step-by-step explanation of proper spelling and grammar, and let my exhaustion take over. This was when I'd drift, letting my vision sweep the room in rocking motions until my eyes eventually closed shut.

I wondered, half-conscious, if Ma had woken up yet. If so, was she watching *The Price Is Right* without me? Was she in the mood to go for a walk? If I were home, would she take me out with her?

When Mrs. McAdams finished the reading lesson, she reviewed some math problems that I didn't, in any way, recognize. Each minute in class felt like an hour. While she spoke, I often killed time dreaming up reasons I'd give the school nurse for needing to be sent home early: stomachache, flu, fever, plague.

They were at least half true. Every time Mrs. McAdams looked over the room to randomly call on a student to answer a question, my stomach was racked with sharp pains and I felt so shaky I thought I might puke.

When the bell finally rang, I quickly stuffed the pages into my bag. I always tried to slip out ahead of the rest of the students. They made me nervous. Walking between them as I left class, tension tightened my whole body. At least, I thought, Ma had finally scraped all of the lice off my head, using Quell and a comb. Still, I was clearly different from them all. They knew it, and so did I; their stares proved it. My dirty clothing hung heavily off my body. My socks were always weeks old, and I wore my underwear until the crotch dissolved away into nothing. I was aware of the stench I gave off, so I knew they must have been aware, too.

Who cares what people think? Daddy had said. *That's their hang-up.* I tried to tell myself their judgment shouldn't matter. I was, in one way, going through life much faster than all of them—who else cursed freely in front of their parents, went to bed anytime they wanted, knew about sex, and could demonstrate, crudely, how to mainline drugs when they were just six years old? This knowledge did give me some feeling of maturity around them. Still, in ways that I couldn't quite put my finger on, the other kids seemed far more *together* than I was, in the sense that they were actual kids. It was intimidating, the way they mingled so easily with one another and made friends, or raised their hands to answer the teacher's questions, exuding so much confidence. Maybe I was growing up faster, but I worried that I might be skipping too many steps along the way, taking shortcuts that left me feeling scattered, full of holes. Different.

It was the feeling that I was different that gnawed at me in the classroom, pressing me deeper into my exhaustion, racking my stomach with sharp pains. I was always grateful for the end of the day, when I could finally go.

Soon I was outside again, and then after a quick walk, I was home, the school day blessedly far behind me. I was just glad to be somewhere I could rest. And I did, all through the afternoon and into the evening; I slept on the couch so that I could be in the center of the apartment, in the middle of everything.

The following month, December, after weeks of explaining to Ma about the way school made me feel down, she allowed me, against what she called her better judgment, to stay home much of the time. Together, we watched game shows and ate mayonnaise sandwiches on the couch again. Daddy slept until early afternoon and became angry every time he woke to find me home. "Lizzy! You stayed home again?" he'd shout, as though he was somehow surprised at what was becoming a regular occurrence. "You have to go next time, okay?" he'd say, never following up to wake me in the morning. He'd just see me at home, day after day, and shake his head in disapproval.

One Thursday, three weeks into my time off, a morning when Lisa had already lost a fight to get me dressed and left for school, there was a hard knock at the door. I was the only one awake for it. From the hallway, I heard two people talking: a woman and a man. They knocked again, louder this time, making my heart race. I tiptoed over to Ma and Daddy's bed. In their sleep, neither of them flinched. Then I heard voices in the hall speaking to each other, something about a bad smell. I knew they were talking about our apartment. Over the last six months or so, Ma and Daddy hadn't cleaned much. Dirt was collecting on everything. A broken window from one night when Ma lost her temper, slicing open her hand as she punched through it, remained broken. To the best of our ability, we staved off rain and snow from falling into the kitchen with the occasional taped-up plastic bag. But it wasn't effective, and the kitchen was often wet and the apartment freezing. Lisa and I both got the flu that winter. Also the fridge had broken down, and ever since, Daddy had put quarts of milk and packages of cream cheese on the windowsill. But what the people in the hallway must have smelled was the bathtub.

Somehow the drain had gotten clogged. Lisa took a shower in it anyway by using a bucket to scoop out just enough of the old water, and then turning the bucket over so she could stand on top of it to make a little island within the dirty tub. She did this repeatedly, but the water she used was never emptied and over the months it had turned black. There was equally dark slime collecting around the tub's edges. If you stirred the water, a swampy smell kicked up.

The knocking subsided momentarily, and the voices slid a piece of paper under the door. After a few minutes, I heard them leave.

At my bedroom window, I peeked out onto the street below. A dark man holding a briefcase and a tan woman in a long coat approached a double-parked car. The man looked up and I ducked back, convinced he'd spotted me. But they just drove off.

Slowly, I tiptoed to the door and lifted the paper up. It ordered the parent(s) or guardian of Elizabeth Murray to hereby phone a Mr. Doumbia regarding her truancy from school. There was a phone number at the bottom, along with a cartoon outline of an adult holding a child's hand. I didn't know the exact definition of truancy, but figured it had to do with me never showing up to school.

I double-checked to make sure Ma and Daddy hadn't heard anything. Then I folded the paper and ripped it, again and again, tucking the small pieces into different parts of the trash, under wet tissues, banana peels, and beer cans, until it was completely invisible.

✦

One night, Ma came home and announced to us that she'd just made a new friend in the neighborhood, a woman named Tara.

"I was just in line at the drug spot to get a nickel bag and I saw this other *white* lady standing there. That's rare, ya know? So I started talking to her." Ma paused, seeming to decide right there in our living room, "I like her."

They'd hit it off so well that they left and used their coke together, at Tara's apartment on 233rd Street and Broadway. Soon after, Ma, Lisa, and I were there all the time.

Tara had a limp, blond mullet, and a light facial twitch when she was irritable. With her bulky sweaters and ripped stonewashed jeans, she might have perpetually been on her way to an eighties hair-band rock concert, if not for her age, which had to be in her early forties. Her seven-year-old daughter, Stephanie, was wild, prone to unprovoked tantrums at any random time, which made Lisa and me make fun of her relentlessly, behind her back. With olive skin, small, dark eyes, and relaxed jet-black hair, Stephanie must have looked more like her father, whom Tara didn't keep in touch with. Ma told me he used to be kind of famous for acting in a seventies sitcom. But for all the money he made, Stephanie, Tara said, got almost nothing.

In Tara's apartment, Lisa, Stephanie, and I played with toys and watched cartoons while she and Ma got high in her kitchen. The noises they made setting up the drugs in Tara's place, I noticed, were different from the way Ma and Daddy sounded; Tara kept up conversation the entire time. Before that, I'd assumed there was some technical reason Ma and Daddy were so quiet. Listening to Tara and Ma, I realized this wasn't so, and it made me wonder whether Ma and Daddy were as close as I assumed they were.

In their time together, Ma and Tara circulated the same three conversation topics: Stephanie's dad, the quality of their bag, and each other's chosen method of getting high. Tara sniffed her coke; I found out that this is what most people did with it. Ma and Daddy were different in that way. I'd hear Ma explain herself almost every time Tara had to watch her use the syringe.

"Good God, Jeanie, how *do* you do that to yourself?"

"Better than letting the powder cut your nose into pieces. You think I wanna be left without cartilage up there by the time I'm fifty?" Ma said.

"Anyway, Jean, he thinks raising a child is as simple as mailing a check whenever you feel like it, which, did I mention, he never does anyway. Well, you know there's a lot more to it than that."

I found out that Ma wasn't a good conversationalist around new people, at least not when she was high.

"I know" was usually all she said back; but that was all Tara needed to keep going.

"Well, his head's gonna spin when I sue the pants off him. Mr. Big Shot, he ain't gonna get away with this," she'd insist, pointing two fingers forward, a cigarette pinched between them.

It turned out that Ma and Tara had a lot in common. They'd both grown up with abusive, absentee fathers, and had kids before they were ready, and they both lived off of government assistance. Above other drugs, they both preferred the rush coke provided them. But they differed in one key respect— the methods they resorted to in order to sustain their habits. Tara gasped dramatically, listening to Ma talk about how much she hated waiting for welfare each month, and how it was almost easier to hustle guys in the bar or to stop people on the street for cash.

"At least I know if I'm out there, I don't have to wait. I *hate* to wait," Ma said.

Tara called Ma's scrounging "panhandling" and said it was beneath them both. But Ma couldn't care less about her pride when she wanted to get high.

"Oh no, Jean, we've got to get you to cut that out. You should meet Ron," she told Ma. "He takes care of me. He'll probably help you out, too. No more begging for you. That's no good," she insisted.

We all met Ron, together, the very next Sunday. He was an older man, mid-sixties, very thin, with pale skin and large brown eyes. His jacket was sparrow-brown, with patches covering the elbows. He used a separate voice for speaking to children.

"Well, hello there, you pretty little ladies. And how are we all doing today?" he said as we sat in a row on Tara's couch, the early-afternoon sun streaking through Tara's sheer curtains.

Stephanie got up to hug his leg. Lisa and I were a little shyer, so we hung back. He tried to win us over with candy. I snatched three butterscotches from his hand and began unwrapping one, fast. He smiled and rubbed my head.

"That's a good girl," he said.

Lisa remained quiet and held her candy in her hand until Ron went back into the kitchen. He winked at her on his way out. She turned to me.

"Don't eat that crap," she said, smacking it out of my hand.

"Why?" I whined.

"We don't know him, that's why."

"You ruin everything!" I screamed.

Right from the start, Lisa didn't like Ron. "He's a stranger," she always reminded me. "We don't know him. Treat him like a stranger."

But was he a stranger if he was Tara's friend? And would a stranger take us out to eat? Would he buy us candy and take us for a long ride in his big, red car? And especially, would Ma warm up to a stranger so quickly?

Ron bought Tara most of her drugs, and she assumed, correctly, that he would do the same for Ma.

While Lisa, Stephanie, and I lay on our stomachs on Tara's plush carpet in front of the TV watching cartoons, Tara introduced Ma to Ron in her kitchen. Soon after, the three of them slipped into Tara's bedroom, shut the door, and didn't come out for a long while. Occasionally, we heard a giggle or a thud, but it was impossible to tell what they were doing. Ron was the first to return to the living room.

"Now, which one of my girls is hungry?" he asked, rubbing his hands together.

Ron took us all to eat at International House of Pancakes, not too far from Tara's apartment, on Broadway. He surprised us by saying we could get anything we wanted—something neither Lisa nor I had ever done before. The notion of limitless food seemed unreal. I ordered a whole stack of pancakes that the two of us could have never finished. So did Lisa. I enjoyed pouring almost the entire syrup bottle onto my unused portion. No one noticed. Stephanie's habit of ordering eggs grossed out both Lisa and me; we'd had enough eggs to last us a lifetime. Between bites, Stephanie drummed her fork on the table and kicked her legs all around.

Ma, Tara, and Ron spoke in whispers over lunch. Ron did most of the talking, leaning in close so he could speak privately to them while resting his hand on their thighs, something that I saw made Ma fidget.

Our next stop was in a desolate area of the Bronx, near abandoned, burned-down buildings, where men wearing flashy jewelry stood on street corners, dancing beside enormous radios. Ron passed Tara and Ma some cash from his breast pocket, and Ma ordered Lisa and me to stay put in Ron's car. She walked over with Tara to give the money to the men and I knew they were buying drugs. Ron turned around and talked to us while we all waited.

"How did you girls get so pretty?" he asked. "You look like a car full of supermodels."

Stephanie squealed with laughter. I concentrated on Ma.

Something about the men she and Tara spoke to made me nervous. I shut my eyes tight and didn't open them until I could hear Ma entering the car. When we were driving again, Tara told Ron they each got a D-I-M-E B-A-G.

No matter how much Ma told Tara that Lisa and I knew all about drugs, she still tried to be discreet around us, and around Stephanie.

"Dime bag," Lisa said. "Tara, I know how to spell."

"Oh, be quiet, Lisa," she snapped.

Back at Tara's, with Ron keeping them company, she and Ma got high for hours.

Ron started coming around in his dusty red car every Sunday to pick us up at Tara's apartment. Our outings became the thing I looked forward to all week long. No matter what else was happening, I'd think of Sunday and count the days. But, taking my cue from Ma, I hid my excitement and never talked about the time we spent with Ron when Daddy was around. More from instinct than thought, I knew that our trips were something Ma didn't want Daddy to know too much about. As far as he knew, we were just passing time with Ma's friends.

Ron must have looked forward to Sundays the way I did, because he was never late to Tara's place. He'd show up at exactly eleven a.m., honking the car horn three times. We'd drive aimlessly, for hours. Tara played the radio loudly from the front seat, so we could all sing along together.

At IHOP again, we feasted on pancakes, sausages, and orange juice, while Ron whispered more mysterious stories close to Tara's and Ma's ears, stories that made them laugh with their heads thrown back.

"That's when you have to up and out if you want to save your own A-S-S," Tara added to something he'd said, slamming her fist on the table, jingling our forks and knives.

"Tara, you're a riot. Only you, man," Ma responded. Always hyper, Stephanie kicked her seat repeatedly. Whenever they weren't looking, Ron's eyes skimmed up and down Ma's and Tara's T-shirts.

✦ ✦ ✦

One day, when Tara was busy doing something else, we met up with Ron without her or Stephanie. He suggested that Ma, Lisa, and I go to his house, out in Queens.

"Come on, Jean." He'd coaxed Ma out in front of our building, tugging on her wrist. "We can pick up a bag. You'll like my place, it's real nice."

The drive there was long; it was the first time I can clearly remember being on a highway. The cars zipping past made the trip seem adventurous to me, but Lisa fell asleep.

Without Tara around, Ma and Ron didn't seem to know what to say to each other. Ron turned his tape player up, a country-music singer's whiny voice filling the car. Ma fidgeted in her seat the whole, silent trip there. Once, I thought I saw him reach across and rest his hand on her thigh, but Ma shifted too quickly for me to get a clear view.

Ron's place was a real house, two stories high, with a front yard and a garage. A thick, glass wall divided into squares separated the living room from the dining room, and viney plants hung from hooks above a large, black piano.

Everything was made of gleaming blond wood. Ron and Ma headed straight for the kitchen. Lisa turned on the TV and we watched cartoons from his huge, black leather couch.

Hours later, I woke up to Ron's rough hand on my shoulder.

"Girls, wake up."

"Where's Ma?" Lisa asked.

"She went to the store for a beer. She'll be back in a little while."

I'd never seen Ron dressed in shorts before. Why had Ma left us behind?

"The store is far from here, so it will be a bit. She asked me to look after you both; she said you needed a bath," he told us, clasping his hands together and lowering his chin with a seriousness that seemed insincere.

Given that it wasn't uncommon for me to go a month or two without washing or brushing my teeth, this struck me as strange. One time, while I was helping to hang up test sheets in class, my teacher noticed a patch of dirt on my neck and told me that when I showered that night, I should make sure to scrub extra-hard there. Though our clogged tub prevented me from showering, I was embarrassed enough to take a washcloth and scrub my neck when I got home. Bits of dirt had rolled off into my hands.

Considering the uselessness of our tub at home, I thought maybe Ma wanted us to take the opportunity to bathe here.

Ron watched us from the toilet, while Lisa and I sat together in the soapy water. Not only had I never seen Ron in shorts, I'd also never seen him without his tweed jacket before. In the steamy bathroom, I saw that underneath it, he was even thinner, in an almost feminine way, with large nipples that showed right through his shirt. I wished he would put his jacket back on and go. The white tiles were shiny clean and the bathroom lemon-scented. As we washed, he kept his eyes just below our necks. Something about that look made me cover myself. I curled into a ball, pulling my knees to my chest. Lisa had a look on her face that bordered somewhere between worry and anger.

"Your mother wants me to make sure that you girls wash every part now," he said. "I want to see every part get squeaky clean. Let's see those feet," he said. "And those legs. Above the water, or else it's not really clean."

Under his instruction, Lisa and I lifted our feet, ankles, calves, and thighs above the water to scrub clean.

"Now, one of the hardest parts to wash is your privates, so we need you girls to stick that way up high in the air and clean every crevice. Come on, I want to see them clean."

"How?" I asked.

"Come on, use your hands to lift yourself up and push your privates above the water," he said eagerly.

"I know how to take a bath," Lisa said, scowling. "You don't need to watch us." Ron swallowed and his eyes darted all around the room; it was the first time he'd taken them off our bodies.

I had already lifted my crotch way out of the water and was washing when she'd spoken up. In a way, I wondered why Lisa didn't say something sooner. I could feel her anger when he first made us get in the tub.

"Now, Lisa, I'm just making sure," he said cautiously. "Liz knows that, don't you, Liz?"

I didn't know anything other than the fact that Lisa was mad, Ma wasn't back yet, and I was getting nervous about the way he kept staring at me.

"Get out! We're fine by ourselves!" Lisa suddenly yelled.

"Okay, then. I suppose big sister is going to make sure that everything in here is taken care of, then," Ron said, backing away.

"Get the hell *out*!" she screamed.

With that, he closed the door behind him. Together, Lisa and I dressed in complete silence.

Five weeks later, Ma had her first mental lapse in more than six years, and Lisa and I were hauled into family services for examinations, during a night I can recall only in fragments.

Lying flat on my back, I watched the doctor take one latex glove from a box—one, not two. It made a snap when he put it on. I'd never seen anyone do that before, wear just one glove. I was going to tell him he forgot the other one. But before I got a chance, he turned away and went back to talking with a blond woman. I couldn't see past them to the counter, where they were fidgeting with something. I just saw their white uniforms, the white walls, and the white papers covering the counter that read my name—Elizabeth Murray—and next to it, my birth date, September 23, 1980. I'm six, I thought, proud of how I counted so quickly. Elizabeth, not Lizzy. No, here my name is Elizabeth.

"Elizabeth, are you hungry? Have you eaten anything today? Would you like some soup, a sandwich? Elizabeth, you can tell us, honey, does your father touch you?"

The night had already been so long; the weeks leading up to it even longer. Ma hadn't been herself. It started with the crying fits. Unprovoked, she'd scream accusations into the air or threats to no one in particular: "Get your hands off! I'll kill you!"

Then one day she just stopped, wrapped all those shouts and tears into her ankle-length bubble coat where she lived, a single member of some far-off world. If you tried to talk to Ma, she'd snap up the ends of the collar with her skinny fingers. Her eyes became electric, a warning to be heeded. She no longer recognized any of us.

When the police came to load her into the ambulance, she thought they wanted the coat. The struggle was brief, no more than two swift hits, methodically placed—a demonstration of the officer's academy training. Our building's hallway filled with her ghostly cries for help. The neighbors' doors creaked open in succession from nearest to farthest. Soon after, when the chaos moved to the windows, locks snapped shut the same way.

"The doctor's just going to do a test. Okay, Elizabeth? It won't hurt; it's just a little uncomfortable. Hold still and be a brave girl, okay?"

A breakdown, I heard someone call it. Not her first, Daddy reminded me; maybe not her last. Lisa and I were placed in a police car—without Daddy—that followed the ambulance carrying Ma as it drove in silence, its signature red light piercing the night as we made our way up University Avenue.

I kept my eyes shut tight the entire time.

I never told anyone that Ma's breakdown was my fault, that I had brought it on by telling what happened. When Ma returned to Ron's house from the store with a six-pack, Lisa called her into the bathroom with us. I thought she would tell, so I did it first, and I watched Ma's face fill with horror. Ma ran out of the bathroom angrier than I'd ever seen her. I could hear her hit Ron across the face. Then she took us home on a long, long train ride, where Lisa told Ma about one time at Tara's when Ron had asked to take Polaroids of her. The conversation embarrassed me. My hair still wet from the bath, I remained totally silent and went to sleep on Ma's lap. For days after that, the questions didn't cease.

"Lizzy, tell Ma about every time Ron made you feel bad, baby. You can tell me, pumpkin, please."

The shame was so heavy, I couldn't look Ma in the eyes, and my throat ached when I told her how afraid I was in the bath, and how worried I was when Ron pinched Stephanie's chest because she'd misbehaved. Then I told Ma about the time he helped me with my zipper, privately, in Tara's room, his fingers scraping against my skin. I couldn't move throughout the whole thing; I froze and could only stare up at the wooden ceiling fan, listening to the click it made on each go-around, counting them as he thrust his fingers inside me painfully. Held firmly in place by Ron's free hand, my privates burned. I bit ridges into my bottom lip to keep from wailing.

I told Ma all but one detail—the fact that I knew it was wrong. I knew that all I had to do to end it was to call out for her. But I didn't, because Ron made things better for Ma, for Lisa and me. I didn't want to ruin that, so I failed to call out. When he'd finished and slipped back into the kitchen with Ma and Tara, I'd used Vaseline from the bathroom cabinet to soothe the pain.

This was how I knew I had driven Ma crazy. I could have stopped Ron before anything worse happened, but I didn't. Then, later, I told Ma about what Ron had done. It was the last straw. Ma snapped.

Now a voice in the doctor's office said that she had brought the breakdown on herself with all her "drug abuse"; that she never gave her schizophrenia medicine a fair chance to work. Only I knew they were wrong. "Check the kids," another woman in clicking heels ordered a nurse. "You should have heard what their mother had to say about their father. Find a doctor and check these kids. We have to find out what's been going on."

With two fingers pointed skyward, like a priest's blessing, the doctor applied a kind of jelly to his glove. The nurse drew metal stirrups out of the table. Each made its own metallic snap when extended.

"Elizabeth, honey, this will be over soon. We just need you to put your feet here for now. Be a good girl and stay still."

My heels rested, caged in cold metal. My legs frogged open to form a diamond, raising the hospital gown into the air—a paper sail to catch flight above the goose-bump breeze that pricked my skin and cooled my thighs. A chill ran over my naked pelvis as the doctor pulled his chair in close.

Lying there, I wanted Ma, the soft feel of her hair in my fingers, the reassurance of her hand holding mine. As the doctor positioned a warm lamp on me, I longed most for her protection, for things to go back the way they had been. If only I had told her sooner.

A sharp pain shot through me as the doctor began his examination in the place Ma and Daddy told me no one should touch, a place I myself had never touched. A place where, even if no one believed it, Daddy had never touched me.

I felt a metal rod tearing me open. I managed only the faintest whimper as his fingers entered me. The doctor's intrusion made a dull ache that sent my back arching. The nurse's press-on nails pinched as she held on to my shins. Tears rolled into my ears.

"That's all, Elizabeth. We'll be outside. You can get dressed now, honey."

A tree of pain throbbed and grew through my abdomen. I descended from the table slowly and carefully, a bright strip of blood coloring my thigh.

Somewhere, in a room nearby, my sister was enduring the same.

I lifted myself back onto the noisy paper to take a look, curling my body into a C. To my horror, the source of the blood was an angry, red gash between my legs. Fear shot through my chest. My eyes raced across the empty room for something to bandage the hole with. I quickly plucked several gauze pads from a blue-and-white medical box. My trembling gave way to panicked sobs.

Tears fell onto the paper gown in spots that expanded on impact. I cried to the ceiling and held the gauze tightly to my wound, unable to imagine ever feeling normal again.

CHAPTER 3

Tsunami Weather

FOLLOWING HER 1986 BREAKDOWN, MA'S MENTAL ILLNESS PROVED to be more menacing than any of us expected. All together, Ma suffered six schizophrenic bouts in just four years, each requiring her to be institutionalized for no less than one month, no more than three. Initially, I regarded Ma's attacks as something to dread for the ways they changed her and for the haunting images her episodes replayed before me.

Ma in a conversation with the characters flashing across our TV screen, the uniformed police officers dispatched to our living room to take her away, standing among our furniture, their boots pressed down on our carpet, their crackling walkie-talkies clipped tightly to those tough leather belts. Curled up on our couch, I passed the corner of my pink nightgown through my fingers over and over, watching when they pulled Ma's wrists together for the handcuffs, as she never went voluntarily.

The beige tiles of the mental ward's stain-resistant floor; Ma's life made uncomplicated, in her assigned room with a bed for sleeping, a square cabinet for "personals," a sink for washing. Ma's big blank eyes unfocused, wide as two boiled eggs, staring ahead at nothing.

As time passed, Ma's drug abuse doubled, then tripled in frequency. The addiction became obvious in every part of her, from her diminished ability to string together whole sentences to that overused spot on her forearm that became perpetually infected, as dark and raw as a cracked plum. I began to think differently of her months in the mental hospital. As long as she was able to, Ma would get high; the breakdowns were the only thing that stopped her.

The posters at school called drug abuse a slow form of suicide. At the pace Ma was going, I was beginning to feel that the mental hospital was all that was saving her. And with each hospitalization came the hope, however futile, that she could remain sober.

On each of her returns from North Central Bronx Psychiatric Ward, Ma seemed ready for a healthy, drug-free life: thicker around the thighs and waist, the dark circles gone from underneath her eyes, and her beautiful black hair shimmery and thick again. She'd make regular trips to Narcotics Anonymous, and over those weeks, the glass jewelry box from Daddy quickly filled with optimistic piles of rainbow-colored NA keychains marking her steps toward sobriety in increments of one day, one week, or one month clean. But they always seemed to halt there.

As inevitably as a shift in seasons, Ma would start to show the signs of another oncoming lapse, beginning with her absence from meetings. She'd linger in the living room too long, flipping channels until six p.m. came and went; she'd miss one meeting, then two, then three, and then when her SSI check arrived, she'd go on a weeklong drug binge that ran us broke. Then she'd sleep that off for days as the phone rang and rang with unanswered calls from her NA sponsor. As it turned out, the coke had a way of counteracting the effects of Ma's psychiatric medication, and enough bingeing would always land her back in the psychiatric ward, leaving Daddy to fill in as a full-time single parent.

Daddy rose to the occasion. Just as Ma had found it easier to manage our finances when Daddy was in prison, so it seemed Daddy was able to stretch the monthly checks in a way I hadn't realized was possible. I learned with some degree of relief, as well as hurt, that all three of us could go an entire month eating dinner each night, and usually with something to eat during the day as well, on that same check that I'd spent years watching Ma and Daddy deplete in only days following its arrival. Had it been possible to feed us this well all along? Humming tunes from his favorite oldies songs, Daddy spent evenings sweating over the oven, cooking up two-dollar steaks with mashed potatoes or pasta for sides. On the two days a week we visited Ma, Daddy gave Lisa and me four quarters each. I always saved half of it in my Pooh bear piggy bank; not so much for any future purchase, but just to be able to drag my hand through the growing pile and know it was mine. Toward the end of this four-year stretch of Ma's hospital stays, I realized that I could measure Ma's time away by counting the quarters. By the middle of the year in 1990, more than once, I had accumulated over twenty dollars in change before Ma found and stole my savings. "Crazy quarters," I had called them, for Ma's craziness. Daddy had more money then too, because he used drugs more conservatively, no more than seven or eight times a week, when Ma was away. In her absence, there were no more multiple drug runs either. Daddy seemed almost content to be sober the rest of the time.

And finally, there was the brief period just after Ma came home, before both of them fully let drugs back in, when they were semi-sober together. The four of us saw movies at the Loew's Paradise Theater, Ma braided my hair, Daddy orchestrated day trips to the library, and the rug got vacuumed.

Though, like a pendulum, I knew Ma and Daddy to be either all to one side—social, approachable—or on their way toward the other—totally removed, inaccessible in almost every way. It was a relentless back and forth, the momentum of their switch determined by the different stages of Ma's mental illness. That was until they broke the pattern in the summer of 1990, a time that marked an alarming eight months of their most severe drug abuse ever. This overlapped, not coincidentally, with the lowest point in their troubled marriage. Their relationship seemed to worsen as Ma lingered in her longest period of sanity in the last four years. The slump went on for so long that not only did it feel permanent, but it also left me wondering about my love for Ma. I found myself wishing, almost daily, for her to lose her mind and be committed again, so that something, *anything* would clear away the haze that had settled over us.

That was the summer before I turned ten, when, after a series of daily shouting matches and sometimes violent arguments, mostly instigated by Ma, that lasted for all of June, Ma and Daddy began sleeping separately. Their most recent fights were based primarily on vague suspicions Ma held against Daddy, declaring him "no goddamn good."

"It's just *him*," she'd say. "He's *conniving*."

Though Ma's doctors deemed her recovery from each breakdown as "full," over her last three or so releases, Ma retained an irrational, vague, but consistent image of Daddy's having something "off" about him.

"It's just his character, Lizzy. You'll understand when you're older."

Unlike so many of the things Ma's mind created because of her sickness, part of me wondered whether or not she had reason to mistrust Daddy. When Ma would go on one of her rants about him, I defended him, but part of me would think about all the time he spent out of the apartment with no explanation as to where he'd been. And sometimes, this one fuzzy memory about Daddy would surface.

In the memory I was maybe six years old and Lisa was about eight. Daddy walked with us down a Manhattan block and I could see that we were heading toward a park. As we got closer to the park Daddy let go of my hand and pushed me toward Lisa. I remember that there was something about him that made me anxious.

"Go with Lisa, Lizzy. She's gonna take you to see Meredith."

I wondered where we were going and why Daddy wasn't going to come with us to the park. With my free hand, I reached for him, but Daddy backed away. His hands were shaking.

"Come on, Liz," Lisa said, pulling on my hand. "Let's go see Meredith. She's right there."

A teenaged girl stood across the street in front of a path leading into the park. She had brown hair and she was waving at us, smiling in a way that implied we were familiar with one another. Years later, Lisa would confirm this memory and tell me that before he met Ma, Daddy had another daughter. We had a sister, named Meredith. Daddy had abandoned her when she was barely two years old.

I don't recall Daddy ever talking about Meredith at home or in front of Ma. She never came to visit. Sometimes it felt as though I made up the memory of her, but I knew I hadn't. And every now and then Lisa and I would talk about how we wanted to meet Meredith again, and get to know our big sister. But no one talked about Daddy's other life before us, or our other sister. And with all the time Daddy liked to spend out of the house, it made me wonder what else I didn't know about him. The feeling this gave me was one of Daddy being somewhat mysterious.

Whether or not his mysteriousness was the actual cause, Ma was often furious with and suspicious of Daddy, and she expressed herself freely, shouting at him, provoking fights. Daddy was more laid-back, having grown indifferent to Ma's fits. "You can take it for only so long before you tune out," he'd tell me, an attitude that only deepened Ma's mistrust and anger. It was hardly a surprise when they finally stopped functioning as a couple altogether. In a way, Ma's moving to the couch felt overdue.

The living room took on a bedroom feel with the addition of Ma's things; cigarettes, matches, keys, and underwear littered the coffee table, among old magazines and crust left behind from food stuck to a fast-growing collection of dishes surrounded by an ever-present swirl of flies. During the day, while she slept and Daddy was downtown, I walked the softest steps past the couch, stopping only to shut the window and keep the draft off Ma, or to cover her naked body with a sheet. Coming in close, I could smell the aroma of sour beer breath circulated by Ma's snoring. When she was awake, Ma walked circles through the apartment and found everything depressing. She made multiple daily runs to the bodega for forty-ounce bottles of Budweiser, which she drank in heavy gulps, breaking occasionally to burst into tears.

Getting high became one of the last things Ma and Daddy did together. When they weren't shooting up, Daddy read by his nightstand, sometimes laughing so loudly I'd hear it all the way from the bathroom. Daddy staved off the fighting, shielded by his newly private bedroom and his books. The only real concerns he expressed were over very particular things. As long as everything was together—his aging, faded magazines stacked in some private but vital order, the empty Sunny Delight bottle beside his bed so he could avoid regular trips to the bathroom at night—Daddy could lie there uninterrupted for hours. He'd have no trouble relaxing, he said, if only everyone would just remember to screw the goddamn cap on the Pepsi, *tight*; or if he could understand why anyone would think two slices of turkey didn't make a sandwich; and if he knew, for certain, that all the oven's knobs were switched *off*.

Whenever Ma and Daddy's fighting became too bitter, Lisa and I locked ourselves in our own rooms at opposite ends of the apartment, her with her music, and me with my books. I sat at my desk, where I could read for hours. I read very slowly through Daddy's true crime books, his biographies and his books on random trivia. Eventually, I began reading fast enough to get through one of his books in a little over a week. And though my attendance at school remained spotty, this made the year-end exams passable. Even if I hardly showed up for class, I could make sense of most literary material put in front of me. After consistently earning high grades on my exams, I was always promoted to the next grade, whether or not I really learned anything in school.

Still, it wasn't long before I looked for an outlet outside of school, outside of reading and our apartment. Right after the first grade, I'd begun making daily rounds throughout the neighborhood in search of something to take my mind off my family. In July 1987, this search had led me to Rick and Danny. Brothers born two years apart, they were mistaken for twins everywhere we went. Both had the same caramel skin, toothy smiles, and identical close-cropped haircuts. I was one year younger than Rick and one year older than Danny, a fact that made me feel I could have been their sister, aside from their Puerto Rican heritage.

We first met on a morning when Rick and Danny were playing on a mattress in the trash on University Avenue. The moment I saw them there, I thought that they were different-looking from the kids at school—dirty, almost wild, like myself—which made it easy to reach out to them.

"Can I get on your trampoline?" I asked Rick as he and his brother bounced up and down in front of me. "Yo, be my guest," he answered, moving aside, smiling. The three of us spent over an hour that day playing together and talking. We were in awe of our similarities. Danny had had the same kindergarten teacher I had at P.S. 261. Kraft macaroni and cheese was their favorite snack, too. Rick also liked hide-and-seek better than freeze tag, and we had the same birthday, even if he was one year older. A few hours later that same day, I found myself in Rick and Danny's squeaky-clean, three-bedroom apartment surrounded by their family, which consisted of their older brother John, little brother Sean, their stepfather, and their mother, whose name was also Liz. She was a kind woman who smelled of oregano and smiled warmly at me as she scooped generous servings of rice and beans onto my dinner plate. Afterward, in the boys' room, Rick, Danny, and I competed fiercely in video games late into the night. Someone had draped a blanket over me on the bottom bunk, where I fell asleep with my sneakers still on.

In the three years since, I'd dug my own half footing into Rick and Danny's crowded family. Through countless sleepovers and Spanish food dinners at their place, family trips headed by Liz to theme parks and to the Bronx Zoo, I'd forged my way into numerous appearances in family photo albums and home videos. It was a quiet pleasure I took, to think that any stranger or new friend of the Hernandezes who might be presented with family memorabilia could see *me* there, in the pages of their albums, posing naturally beside the boys at communions, or with my arm slung around their grandmother at casual family outings, Rick, Danny, John, and Sean there with me, aging together as the pages progressed. My favorite images were of Rick's and my mutual birthday parties. Liz always remembered to have the bakery write both our names in scripted frosting along the top of the pineapple Valencia cakes. Dozens of pictures captured the two of us blowing out double the amount of candles, Liz clapping wildly over us, her hands frozen in a streak of motion, vivid and persistent as hummingbirds' wings.

I cherished Rick and Danny's family, yet in the time I'd known them, I had never mentioned my own family or given any real details about my home. It's not that Rick, Danny, or Liz never asked, so much as I was good at guarding my secrets, either immediately changing the subject or touching up aspects of myself that might tip them off. I used rubber bands to make sloppy ponytails from the golf-ball-size knots dangling in my hair. For the embarrassing dirt spots along my neck, the moment I entered their apartment I made sure to use the bathroom, where I scrubbed my neck over the sink until the dirt rolled off in little threads and my skin turned bright pink from the harsh rubbing. And to cover the rank odor that rose from my rotten sneakers when I removed them for sleepovers, I always tried to stick my shoes in some far-off corner in the apartment, in the boys' closet or behind the garbage can in the kitchen, where Liz might mistake the smell for trash. If I could hide the things that made me feel different, I could relax more and feel like I really belonged. Equally, when I returned to my own apartment, I withheld things from my family, too.

Instinctively, I knew that I should not allow Ma and Daddy a full view of my experiences with Rick and Danny, and especially with Liz. When Ma was plastered to the couch, flies buzzing over her head, cigarette butts floating in her nearby bottle of beer, it just didn't seem right to tell her that I'd spent my day at a picnic or at the pool, playing in the sun, eating home-cooked meals with Rick and Danny's family. The same went for Daddy and Lisa. Any joy I managed outside of our home felt, to me, like a form of betrayal. I found that I was always hiding; there wasn't room for my full self in either my own apartment, or in Rick and Danny's place, or in school, or anywhere I went. It all had to be kept separate. If I wanted to squeak by unnoticed in class, or be a "good" daughter at home, or a "normal" person to my friends, I needed to tuck away parts of myself.

More and more, the summer I was nine years old, I itched to be outside, to be a part of what went on in the world. The Bronx streets surrounding my building were magnetized, with their moving crowds and winding back alleys, littered from ground to sky with outdoor clotheslines flapping vivid purples, greens, and golds, like new flags. I yearned for movement, for an outlet of some sort, and my friendship with Rick and Danny—when we were not in the company of their parents—fast became a channel for these restless feelings.

The three of us roamed the Bronx, wandering until our feet ached, walking just to see how far we could walk, down the Grand Concourse, along Jerome Avenue, beneath the number 4 train tracks until they curved underground, miles away from University Avenue, near Yankee Stadium. There, the Bronx met upper Manhattan and the street signs read unfamiliar names; the red- or tan-bricked buildings became ragged auto body shops fed by traffic streaming in from the nearby highways. Then we'd turn back and take an entirely different route home, while the sun set on the Bronx and the streets took on a dangerous quality, boom boxes crackling in darkened side streets, brooding strangers clustered under street lamps. Often our play turned to mischief. Together we became troublemakers, street kids, what older people called derelicts. As time passed, our favorite kind of thing to do together became anything outrageous, anything dangerous, and especially anything we were not supposed to be doing.

There was the time that we accidentally burned down the storage shed at the old-age home. It started at Rick and Danny's apartment, where we'd watched a movie about cave explorers. While the men climbed and maneuvered their way through the dangerous enclosures, Liz served us Kool-Aid with ham-and-cheese sandwiches for lunch. "Here we are," she said, "for the three musketeers," something she always called us. Later that day in Aqueduct Park, I had an idea to make exploration tools of our own with a thick tree branch and bundles of paper bags, rubber-banded to the top. I used Rick's lighter to ignite the "torch." Our task, I informed the boys, was to "investigate" the tool shed outside the local nursing home, which was dark and mysterious enough to qualify us as real-deal explorers.

While climbing through a hole in back of the shed and carrying our torch, we inadvertently set fire to the shed within seconds, causing the alarm in the main building to go off. I was the first to back away, while Danny stood awestruck before the bright, spreading ball of flames, half believing his eyes.

"Yo man, it's on fire!"

I grabbed their shirts, tugging them hard.

"Run!" I shouted, *"Now!"*

We ran at top speed in silence until we reached a nearby van, large enough to conceal the three of us behind it, where we rested our palms on our knees and gasped for air. From there we watched, petrified, while firemen raced to hose off the tool shed, with a couple dozen elderly people crowding the sidewalk in their robes, stunned out of their bingo session, Rick guessed.

We explored the area beneath the 207th Street Bridge, and walked beside the Metro-North Railroad, where we could place stones along the train tracks so that they would go flying on impact. We ran clear across the Cross Bronx Expressway for the thrill of dodging speeding cars. I navigated our neighborhood rounds, sometimes directing us into supermarkets to stuff our pockets full of candy bars, making sure we exited at separate times to be discreet; I could devour three whole bars of chocolate within five blocks of leaving the store. We threw fist-size rocks clear through warehouse windows, savoring each loud burst followed by the acoustic clank of the falling shards. Laughter bonded us in these moments; courageous pranks were the highlight of our outings.

On a day early in July 1990, we spent hours dipping in and out of apartment buildings along Grand Avenue just to remove every last doormat from every last doorstep and dump each one down the elevator shaft, pausing to listen to their floppy descent. We kept the laughter to a minimum and made it to the ground floor undetected.

Standing in the lobby, eager for another thrill, Danny began popping open someone's mailbox with a screwdriver that he kept in his back pocket. My eyes caught a metal curtain rod leaning on the wall. I picked it up and passed it to Rick.

"Test this out," I said. He stared at it and then looked to me for clarification. I motioned to a mysterious, mousetrap-size compartment on the inside frame of the open elevator door.

"Yeah, try that," Danny said, fanning envelopes high in the air.

Without hesitation, Rick hooked the end of the thin rod into the box. Instantly, a bright spark flashed and crackled at the point of contact. Rick stumbled backward in a way that appeared totally involuntary. He looked down at his hand and spread his fingers, which were dusted black. Danny laughed first, and then we all did, hard and hysterically. Our voices boomed up the stairs and echoed back down at us. I could smell the faint odor of smoke. Rick shrugged his shoulders.

"At least I did it," he said, his eyes still wide with shock. There was a pause.

"Yeah, you did," Danny said, laughing.

Unlike the guys, I had no curfew and I coaxed them to stay out too late, disregarding their mother's rules. It's not that I wanted them to get in trouble, so much as I didn't want them to leave. Sometimes we would stay out until the dark sky grew light again—what we in the Bronx called "breaking night."

On the evenings when the guys eventually did go home, I was left with nothing to do. Walking back as slowly as possible, I replayed images of our day together. Entering our building, and then 2B, I mapped out plans for the next day. Maybe we would sneak into the movie theater and movie-hop all day, or go to the Bronx Zoo on Wednesday, free admission day.

Compared to the dry summer air outside, our apartment was thick with a humid odor primarily coming from our bathroom; the tub was still clogged and more pungent than ever. Daddy even nicknamed the black substance inside "the Blob." The house was completely dark, except for the TV, which was barely audible. I knew Lisa was in her room because I heard Debbie Gibson music coming from her cassette player, turned low. Walking to the back of the apartment, I followed the sound of Ma sniffling in the pitch-black bedroom, where all I could make out in the darkness was the orange tip of her cigarette. Her sad records were on again, something she called *Cry of the Humpback Whales*, which meant she'd already gone through Judy Collins.

"Hey, Ma," I spoke to her cigarette light. There was a pause, and then I heard her draw in a deep breath, followed by the swish of her beer bottle.

"Hi, Elizabeth." The screeching of the whales peaked, drowning out the end of her greeting. She used my full name only when she was slipping back into a schizophrenic episode, so hearing it made me nervous.

"Ma, what's wrong?" I took just two steps into the room, feeling around for the mattress. I sat on the very corner of it, as close to the door as possible. As Ma spoke, I circled my fingers along one of the exposed mattress springs.

"Oh," she said, half laughing. "I just . . . I don't know, Elizabeth. I'm lonely." The tip of her cigarette glowed brighter.

"Where's Daddy?"

"Who knows," she replied flatly.

"Did you guys have another fight?" Still charged up from being outside, I swung my feet back and forth.

"Your father is not a caring man. Did you know that, Elizabeth? But I guess I'll tell you more about that one day, when you're older," she said. The tip became a streak of light as she waved her hands in the dark for emphasis.

"I want to know about Daddy now," I said.

"No, you'd just defend your *daddy* . . . and you'd think I'm lonely. Well, I just need to be loved . . . you know, people need to be *loved*," she snapped, raising her voice and taking another sip from the bottle. The record player continued to spin, filling the room with sounds of a deep, moving ocean, pierced by screeches from enormous, invisible whales.

My heart beat faster. I didn't like it when she got this way, reclusive with a streak of meanness. All the signs of an oncoming episode were there, the same as in all her previous breakdowns. The last time she'd been completely delusional; she came across the electric bill and mistook it for her SSI check, and herself for Con Edison, the name of the electric company. I made the mistake of addressing her as Ma then. *"I'm not your mother, I'm Edison, you little bitch,"* she'd said. *"And you are not getting any of my money. So back off!"* This, while her real check sat uncashed, hopelessly lodged in her pants pocket while the fridge remained empty for weeks. A couple nights later when our stomachs finally ached from hunger, and it became too awkward to knock on 1A and ask for leftovers again, Lisa and I split a tube of toothpaste and a cherry-flavored ChapStick when we got hungry.

Sitting there, I identified her current phase in the cycle. This was the part where she was almost finished speaking to, or even recognizing, us. Soon, I thought, she would revert to near-silence, talking only to herself or to the people she believed to be there with her. We'd have to wait until she was far enough gone before she could be legally taken against her will. Then, Lisa and I would clean the house as best we could, taking down the garbage in big bags, spraying the rooms with air freshener and making sure to shut the bathroom door, tight. Daddy would call the ambulance and the police, and she'd be on her way out again. Based on her behavior now, I guessed she had less than a month.

"Well, *I* love you very much," I told her, using my most caring voice.

"No, Elizabeth, I need a man to love me. Okay? Is that okay with everyone? I just need a man's love." She began sobbing. "I need a man's love," she repeated over and over.

"Daddy loves you," I said. In the darkness there was no response. "He does love you," I whispered, more to myself than to Ma.

One Thursday afternoon, when I was tying my sneakers on my way out, there was a sharp knock at the door. Immediately falling into the mode I devised for would-be social workers, I cautiously approached the door, tiptoeing, ready to peer out the peephole. To my horror, Ma—by this time not in her right mind, dressed only in an obviously filthy, extra-long T-shirt—had gotten there first and was already unsnapping locks. Given the extent of the mess spread everywhere—rotten garbage, old clothing, a thousand cigarette burns and butts on the matted carpet—I panicked. The door creaked open and my body went limp when I saw who Ma had let in—a twenty-something-year-old white man in a starched suit, undoubtedly a social worker obligated to report our unfit living conditions.

Unable to fix the larger mess, I ran to clear a kitchen chair for him and was wiping the surface down with a towel so he could at least sit somewhere. Just then, Lisa emerged from her room and shocked me, greeting him by name.

"Matt, right?" she asked casually. Had *Lisa* called Child Welfare on us?

"You're Lisa?" he asked, in a voice that sounded surprised.

"Yeah," she told him. "We can go sit in the living room, the coffee table should be good."

Baffled, I ran to throw on a long-sleeved shirt so I'd appear a little heavier, a tactic I picked up after one social worker had commented on my low weight and threatened to remove us if I didn't show improvement. Lisa sat on the couch, on top of Ma's jeans, tucking her long hair behind her ears. Ma joined her. I sat near the social worker, in a kitchen chair, where I felt I might best supervise the situation. The front door slammed, Daddy returning from the store. My stomach tightened into a knot.

He came whistling into the living room and stopped in his tracks, seeing the stranger who was now searching for a clean spot to set down his briefcase. I prayed he wouldn't notice the roach crawling near his shoe. "Oh, hi," Daddy said, his mood noticeably dropping, his tone sharp and deliberately unfriendly.

"Hello, sir, my name is Matt," the man answered, reaching for Daddy's hand. His manner was far too polite, nonauthoritative, I thought; something seemed off. By the look on Daddy's face as they shook hands, I could tell that he noticed, too. I finished moving some plates over to clear room, but the man had already placed the leather case on his lap instead.

Just then, my heart sank into my stomach as I caught a glimpse of Ma, obliviously easing her legs wide open for comfort. Daddy flashed me a warning glance and pulled up a chair opposite me, filling the last remaining space around the coffee table. I realized that it was the first time in a long while that we'd all sat down together. The room was silent. We waited, staring at Matt.

"Well," he began, his eyes taking a full sweep of the room, over the filthy, partially intact Venetian blinds, the busted garbage bags spilling out over the floor with dozens of roaches darting in and out. He tugged the collar of his shirt and cleared his throat.

"I . . . I've been asked to come here today to share with you some exciting opportunities offered—ahem—from *Encyclopedia Britannica*."

All the tension in my body loosened, but only for a moment. Before I could draw any relief from realizing this man was no social worker, I caught sight of Daddy and tensed right back up.

"*Excuse* me," Daddy said, raising his eyebrows, leaning in way too close to the man. "*Where* did you say you were from?" Daddy's arms were folded over his chest, his chin dropped, his eyes suspicious.

A moment from three weeks earlier struck me. It was late at night. Lisa and I had been watching a *Honeymooners* rerun when a commercial for *Encyclopedia Britannica* filled the screen. A girl and a boy struggled with their homework and repeatedly turned to their parents, two neatly dressed professional types, for help. "Look it up, dear," was all the parents would answer to each of their children's questions. The children did look it up, with the trusty help of *Encyclopedia Britannica*. And when they received A's on their papers, the family gathered to celebrate in the living room, beside a crackling fireplace with a coffee table much newer and cleaner than ours.

Lisa's attention had been fixed on the screen. Then, when the narrator invited us to have a free home presentation, which would include two *free* volumes—I remembered now with a certain degree of helplessness—Lisa had grabbed a pen and jotted down the number. It never occurred to me that she would actually call.

"These are our brochures," Matt said, pulling glossy materials from his briefcase. "You can all have a look."

Every other moment, he ran his finger through his neat, gelled hair and licked his lips before speaking.

"Would you like a glass of water?" I asked. I wanted so badly to communicate that at least *I* was normal.

"No. No thank you," he responded right away, without even looking at me. I could feel my cheeks flush hot. "This is for all of you," he said as he distributed to us, counterclockwise, one pamphlet each. Before it was her turn, Ma snatched Lisa's copy straight out of his hand. The man jumped, only a little, and quickly continued passing the pamphlets out, reaching a wide space around Ma to get to Lisa. I could feel myself start to sweat.

He was sweating, too, obviously so. I could tell from how he cleared his throat between almost every word that he was also choking on the rancid smell from the bathtub. Lisa got out her glasses to look over the brochure. If she felt awkward, I couldn't tell at all.

"The benefits to owning your very, ahem, *a-hem*, very own set of *Encyclopedia Britannica* are, a-hem truly beyond measure. Education-wise—"

Daddy clenched his pamphlet tight in his fist, his knuckles whitening, and interrupted, "Yeah, okay, okay, yeah," every second or so, as though to speed him up.

As the man spoke, a couple of flies from the garbage buzzed past his face. He pretended to open a pamphlet, swatting at the flies with its pages. I thought I would die right there when Ma spoke.

"You think you can just come here and get away with that?" she said, sneering at him.

"Ex-excuse me, ma'am?" he stammered.

"Nothing," I said quickly. "Nothing, please finish. I mean, go ahead, please."

Ma's eyes were too wide open to look sane, and she was nodding her head at something unapparent to anyone but herself.

"Ma!" Lisa said, looking up from her reading. "I *told* Matt to come, that's why he's here." Ma continued to stare at him without flinching.

Regardless of Ma's state of mind, Lisa always addressed her as though things were perfectly normal. Then, when Ma's actions conflicted with whatever logical outcome Lisa expected, she became livid. I found the pattern just as frustrating as it was irrational. Not only was Ma obviously insane, but it seemed as if Lisa was detached from reality as well. So much so that her behavior could, at times, make me feel like I didn't have an older, but instead a younger sister.

"How much is everything?" Lisa continued, looking up at the man, who was shifting uncomfortably under Ma's unrelenting glare.

"Well, luckily, *Britannica* offers a variety of payment options—"

Daddy crossed his arms again and smiled smugly, interrupting.

"So tell me, sir, would this be the exact same set available in the *public library*, down the block?" Daddy had a way of engaging people as though they were attempting to take advantage of him, but he wasn't going to let them get away with it.

"Well, uh, really the luxury of owning your own set cannot be, ahem, underestimated. To answer your question, ma'am," he addressed Lisa, "there are several payment plans, ahem, packages that make it possible for nearly anyone . . ."

Forgetting Matt, Ma absentmindedly dug her pointer finger up her nose. He pretended not to notice, but gave himself away with a frown when she wiped it across the arm of the couch. I might have been the only other one to notice. I wished then that I could somehow explain to him—*I* knew what this must look like; *I* got it. I kept offering the man my gaze, so that he could see that I understood, but he would only glance my way for brief moments before looking away again.

"Well, what if we want only certain volumes?" Lisa asked. "Like your special editions on the presidents, or the wars?"

What was my sister thinking? What apartment had *she* woken up in every morning? If we went days without a solid meal, why would it matter if we wanted to look up the Peloponnesian War, or what year Abe Lincoln was born? Watching her nod at the man's proposals of payment plans that I knew we could never afford, just as he was probably aware we would never accept, while Ma ate her boogers and Daddy shifted every five seconds, I needed for Lisa to realize the extent of this foolishness, to see it clearly, the way I did.

I'm not sure who was more relieved when the whole ordeal finally ended, Matt or me. During the following three and a half months Ma spent in her next hospital stay, whenever a *Britannica* commercial came on, Daddy folded his arms, privately indicating Lisa to me with his eyes. Each time, I relived the humiliation of our first-ever house guest all over again.

To Lisa's great disappointment, our two free volumes never came.

Five days after Ma was again committed, the next month's check had yet to arrive. I searched our cabinets to find them totally barren, not a scrap to eat. I was starving. When my stomachache turned to something more like stomach-fire, and I felt shaky all over, I decided to head out to see what I could do about my situation. I had in mind an acquaintance of Rick and Danny's, a boy named Kevin, who, even though he was not much older than me, always had money in his pocket and talked endlessly about some job that he had.

Because it was already ten in the morning, and Kevin was never seen hanging around the block during the daytime, the guys and I rushed over to Fordham Road and University Avenue, where we might be able to catch him on his way out to work. We found Kevin at the number 12 bus stop, in front of a part of Aqueduct Park that everyone called Dead Cat Alley. Guys from Grand Avenue used that area to set their pit bulls loose on rounded-up stray cats, whose bloody and disfigured corpses could be found scattered across the cement most Sunday mornings. I went near the alley only when I had to; the sight of one limp cat body, a patch of blood wetting its fur, gave me nightmares.

When we crossed from University Avenue onto Fordham, Kevin had just exited from the front of a bus and the driver had yelled something I couldn't hear before pulling the doors shut and driving away. Kevin ignored the driver, and when he saw us coming, he did not seem at all surprised. From the casual look on his face as we approached—drooping eyelids and a bored, steady face—you'd think he'd been expecting us. I let Rick do the introduction.

"Yo, uh, Kevin, man . . . this is my friend Elizabeth. Yo, uh, bust it, we wanted to find out about that job you got."

"You guys wanna make some money?" he asked, a smile spreading across his face. Rick and Danny half shrugged, half nodded.

"Yeah," I responded immediately, stepping forward. "I do. Will you show me where?" I felt as if acid were eating away at my stomach. "I'll work anywhere," I told him. "Can we go now?"

Kevin taught us how to hop the bus. We waited, standing off to the side, a few feet away from the back door, so as not to get the driver suspicious. Then we rushed in the back door as exiting passengers clustered, blocking us from sight. Our destination, Kevin informed us, was the self-service gas station just beside the Bronx Zoo, where Fordham Road split into the highway. There, we could run up on customers and offer to pump their gas, hoping for a tip.

Kevin prepped us the whole bus ride there. I nodded and listened quietly, hoping to mask my hesitation. When I realized that Kevin's "job" was more hustle than legitimate work, the hunger in my gut made room for anxiety. But I kept a straight face, sucked up my worry, and listened to Kevin's advice while the bus chugged down Fordham Road.

"Just stand there and look at 'em like you're dumb, like you don't get that they'd even *think* about not tipping. Make 'em feel cheap. They'll give ya somethin', especially a white girl. You guys'll get somethin', too, we all will. Just grab the pump and don't let them tell you no."

It actually worked. In the beginning, it took me a while to get the hang of hooking the nozzle into the tank's opening without spilling gas all over the ground. But in a few hours, I was a pro. By dark, I'd made more than thirty dollars, more money than I'd ever had at one time in my life. It wasn't easy at first; the station's legitimate workers occasionally took a break from their post behind Plexiglas to chase us away. They said we were trespassing, and they were going to call the police. But the four of us were too quick for the two of them; to our advantage, only one was allowed to leave the booth at a time. And with our system of serving as lookout for one another and our agreement to scramble in separate directions in order to cause confusion, they couldn't catch us. It was never more than five minutes before we returned to our spots. Kevin, I noticed, gave them the finger the moment he caught their glares from the booth again.

The drivers' initial reactions to me were off-putting, and my confidence suffered with each rejection. My voice became a shy quiver and I had to repeat my request a couple times before they understood it. "You want to what?"

they'd say. "*What* about my gas?" Or, worse, they just silently looked confused until I got up the nerve to say, loud and clear, "Can I pump your gas for you?" I'd been turned down more than a few times during those hesitations. Eventually, I realized that I had to act confident, and this made courage easier to summon. Before long, I was reaching for the pump and, with a polite smile, saying, "Let me get that for you." This worked almost every time.

Enlivened by the rush of earning my own money, I stayed behind far into the afternoon, long after Kevin, Rick, and Danny left for home, allowing myself only one break to buy a Happy Meal from the neighboring McDonald's. I'd almost drooled on myself waiting in line for that cheeseburger; I ate it in a few bites on my way back to the pump, licking my fingers clean. It was one of the most delicious meals I'd ever had. My stomach pains eventually subsided and I went back to work, staying at the station for hours longer, until the sky turned sapphire and the night breeze ran goose bumps down my arms and legs. Finally, I walked back to the bus and headed home. During the whole free ride back, my mind raced, replaying the day and thinking about all the new possibilities I'd just discovered by making my own money. The experience was exhilarating.

It occurred to me that Kevin might have brought us along to solve the only obstacle he could not overcome alone—the issue of the gas attendants chasing after him. Since he'd had us to look out, Kevin was able to spend the day making all the money he could, with hardly any interruption. We worked with Kevin for that one day, and after that, I never spoke to him again. But something about my brief encounter with him gave me a sense that I could do something to change my situation. Though he wasn't my friend, I admired how Kevin had found a way to do things on his own, how he looked at not having money—a situation that most people would see as fixed—as something he could overcome. What else wasn't set in stone? I wondered what other opportunities were out there for me.

Along Fordham Road, stores glowed against the night. Through the bus window, I saw shoppers streaming in and out of them, clutching bags filled with newly bought merchandise. I considered how often I'd gone by that gas station on the bus with Ma, never thinking there was a chance for me to do something about my hunger. Now, as I rode past these businesses, I wondered what else I hadn't seen. Surely there must be managers inside of each store who were able to employ whomever they chose. Though I knew that at nine, I was not old enough to be officially employed, maybe with a little convincing, some bosses wouldn't mind having me sweep their floors or clean in back for tips. Maybe we didn't need to be out of food all the time, even when the check ran out. Of all the businesses, I thought there must be at least one place for me, somewhere.

Riding up Fordham Road, I rested heavily against the bus seat, soothed by my exhaustion. Change weighted my pockets, rolling over my thighs in my shorts—more than enough to buy Chinese food for Lisa, Daddy, and me. I began to work out the next day in my mind. Leaning my head against the window, I drifted into a light, easy nap made sweet by the new idea that I could have some say in what happened to us, after all.

The next morning, with twenty dollars' worth of leftover earnings tucked away in my room, I walked up and down Fordham in search of work. With station attendants chasing me at the gas station, it could never be a real job; I wanted something I could count on, something consistent. I entered each store and requested a conversation with an employee, trying to look as serious and responsible as I could. But no matter how hard I tried, I couldn't get one person to take me seriously.

"*You* want a job? You asking for someone else, or *you* want a job?" Though I made every effort to be clear—yes, I was hoping you might have something; doesn't have to be a real job or anything, maybe you need someone to sweep up here—the responses at Alexander's, Tony's Pizza, and Woolworth were the same. No one seemed to want to bother with me. Some even laughed outright.

"You have to be *at least* fourteen, kid. How old are you—ten?" One woman leaned over the counter to pat my head and smile, a thick gold chain resting between her coffee-colored breasts. Laughter from the entire cashier's section followed. I stomped away, embarrassed, deeply frustrated. I was sure of my ability to work, if they would just allow me to; though the more I was rejected, the more self-conscious I became. I began noticing my tangled hair, my dirty, cracked sneakers, and the dirt caked under my fingernails. Yesterday's exhilaration was beginning to seem foolish.

I walked so far down Fordham—from rejection to rejection—that I ended up at the end of the shopping area, well on my way back to the gas station.

I hadn't originally intended on going to the station, given the problem of dodging the workers. Rick and Danny had let me know yesterday that one day's work had been more than enough for them. At least, I thought as I walked toward the pumps, I probably wouldn't have to come home empty-handed if I took a shot at it.

I decided to work into the early afternoon, pumping gas until just after lunchtime. Then I would make my way back uphill until I reached the Grand Concourse, where there was a whole strip of stores I could try my luck at.

Apart from constantly looking over my shoulder to check for the station attendants, the first two hours of pumping gas went by smoothly. I learned that early-morning traffic from the Bronx Zoo brought a rush of families to the station. I jumped from van to car to station wagon, each packed with its own family. There were babies screaming, adults counting money, children my age fighting in backseats who looked at me with curiosity, the smell of ripe diapers and fast food rising toward me from their open windows.

Change from my tips crashed against my thighs as I ran, weaving between gas pumps to rush up to people. Missing a customer meant missing profit, so I wasted no time. Soon I delighted at how I could afford anything from the McDonald's. I thought, as I saw a bus pass, that I could even go far away, if I felt like it. As long as I was able to work, I was beginning to feel as if I didn't have to be stuck anywhere. I had options. Yesterday's excitement returned to me, and I raced back and forth from one customer to the next, fattening my pockets, oblivious to the passing hours and the station workers.

By one o'clock, I had made almost as much money as it had taken me the whole day before to gather, but I'd been chased out of the station three times. The final time I had decided not to come back, when a station worker grabbed the back of my T-shirt, screaming at me, threatening to have me arrested. He tried to drag me back into the booth with him, but I thrashed around, shook loose from his grip, and escaped, pumping my skinny legs as fast as I could, letting his insults fade as I gathered distance.

I rested to catch my breath on a bench at the foot of the hill, where I counted twenty-six dollars in tips. My skin had turned dark pink and sensitive from hours of standing in the sun. Stuffing the money back into my pockets, I resumed my search along the Grand Concourse, pushing my way through crowds of people whose elbows and heavy shopping bags brushed painfully against my sunburned arms. Warm sweat spots dampened my T-shirt beneath my armpits and the top of my back, then turned freezing cold each time I entered another air-conditioned store to ask the same question over and over again.

As the afternoon wound down, my luck at finding a job on the Concourse turned out to be no better. I couldn't locate one person to take me seriously. Finally, I started on my way home. As I walked, I tried to come up with another possible location to search for work, maybe on nearby Kingsbridge Avenue, or over the bridge on Dyckman, but doubt began sinking in.

I entered through the automatic doors of Met Food supermarket four blocks away from my building, into air-conditioning. Stealing was something I knew I could do. I would take a package of steak and a stick of butter. I could afford the food with my tips, but until I was sure I could earn money consistently, I did not want to spend any of what I had. In the meantime, I would settle for taking things; after doing it so many times with Rick and Danny, I was sure I could manage without getting caught.

The supermarket was packed with evening shoppers, which made me all the more confident that I could slip in and out without being noticed. Customers stood in long, winding lines and stock boys in white coats stained with cow blood weaved their way through, carrying crates high up on their shoulders. I searched for the manager and the assistant manager, the only two people I knew to be on the lookout for shoplifters. Instead, I caught sight of something else—kids only a few years older than me standing at the end of the cash register counters, dressed not in workers' uniforms but in their regular clothes, packing grocery bags for tips.

I counted four baggers, and saw that all four had a few things in common. They were all boys, either Latino or black, and all had a container where customers dropped change before exiting. My impulse was to take one of the two empty counters, but instead I stood beside the bread rack up front and watched to learn how the job was done. Single bags were used for eggs and bread, which were packaged alone. Heavy items were spread out with items of medium weight. Smiles and polite conversation prompted tipping. I took in one deep breath. With a mixture of excitement and fear, I approached a register.

The cashiers were a string of young Spanish girls in tight clothing and baby blue aprons, all wearing similar gelled hairstyles. At the counter where I took my place, the girl smiled sweetly. We exchanged no words, but her gesture told me I was welcome. I peeled a plastic bag from the bag rack and before I could think or do anything, she reached over and began sending items rolling down the counter toward me. A cake box and cold cuts slid over; cans of soup and a bottle of Pepto-Bismol followed. A stout, middle-aged man watched his purchases ring up on the register through thick, bottle-capped glasses. I was glad he didn't seem to notice me touching his things.

Boxes have sharp edges; they need double bagging. Cold cuts fit on top and don't weigh the box down, so it all gets packed in together. Only two cans, they go together . . .

Somehow, I was able to finish before he was done paying, and this made me feel proud. But when I passed the neatly packed bags to the man, now staring right into his eyes, he took his receipt from the cashier and headed for the door without so much as glancing down at me. I continued to follow him with my eyes, half expecting he'd realize his mistake and turn back. But he kept on going. Frustrated, I remembered that each bagger had his own change-packed plastic dish.

Leaning over the partition of his booth, a manager shouted, "Attention shoppers, we will be closing in ten minutes. Thank you for shopping here. Good night!" Under the metal counter I found a half-pint container. I fished in my pocket for some change and quickly dropped it inside.

A large woman in a floral muumuu and her children pushed three carts full of groceries to the counter. Scanning the enormity of their purchase, it seemed they'd spent the entire day inside the supermarket, gathering food. I panicked, seeing the large mass of items rolling swiftly toward me. The children unloaded the carts so much faster than I could pack the items. Their mother waved a stack of coupons in the air, rippling the loose skin on her arms.

"I got coupons, so *don't* let me catch you overchargin', miss."

The girl hardly looked up from punching in the numbers.

"Thass right," the lady emphasized. "I got my eye on you."

One of her three children began an argument with another. The woman spun around and whacked the boy in the back of his head, putting an abrupt end to the argument. "Unpack the goddamn food and behave yo'self!" I could feel my insides tighten; I wasn't sure a tip from her would be worth the trouble.

The woman returned her glare to the register. Chips, dip, pudding, various slabs of meat, and two-liter bottles of Pepsi rolled to my end of the counter and clunked against the partition. I worked fast, avoiding eye contact in spite of my hopes to be tipped.

Meat with meat, cereal fits with bread. Gallons of milk get individual bags.

I finished the job as the cashier sorted through the woman's coupons. Looking down over the packed bags, I felt another small jolt of pride. Each one was neatly arranged, the weight distributed evenly, the items sorted in the correct clusters. I stood still, waiting.

That's when I spotted a yellow Lunchable package protruding from the grocery bag closest to me.

Pink bologna meat, a row of crackers, and a small block of cheese sat behind the plastic. I could imagine the texture of the meat, the bland taste of the cheese.

Looking at the package, I realized how hungry I was. I stared at the food and suddenly felt a deep craving for it. My mouth watered. All around me, the supermarket was finally closing. A couple of cashiers were counting out their registers for the day. Someone pulled the gate down over the window outside, and I realized I would not have time to pick up my own food, as I had hoped.

I leaned down and pretended to tie my sneaker. No one was looking; the cashier made conversation with a stock boy while the woman organized her food stamps. I let go of my laces and very quickly slipped the Lunchable out of sight, underneath the metal counter where I'd found my change dish a few minutes before. I rose, smiling stupidly for everyone who wasn't watching, my heart pounding.

"Let's go, kids," the woman shouted, clutching her receipt. "And we *ain't* stopping at the quarter machine. So don't ask!"

I passed the heavy grocery bags into her hands in groups of two. She handed them over to her kids. I thought I might die when I realized she was speaking to me.

"Look at that smile," she said, looking down at me with affection.

My guilt made it hard for me to look into her face. "Here you go darling, this is for you."

Leaning over, she placed a moist, limp dollar bill in my hand. I forced another smile, and said, "Thank you, ma'am."

"Such a pretty smile," she repeated. "Now let's go kids!"

She charged out the automatic doors, children teetering and straining under the weight of the bags as they followed behind her, the smallest one wobbling like a penguin.

I tucked the dollar away and waited a moment to make sure they were gone before sliding the Lunchable into a new plastic bag. The other baggers had already gone for the day; only the cashiers sifting through their day's count remained.

In the clear, I grabbed the bag and exited. I walked home much faster than I needed to, looking over my shoulder until I reached University Avenue. Two blocks from home, I tore open the package and shoved crackers, bologna, and cold, delicious cheese into my mouth; filled with guilt and giddiness, I consumed the food in just a few quick bites.

The rec-room phone in North Central Bronx Hospital's psychiatric ward rang until the ringing dissolved into a distant hum. At home on my side of the line, the receiver grew hot against my ear. There was a calm I found in dialing and redialing the same seven numbers on our rotary phone, just to hear the connecting click and the rolling noise of the ringing go on and on. Nearby, Daddy was watching a game of *Jeopardy!*, slapping his knee with all of his correct answers. Resting my head on the table, I let the ringing lull me into a light sleep.

In my dream, Ma, miniature and far away, was screaming for my attention from someplace remote. "Lizzy," she called over and over again in a tinny voice, "Lizzy, is that you?" I snapped out of sleep, realizing she was actually talking to me from the phone, which had rolled halfway across the table. I grabbed it.

"Ma?"

"Lizzy, I thought that was you, pumpkin. We were in friggin' arts and crafts again. I made you something. A cup. It's not as good as I wanted, but I couldn't see the board."

"Pottery? You can *make* cups?" The idea impressed me; it made her seem unusually capable. "Are you feeling better, Ma?"

"Sure. I guess. Well, actually I'm havin' a hard time. . . . I just need a little bag. It's been a while, ya know? They're like the goddamn gestapo over here, these nurses. I can't even get a cigarette from anyone. I just don't feel that great right now, I guess."

Ma complained that the staff was always placing her on smoking restriction for "bad behavior," like cursing or showing up late to group.

"I feel like a goddamn inmate," she said. "They don't know what it's like to need a smoke and not get one. They never had to go without, ya know?"

"I know, Ma."

The shift down in rank Ma suffered as a resident of the psychiatric ward was a tricky issue to manage. North Central Bronx staff came to know Lisa and me by name; they inquired about school, commented on missing baby teeth, and remembered birthdays. But I resisted their kindness. Something about their interest, alongside the authority they exerted over Ma, made me feel like a traitor. So I pretended not to notice when they charted "behavior points" for Ma on the bulletin board, or spoke to her in a voice most people used to discipline their children. I turned away rather than watch how she was made to stand ten feet behind them, tapping her foot, dressed in hospital booties and faded sweaters from the lost and found, watching while they locked and unlocked ward doors to permit her access to places. There was just no way to acknowledge the people who contained Ma without acknowledging her confinement; no clear way of addressing them, I worried, without belittling her. So I always stood off to the side, looked to the ground, and only whispered my answers to staff during visits.

One thing that helped to make the tension easier was watching other patients: the sweaty Chinese man who stuffed all the checkers into his pants in slow motion, or the old woman with pursed lips who paraded the "runway" through the ward's halls, or the man who faced the wall and let a continuous strand of drool spill out of his mouth. Whatever planet these people were on, I knew Ma would be doing ten times better in just a month or so, with medication. Her illness came in bouts, not like these people. Watching the other residents, I counted on the difference I could trace between them and Ma; it assured me that things could be worse, that Ma would come back from this.

"Ma, listen, when you come home, we're going to McDonald's." I'd been searching for a place in the conversation to tell her about my new job.

"Yeah, Lizzy. No problem."

"No, Ma, I wasn't asking. I was *saying*; we can get McDonald's when you get home. It'll be my treat. I got a job."

"What, pumpkin? Really? You know, I used to work on a farm when I was a kid, for only a little while though. It was part of one of my foster care placements for like six months."

She was sane again, safe. I could hear it in her voice.

"We milked cows, it was dis-gus-ting. But everything tasted fresher than when you buy it at the store, ya know? You have no idea how old canned string beans really are."

"So you're coming home soon, right? You're well enough to come home, I can tell. You sound good."

"Soon, Lizzy. Tuesday, the doctor said. Tuesday."

"*Really?* Promise?"

"Sure, pumpkin."

"Okay. So that means you're coming home this week no matter what, right?"

"Yeah, Lizzy. Hey, I love you pumpkin, put Daddy on the phone now, okay?"

"All right, Ma. I love you, too."

Daddy took the phone and released a heavy sigh into it, keeping his eyes on the TV. "Hi, Jean," he said. "Don't worry. Yeah. Yup. Yeah."

While they spoke, I skipped over to Lisa's room and pushed my way inside, calling out her name.

Seated on her bed, Lisa quickly clutched a blanket, covering up her chest. She was shirtless. I immediately stepped back out the door.

"Oh. Sorry."

"Could you watch it, Lizzy, I'm getting dressed," she snapped.

A crinkled plastic bag lay on the bed near her; the center of the bag read YOUNG WORLD in rainbow letters.

"Sorry. It's just, Ma's on the phone. She's getting out."

"Give me a minute," she said, avoiding my eyes, "and close my door."

"Okay," I told her, backing away.

The door shut and bounced open just a crack, so that it bled light into the dim hallway and still provided a view into Lisa's room. From down the hall, I could still hear Daddy "uh-huhing" into the phone every minute or so. I pretended to take a few steps away from Lisa's door but remained close, watching. After a moment, she lowered the blanket, revealing a pale pink, lacy bra half drawn across her chest. The sight of it shocked me. She'd never mentioned anything about a bra before. Though the other day, I remembered her fishing for coins between the couch cushions and counting out some singles she'd saved. Ma owned only one dirty bra herself. Up until just then, I hadn't given much thought to the idea that we would both need to buy them one day, too.

Lisa pulled either side together and pinched her fingers on a small, plastic bow in the bra's center, fumbling to close it. Her thick hair was held in the teeth of a hairclip, high up on the back of her head. The bra popped out of her grip twice, and she started over again, until finally it clicked into place. Seeing her topless, I almost backed away. Nudity had become strange around the time we stopped taking baths together, when I was three and she was five. But the bra was too mysterious; her relationship with it too intriguing not to watch. She was becoming a woman, I thought, like Ma. I felt betrayed, like the first time I'd spotted a box of tampons on her nightstand. Maybe if we were closer, if we spoke to each other more than a handful of times each month, then maybe she'd trust me with her secrets.

By my behavior, my wearing shorts and T-shirts, and especially my body, I thought, I might as well be a boy. Climbing trees or getting filthy with the guys, I was often called "tomboy" by other kids. It was a term that made my face hot and my heart beat fast. Just because I was active and enjoyed being physical, I didn't see why this got me compared to a boy. Yet I felt nothing like the girls who wore frilly dresses that left them sitting motionless, legs folded, gossiping on chairs and other clean surfaces all day long. Still, I didn't feel male, either. I was neither one, I thought—an outsider. A girl-boy. Watching Lisa made me feel even more displaced.

Lisa took off the bra and pulled a T-shirt over her head. Then she took a wire hanger out of her closet and hung the bra up with care. Her walls were covered with posters from teenybopper magazines, airbrushed boy pop stars and feathery-haired female teen idols. Lisa took a small, broken piece of mirror and walked back to her bed, puckered her lips at the glass, and batted her eyes.

I leaned against the wall and looked down at my own chest, which was as flat as Rick's or Danny's. I was wearing a Ninja Turtles T-shirt and black, high-top sneakers. My hair was tangled in several large knots. Inside, Lisa began applying lipstick. It was a bright pink, which she lightened by pressing her mouth over a napkin. She plucked at her bangs and smiled wide for the mirror.

I reached out and almost knocked on her door, but stopped when I realized I had no idea what I would say. Instead, I just stood for another moment or so, staring at my big sister.

I was jolted out of sleep on the couch by our front door slamming. I looked up to see Ma storm through the apartment, teary-eyed, distraught. She tossed Lisa's winter coat onto a chair near me and plopped onto her bed. I got up to shut the TV off and went to see what was wrong.

As I stood in the doorway, Ma shut off the light in her room and began crying. She did not acknowledge my presence.

"What's wrong, Ma?"

"Lizzy?" she asked, in a tone that implied she was surprised to find me in our apartment.

"Hey, Ma . . . what's wrong? You okay?"

"Nothing baby . . . I'm having a bad night," Ma said, kicking off her shoes in the dark. "This guy . . . I thought I could trade him . . . I was going to use Lisa's coat, but they wouldn't. I walked all that way there and I didn't even get a bag." She burst into tears, wailing in pain on her bed. Hearing it broke my heart. I hated that there was nothing I could do to make her better when she was this way.

"This guy" that she was talking about was one of the local drug dealers, and the "trade" Ma was referring to was Lisa's coat for a small bag of cocaine, a type of bartering that was typical for Ma. On a regular basis, when Ma had no cash, she scoured the apartment for all manner of semi-valuable objects to present to local drug dealers for bartering consideration. Gun-wielding, illegal-drug-trade-working, criminal-record-having drug dealers around our block became so used to Ma showing up and badgering them to trade her drugs in exchange for everything from old shoes to alarm clocks that they gave her a nickname—*Diabla*, Spanish for She-devil—to capture her relentlessness.

As though she had no idea the dealers were dangerous at all, Ma waited in line behind paying drug customers, and when it was her turn, rather than set down cash on the dealer's table for her purchase, Ma fearlessly placed down whatever item she had managed to dig up: VCR, video games, toys, groceries. And she began making her case, unwilling to leave, even as the drug dealers threatened her. I have no idea why they didn't harm her, or if they did and she just didn't tell me. But I do know that a dealer familiar with my parents had once asked Daddy to make sure to come get the drugs for the two of them, and leave *"Diabla"* at home, she was bad for business. Sometimes, the guy told Daddy, they gave Ma just a small hit to make her go away.

On this particular night, when Ma attempted to sell Lisa's winter coat, the drug dealer had refused, not based on the value of the coat, but on principle.

"Yeah, everybody's got a high horse apparently," Ma said. "He gave me *this* crap," she said, handing me a strange coin in her frustration, "and he preached at me . . . Like he's so good."

Seeing that the coat was the size of a child's, the drug dealer handed it back to Ma along with the single large coin, and he told her to go home to her kids, which made Ma livid. Ma would later explain to me that it was one of those coins people got in Narcotics Anonymous for reaching a given number of days in their sobriety, as a symbol of their progress so far and for struggles yet to come. In no way did Ma seem to appreciate the irony of being given the coin by a drug dealer. Collapsed on her bed, shaking from withdrawal, she was just consumed with pain, hurting from the need to use.

I stayed with Ma until she fell asleep, then I went into my bedroom and got under the blankets, where I turned my attention to the coin as I lay in bed. Later on, I would keep the coin tucked away in my dresser drawer for years. From time to time, I'd take it out just to run my thumb over the engraving and to marvel at its mystery, the "Serenity Prayer" on back:

God grant me the serenity to accept the things I cannot change, the courage to change the things I can, and the wisdom to know the difference.

While I didn't exactly get the meaning, I recognized the music of this prayer as familiar to me from Ma's countless NA meetings. There was a structure to the meetings: Addicts always recited the serenity prayer in unison, clasping hands together in the basements of urban churches while their children, Lisa and me included, rummaged through the free donuts and too-sweet lemonade. Once at the beginning of the meeting, and then once more at the end, *God grant me the serenity* . . . It was a staple of all NA meetings, along with the testimonies from those who had forsaken addiction, those who had "worked the steps" and "beat drugs," the testimonies of those who had "made it." Standing in front of the room, each recovering addict's story took on a familiar shape: there was a lifestyle that wreaked havoc on self, family, and loved ones; the redemption that brought them successfully through NA; and in between, a dark and frightening low—one moment of demarcation between old life and new, characterized by the person's absolute bottom.

These former addicts who "had recovery" would sometimes make their way over to Ma after meetings. They wanted to help her, and I could feel them using me and Lisa as a way to reach Ma. One man stands out in my memory, a white guy with green eyes, impossibly tall. He crouched down to look me in the eyes and asked if I liked cookies. With several in my hand and one stuffed in my mouth at that very moment, I couldn't discern if he was being playful, or if I felt accused. I stared back stupidly. He smiled and stood to talk to Ma about sobriety. She chain-smoked and eluded eye contact while he spoke, shifting back and forth (a side effect from her schizophrenia meds), as he tried futilely to connect. Ma was fresh off another release from North Central Bronx psychiatric ward at the time, and her sobriety was hitting its predictable threshold. We would end up accompanying her to the drug spot right after the meeting that night. But for a few moments this man's message was as clear and powerful as it could be to someone who was unwilling to listen.

"You know how you know for sure when you hit bottom, miss?" he asked. "You know you hit bottom when you stop digging! That's what my sponsor told me." His attempt at eye contact was earnest, but his words just couldn't get to her.

Later that night, Ma sold the toaster and my bike for a hit.

After years of experience, I knew that there were a few existing versions of Ma, roughly five personalities in total. There was crazy Ma, drugged-and-drunken Ma, sober-and-nice Ma, check-day-happy Ma, and pleasant, fresh-out-of-the-hospital Ma. This last one was maybe the most appealing version, though she had a lifespan of roughly two weeks.

Back home, at the outset of this alter ego, she would entertain us with hilarious stories about other people on the psychiatric ward, each anecdote making her laugh in a breathless way, the edges of her mouth turned down, her fist slamming the countertop as she doubled over at her own jokes. She still carried the smell of that hospital-assigned soap on her skin and hair, something I loved to smell when she hugged me so frequently, having just come home to us. This Ma smoked less; she fussed over the symmetry of the living room curtains. She might pass through the apartment humming, and then pause at the couch to kiss me on the forehead on her way down the hall, just because. Simply being home was enough to make this version of Ma happy.

But this time was different. This time, the hospital sent us back a stranger in Ma's place, one that did not seem to fit any of the previous versions. They dressed her in the same clothes, delivered her to the right address, familiarized her with our names and her surroundings—only they forgot part of her personality. The first thing I noticed was her absolute stillness, the way her limbs carried her too steadily through the front door, like a model balancing a stack of books on her head. None of her usual fidgeting; the jumpy quality was totally removed from her mannerisms.

Ma went through all the motions, extending limp hugs to us one at a time. She managed a smile, though most of her face wouldn't cooperate. "Are you taking a different drug?" I asked as she unpacked in the most awkward silence.

"I don't know, Lizzy. I might be."

Lisa was more aggressive; she came with question after question. Ma said little, and walked away from Lisa mid-sentence, her eyes searching the wall, the ceiling, the floorboards, anywhere but Lisa's eyes. Daddy was obliging, or else Ma was; they shared a bed for almost a week. Then Ma returned to the couch, or she took a seat by the window, where she could sit for hours, wide-eyed, hair pulled back, her body steady, frozen in her rose-colored robe, like one of the mannequins in a Macy's window, a picturesque display of sadness. Outside, the weather seemed to match her mood.

It rained that entire first week she was home, overflowing potholes and washing old beer cans and cigarette butts clear from the gutters. It rained so much that the weathermen diligently provided updates on commercial break. The sky was so gray it seemed to be evening all day long. On the third straight night of the rain, Ma commented that it was "tsunami weather," exaggerating its significance.

"Wherever tsunamis hit, this is probably what the weather looks like," Ma said, while we sat together one evening to watch the rain pimple the asphalt in the alley.

"What's a tsunami?" I asked, more in an attempt to gauge her mood than in sincere curiosity.

She picked at tiny pieces of ancient paint, chipping it off the windowsill, the scent of rain riding in with each cool burst of wind. "A tsunami is a really big wave that kills people and destroys houses and villages, Lizzy. It's huge, the size of a mountain."

Sometimes, the randomness of what Ma offered in conversation made her seem like a stranger. I both did and didn't like learning things about her this way. It was like bobbing for pieces of Ma in the dark space that was her past. It was all too indistinct, with no rhythm to what she shared. I could learn something important about Ma as easily as I could not learn it. The thought of how much I didn't know about her bothered me; it made us feel separate, and I hated that.

"How does it destroy stuff if it's only a wave? Waves are in the ocean, and villages and people are on the ground."

"Yeah, but this wave is different, Lizzy. It's not like at the beach, ya know. It's a lot bigger." Lightning flashed through our window, illuminating old water stains like a stencil on the glass. It was followed by a deep crack of thunder that set off car alarms outside.

"How big are they?" I asked, draping a sheet over my shoulders for protection.

"Huge. So tall. As tall as our building, like six stories, or sometimes even higher." Ma extended her arm above her head. Her faced tensed with emphasis. "I'm telling you, Lizzy, like this. They're huge. They darken the whole sky before they drop down."

"Wow. Have you ever seen one?" I fished to link the information to Ma's life.

"Oh no, hell no, they happen only in places far from here. But I used to have nightmares about them all the time. After I saw this news report on tsunamis when I was a kid, I always dreamed I was swimming as fast as I could, with this huge one right on my back. And I never made it out; the wave took me every goddamn time."

"Do you dream of them now?"

"Every now and then. Last night. I guess the rain has me thinking about them."

"Why don't people just leave before it comes?" I asked. Ma stared again out into the alley.

"They would if they knew when to expect it, but they can't. It takes them by surprise, and then it's too late to get away. I'm going to get some sleep now, pumpkin. I'm tired."

"But Ma, no matter how fast they run?"

"No matter *how* fast they run, Lizzy. Once they see it coming, it's already too late to escape."

Ma and Daddy plowed through Ma's saved-up welfare check in just a matter of days. For Lisa and me, they'd purchased thirty dollars' worth of groceries, but just under a week later, money was scarce, and we had to be careful about our portion sizes again. Each day that I tried to work in Met Food, every slot was full. So Lisa and I divided what was left of the food. That night, I made myself peanut butter and jelly sandwiches out of my supply, while I worked on a diorama assignment for Ms. Benning's class. The rain was still coming down in noisy sheets, blowing bursts of cool air onto my legs and arms from the open living room window.

In fifth grade that October, we'd read *Charlotte's Web* for the fall reading fair. I was using construction paper from the art lounge to cut and paste careful sketches of Charlotte, Wilbur, and Templeton into a shoebox for a depiction of the scene where Charlotte weaves the word *humble* into a web. The three best models from each class were going to be displayed in the school lobby for the month of December, where everyone would see them. Tomorrow morning, first thing, Ms. Pinders, the school librarian, was going to pick the winners. If I made the characters vivid enough, I was sure that my diorama had a chance.

I spent all night on the finishing touches: Elmer's glue joined Popsicle sticks to form the barn's low fence. Pencil shavings sat in for tufts of hay. Every so often, I stepped back to take in my progress, pleased with how well it was coming along. As I worked at the living room table, Ma and Daddy stormed in and out of the apartment behind me, headed to bars or to cop drugs. It was clear from their aggressive but indistinguishable conversation that something was up. Just what it was remained unclear. More than once, Ma staggered out of the apartment in tears, headed for the bar. From my window, I'd watched her dissolve into rain so thick, it concealed University Avenue.

Finally, around four o'clock, my arms grew tired and my eyelids heavy. Though neither Ma nor Daddy was home, I went to bed. Once the finished diorama sat safely on my dresser top, I made my way through my darkened room, under the covers, my head sinking into the pillow. Outside, cars whizzed by, casting fast-moving shadows on my empty walls. A gate rattled in the wind, barely audible over the pouring rain. The repetitive *clink* carried me into sleep until a closer, more urgent sound brought me back, waking me—Ma's beer bottle tipping and sloshing with the tapping of her foot.

"Hey, pumpkin." Weighing down the corner of my bed, Ma sat with her legs crossed, the remainder of the mostly consumed beer in her hand.

"Hi, Ma." Rubbing sleep out of my eyes, I became instantly ready to console her, to listen well to whatever was wrong.

"You want to talk? Are you okay?" I asked.

Tears streaked down Ma's face, shimmering in the moonlight. She rubbed them away harshly with the back of her hand. She said nothing, only taking in deep breaths and letting more tears fall. I always knew what to do when Ma spoke, but this silence thing was new. It made me tense, clumsy.

"Ma, talk to me. . . . You know, I love you. Ma? I love you. Whatever it is, you should talk to me. Did someone say something mean to you at the bar? You know I want to hear it. . . ."

"I love you, pumpkin. Don't *ever* let anyone tell you you're not my baby. You got that? No matter how old you get, you are always my baby."

"Ma, please, what's wrong?" Watching her face contort in some private pain, I wished for one of our better nights, when Ma let her thick, curly hair dangle down to brush my cheeks while I lay in bed. She'd tickle me until I burst with laughter. But sometimes she just didn't have it in her. I knew those nights did not come easily to her. And she needed my help through the harder ones, like this, when memories of her past caught up with her. This was when I needed to listen, to soothe her, when she needed me most.

"Ma, I love you. You shouldn't cry. We're all here, we all love you. Whatever it is, it'll be okay."

I searched her eyes for recognition, but she was somewhere far away. I could tell that this was going to be one of our long nights, when we talked until the sky lightened and the birds were the only noise outside. The thought alone exhausted me. I thought of Ms. Pinders and the fall reading competition in the morning, and I wished for some way to make Ma as tired as I was. Maybe then she'd just fall asleep.

"Okay, Ma, talk to me." I grabbed her hand; it was wet with her tears.

"Lizzy, listen. I'll always be in your life. *Always*. When you get big—" She suddenly sobbed, letting out a heavy moan that scared me. "When you get big and have your own kids, I'll babysit them. I'll watch you graduate from school. You will always be my baby. You know that? No matter how big you get, you'll always be my baby."

"Let me hug you." I began shaking, but tried hard to conceal my fear. "I know you'll always be here. I'll always be here for you, too. Don't worry so much, Ma."

"Lizzy, pumpkin, I'm sick. . . . I'm sick, I have AIDS. They diagnosed me at the hospital. Daddy thought it would be better not to say anything until I got sick. . . . They gave me a blood test. I have AIDS, Lizzy."

Television images of pale men spread out on stretchers came to mind; people on cots, limp with sickness. I remembered someone saying that all AIDS patients eventually died. It took me only a moment to connect the images and the word *death* with Ma. Was Ma going to die? A hot quiver shot up from my stomach, and I burst into tears.

"Ma, are you going to die? Are you going to die, Ma?"

I was fully awake. I watched the rain fall behind Ma as she continued to cry, illuminated by the streetlight. It made a silhouette of my mother, like a stark, vacant painting. Only a few minutes ago, the rain fell just as steadily and Ma wasn't dying. Somehow, my bed and my furniture all stayed in place, the shadows of my window guards remained stationary along the wall, but Ma had changed.

Ma gathered me into her arms, digging her beer bottle into my back. Hugging each other, we shook with quiet sobs on my bed for long, disbelieving moments. My mother and this thing, both seated beside me, both in my arms. Holding her, I held it, and shared her, took what I could get away from the alcohol and from the disease.

"Ma . . . you can't go."

"Not right now, pumpkin. I'll be here for a while. At least a few years."

"*What?* No, Ma!"

Now it was me who was sobbing uncontrollably, choking on my own tears.

"I mean, I'll be here for a long, long time. Don't worry, I'm not going anywhere. I love you, pumpkin. I'm not going to die. Mommy's not going to die for a long time. I might not even have AIDS, who knows. Never mind what I said."

But it was too late. I knew Ma too well, with her inability to keep secrets. I was sure it was true. She couldn't just take it back. I wished so badly that this was a delusion, a sign of another oncoming episode, but I knew this was real.

"But you just said . . . Ma, don't lie to me. Are you going to die?" I coughed and choked on my tears; I was hysterical.

Abruptly, Ma stood up and reached for my doorknob.

"Forget it, Lizzy," she said. "You get some sleep now. Never mind what I told you. Who knows *what* I have. These days, no one knows anything. Don't worry, I was just kidding. It's fine. I'm fine," she said, taking another drink from her bottle. "We'll be just fine," she added, before stepping out and shutting the door.

"Wait," I screamed. "Wait! *Ma!* . . . Maaaa!" I knew she'd left because I failed to give the right response. That must be why she'd left. I hated myself for whining, for being so needy. Whenever I needed too much, it always pushed Ma and Daddy away. I should have known better. I called out to her one final time, "Maaa!"

But as loud as I yelled, and as much as I cried, she did not come back. I couldn't find it in me to chase after her, either. Something about climbing out of bed would make the moment more real.

I drew deep breaths and tried to quiet down; I gripped the sheets to ease my trembling. The silence made the room feel emptier than it had before. Only ten minutes ago, I was asleep and Ma didn't have AIDS.

As much as I wanted to hold things together, I was always letting them fall apart. I tried to help Ma, to give her what she needed, but maybe I only made things worse. Knowing what she needed the money for, there were countless times I still gave Ma my tips from packing bags or the dollars taped inside my birthday cards sent from Long Island. It hit me then, like a hammer to my chest, that maybe I'd driven her crazy *and* paid for the needle that infected her with AIDS, too.

"Idiot," I said out loud. "Moron."

I hurled a pillow across the room, smashing the pieces of my diorama. The Popsicle stick fence, still glued together, clacked onto the floor, snapping in half.

CHAPTER 4

Unraveling

IF OUR APARTMENT HAD BEEN A WORLD UNTO ITSELF BEFORE, THEN by the time I was nearly twelve years old, the four of us came to live on entirely different continents, separated in our own locked rooms, detached and floating so independently from one another that I worried we might never come together again. I spent the majority of my time out of the house, hanging out with friends or packing bags and pumping gas. Lisa, in her room, blasted music from her radio, her door permanently shut. Daddy had his trips downtown, and his long walks around the neighborhood. And Ma made a new friend to keep her company, a detestable man whose presence in our apartment drove a wedge between us at a fragile time when we were already farther apart than we could afford.

Leonard Mohn was a flamboyant, bone-thin man who resembled Munch's painting *The Scream*. He had small tufts of hair on either side of his bald head and his eyes bulged from his sockets as though he were being strangled. He was jittery and impatient, and suffered from a mental illness, not unlike Ma's, which he treated with all sorts of colorful pills. He and Ma met and became good friends in the bar one night when they discovered they had the same taste in men. Together, Leonard Mohn and Ma took over our kitchen and transformed it into something between a grievance group meeting, a smoking lounge, and what addicts like to call a shooting gallery; a place, usually deserted, where people go to mainline.

Their routine together was consistent with each cycle of government checks: Daddy was the gofer; he ran to cop the drugs, while Ma and Leonard sat in the kitchen moping about life, guzzling large bottles of Budweiser, setting up the works, and waiting for Daddy to return so they could get high. This sequence was repeated for two nearly sleepless weeks (the time it took to run through both Ma's and Leonard's checks combined), until dark rings surfaced under their eyes and between them, there wasn't a single dollar left to spend. Leonard could be expected back when the checks came in again, either his own or Ma's. He didn't stick around much for the mid-month grubbing from bars. In his absence, Ma slept for days.

Daddy, Ma, Lisa, and me all made fun of Leonard behind his back. I don't think any of us liked him, not even Ma really. With his shrill voice, obsessive self-concern, and obvious disgust for children (despite the fact that he was a substitute schoolteacher), he wasn't exactly likable. But Ma and Daddy did not make decisions based on what they liked or didn't like, just as they didn't make decisions based on what was good or bad for our family. Instead, Ma and Daddy made decisions based on drugs, and Leonard was a resource, if nothing else. The more he was around, the greater the check money and the more they could get high. So on the nights when I took long walks with Daddy, tagging along for his drug runs, he'd make me laugh hard by imitating Leonard's over-the-top effeminate voice and his incessant whining, while simultaneously teaching me how to press the bright beeping letters of a Chase ATM, while we typed in Leonard's PIN, "WATERS," to get out cash for their next round of coke. I could always make Daddy laugh when I did my imitation of Leonard, bulging out my eyes big and doing my best version of his voice whining to Ma in our kitchen: "Ooooh, Jeanie! Oh, life's so hard, oooohhhh."

Daddy would smack his knee and crack up laughing in the empty ATM carrel, receipts and trash strewn about our feet, as we were totally alone in those predawn hours. Then he'd ask me to do it again and again for our whole walk to the drug spot and home. When we'd get back to our apartment, you could already hear Leonard's shrieking voice all the way from out in the hallway, before we even put our key in to open the front door.

"If not for the kids, Jeanie, my job would be great. Oh, the little beasts," he'd say. "I just wish I could give them a good wallop when they get out of hand, the monsters!"

Leonard was as strongly disapproving of the idea of having children as he was pessimistic and dramatic. And he wasn't at all reserved about saying so. Throughout his visits, I could hear him complain to Ma, using a stage whisper from the very next room with the door open.

"Jean, they're such little ingrates. I don't know *how* you do it." He always sucked on his cigarettes audibly, making a small kissing noise when he pulled them back. "I can't even take them at work. God help you with them here in *your home*."

"Oh, Leonard, stop it," she said, weakly.

This was the single response Ma came up with. I'd like to think it was Leonard's check money that kept Ma quiet, but I'll never be sure why she sat there complacently, sipping her beer, oblivious to his verbal attacks on us.

If it had been only this nasty attitude of his that I had to deal with, I probably could have tolerated Leonard Mohn. But what escalated him from irritatingly difficult to impossible to deal with was this one recurring conversation he shared with Ma, regarding their shared status as HIV positive. That conversation was too painful to overhear. It made me need to escape him, to escape her.

The subject always came up just as their coke was wearing off, in that stage when the high had lost its thrust and reality came flooding back in a wave of melancholy.

"Jeanie, my heart is racing. Jeanie, hold my hand." Even if she hadn't held mine in years, even though the last real hug she gave me was on that night she told me of her diagnosis, she'd sit there and clasp Leonard's hand, crossing their fingers through each other's.

"Jeanie, I just don't want to get sick," he'd say. "Well, we're going to get sick, but at least we won't ever have to be old. No, we'll never have to have that happen, thank God. Aren't you grateful for that, Jean?"

Most times when they talked like this, I was no more than ten feet away, lying on the couch, well within earshot. Close enough so I could smell the sour beer, see the fog of cigarette smoke streaming out of the doorway, and hear every distressed word of his, spoken so blatantly, distorted by his tears.

"Oh, Jeanie, in a way it could be a blessing. The good years are all gone before forty anyway."

"I know, Leonard. That's one good thing," she'd agree. "We'll never be old."

Any delusion I had that Ma's and Daddy's drug habit was somehow harmless vanished with her diagnosis and the intrusion of Leonard. I eventually outgrew my tolerance for being witness to all of this: my parents' naked arms under our flickering fluorescent light; the very moment a needle punctured their flesh, thin and vulnerable as grape skin; their blood drawn up the syringe in a red cloud, and then shot back in again, causing that electric rush to overtake their faces. Then, blood all over—blood speckling the walls, across their shirts, onto our newest pack of Wonder bread, on the sugar jar. Maybe worst of all was watching them overuse one spot on their bodies, the way it swelled and began to darken, to shine, and even to smell. The way Ma searched desperately for a clean spot on her feet or between her toes. Far more than the gore aspect was their desperation that grew more obvious to me over time. That's what the whole thing was—an ongoing movie of their desperation playing out in front of me, as though I were seated alone in a dark cinema, watching an eerie slow-motion black-and-white film of their lives crashing and burning. It wore on me, and where I had once tried so hard to be involved, I now grew tired and longed to go anywhere else in order to escape it.

When Ma and Daddy went on their late-night binges, I stopped coming with Daddy and I never explained to him why. Instead, I was compelled by a distinct feeling of resistance that sent me slipping out the front door quietly to take aimless walks along Fordham Road, up and down the deserted shopping strip, by myself. Some nights I searched through plastic trash bags along the sidewalk for defective store clothing, a trick Daddy had taught me. I filled my backpack with damaged or inaccurately stitched clothing while my parents made their runs, occasionally staying out until the sun began to rise. One night while I was foraging for clothing, I actually saw Daddy walking briskly down Fordham Road and I said nothing to him. I did not call out his name but instead just stood in front of the trash bags watching him walk at top speed toward Grand Avenue. Calling out his name would have made me sad for some reason; not calling it out made me sad, too.

Some days, children at school made jokes about my messed-up clothing, the pocket sewn onto the back of a shirt or a short pants leg on my too-large jeans. Most days, I avoided school and walked a different route entirely, arriving early in the morning at Met Food, so I could stand alongside the cashiers to watch the manager unlock and raise his gate for the start of business.

It's not that I *never* went to school, but more like I passed through it the way a net passes through water, passively snagging whatever happens to drift inside. Any formal education I received came from the few days I spent in attendance, mixed with knowledge I absorbed from random readings of my or Daddy's ever-growing supply of unreturned library books. And as long as I still showed up steadily the last few weeks of classes to take the standardized tests, I kept squeaking by from grade to grade.

Cutting school, I walked or rode the subway, traveling all over the Bronx and Manhattan just for the feel of sitting among crowds, to hear the sound of conversations, arguments, panhandlers singing, and my favorite sound of all, laughter. I could disappear in the crowds of people—who would notice a short skinny girl in need of a shower, with knotty, filthy hair, if I slung a hood over my head and walked with my eyes downcast, invisible? Even though I worried about getting picked up by truancy officers, it was worth the risk. I just needed to have life around me—the pulse and vibration of people out in the world doing things. I traded school for this. I traded my home for this. Soon, I accumulated two steady absences: one from school and the other from our apartment.

Sometimes, I had company. Rick and Danny abandoned class to ride the number 4 train with me, back and forth on its Lexington Avenue line, for hours. This was a different kind of cutting school; not peaceful like my solitary trips, but marked by adventure. Together on the train, we swung on straps and kicked open empty conductor's booths to use the PA system, announcing that sandwiches and drinks were being served in the last car. We broke stink bombs—little glass tubes containing the foulest-smelling liquid—onto the floors of crowded cars, delighting in people curling their faces in disgust.

Bowling Green was the only station where we ever deboarded (unless we were being chased by the conductor). Here, we hopped on the Staten Island Ferry; if we rode on the bottom deck, forward bound, the sea breeze drizzled on our cheeks and the ocean split and foamed beneath us. Return trips to Manhattan cost two quarters, a fee easily averted by hiding in the men's room (I was outvoted by the boys two to one), sneakers jammed against the stalls to support our weight while the ferry staff made their rounds in search of fare beaters.

The ride home always snapped me back to reality. Surrounded by hordes of commuting schoolchildren, dressed in crisp uniforms or the latest fashion,

I always felt lonely. I worried the whole hour-long ride home about what might have gone on in school, what I'd missed.

A surprise visit from a caseworker could come on any day, like the day I returned from the ferry to find Ms. Cole in our home. It was her second visit to our apartment that month. Ma had let her in half an hour before I returned. They were in mid-conversation when I walked through the door, clutching my book bag like a prop. Before I passed through the doorway into the living room, I'd already smelled the lilac aroma of Ms. Cole's perfume, distinct from the musky smell emanating from the rest of the house.

She was the first to speak, establishing her dominance over Ma and me. "Nice to see you, Elizabeth," she said with a raised chin, her gaze fixed on me. Her legs were crossed, her hands resting flat on her knee. Daddy's fan had been hauled out from the bedroom. It looked unfamiliar propped in the living room window, aimed at Ms. Cole. It stirred the ends of her feathery weave as she spoke.

"Elizabeth, I'm here today because even though you promised to go to school, I got another call. Mrs. Peebles hasn't seen you in almost a week. Now I want to hear what you have to say for yourself. Why haven't you been going to school, Elizabeth?"

Her question struck me in its directness and in its airtight logic. In one way, it made sense for her to ask it, but in another way it made no sense at all, given the chaos we lived in. Because if logic were enough to change things, I suppose she could just as easily turn to Ma and ask, Why are you on drugs, ma'am? Why is the fridge empty? Why did you let yourself contract HIV when you have two daughters and a whole life ahead of you? Ms. Cole could have asked any one of these questions, too. Instead, she chose this one question, out of all the possible question marks we lived in as a family, and she directed it at me.

I looked to Ma, who sat hunched in her chair, eyes half-open. "I can't do anything, Lizzy. You just need to go to school. You have to." She addressed the last part of her statement to the wall. Ms. Cole patted the coffee table, clicking her gold ring against the glass.

"Have a seat, Elizabeth," she said. I hated her for calling me Elizabeth, for coming into our home and bossing us around. Obediently, I sat on the edge of the table. She gave me a look that implied she was getting down to business. If

I hadn't seen the same expression so many times before, I probably would
have taken her more seriously.

"You *need* to get to school, Elizabeth. If you don't go, I'm going to take
you; it's as simple as that. Your mother told me she sends you to school and
you don't go. Well, that needs to change. And you and your sister need to
help your mother out and clean up this mess. Tell Lisa that. I mean it. This
house is *disgusting*, an absolute pigsty."

. I could tell from the way she used the word *disgusting*, dragging it out,
smiling, that it made her feel powerful to say so. Ms. Cole liked her power
trips.

"I don't know how you even live here. You're old enough now to *do something about it*." She raised her voice momentarily, but then said with an unsettling calm, "There are places for girls like you."

This part of the lecture was hardest to hear. She was just the type of
person Rick and I would chuck a water balloon at from the roof, I thought.
I imagined her reaction: the shriek she would let loose on impact, how it
would flatten her cheap hairdo. I'd do it myself, I thought, and I'd fall down
laughing.

"You won't like the homes I can put you in. And let me tell you, if you won't
clean here, you *will* clean there. They'll have you scrubbing toilets. And the
girls there are violent." I saw myself doubled over toilets dirtier than my own at
home, blackened along the edges, slimy and slippery. Large, evil-looking girls
dressed in rags stood behind me to supervise. "But I'll take you out of here if
that's what you want. All you gotta do is not attend school and you *will* go."
Here came her favorite part; you could tell by the half smile on her face, like she
worked all day just to be able to deliver this one line. "It's shape up or ship out,
Elizabeth; pick one," she said.

Her face twisted into something between revulsion and exasperation.
"Don't you want to get your life together, young lady? You ever think about
that?" She enjoyed this; I could sense it coming off her, like heat. There wasn't
a trace of good intention in any of it, I knew in my gut. Like so many social
workers who disciplined me, Ms. Cole enjoyed being angry; she savored the
performance.

Where was the caring that would have made her words effective? *"Get your
life together."* People said things like that all the time, but who could explain,

nuts and bolts, what they meant? Who was trying to *show* me why I should care about school and keeping an apartment clean? Didn't adults see the size of those words, the way they were bigger than my understanding, and how the gaps between were wide enough for me to fall deep inside them? What was the connection between what I woke up to every day and the vague goals she expected of me? What was she talking about? If an education and a job were so important, then why didn't my parents have either? *"Get your life together."* What did that even look like? Was I supposed to make sense of that myself? If not, how could I decipher it from Ms. Cole's lectures? Especially when she explained things to me with such angry self-righteousness.

I was furious, but I did my best to appear calm, especially as Ms. Cole delivered the punch line when I walked her to the front door, briefcase in hand, her long, curly nail wagging at me.

"You know, Elizabeth, if I really wanted to, I could take you today. Actually, I could come in here and take you any day I want to. Remember that. I'm just being nice."

If this was her being nice, I couldn't imagine Ms. Cole's idea of antagonistic.

Back inside, Ma was already lying down, pillow drawn over her head. The clock said it was just before three; Lisa would be home soon. I was shutting my bedroom door when Ma spoke, muddled from under the pillow.

"Lizzy, did you pack groceries today? I mean do you have any cash? I could really use five bucks."

"No, I'm broke today, Ma."

She turned over and made a noise, half moan, half grunt. There was a penny stuck to her butt cheek. A tremble ran up my body, then quickly subsided. I didn't know whether or not I wanted to be upset at her, or if she just made me sad. I went to my room and sprawled across my bed, realizing that I felt only numb. Ma began crying into her pillow, loudly. I stared up at the ceiling and felt absolutely nothing inside.

That night, Leonard Mohn came by with a paycheck. He, Ma, and Daddy binged for hours. In my bedroom, I could hear them make their rounds, beer bottles clanking, footsteps, the front door opening and slamming continuously.

At one point, I came out and called Rick and Danny's house. I cupped my shirt over my nose to filter the cloud of cigarette smoke and made plans with the guys, to hang out until the sun came up. We might sneak into the movies or just walk and see what we could find to do.

As I pulled my sweater over my head to get ready, something in Ma and Leonard's conversation caught my attention. They were whispering about something, about someone. Leonard's neurotic foot-tapping drowned out some words. I stood perfectly still and listened.

They were discussing a man Ma knew from the bar. From what I could tell, someone she had known for a while, and had recently begun to connect with. His name, or the nickname that everyone knew him by, was Brick.

"I don't know, Leonard. He listens to me, ya know. I like that. I've missed being with a man who listens. We have a good time together, ya know?"

It was a man Ma was *seeing*.

"Oh Jeanie, don't let go of a man who makes you feel good. I wouldn't. Men with careers are so much more mature." Leonard whispered the next part: *"Go for it, Jean. You deserve better."*

I could have thrown Leonard out of the house with my hands. There he was, one minute smiling in Daddy's face and the next, telling Ma to go for another man. He was as two-faced as he was mean. Listening to them continue, it took me a while to fully grasp what had been going on, but I soon understood that Ma had been seeing this man for a while. I eavesdropped, hearing her describe the money he spent on her, their lovemaking, and how much she liked the fact that he didn't use drugs at all, he just drank to ease his nerves sometimes. The descriptions became more fleshed-out as I stood there, each detail bringing Brick closer to being a real person, all the while threatening Daddy, and the foundation of our family.

Brick made a good living, with benefits, working as a security guard at a fancy art gallery in Manhattan. Ma boasted that he had been in the navy. In a neighborhood much nicer than ours, Brick had his own, large, one-bedroom apartment and was single. And apparently, I was not the only one spending nights far from home. I got the sense this must mean that Daddy knew.

My eyes made a full sweep of the apartment. In my absence, the house had gone from bad to awful. Everywhere, there were signs of deterioration: busted lights, empty beer bottles, and cigarette butts littered the carpet, more so than ever before. Moistness hung in the air. The grime had an airborne weight that you could feel as you breathed. With Leonard there as Ma's new shoulder to lean on, with his money, my parents were getting high two and a half weeks out of the month, nonstop. Guilt struck me for all of my drifting; I'd abandoned my role in the apartment and in doing so, I'd let things fall apart.

Daddy came in through the front door, whistling. Ma and Leonard got quiet. I opened and shut my own door, coughed, took a step out into the living room. Ma walked through the room and went to remove her worn-out leather belt from a doorknob to use for an arm tie. "Just a second, Petie," she called over her shoulder. Daddy was counting off change for a twenty to Leonard.

I opened my mouth, intending to say something to her, but shut it quickly when I realized I had no idea what. The beginning credits to *The Honeymooners* filled the TV screen, the theme music crackling. In no way did Ma's gestures suggest that she knew I was in the room. I coughed, loudly. She glanced at me, for just a moment. "Petie, I'm getting first," she said, marching back in with the belt.

Something had stolen away the affection between Ma and me and reduced our interactions to casual, distant ones. Since her diagnosis two years ago, our dynamic hadn't been the same. I never discussed with anyone what Ma told me that night. Most times I told myself I might have dreamed it; I figured she never told Lisa because otherwise, I was sure she would have said something. It felt as if Ma and I shared a dirty secret, and this seemed to make her afraid of me. The distance she kept told me so. We hardly knew what to say to each other anymore, maybe because so much went unspoken.

Daddy got Ma high first. I could hear her begin to sniffle. Leonard Mohn was next. Daddy took his high to the bathroom, away from them, as he often did. I stood up to go meet Rick just as Leonard began wailing through his high again.

Telling me about her HIV had made me part of the landscape of painful things Ma shot up to escape. I was as certain of this as I was heartbroken by her abandonment. And when I was being honest with myself, despite tremendous efforts not to admit it, the knowledge of her disease made me want to avoid her, too. Being in Ma's presence was being near the disease, near the knowledge that I was fast losing my mother—information that was just too painful to feel.

I slipped on my backpack, passing the kitchen. Leonard whined from inside, shouting, "Oh, God, Jeanie, my heart is beating so fast. Hold my hand."

Seeing her clasp his hand sent an ache deep through me. I left quickly, just in time, I was sure, to avoid hearing that same, awful conversation again.

It was a weekday, less than one month later, when I met Brick. Ma let me cut school and brought me down to the art gallery where he worked so that the three of us could eat lunch together, his treat. As we exited the train on Twenty-third street, Ma began fidgeting and appearing obviously uneasy.

"Lizzy, do I look all right? You think this sweater is nice?" She wore a fuzzy pink V-neck sweater and hip-huggers, and she hadn't had a drink or shot up all day. Her long, curly hair was pinned back neatly. It was the first time in years I'd seen her out of her T-shirts and filthy jeans.

"Yeah, Ma, you look real nice. Don't worry. Why are you worried whether or not he thinks you're pretty? Who really cares what he thinks," I said.

"I do, pumpkin. I like him."

The words, in their directness, shocked me. It had been a while since Ma and I had been straight with each other; it felt like she was testing it out on me.

"Your ma likes somebody. I haven't had a crush in years." She smiled nervously, discarding Daddy altogether.

I knew it was more than Brick making her nervous; it was me, too. After Lisa left for school and Daddy went downtown, it had taken me at least half the morning to convince Ma to let me join her. For the first time in a while, it was just the two of us—even if only for the time until we met up with him and right after, it was just us. I knew she felt awkward because so did I. And though I found myself snapping at Ma, I longed for her to hold my hand, to talk to me, to walk me through this experience. I wanted her to want my opinion, to ask how this whole thing made me feel. But instead, all the way over she'd spoken only about him; of how he was career-oriented, stable, a real family man. I kept quiet and worked out a half plan in my mind: I would check Brick out, and by my disapproving response, Ma would see his flaws, see the flaws in her thinking, too. Our family would be saved.

While we walked, Ma's descriptions of the gallery seemed full of awe and admiration, as though its professional status were somehow a testament to Brick's stability. We crossed the street toward a narrow and very tall building, the levels of which were divided floor-to-ceiling by large windows, through which I could already see paintings and sculptures. Ma rushed me in through the side door, an employees' entrance leading to the gallery's coat check, where Brick worked, nine to five, alternating between hanging people's overcoats and standing watch over art.

"Everyone has to get a ticket if they wanna walk around inside the gallery during a show, Lizzy. Normally, you have to pay for 'em, but don't worry, Brick will get us those for free." She spoke with pride. I found that the more familiarity she expressed with him, the more of a stranger she felt to me. It made me regret spending so much time being distant. I panicked at the thought that she'd found something more exciting than us. She'd never talked so much about me or Lisa, or expressed pride over how hard *I* worked. As I watched Ma expertly navigate her way through the employee area and confidently maneuver a path to his post, I was suddenly aware of the numerous private visits she'd been making to the gallery. I felt somehow betrayed.

Brick was a bald, stout chain smoker who said very little, but nodded in agreement to most of what Ma had to say. He wanted her; I could tell by the way he stared openly, shamelessly, at her face, her body. I didn't trust him. I was suspicious of strange men who bought you things; I assumed they were out for something, like Ron.

We ate together at a nearby diner, down the block. I was allowed to pick whatever I wanted from the selection of soups. With my complimentary gallery ticket stub set on the table in front of me, I ran my spoon in circles through my cream of mushroom soup and watched them flirt. Brick slid his hand over Ma's at the lunch table, right there, rubbing it while she talked, in front of me. His nails were deep yellow, chewed to the quick. Even his fingers looked a bit gnarled at the tips, as though he chewed those as well.

She stared into his eyes while she spoke, not breaking away for a moment. I hadn't known Ma was capable of such a long attention span.

"I told Lizzy about how big your apartment is, how you get lonely living there by yourself," she said.

He gave her a confused smile and said in his five-packs-a-day voice, "Jean, I'm okay."

She slapped his shoulder playfully. "Oh, I know you get lonely, Brick. He tells me he does, Lizzy," she said, looking back at me for a moment. "You get lonely, Brick, you told me so." Her laugh was nervous.

When we initially entered the gallery, headed for coat check, I had mistaken a younger man for Brick, a mildly handsome, dark-haired man standing beside him, until Ma approached Brick and threw her arms around his thick neck. He'd been stuffing a tip in his pocket when we arrived. Over Ma's shoulder, as they hugged, he'd given me a small "*Shhh*," with a wink and a smile that revealed a damaged set of yellowish teeth, as he pointed above to a tiny, silver sign that read: NO TIPPING, PLEASE. Ma couldn't stop smiling and holding on to him, while I'd stood there, waiting, shifting my weight from foot to foot.

Before we could go to lunch, I was instructed, because of my sharp vision, to be lookout while Brick snuck us to a deserted area and pulled a large bottle of beer out from under a trash bag in a black wastebasket, quietly, secretly. While he went to the men's room to drink it down in a locked stall, Ma assured me, "He just has a few every now and then to calm his nerves. You know, working a full-time job has got to be real stressful."

Watching them at the diner table, it was difficult to stomach their physical contact. Seeing Ma slide her hand playfully over Brick's thick, uniformed thigh, I realized that in my whole life I'd seen my parents kiss only twice, a brief peck both times. Now her roaming hands over Brick's thick body seemed not only a violation to Daddy, but of who Ma was. The difference made me lonely. I almost reeled in my seat when she continued discussing Brick's extra living space. I couldn't help interrupting. "Can we go now, Ma? Please?"

When the full hour was up, we walked Brick back to the gallery, where Ma kissed him affectionately. Then she and I circled the floors together for a long time after. I refused to look at her, but kept my eyes trained on the walls as we walked. She kept trying to talk to me, but I pretended not to hear. When we made it to a section that a nearby employee called "contemporary art," which was only splashes of paint or solitary shapes on stark white canvases, Ma was up to the part about how wonderful Brick was, if I'd only get to know him, for the third time.

I continued to pretend not to listen as we moved along from the first floor to the second, until finally, when we entered an area dedicated to an artist's re-creation of historical Egyptian artifacts, I cut her short.

"Ma, I'm sorry, but I don't really want to get to know him. I'm fine with not knowing him." I kept my back to her and let my eyes trace the details carved onto a contemporary version of a mummy. "I know he's your friend, but maybe you shouldn't spend so much time with him. Okay?" She took to silence, a moment passed, and she asked a stranger for the time. We walked into a clay rendering of a small tomb, the ceiling and four walls covered in pink hieroglyphics turned orange by track lighting.

"He gets off work soon, maybe we can all take the train together," she suggested, standing so that she blocked the entrance of the tiny enclosure.

"This is nice, right, Ma?" I asked, scanning hieroglyphics inscribed in clay for several rows in front of me. "We had a worksheet translating some of these in school once. Maybe I can remember a few. You know, some of them are spells to scare off grave robbers. Creepy, huh?"

"Look, Lizzy, I've been thinking about getting off of drugs . . . I am, I'm going to get off drugs."

"I know Ma . . . ," I said gently, hoping not to discount her. "Any way I can help, you know I would."

"You mean that, pumpkin? Because this time it could be for real. I just need to be somewhere where there are no drugs. Ya know?" she asked, crouching down to the floor where I sat crossed-legged, pretending not to know what she was getting at. Her face was clean and her eyes were wide and aware. It occurred to me then that she actually hadn't shot up in almost a week, even if she had been at the bar several nights consecutively, drinking White Russians, her new favorite. I wondered if maybe she was serious this time.

"If you don't want drugs around you, then don't bring them into the house," I said, turning my head away from her again. "It's simple, if you really want that."

"But your father will bring 'em into the house, Lizzy. He'll keep using, and then I won't be able to keep from using too. I can't see that stuff in front of me and not do it, no way. Not a chance." No response came to mind, whatsoever. I knew she was right, and I couldn't remember ever hearing Daddy say a thing about stopping. I began feeling claustrophobic within the small space. Speechless, I ran my hand over the Plexiglas that protected the delicate art, tracing my fingertip to a stiffly drawn, armored soldier who looked out bravely into nothing in particular.

"I don't want to move, Ma. I don't want to leave Daddy," was all I could think to say.

"I'm not just going to go, Lizzy. I'll give your father a chance. Maybe he'll stop using too, and then we won't have to go anywhere."

Her hand appeared on my shoulder. "You know, Lizzy, I'm not always going to be here. I'm not well, baby, you know that. I need to stop living like this. I want to be around to watch my girls grow up. So . . . some things have gotta change."

Tears gathered in my eyes, fell from my cheeks. I finally turned to face her. Ma let herself fall on her butt with a thump. Sitting on the floor across from me, she took my hands in hers and squeezed them tightly; her touch was warm and reassuring. The rare thrill of Ma being totally present to my needs was something I wanted badly to last.

"Yeah Ma, maybe Daddy will stop using," I said.

"He just might, Lizzy."

We sat in silence for a moment, both knowing full well that neither of us believed he would.

I didn't expect to graduate sixth grade and go on to junior high school, given all of my absences, but somehow I did. Apparently some of my classmates shared my surprise, because the day that they saw me receiving a diploma alongside them, comments flew. "They passed *you*, Elizabeth?" Christina Mercado had commented, turning to her friends. "Damn, wonder why we even bothered to show up if they were just *givin'* these things away. Know what I mean, girls?" For years, each time I sat down near Christina or any of her friends, they collectively fanned papers in front of themselves and coughed excessively, to draw attention to my dirty clothing and obvious need for a shower. Or they'd hiss at me in the halls and sketch pictures in which bugs infested my hair and waves of bad smells rose from my body. As I sat in the auditorium, sweating in my shiny graduation gown, and the principal called each student's name, they laughed at one of the last comments Christina would ever make at my expense. I was glad Ma, Daddy, and Lisa weren't there to witness it.

While I accepted my diploma, Ma lay flat on her back in bed, recovering from a night of White Russians. Daddy was off on one of his private excursions downtown, one of his infamous outings that used to irritate Ma, back when she cared what he did. After the service ended and parents were snapping pictures of their children with their teachers and friends, I left quietly through the side door. In the hallway of my building, I removed my cap and gown before entering my apartment so that Ma wouldn't feel bad for missing the ceremony. When Ma woke up later that evening, apologizing for not showing up, I assured her, "It was so boring, Ma, you would have hated it. I was glad to get out of there. I wish I could have stayed in and slept, but I didn't want to make my teachers feel bad, ya know?"

It seemed like no time at all between my graduation and the day that Ma stood over my bed wearing a form-fitting T-shirt, her hair combed back neatly, asking again and again for me to come with her to Brick's apartment.

"Pumpkin, I gave it my best shot," she said. "Please, baby, come with me."

But I clutched my pillow and did not budge from my bed. "I'm not going, and you shouldn't either! We're a family, Ma. You can't *leave*!" I shouted. "Please, Ma, stay here," I begged her, crying. "Stay home, stay here with me, please." I didn't stop pleading; I even shouted at her from my bedroom window until she and Lisa got into the cab. I couldn't remember ever being so honest about something I wanted before, and still it had no effect on her. It seemed Lisa had been as ready to go as Ma was, because she placed two pillowcases full of clothing in the trunk, stuffed so full that they told me she had no intention of coming back. Before pulling away, Ma rolled down the taxi window.

"I'll be waiting for you, pumpkin!" she shouted. "Whenever you want to come, you can." And with that, the cab drove off, and they were gone.

Throughout those first few months that Daddy and I spent alone in the apartment, I busied myself with upkeep. Using ripped-up old T-shirts and scalding hot water, I wiped down the tabletops of the living room and kitchen. I cleaned the dishes and took out the trash. Each night, when our favorite shows aired, I went over to our black-and-white television and snapped it on, turning the volume up. Whenever it got dark outside, I flipped on the lights in every room of our three-bedroom apartment, and I turned on Lisa's abandoned radio (too large for her to take with her) so that it spun pop music into her empty room. The noise and light imitated a full household in my mother's and sister's absence.

Daddy never said he was sad that they left. He never complained. Though he was quieter than usual those days, even for him. When he wasn't getting high, Daddy slept throughout the day with the curtains drawn and the lights off in his room. Most of the time when he was awake, he wore his loneliness on him like an old jacket. I could see it in the hunch of his shoulders, and in the way he avoided any mention of their names.

Sometimes when Daddy left for downtown, the moment he vanished over the bend of University Avenue, I opened a drawer that held a few pieces of Ma's old clothing and selected an item to wear around the apartment. Mostly, I enjoyed sitting in Ma's rose-colored robe—which dragged on the ground wherever I walked—and eating bowls of cornflakes while watching *The Price Is Right*. I was sure she'd return any day to join me, sorry for her absence, ready with assurances that she would never leave us again. Wearing her clothing was my way of summoning her, just for the meantime.

By the time I started Junior High School 141, our phone was back on for a short while and Ma had called at least four times to describe how clean Brick's apartment was. "Bedford Park is a much better neighborhood, Lizzy. Lisa thinks so, too." She always placed her calls when she was at the stove. Living with Brick, Ma had taken to cooking. "I haven't used coke in months. Do you realize that, Lizzy? I feel great. I told you, I only needed to get away from it to stop," she said, deflating my argument before I could even get the words out of my mouth.

In the background, I heard Brick prodding her, "Jean. Jean, the pork chops. Jean!" The grease crackled loudly and she returned her attention to me. "I have to go now, Lizzy. We're about to eat. I love you, pumpkin!" My heart dropped. "I love you too, Ma." And then instantly, a click, and the hum of a dial tone.

♦ ✦ ♦

Junior high was a whole new system to adjust to, one I hoped to manage the way I had managed grade school—squeaking by with my performance on the annual standardized tests. That fall, I began taking half-hour bus rides, packed with wild twelve- and thirteen-year-olds, for the whole first month that I actually attended.

Though, as with grade school, I eventually found myself absent more than I was present. The only difference here was that with the long distance to travel and the jarring experience of now having several teachers to deal with, I was actually absent all the time. My truancy got worse than ever. On the rare occasions that they did see me, some of my teachers didn't even know my name, and I did not know theirs.

In those first few weeks of the semester, whenever I would return to school after a few days of absence, I'd find several handwritten notes stuffed into my student mailbox, summoning me to meet with the school guidance counselor to discuss my truancy. While the notes made me nervous, I just ignored them. I carried the thick office stationery as I walked to the bus stop and I shredded it into a thousand tiny pieces that I released behind me.

I was good at that, tuning out official notices from school and Child Welfare—just as I had grown accustomed to tuning out the barrage of "official" people who always seemed to be pushing themselves onto our family: social workers, Ma's caseworker at welfare, disappointed teachers, and guidance counselors. They had never really felt like separate people. Instead, to me, they felt like one disapproving entity, one voice repeating the same threats to take me into "placement," shaking their heads at my mistakes, telling my family how to run our lives. I responded to them uniformly, disposing of the mail they sent and barricading myself in my home.

Daddy made regular day trips downtown to see his friends, and I spent my days content to lie on the couch and watch television. Sometimes, I'd scour Ma's dresser drawers in search of things to remind me of her. Other times, I was content just to sleep, wearing Ma's robe like a big warm blanket.

One day, while Daddy had gone downtown for something, I spent the afternoon sifting through the contents of his and Ma's closet. I discovered a huge stash of Ma and Daddy's seventies things packed deep inside. Behind crates of dusty records and eight-tracks, there was a plastic bag stamped FARMERS' MARKET, with a picture of an old guy wearing overalls and plowing a field of hay on the side. I dumped the contents out across Ma's and Daddy's bed: a set of matching turquoise pipes for smoking, a teardrop-shaped pendant of amber, a museum ticket stub, and a thick stack of old photographs, the corners of which had begun to curl with age. There were three dinky silver rings, the smallest of which had a peace sign carved into it, and which fit right on my finger. Scattered between the pictures were grains from their pipes, which gave off the acrid scents of tobacco and weed. Most of the people in their pictures were unrecognizable to me—twenty-somethings wearing headbands and tie-dyed shirts, posing in city parks or beside old Volkswagens. Proof that Ma had had a life before me, and an uneasy reminder that Ma could build a life after me.

I found one faded shot of Ma and Daddy together, taken in a newer version of our kitchen. Daddy had dark, wide sideburns that connected to a fuller head of hair. Ma wore an Afro and a paisley blouse; neither one of them looked up for the picture, but lowered their eyes and heads as though they'd received bad news.

"You look miserable," I said to them. "You *are* miserable."

But I thumbed through the rest of the stack only to discover a cluster of pictures that proved there had actually been much happier times—such as one photo of them standing together in a living room that I did not recognize. In the picture, they were both smiling brightly with their eyes shielded behind large, red-tinted sunglasses. Ma and Daddy had on matching his-and-hers leather coats and were holding hands, something I had never seen them do. Another picture showed Ma in a fit of laughter. She was sitting cross-legged on a thick, orange rug, wearing a white T-shirt and tiny pair of jean shorts. Her head was thrown back in a moment of joy. Curled around her shoulders and propped up by her petite hands was a long, muscular snake of some kind. In yet another photo, Ma was blowing out candles on a birthday cake. There were several people surrounding her that I did not recognize, their clapping hands frozen in streaks of motion. Daddy was standing beside Ma, his arm over her shoulder; he was leaning in to kiss her on the cheek.

That one gesture captured in that photograph was the single greatest act of affection I had ever witnessed between my parents. I felt like I was looking at strangers.

But my favorite picture, by far, was a black-and-white headshot of Ma that had been taken when she was high school age. With a brooding look on her beautiful face, she could have been a model, I thought. The photograph drew me in and I stared down at it for what felt like forever, at this single moment of Ma's life before she went and accidentally made children, before mental illness, welfare, and even before HIV. I wondered if this was where she was always running back to: her old life, happier times that had nothing to do with children, a truant daughter interrupting her, driving her crazy, holding her back, making her sick. When I finally packed everything into the plastic bag again, I took that single headshot and slipped it into the back pocket of the jeans I wore under Ma's robe.

Placing the bag back onto the shelf turned out to be trickier than pulling it down, so I grabbed a chair from the kitchen and stood on it to see high over the crates of records. As I did, my eyes caught sight of something I had missed before, an old, dust-covered wooden box situated on the very back of the high shelf in my parents' closet. I returned the Farmers' Market bag to its place and lifted the wooden box out from behind the crates of records; it was much heavier than I had expected, given its small size. I climbed down from the chair and sat on my parents' bed, where I placed the box on my lap.

Inside, there was a scrapbook held together by rubber bands so old that they snapped when I pulled on them; a few pictures slipped to the floor. "*SAN FRANCISCO*" was scribbled across the tops of the remaining pages of the scrapbook, in my father's bold handwriting. On each page, there was picture after picture of Daddy looking even younger than he did in the photographs with Ma, his head nearly full of hair. There were shots of him pointing to the Golden Gate Bridge in the distance, relaxing on a beach, cooking hamburgers with friends at a barbecue, and laughing at parties.

In one photo, Daddy was standing in front of a place called City Lights Bookstore, in a row of four well-dressed men who were playfully serious for the camera, their chins bucked up, eyes squinting in the sun.

There were also two black-and-white pictures of Daddy, and on the back of them, unfamiliar handwriting stating three words, "*AT CITY LIGHTS.*" In one, Daddy is reading by himself, seemingly unaware that he is being photographed. In the other, he is part of a group of serious-looking people all seated audience-style before a bearded man, whose arms are raised in a gesture that implied storytelling.

Paper-clipped onto the back cover of the scrapbook was an old, faded letter, the return address of which I recognized as my grandmother's, on Long Island. I unfolded a brief, handwritten note in which she informed Daddy of her surprise the day she had received his tuition check, returned by his school in the mail, uncashed. In the short note, she explained that Daddy's former roommate had given her his forwarding address in California, and she asked when he intended to continue his studies and how long he would be "vacationing" out west. She signed it *With love, your mother,* just as she had signed every birthday card she had ever mailed to him at our apartment.

Clipped to Grandma's letter were two more letters; these were unopened and not addressed to Daddy, but rather were from Daddy, to a Mr. Walter O'Brien, in San Francisco. They each were stamped RETURN TO SENDER. In my entire life I had not seen Daddy write a letter to anyone, and I wondered what they could possibly say, but I knew I was already snooping and that I couldn't get away with opening them. So I thumbed through the postcards. One featured a photograph taken at the bottom of a very curvy hill, and it read LOMBARD STREET; it was sent to Daddy at a New York City address from a woman whose name I no longer remember, telling my father that she missed him and his "bad taste" in poetry. She also wanted him to know that their friend Walter missed him too, and that she hoped he would return to San Francisco. *Daddy liked poetry?* I couldn't imagine it. With his true crime and trivia books, all he ever seemed interested in were facts, and usually dark ones, or those absent of deep meaning. Poetry didn't fit.

I gathered up pictures that had fallen out of the scrapbook. There was one photo of a baby girl wearing a pink dress. At first, I thought it was a photograph of me, only I'd never seen it before and the picture was badly faded. Then I flipped it over to find that the writing on the back read, *Meredith.*

My chest tightened. I stared at the photo for a long while, comparing Meredith's face to the foggy memory I had of her that day in the park when Daddy had directed Lisa and me to walk toward our big sister. I stared at Meredith's face as a baby and compared it to Daddy's. Taking in her complete vulnerability as an infant, I wondered where she was now, and how Daddy could have left her behind, and why we never talked about her. It filled me with a deeply unsettling feeling to wonder what else he was capable of doing.

In the last few photos, I found one that read *"Peter and Walter, July 4."* I flipped it over and saw a picture of Daddy smiling. In it, his eyes were so bright, it was as if they were smiling too. The other man in the photo, Walter, was handsome, slim, and even younger-looking than Daddy. He was fair-skinned, with red hair and freckles. He was also smiling, and he had his arm around Daddy's shoulder. In the background, I saw people carrying American flags in a park that did not appear to be in New York City, but rather someplace I had never seen before. It looked as though everyone was having a picnic.

Finally, I reached the last photo—a Polaroid at the very bottom of the stack, underneath the pictures. At first, the image confused me. I stared at it for some time because my mind simply could not make sense of what I saw. Slowly, though, the reality of it seeped in. First, I understood that I was looking at a picture of two men kissing. I then processed that the red-haired man in the picture was Walter. My father's friend Walter. The Walter mentioned in the postcard. The Walter of the returned letters. Walter was kissing another man, and that man was Daddy.

Without thinking, I sprung to my feet in a sudden panic and stuffed the letters, postcards, and pictures back into the scrapbook and slammed it shut. I jammed the scrapbook into the wooden box, *fast*, as though if I moved quickly enough, I could pack my discovery back in there with it. I returned the whole thing to the very back of the closet, put Ma's robe back in its place, and ran to my room.

On the bed, my head buried in my pillow, Ma's warnings about Daddy came roaring back to me. I remembered all the times she accused him of being secretive and not loving her. I thought it was her illness making her paranoid. I had defended him and felt sorry for his having to put up with her irrational meanness. *Did I really just see that? Was that real? Did Ma know?*

I cried hard into my pillow. I cried out all my hurt over missing Ma and Lisa. I cried out deeply unsettling feelings. I cried because, buried in the back of the closet in the bedroom Ma and Daddy had once shared, was evidence that I didn't really know my father. Was he still seeing this Walter? Was he seeing some other man? Had he ever loved Ma? Could Daddy have given Ma AIDS?

Those next few months, I began spending a lot of time in my room with my door shut. Each night when Daddy returned from his drug runs or his time

spent downtown, I'd step out briefly to receive the take-out food that had become our routine dinner, fried rice or a slice of pizza. We'd make brief conversation, and then when Daddy was ready to get high in the kitchen, I'd retreat
into my room, where I could eat in privacy. When he brought home a second,
smaller TV set from the trash one day, he let me keep it in my room. I explained
that the couch wasn't comfortable anymore. Sometimes at night, before Daddy
went to bed, he'd tap lightly on my closed door to say, "Good night, Lizzy, I
love you." From the other side, I made him wait just a few moments before I'd
finally answer ". . . I love you too, Daddy."

A few months later, when I was thirteen years old, Child Welfare finally took
me into custody. When they came for me, I didn't put up a fight. In someplace
deep inside of me that is hard to think about even now, I do believe that my
heart broke when Daddy didn't put up a fight either.

In response to numerous calls regarding my truancy from Junior High
School 141, two unsmiling male caseworkers wearing starched suits appeared
at our door to escort me by car to "placement." One introduced himself as Mr.
Doumbia, and the other was nameless. While Daddy signed the papers handing over legal custody of me to the state, I had ten minutes to pack whatever
I could into a book bag. In a tearful panic, I'd taken some clothing, Ma's
bronze-colored NA coin and that one black-and-white picture of her, and that
was it. Daddy's hug was stiff and nervous at the door. "Sorry, Lizzy," was all
he said, his hands shaking with tremors. I hid my face from him because I
didn't want Daddy to see me cry. If I just had gone to school, this never would
have happened.

In the backseat of the car, I sat with a bag in my lap. No one spoke a word
to me. I tried to figure out what was going to happen next by listening to their
conversation. But I couldn't make out much through their guttural accents,
which were drowned out by the roar of the car engine. My eyes were darting
everywhere, up and down the Bronx streets that we drove through and which I
did not recognize. They took me to a massive, anonymous-looking office
building made of tarnished bricks, with no sign above the entrance, I noticed
as we walked in.

I was brought to a small office that resembled a doctor's examination room, but without the examination table. "Sit here," a tall woman said, pointing to a chair, before walking away and leaving the door wide open. The walls were bare. The window was barred with a thick, rusted gate, and the sun illuminated a small, trash-filled back alley behind the building. From my chair I could see another girl seated alone in the hallway, hair in cornrows, wearing sweatpants. Her eyes were lazy; she looked the way people in Ma's psychiatric ward looked when they were doped up on medication. More than a half hour went by, and no one returned. I got up and dared myself to walk over and speak to the girl.

"Hi," I said. "What are you here for?"

"They think I stabbed my cousin. I'm sick of this shit," she muttered, not looking up at me.

"Oh . . . sorry," was all I said, and after a moment I went back to my seat. I don't know how long it was before the tall woman came back, but when she did, she shut the office door and it was just the two of us alone. She opened a file under her desk lamp, read something, and then she turned, looking at me from over the top of her glasses. It was the first time anyone had looked at or spoken to me since I had gotten in the car.

"I need you to undress," she said, followed by nothing but silence.

"Get naked?" I asked.

"Yes, I need to examine you. Please undress."

The last thing I wanted to do was take off my clothes, but what else could I do? What wouldn't I have done if she told me to? So I did. She flipped through a couple of pages from the folder while I stacked my clothing on the extra office chair. I stood slightly hunched over in the chilly office, rubbing my arms to smooth away the goose bumps, and I waited for my next instruction.

"Your underwear, too. Everything."

"Why?" I asked, pulling my underwear down. "What's this for?" If someone had just talked to me like a human being and walked me through what was happening, that would have helped so much, made it so much less frightening. But instead, she talked to me with a stiff office voice that told me I was not a person, but a job, to her.

She didn't answer my question directly, but looked up from the page again and began to recite what felt to me like a practiced script.

"Elizabeth, we will be examining you today and I will need to ask you some questions. All you have to do is answer honestly. Can you do that?"

"Yes," I said, standing there completely naked, repulsed by the feeling of her eyes on my skinny body.

Looking up from her notes, with the tip of her pen she pointed to a bruise on my shin and asked, "Where did you get that, Elizabeth?"

There were lots of bruises on my body. I was naturally pale and always bruised easily. Every time I came back from playing outside, I had a bruise somewhere, so how was I supposed to know where one particular one came from?

"Um . . . playing outside?"

She wrote something down. "And that one, and this one," she asked, pointing to two more on the same leg, in approximately the same area.

What was the right answer? What would happen if I said I didn't know? Would they think Daddy beat me? If so, could I never go home again? What was at stake? The whole thing was so unclear, and the less clear it was, the more she was in complete control of me, and the less I trusted her. Why wouldn't someone just talk me through this?

"Um . . . my bike, from getting on my bike and hitting my leg."

This went on for a while. I was asked to turn around, raise my arms up, and extend my legs. Finally, I could put my clothing back on and sit down. She walked out, and a Latino man entered to bring in some food. He didn't say anything to me either. He just nodded and placed on the table a mound of something wrapped in cellophane; inside it was one thick slice of ham and one thick slice of cheese encased in a tough-to-chew roll. He gave me a juice box and left as noiselessly as he'd come. Eventually, Mr. Doumbia appeared in the doorway, and it was time to go. Back in the car, I curled my arms to my chest and stared out the window in a passive daze, at nothing in particular.

Saint Anne's Residence was a plain but stern-looking brick building on the Lower East Side of Manhattan. It looked like a cross between a public school and a home for the aged. I would find out later from other girls in the home that St. Anne's was a "diagnostic residential center"—a place where girls with histories of behavior problems like truancy, mental illness, juvenile delinquency, and other issues were sent to be "evaluated" before being sent to a more permanent placement. This evaluation process was supposed to involve sessions with all kinds of mental-health professionals, and there was a rumor that it took at least three months to complete.

My time in that group home—nearly a whole season—comes back to me now only in flashes of smells, images, and sounds. I was, for that period of time, a witness more than a participant in my life. And even if I try hard, I can only remember certain pieces.

I can see the day I was sent there, those two looming male caseworkers walking me in, sandwiching me between them. The way they pressed their picture IDs to the receptionist's window to get us buzzed in. The automated unlock-then-lock click of the doors, like the sound I'd heard in Ma's psychiatric ward. The heavy feeling in the pit of my stomach when I wondered, did these people think I was crazy? If I was sent to a place like this and no one would talk to me like a human being, did that mean that something was wrong with me? There *must* be something wrong with me.

A thick, bald troll of a woman nodded acknowledgment at my escorts, and they turned back to the door. When it clicked open, a gush of city sounds filled the otherwise noiseless entryway, sounds made by people who enjoyed freedom. In that moment, I could feel the shift in rank; I was no longer one of them.

This wasn't okay. I shouldn't be here, and Daddy was too fragile to be alone. I was sure I knew the subway system well enough to find my way back to him, if only I could get away from these people. But when I looked, I saw that attempts to escape were anticipated, and precautions had been taken accordingly. Each window was covered by gates the shape of fly-screens, and they were rock-hard. Everything was so sterile and bare that hiding was impossible.

"Call me 'Auntie,'" the woman said. "I'm in charge. You gonna stay on the third flo'. Stay outta trouble and you'll be a'ight. . . . Do you hear me, girl?" Tears caught in my throat. I nodded.

Upstairs, melancholy girls walked while being supervised through corridors lined with rooms, two or three beds in each. "This'll be your room, with Reina and Sasha. We don't tolerate no disrespect! Lights out at nine, breakfast at seven, and no missin' class. No fuss. Anything else, ask them." She indicated the girls with her nose.

Reina was dry and dark, with a narrow face and lanky body, and her head was topped with fuzzy braids. She spent all her time talking about girls who "run they mouth and get what's comin' to them . . . know what I'm sayin'?" She often paused for confirmation.

"Yup" is all I ever said back to her incessant talking.

Sasha, my second roommate, was extremely quiet, especially around Reina, and she had every reason to be. Whenever Sasha left for the bathroom, Reina immediately started in on her, going on about how "ugly" or "full-o-herse'f" she was. "Now me, I was a model befo' this place, and my clothes was bangin', before the home messed 'em up, but you ain't see me akin' like I am betta' then all-yall! Let her keep it up, I *will* smack that bitch."

It was true that style was not an option in St. Anne's, because everything valuable was inevitably stolen, and all clothing was washed together in scorching, color-draining water. But Reina was no model, and Sasha's silence was more strategic than egotistical.

Reina looked at me like she was trying to decide what to do with me. "I like you, white girl, we could be tight, watch each other's backs, know what I'm sayin'?"

"Sure," I told her.

The first night, as I sat at the dinner table, quietly delighting in a single moment's pleasure of eating a warm meal, a sudden liquid heat erupted in my lap, scorching my abdomen. It burned like fire and I screamed in pain. Reddish soup had soaked through, leaving only a few carrots and rice grains clinging to my shirt and jeans. A group of girls gave themselves away, departing backs hunched over with laughter. But they were not alone; one of the girls at my table muttered, "white bitch," under her breath.

The end of the day was marked by standing in a long line, waiting to join a row of girls brushing their teeth before white, sterile sinks that sat under hanging fluorescent lights in the bathroom. The windows were guarded in there, too. I could already tell which girls were dominant by the way they took slightly longer washing up, exaggerating their movements, leisurely fixing their hair while we all waited for our turn. Everyone else quickly splashed water over their faces, grazing their toothbrushes over their teeth in mechanical motions.

The smells of toothpaste, shampoo, and Tone soap were strongest; the butter-colored bars were distributed to us in the shower line. One by one, we waited, barefoot on the tiles, holding our towels, for the night watch to call out our names off the clipboard and count on their stopwatches the minutes we were to shower. The distinct cocoa-butter scent of Tone filled the space between all the stalls, emanating from behind the plastic curtains that separated us, thickening the foggy steam.

No one loitered because Auntie's omniscience made it seem as if she was right behind you, ready to speed you up with a threat at any time. So the main hallway remained totally empty, pyramids of light shining out of each open bedroom door.

"Raguìa-Lauryn-Elizabeth, this ain't yo' personal bathroom. Now hurry up befo' Auntie lose her temper! You ain't no snails." It was the first time my hygiene and bedtime were ever enforced; it felt strange to know that people showered every day, and to be one of them. But I loved the feeling of being clean and the brush of laundered clothing on my skin. Auntie made sure everyone's lights were off promptly at nine; as a backup, a staff member sat in the hallway for a night shift.

One of the hardest things to deal with, it turned out, besides the confinement, the half hour a week of phone time, and the minute-by-minute routine, was the thunderous call of Auntie's voice from morning till night, accompanied by the jingle of keys that clicked on the waist of her one, permanent house dress. Each morning all twelve of us woke no later than six thirty, *or else*, to the sound of our doors flying open, the flicker of fluorescent lights over us, and, of course, Auntie screaming.

"Besta get up now, *girls*! Get up, get up, get uuup!"

Occasionally came the sounds of a girl (usually new) who refused to leave her bed and was consequentially dragged, kicking and screaming, out of it.

"Don't test Auntie, 'cause Auntie don't play. You try this on Auntie, you see what Auntie going to do."

"Why don't you start by telling me how you feel about being here."

"Stuck," I replied, ignoring the disappointment on her face as moments dragged on and I stayed silent. The long hand on the Prozac clock ticked patiently; instead of the 12, there was a picture of a bright green-and-white pill.

Dr. Eva Morales drank her coffee from a Cornell University mug, which never traveled anywhere in her small, windowless office except to her mouth and back onto her coaster, a doily the same exact shade as her bright pink lipstick. Our sessions, like every other girl's sessions, ran for forty minutes, three times each week, for the entire time I remained at St. Anne's Residence.

"Consistency brings progress and progress is marked by consistency," Dr. Morales would chirp, nodding her head to each syllable on an angle determined by the seriousness of our current topic—which was usually my "discipline problem." However, sometimes she took the opportunity to explore other things: "Doesn't that hair in your face bother your mother?" And, "If you stay this shy, you'll never make any friends."

Her expression had only two variations: the sympathetic frown (one hand cupping her cheek) and the pensive look (biting her lip and steepling her hands). I wished for anything other than the pensive one, for an irritating affirmation never failed to follow it: "Life is about taking charge, and being responsible for oneself."

As though I hadn't been responsible for myself almost my whole life.

She was so disconnected from anything she was saying that I sometimes felt the entire session might just be *for* Dr. Morales, a forum for her to practice phrases she learned in her training. As a result, I spent half my time in her office appeasing her, nodding unwavering agreement and faking my own connection to her insights.

"I want to help you, but everyone knows, you can't help someone who won't help *you* help them." Her eyebrows perked up; she was trying to draw me out of a long silence.

"I understand," I constantly told her.

I practiced my best attentive face so that I wouldn't have to suffer through her repeating herself. That's what Dr. Morales and I did for our forty minutes—"understand" each other for the sake of progress. I understood her because if I did, I'd be closer to getting home. If she was my ticket back to my family, then I would show her that I didn't deserve to be at St. Anne's Residence another minute.

So I burned our time together making responsive faces and nodding endlessly, as though I was moved and enlightened by her affirmations. Yes, I did think that it was time to start caring about my future. Yes, now that you mention it, I did want to be an educated young lady and to take advantage of my potential. Yes, you are effective at your job and I am changing because of you, Dr. Morales.

One afternoon later that week I found out what Reina had meant by having me "watch her back," when Auntie slammed open our door fuming, dragging Sasha behind her, soaking wet and sobbing, her eyes bloodshot.

"Don't neither of you girls try playing no tricks on Auntie!" Her beady eyes darted from me to Reina. With that bald head and pushed-up nose, she looked like a bulldog with its ears clipped. "Which one of you put bleach in Sasha's shampoo bottle? Don't make Auntie guess!" Reina insisted that it wasn't her, in a way that was so convincing, for a moment I doubted myself.

"Elizabeth did it! I told her we don't ak like that here, but Auntie, she just don't listen." With an exasperated shake of her head, she added, "She told me to leave her alone if I didn't want no trouble fo' myself, but I'll be damned if I am going to take blame! Auntie, cross my heart and swear to die, I didn't do it." At that, Auntie was convinced.

"I would nev—" I began.

"I don't care where you came from, but ain't no way that mess goes down here—you ain't gettin' away with none a dat on Auntie's watch. You come with me!" I followed her shiny bald head out of the room, past Reina's smug smile.

I ended up in the "quiet room," a six-by-ten space with bad light and itchy carpeting, where girls were dragged and locked in when they misbehaved.

There was one small window, barred like the rest, through which an eerie light came in. It faced the brick siding of the neighboring building, and only if I strained could I see a slice of sky. The room smelled of dried sweat and urine, and I rationed my breathing as I sat, furious, crying in the miserable room. "I hate this place," I said aloud to myself. "I hate it."

After Reina's bleach prank, I was moved away from her and Sasha, to a room with only one girl. Her name was Talesha; she was fifteen, two years older than me. She had small, down-turned eyes, coffee-colored skin, and a six-month-old son. Because of her age, Auntie figured I "wouldn't try none a dat sass" on her.

As I brought a garbage bag of my stuff to the new room, Talesha held the door open, smiling. Long, slender braids cascaded behind her shoulders. She had full hips and inch-long metallic purple nails.

The minute the door shut behind us, she bounced onto her bed and exclaimed, "Reina's got issues out da ass! Girl, I know you ain't do that bleach trick . . . especially being the only white girl here, you'd have to be crazy to pull somethin' like that. You don't look crazy." Her eyes were soft.

"I didn't do that to Sasha," I said.

"So why are you here?" she asked. "Where's your family?"

I didn't know how I wanted to answer her, and I didn't want to tell her about Daddy or even to think of him alone on University Avenue, because of me. So I just shrugged my shoulders and unpacked my things.

Talesha had been in foster care for over a year now. This was her second time back at St. Anne's, and she knew everything about everyone. Living with her, I was privy to the former lives of many of the girls, and even Auntie. It turned out Reina's mother was a crackhead, who showed up broke at her dealer's apartment and traded Reina for some rocks.

"Her mother was like, 'Reina can clean your house for you.' Yo, they was like, a'ight, let her fix up the house, that's worth something. But girl, Reina's mother never came back, she just bounced with the rocks and thass it!"

Listening to Reina's story, I felt lucky to have Ma. She would never do something like that.

Talesha went on, "And another thing! Did you know that Auntie useta have thick, long dreadlocks, but then she got sick and they fell out. She put them in a big plastic bag, and till this day keeps them behind the couch in her office!"

"No! Serious?" I said.

This I refused to believe, until a few months later when I actually saw Auntie proudly showing them to other staff. She pulled the long, raggedy things out of that plastic bag, like toy snakes popped out of a fake can, and she declared, "There's Indian in my family. My father's Cherokee, so I can grow 'em back whenever. They looked good on me, too!"

But more than anything, Talesha talked about her baby son, Malik. Often we would lie awake hours after lights-out as I eagerly listened to what it was like to have a boyfriend and become pregnant. "It's nice. When you start showing, people get up out they seat on the bus and treat you real respectable. And there's always someone to love you when you have a baby, and always somebody you could love, too."

Many nights, I'd lie awake and listen to Talesha cry softly, telling me how much she missed her son. And about how she hated her mother for forcing her into the home and keeping the baby herself. Sometimes we'd stay awake and she'd tell me about how good life was going to be when she got out and got Malik back. They'd get a house somewhere upstate, near Peekskill, where Malik could play in a beautiful yard. Sometimes, long after Talesha had gone to sleep, in the total silence of the pitch black room, I cried, thinking of my family. Daddy alone in that big apartment, Lisa drifting so far away from me, and the AIDS virus making its way through Ma's body minute by minute, with nothing I could do to stop it.

I was discharged from St. Anne's just as spring arrived and cherry blossoms were budding on the trees along the Lower East Side. I don't know if it was Auntie, Dr. Morales, or Mr. Doumbia who made the final decision on my release into Brick's custody, but I was more than happy to get out of there. Other than leaving Talesha behind, there was absolutely no sadness I felt about going.

"Good luck, girl. I'm gonna miss you," she said, giving me the warmest hug I'd had in a long time. I thanked her for everything, wished her luck, picked up my garbage bag of clothes, and went downstairs to meet Mr. Doumbia.

It didn't hit me until I was on the street outside of St. Anne's, standing on the sidewalk surrounded by all the noise of a busy Manhattan day, that I had no idea what my life was about to look like. Even though I was "going home" to Ma and Lisa, I was not returning to anything I knew. On each of our weekly phone calls, Ma had promised that living with Brick was the best thing for me—for us. But now, her "us" no longer included Daddy.

I settled into the backseat of the taxi next to Mr. Doumbia. As I listened to him give the driver my new address on Bedford Park Boulevard, I was aware of a very familiar feeling spreading through my chest. I was afraid—to the point of certainty—that far from "going home," I was just being shuttled to another place I didn't want to be.

Stuck

BRICK'S ONE-BEDROOM APARTMENT WAS CLUTTERED WITH ENDLESS rebate paraphernalia; proofs of purchase for just about anything you could buy in a supermarket. Marlboro, Newport, and Winston T-shirts were flung in lazy piles all over the place. His bowls were a multicolored, plastic, collector's set of overturned baseball caps earned from the carefully cut bar codes off the backs of Apple Jacks boxes, which sat untouched in the cabinet. Whole, boxed, bulk orders of Pepsi and Franco-American gravy were opened, stripped of their labels, and stuck in random spots for later use. Mass purchases of Duncan Hines cake mix had afforded Brick free subscriptions to *Sports Illustrated* and *Better Homes and Gardens*. Strewn around everything, placed on both sides of the two dirty couches, were countless ashtrays, filled to the brim with rubbed-out butts and struck matches. I knew Daddy would have commented that there wasn't a single book in sight.

The morning I arrived with Mr. Doumbia, Ma was spreading a generous serving of mayonnaise across Brick's roast beef sandwich as he sat, waiting to be fed. Smoke from their cigarettes filled the air. Through it, the Platters sang "Only You" from a junk radio on the table. Lisa had opened the door and greeted me with a limp hug. She was wearing dark lipstick and gold hoop earrings that seemed bigger than her face.

"Pumpkin!" Ma cheered when she saw me. "You're here!" She wrapped her arms tightly around me, still holding the greasy knife in her hand. Hugging her, I immediately felt the weight loss, her delicate body like a child's in my arms. I was growing taller than her, larger. The difference struck me, made me feel somehow older than she was. "I missed you, Ma," I said softly into her ear, while I watched Brick behind Ma, signing papers that Mr. Doumbia had fanned out across the kitchen table.

"Feel good to be free?" Brick asked, choking on a laugh through his smoker's cough. His question made me feel gross and I didn't answer him, but pulled back to see Ma smiling at me, looking into my eyes. "I'm *so glad* you're here, Lizzy."

"Don't forget." Mr. Doumbia removed his sunglasses to speak, a toothpick wagging from his bottom lip. "This is a probationary trial. We'll see how school goes, then we'll know if the placement is working or if Ms. Elizabeth cares to return to the system."

Even though school at St. Anne's had been no more than a sewing class in a spare room with a woman named Olga, I had technically passed the seventh grade in the system. The day after my arrival at Brick's, I was scheduled to start the eighth grade at Junior High School 80. Ma had to register me. "Penny Marshall and Ralph Lauren went here, ya know," Ma told me as we crossed Mosholu Parkway headed for my new school. "Only his name back then was Lipshitz. Imagine, Ralph Lipshitz clothing. Like anyone would buy shit." I didn't laugh. "It's a really good school, Lizzy. I wish I could go back to school. I never finished high school, ya know. I hope you finish," she added, more to herself than to me. I was unsure if I could finish a straight week of school, but the thought of returning to St. Anne's made my stomach lurch.

Security directed us to a small office, where we waited to see the guidance counselor about my class placement. Kids were changing classes, swarming in and out of the office. Looking at their backpacks and bright clothing, seeing them laugh and chase one another through the halls, I felt older than all of them. Stepping in the office just then, I suddenly realized that I was embarrassed by my mother.

She spoke in loud shouts over the heads of the passing children, entirely unaware of her language, telling me obscenity-laced stories about her new friends in the neighborhood bar, Madden's. Since getting off cocaine, she'd been consistent with taking her meds but they gave her a nervous twitch, as though her arms and legs were being jerked upward by invisible strings. The scars on her arms had never been so obvious to me until we sat under the bright lights of the junior high office; punctured and injected thousands of times, they'd healed into light purple marks concentrated mostly over her larger veins. Seated there, I was sure everyone would know they were track marks.

Another student, a boy my age, waited across from me with his mother. The mom was neatly dressed in a feminine business suit and pumps. While Ma spoke, the woman shifted uncomfortably, running her fingers repeatedly over her thin necklace and whispering to her son. Ma had recently cropped her hair into a short mullet, and she had on one of Brick's rebate T-shirts that read MARLBORO, WHAT IT MEANS TO BE A MAN. I shrank in my seat.

When the counselor came out to take the next in line, she called out the boy's name. Ma rose to cut in front of the boy and his mother, hearing only the word *next*. "No, Ma, *they're* next," I stammered, but the woman waved us ahead. "No, no, you go ahead." Ma had already taken a seat in the office, oblivious.

Junior High School 80 segmented its students, like most other schools, into "top" to "bottom" classes. That is, smart to dumb classes, which they coded with names like Star, Excel, and Earth levels.

"You're here so I can determine what level class is most appropriate for you," the counselor, an older lady with bookish features, explained.

"Well, she's smart," Ma said decidedly. "Put her in your smartest class, that's where she belongs." I was hammered with guilt. Here I was trying to figure out how I could disassociate myself from Ma, and there she was, sticking up for me, proud of me for no real reason at all.

The counselor's laugh was insulting. She explained that finding my placement was a matter of looking over my records from the last school I'd attended. I fumbled nervously with my hair scrunchie, twisted between guilt, nerves, love for my mother, and fear that I would only disappoint her, prove that her faith in me was unfounded.

It took only a moment for the counselor to skim my file before cheerfully announcing, as though to make it sound fun, "I think we have the perfect place for you, dear." She pulled out the Earth class availability list and began writing my name on some official form, beside the name Eight Earth One, which, she informed me, was a "solid" class.

"They're at lunch just now, Elizabeth. You can join the Earth program with Mr. Strezou when they return at twelve," she said, passing me a note for my new teacher. As Ma and I rose to leave, she added, "I hope you go to school from now on; it would be a shame if you didn't. You're not getting any younger, dear, and these things have a tendency to go either way."

Ma and I lunched outside on slices of pizza and watched cars zip by, seated on a metal grate in the grass just outside of the school. Nearby, behind the chain-link fence bordering the schoolyard, children screamed and played. I ate my pizza quickly and watched Ma smoke, her slice barely touched beside her. A woman crossed the street with three small children and a stroller. There wasn't a piece of graffiti anywhere in sight. Bedford Park was so different, I thought; everything was.

Ma decided to tell me stories of when she was in junior high, about how she and her brother and sister would go to the others' classes and tell the teacher a sob story about how sick the other was, so they would get excused from class. Then they would all meet out behind the school and go shoplift or sneak into the movies all day. We shared a laugh, but Ma became serious with me quickly.

"But I wish I'd done things differently, Lizzy. I regret not going and I can't change that now, it's too late. Don't do that, Lizzy, you'll end up with no goddamn options when you get older. You don't want to end up stuck," she said, shrugging her shoulders.

"Why, are you stuck, Ma? Do you feel stuck living with Brick?"

"We're lucky to have him" was all she said, and I let it go.

Ma's complete vulnerability occurred to me again. There was something about sitting out there with her, under the open sky, in this unfamiliar neighborhood while we ate lunch paid for with this strange man's money, that made me see Ma's small size, her near-blindness, her total lack of capability given the odds against her. She really had no options other than moving in with Brick. If Ma felt she had to leave our home, where else would she have gone? What else could Ma have done for herself, for Lisa and for me? She'd used the word *stuck*. Maybe I shouldn't bother her about Brick, I thought. Just for now.

We sat in silence and I drifted for a moment. Someday, I thought, I'll pass this schoolyard and she won't be around anymore. The thought had caught me off-guard. I decided to create a mental snapshot of the moment: us sitting by ourselves, eating. Ma's body, full of life and motion. We loved each other; nothing could change that. "I'll always be in your life . . . No matter how old you get, you'll always be my baby," she'd assured me that awful night on University Avenue when she told me that she had AIDS.

I reached down and plucked two fluffy dandelions from the patchy grass at our feet, then passed her one. She held it in the same hand as her cigarette and studied it curiously. "Thank you, Lizzy," she finally said.

"Make a wish, Ma," I laughed, "but don't tell me what you wished for, or it won't come true." I pretended not to notice her embarrassment. We held hands and blew dandelion puffs into a thousand directions; some fluttered and stuck in her dark hair. I thought of wishing to have more options, to do well in school. But I wished for Ma to be well again instead.

I never found out what she wished for.

Eight Earth One was comprised of students who'd been teamed together since the sixth grade. So the twenty-five-plus thirteen-year-olds in my new class were divided into tight cliques, several small groups of best friends. The afternoon I walked in, clutching my note from the office with my red book bag slung over one shoulder, our teacher, Mr. Strezou, was conducting a math lesson. He was in his mid-thirties and wore a dark blue button-down shirt with worn khaki pants and loafers. Skimming my office note, he crinkled his brow into a dozen lines.

"Welcome, welcome . . . Elizabeth."

I nodded without saying anything back. Disappointing teachers was so much worse than never getting to know them at all. I decided, before I even walked in, to avoid connecting with the teachers at 80.

"You can take a seat wherever you like," he said, crumpling the office stationery into the wastebasket and returning to the next math problem. "Who can get number four?"

All but one seat was taken in the noisy classroom; keeping my eyes on the ground, I plopped into the seat and hoped to go unnoticed.

Someone had carved the word *Phreak* into my new desk with a pen, scratching the soft wood with angry little lines. As I ran my fingers over the inscription, someone began taunting me. Giggles, familiar to me from grade school, stirred up one row behind me. Heat flushed my face and a lump surfaced in my throat. Here we go again, I thought. I took in a big breath and hung my head, hoping to stick it out until the bell rang. Somehow, despite my having learned at the group home to shower daily, to change my clothing and underwear, and even though I wore Lisa's old clothes instead of my defective ones, I'd managed to attract the same kind of negative attention. I ran down a mental checklist of what I could possibly have done, when I realized that the laughter wasn't directed at me.

I turned around to see a pretty Latina girl and a white boy sitting beside each other shooting spitballs back and forth at close range. Something about their playfulness drew me in; they simply looked so happy. The girl shot another spitball and missed, accidentally sending it across the crowded room, into another girl's hair. No one seemed to notice. The fugitive sight of it there caused them to laugh so hard together that I couldn't help but laugh, too. I saw the Latina girl catch me staring. I turned away quickly. My heart started to pound quickly.

As Mr. Strezou tapped out math problems across the blackboard, I could hear the girl telling vulgar jokes to the boy. Something about it reminded me of Ma's dirty jokes, the ones she came home telling after a night of White Russians. I was sure Mr. Strezou could hear the girl, and I wondered if she was provoking him. I watched, oddly entertained, waiting to see what he might do. Then, out of nowhere, the girl spoke directly to me. I thought she must be addressing someone else, but she leaned forward, swatted her hand on my desk, and came in close.

"You know, next month is my thirteenth birthday. I'm going to celebrate by wearing a trench coat to school." I wasn't sure how to interpret her smile; no one really ever talked to me unless I was being set up for a public joke at my expense. I waited to see what she would do next.

"You know what I mean," she went on. "*Only* a trench coat. Then I'll flash all the teachers." She grabbed the collar of the white boy and laughed into it with him. I laughed, too, this time openly, along with them. Had she really just spoken to *me*? This is when you should say something back, I told myself; say something.

"Are you really going to do that?" was all I could think of. "That would be so funny," I added. Mr. Strezou called out, "That's enough, you guys. Especially you, Bobby, *cut it out*. Samantha, I need you to get this one, number nine." He extended the chalk outward.

"*A'ight*, I got it. Check this out." She snapped her fingers, rising from her chair and striking a showgirl pose, which included a full sweep of her curvy body and another flash of her bright smile. As she stood, revealing her full profile, I saw that I'd underestimated her beauty. The boy, Bobby, laughed hysterically watching her.

"It's right here," she said. Raising the tips of her fingers to a gathered pinch, she exclaimed, "Arrsh!" and sat back down, abruptly.

"Um, I don't really know it, Mr. Strezou, sorry. Can't help you out there actually," she told him, as though the answer were somehow for his benefit. The class was a mixture of silence and laughter, with the exception of a few kids in the first row who sucked their teeth. A dainty girl rose and accepted the task in her place.

When class let out, I followed Samantha through the crowd and started down the stairwell that was parallel to hers, pretending to travel close out of coincidence. I wanted her to notice me again. Together, we began circling the caged, symmetrical staircases, making the rounds until we shared in a laugh, and then the circling became a kind of game, a race helter-skelter to the bottom. When we got there, side by side, heaving for breath, we became friends.

"What's your name?" she asked, pressing her palms to her thighs. I almost said Elizabeth, but thought again when the name echoed in my head from the mouths of angry social workers, angry group home girls, and, worst of all, Ma's crazy voice, the voice from her breakdowns.

"Liz, my name is Liz," I said, testing out the shape and feel of it.

"Well, good to meet ya, Liz. I'm Sam."

"Cool. Do you want to walk together?" I offered, motioning toward the double doors.

She must have said yes, because we ended up walking together, but all I can remember is that big, bright grin of hers, smiling at me.

The next day, I sat alone at the far end of the cafeteria table, arming myself with a book, avoiding contact with the other kids. A foam lunch tray sat beside me and I was picking at my food when, out of nowhere, someone's fingers landed—*splat*—in my applesauce. It was Sam.

"You don't wanna eat this," she said. "It's poison, I think they're trying to kill us." I laughed and looked up, smiling ear to ear. I loved how bold Sam was; she could make an ordinary day suddenly thrilling. She flicked the sauce off her fingertips. "Scoot over," she said, plopping her sketch pad down on the table. Sam was penning a picture of a pouting fairy with a voluptuous body and a set of complicated butterfly wings. She was wearing what looked like her father's button-down shirt. Undone in the front and draped over her woman's body, it made her look like one of those girls in movies who look sexy in too-big men's clothing. The sleeves were rolled up midway, revealing colorful, small, red-and-yellow ink drawings of flames scrawled onto her arms.

"That's so cool," I said, lifting my bag to make room for her lunch tray.

"She's a slut, and her name is Penelope," Sam answered without looking up. "This girl would do anyone, even Mr. Tanner, in two shakes of a lamb's tail."

I laughed instantly, almost too loudly. Mr. Tanner, an older, head school figure with gray hair and rough skin, had entered the cafeteria right on cue. A moment earlier and her comment would have been different. She's quick, I thought. We watched him stop and cup his hands, forming a bullhorn. Hundreds of kids across the cafeteria all fell into a hush. He spoke, and to my surprise, the cafeteria called out with him, "The outer yard is now op-en." Sam rolled her eyes, returning her attention to the page; she was coloring the fairy's wings in emerald. Her attitude was either temperamental or mysterious. "How long have you been drawing?" I asked. Kids began filing out into the schoolyard, holding apples or gulping down the last of their pints of milk. "I mean, your stuff looks good."

"Eh, it's all right. What I really want to do is be a writer," she said. "If I write one book by the time I'm thirty, I can die in peace. In fact, I'll kill myself."

Almost everything she said was dramatic in that way. Over the years of our friendship to come, I would see her offend numerous bystanders with foul language, loud belches, and general socially unacceptable behavior. Back then I savored her rebellion; it made me feel accepted, understood somehow. Something about how offbeat she was synched up perfectly with how different, how separate, I felt from everything. Just by watching her be weird and borderline offensive was like testing out my own weirdness on the world, except when I was with Sam, the world's rejection mattered less because we were with each other. This made her courageous, almost victorious, in my eyes.

"What kind of things do you want to write about?"

A boy sat down near Sam, interrupting us. He was black, dressed in semi-baggy jeans and a Tommy Hilfiger shirt—the typical urban style that boys my age wore, but neater and more put together.

"What radio station would you guess I listen to?" he asked me, an eager look spreading across his face.

It was happening again—another student speaking to me. I searched for his motive, too, and decided that sitting next to Sam made me look cool. It was as if I'd borrowed some of her allure for myself.

"Come on, guess," he insisted.

"Um, I wouldn't know, really." I tried to look laid-back, like someone who casually made friends this way all the time. I said, "You can't really guess those things, not accurately anyway." Plus, I was embarrassed by the fact that I never listened to the radio and couldn't name one radio station if I tried to.

He seemed satisfied. "Didn't think you'd get it. *Z100.* The answer is Z100. Most people think because I'm black, I like hip-hop," he said. Sam looked up from her drawing and pointed a pen right into his face.

"You're a strange one . . . you go by your last name, Myers, right?" The boy smiled, bowed his head dramatically, and said, "Yes. And I like your drawings, Sam." It didn't surprise me that he knew her name, although she wasn't sure of his. Sam must draw attention from guys all the time, I thought.

Bobby, the white boy who'd been flirting with Sam the day before, slid down to our end of the table, too.

"Whatcha guys doin'?" he asked, smiling at me, and then turning to Sam, who poked her tongue out at him. "Hey," he yelled. She exploded into laughter, so did he, and then so did I.

Bobby's hair was a wavy brown puff that sagged over his hazel eyes. He had this perpetual smirk on his face, a sort of half smile, as though he was always about to laugh at something. Any time I looked at him, that little half smile made me always ready to laugh at something, too. Sitting there with him and Sam instantly made me happy.

Another friend was with Bobby, a tall guy in baggy jeans who introduced himself as Fief. "They call him that because of that cartoon mouse in that movie," Sam told me. "'Cuz of his ears, he looks like him." Fief was Irish, slightly red-faced, with slightly big ears. He resembled someone who might have been in my family, I thought.

"'Sup, guys," he said, sliding over.

For the entire duration of our lunch period, we talked as a group, apart from the hundreds of kids around us. I was one of them, jumping in, making people laugh, suggesting plans outside of school. When the bell rang, we walked upstairs together, parted in the halls, waving back at one another until we passed through our individual classroom doorways, out of sight. For the first time ever, I had no doubt that I would be at school tomorrow.

Brick's work schedule dictated the routine in his house, and every day was a carbon copy of the last. Each morning, I awoke at 7:15 a.m., to the oldies DJ playing "Happy, Happy Birthday" for the daily birthday movie ticket raffle. As the radio called out listeners' names, a thick cloud of cigarette smoke from Brick's Marlboros came floating above Lisa's head and mine, in the living room where our bunk bed was stashed in the corner. I could hear him shouting for Ma to wake up.

"Jean, Jean," he'd grumble. "It's morning; time to go." She'd prepare the coffee and get us on our feet while he showered. It was the closest I'd ever come to having a responsible routine. Certainly it was unique to Ma, who always had trouble waking up, until Brick yelled moistly into her face and sometimes pulled her off the bed with a rough jerk of the arm in order to make her listen. I knew that what caused her exhaustion was no longer drugs (she finally wasn't using any), but the illness progressing. From overhearing their conversations, I knew Brick knew she was ill. But he didn't show any awareness or sensitivity in the way he treated her. Watching him in his wrinkled, too-tight boxers standing over her small, resting body revived a growing sense of anger I'd felt since I'd first met Brick. Anger that arose in me each time he'd called Ma away from the phone, interrupting our delicate conversations, back when she'd first left. No one had ever bothered Ma while she slept, especially not Daddy. He never needed anyone to start his day for him, much less feed him. Thinking of his independence sent a wave of worry through me. Was he doing okay on his own? The phone had gotten cut off on University again and we hardly spoke anymore. I both wanted and didn't want him to see the way Brick was treating

Ma. I also wondered whether Daddy's lack of attention, his life of secrets, had caused Ma to gravitate to Brick in the first place. But this couldn't have been what she'd expected.

Soon after, Brick and Ma would head out together, him to work, Ma to the bar, where they came to know her so well that she was served before the general customers came knocking, while the glasses were still being wiped clean and last night's stools had yet to be lowered off the counter. There was no real reason for her to get up in the morning except that Brick said, "This is when people wake up," and so she did. To kill the time, she went to Madden's and drank. By noon, she would return home, drunk beyond the capacity for speech.

Lisa beat everyone at getting up in the morning, except that it was not like before, when she made it a point to get me up for school, too. Maybe it's because we were sharing a space—the living room—for the first time, but Lisa was more aggressive with me than ever. She had developed a hair-trigger temper with me, snapping if I asked her even the most basic questions.

"Lisa, is there any more toilet paper?"

"I don't know, Liz, you live here now, too, can't you figure it out?" I couldn't help but feel as if I had invaded her space.

She readied herself at around six a.m., staring into a large mirror on the side of Brick's living room wall. But instead of searching her image or experimenting with facial expressions, Lisa approached her reflection the way an artist would her canvas. The process was graceful, and each time the transformation surprised me. She began with a dainty zippered bag from which she pulled all types of soft pencils and wands. First she lined her lips, then filled them in with a bright creamy red. Sometimes, if she was going out with her new boyfriend, she drew symmetrical upturned tails at the edges of her dark eyes, like Cleopatra's. Lisa's vision had worsened but then stabilized over the last few years, causing her to lean in, allowing just enough room between herself and the mirror for whatever tool she was using. She left in a brilliant flash of glistening gold hoop earrings and tightly gelled hairstyles, going either to school or—in the evenings—to a life she'd carved out for herself elsewhere.

Many nights she'd return with a faded version of the vivid artistry she'd left with, dark pigment rimming her lids, dull pink smudged around her lips like runny watercolors. I didn't dare ask about the dense maroon blotches, like bruises, spotted around her neck, but quietly willed her to sit on my bottom bunk and confide in me about her boyfriend, and what being seventeen was all about.

"Do you have MTV?" Sam asked the first time she visited Brick's house. On television, O. J. Simpson was crossing and uncrossing his legs in an LA courtroom. A camera zeroed in on his facial expressions as some new evidence was being revealed. We were cutting school for the day. I'd managed to be in semi-regular attendance for almost two months, so I didn't think it would be too big a deal to miss a day or two at this point. Lisa wasn't home yet, and Ma had already returned from the bar and passed out on Brick's bed, bordered by an impossible amount of loose laundry, crates of cans, and stacks of old magazines. We sat on the couch in the living room, Sam painting her toenails a glossy black.

"I think we might have it, but you have to check. I've never had cable before."

"Anything but this," she said, hitting some buttons on the remote. A jumble of guitar strings shot out from the TV speakers. Sam curled her foot to her chest and puffed out her cheeks, blowing on her toes.

"This is a cool place," she said. "Your mom's boyfriend is almost never here, for real? And your mom sleeps all day?"

"Yeah, pretty much."

"Sounds great." Even though it didn't feel great to live under a stranger's roof and to have Ma drained of all her vitality, I knew from my one visit to Sam's house why she thought so. I wasn't delegated responsibility over a younger sibling. I didn't have to deal with the intimidating father she described, around whom everyone at her house walked on eggshells. I hardly had to deal with adults at all, apart from my caseworker's checkups.

Leaning on the arm of the couch, Sam reached to the back of her head. With one jerk of a single brass pin, her light brown hair, phone-cord curly, soft as silk, dropped from a tightly wrapped bun down to her waist. Colorful rubber bands were worked into a single, thin braid within the larger mass. Together, the range of color in the braid made a complete rainbow.

"Oh my God," I marveled. "Damn, look at your hair. I had no idea it was so long. It's really nice."

"It's a bitch to comb, I'll tell you that much. My dad is the one who's in love with it. If he likes it so much, he should grow his own," she said, unraveling the bottom of the braid with her fingers. The smell of peach conditioner carried up to my nose.

A Nirvana video came on; Kurt Cobain filled the screen. "Oh, he is so hot," Sam said, perking up. "Oh my God, I would so do him."

The comment had taken me off guard.

"Yeah . . . I guess he's cute," I said. I didn't know how to join in here; boys hadn't occurred to me yet. They might as well have been bigger versions of females. The only difference to me so far was that every so often I found myself staring a little longer at one, or feeling slightly more curious or impressed by things they did. But I couldn't say I'd ever really been *attracted* to any boy. I watched Kurt's face, covered in blond stubble, as he strummed his guitar in wide circles for the camera. Studying his features, I imagined what it might feel like to cup his cheek, to hold his hand. Suddenly, his face became Bobby's face, smirking his half smile at me.

"Yeah, I guess I would say he's definitely hot," I told Sam. I didn't know why what I'd said embarrassed me so much. But from her face, there was no sign that she noticed.

"God," she said, biting her fist. "Damn right." She turned the volume way up.

"Pass me that," I said, reaching for her nail polish. Holding the jar, I worried that Daddy would somehow see me all the way from University Avenue and think I was being girly. I shook it back and forth in motions that matched the grating noise of the guitars, then twisted the top open and shouted over the music. "Yeah, I would so do him, too."

Sam and I spent every day together. Ours was a hasty, overnight bond that we both swore would last until we grew into old ladies, pushing ourselves around some resort in Florida with walkers. In the meantime, we planned the next fifty years of our lives together. Right after high school, we would hitchhike to LA, where we'd become successful screenwriters, then eventually move to San Francisco when Hollywood became lackluster, after making more money and visiting more countries than we ever knew existed. Our neighboring houses would be on that winding hill in San Fran that I'd seen in Daddy's post-cards, and in Rice-A-Roni commercials. After our children (three each) grew up and moved away, we would buy big, old-lady sunglasses to wear through-out our sixties, and we'd tan on beach chairs in our connected backyards until our skin turned into living leather. New York would have to do for now.

In a way, though, what we hardly realized was that we'd begun our shared lives already.

Little by little, Sam began filling up drawers at Brick's apartment, packing her sketch pad, tapes, shoes, and clothing into sloppy piles that mingled our things completely over time. Together, we wandered Bedford Park at all hours of the night. I always suggested she take us by Bobby's, where we threw pebbles at his window. My heart would thump, waiting for him to appear. TV light flick-ering from his darkened room, he'd lean out to whisper to us, throw down bags of chips, and talk about wrestling or his latest video game endeavor.

Sometimes he'd have Myers and Fief over, and they'd sneak out to join us in the parkway, where we'd make fun of teachers and take turns telling sto-ries. I told them about my adventures with Rick and Danny, about the fire at the old folks' home and how Rick got electrocuted.

"I just told him 'test this out,' and he did it. His fingers were burned like toast!"

Sam's favorites were the stories of the serial killers Daddy told me about. She liked hearing what psychologists believed motivated them to commit their crimes. It thrilled me to see my new friends get as scared as I was when I first heard Daddy's stories, or to see them crack up in hysterical laughter at the very mention of Rick's name.

But mostly, Sam and I were alone. We made rounds to the all-night diner on Bedford and Jerome, where we befriended the Mexican night manager, a stout, often drunk man named Tony. There, we fended off the cold and shared bits and pieces of our lives over plates of French fries smothered in mozzarella cheese and gravy, the diner's ancient speakers crackling Mexican boleros through the air.

On those nights we spent together wandering around outside, Sam con-fided in me some very difficult things that were happening in her home. The exact details of these events she shared with me are private; however, I will say that she needed to be away from home, for her own good reasons. And the things she shared inspired me to want to take care of her, out of my growing love for our friendship, for the sisterhood we were building together. If she felt she could not go back home, I told her, she could always stay with me.

I began to sneak her in for sleepovers, without Brick knowing it. He had firmly warned me not to have any guests past ten o'clock, but given that he went to sleep precisely at nine thirty, the rule was easy to break. We took a bed sheet and strung it along the side of Lisa's and my L-shaped bunk bed. Then, with an old paisley quilt from Brick's hall closet, I cushioned the ground for Sam's resting spot. All we had to do was open and then slam the front door in the evening, to give the impression she'd gone home, then tiptoe back through the room and conceal her. With Sam's legs tucked beneath the top of the bottom bunk and her torso sticking out beside my head, I would pass her half my TV dinners, whole glasses of Pepsi, Oreos, or any of Brick's endless rebate supplies.

I found that as wild as Sam could be, there was also something puppy dog-like about her, as though threaded through her tough, eccentric outbursts were subtle indications that she needed caring for. It was in the way she could walk into an elevator and never press a button, but just wait there for me to do something; or how when we crossed streets, she never navigated, but walked blindly by my side, in total trust. If I made one bad move, I thought, a truck would flatten us both; it was all in my hands. She was fine with that, and that was fine with me.

At night, under my bed, sometimes I could hear her crying softly. But whenever I asked her what was wrong, she'd brush it off, say it was just her allergies or that I was hearing things. But I knew better. Sometimes, when she snored in her sleep—a cute little whistle—I'd reach down and touch a piece of her hair, run it through my fingers, stare at how, in the darkness of our room, the moonlight turned it glossy as polished onyx. I will keep her safe, I told myself.

✦ ✦ ✦

One evening, while I poured myself soda in the kitchen, muffled shouts came from Brick's bedroom. No one responded to him, yet the muffled noises continued and sounded like half of a conversation. As I walked over to investigate, bits and pieces became decipherable.

"In *my* own goddamn house, *I* can't even find a clean fork . . . didn't ask for this . . . if you or those lazy girls of yours . . . group home . . ."

Was he yelling about unwashed dishes? All around me, dirt was ground into the floor; newspapers, yellowed with age, were scattered across the room; empty boxes of doughnuts and potato chips trailed from his bedroom as I walked an obstacle course around his crates of supplies. Brick complaining about a mess seemed insane.

Besides, my mother hardly ever dirtied a fork. The closest Ma came to eating food were the cocktails and sedatives she took randomly throughout the day—she never had an appetite anymore. Even if I put hot bowls of New England clam chowder on the nightstand (her favorite) or cut the crust from her tuna-fish sandwiches, the bowls were returned chilly and full, the tuna untouched. Sometimes I did leave piles of dishes, and I knew that was my fault. But could he really be screaming at Ma about it?

Through the cracked door, I peered in and saw that he was waving around a roll of paper towels, screaming, frantically sweeping it over Ma's depleted body as she lay motionless, one arm protectively drawn over her head. He was in his underwear, a white T-shirt straining to cover his large, hairy stomach. A pile of dirty forks, which he must have collected himself, was clumped on the nightstand. He raised the paper towels over his head and grumbled, "You hear me, Jean? Do you?" thunking the roll on Ma's head and face. I darted inside.

"What the hell are you doing?" I yelled. "She's sick. Don't touch—"

Before I could fully step into the room, Brick grabbed the door. "Goodbye," he interrupted, slamming it with a force that broke against my foot, scraping the skin on my toes so hard that the cuticles peeled back in chunks. A surge of pure heat seared through me as I hobbled on one leg, holding my damaged foot in my hand. I almost screamed in pain, but held it in for Ma's sake. Black nail polish had chipped off on three of my toes; red blotches were rapidly forming under the nails in its place. At the sight of it, I tried, unsuccessfully, not to tear up.

Shoes would have been too painful. I tore open the hall closet and found a pair of oversized slippers, put them on, and stormed out, hysterical. Outside, the sky was transitioning from sunset to night. I started down the street, only half sure of where I was headed. When I passed strangers, I turned my face away, blocking my tears from their sight. Thoughts broke loose, swarming in my mind like a jumble of angry bees.

Ma was in a living hell and as much as I wanted to, I could not protect her. He was impatient with her at a time when she needed gentleness, when she needed someone to take care of her. And he didn't need or want us there either; we were a burden. That much was obvious. It didn't matter anyway because all I had to do was miss enough school and I'd be sent back to the home and Brick could be done with me. Mr. Doumbia was waiting if I messed up.

"You'll end up just like your father, a no-good junkie drop-out," Brick had taunted me once. This one day I couldn't find the toilet paper, only I was sure we hadn't run out because there'd been an enormous economy pack. Later, Brick screamed at me about flushing the toilet after we went, then he revealed the pack on the top shelf of his closet. He had *hidden* the toilet paper because someone had forgotten to flush. Not that I didn't know already that something was off about him, but I realized then that he was as crazy as Grandma. Now he was putting Ma through a small hell over a pile of forks when she couldn't possibly be weaker. The man was controlling and unstable, and Ma was powerless against him. I had to be away from it, from him, from Ma's disease. It was too much.

A light sheet of rain drizzled down as I crossed Bainbridge Avenue, the wind whipping against my jacket, chilling me but seeming to strike fire along my foot. Across the sidewalk, people toted briefcases or clutched umbrellas on their return from work. I stumbled past them with my head held down, hiding my tears.

It hit me then: I couldn't remember the last time Ma and I had had a conversation. All we'd been saying to each other was "Hi" and "Bye." Our last real talk may have been five months ago, when she signed me up for Junior High School 80.

The thought sent more tears streaming down my face; I couldn't control it. Up until that moment, I told myself that I was handling her illness better than this; I prided myself on it. But avoidance allows you to believe that you're making all kinds of strides when you're not. I thought I had dealt with my feelings of pain over my mother's AIDS, but the image of her lying helpless under Brick's rage brought it all back. Like an exposed nerve, I felt the reality of her sickness jabbing at me. AIDS just wasn't ever talked about in my family. Ma and Daddy didn't talk about it, not even Dr. Morales brought it up, and certainly Brick didn't talk about it. He watched Ma take her medication, could see her getting weaker, but he still made demands on her. Judging by the condom wrappers I found lying around, I am sure that for as long as Ma could manage it, they were even having sex.

No one was talking about her AIDS, even as it was eating away at her in front of us. Yet it was as tangible and present as the shaky foundation we stood on with Brick. Ma's rapid deterioration and her sickness, like the sickness of our collective denial, was real.

Two weeks before, I'd been sitting in the kitchen alone when Ma burst in, crying, trembling. She went straight for the top of the fridge without noticing me, reaching for her fat brown paper bag of medication. The eruptive entrance and her raw, obvious pain had frozen me still. I watched her struggle with a childproof top. I didn't dare speak for fear of embarrassing her. When the bottle finally popped open, the pills spilled out over the table, landing with dozens of little clicks against the wood. With great difficulty, Ma plucked up two, placed them on her tongue, and with one deep inhale, she paused her crying just long enough to swallow. In doing so, she caught sight of me.

"Ma" was all I said, one perfectly useless syllable, and nothing more.

"You're too young for this," she told me, raising her hand even as it shook. "I'm sorry. You're too young."

I stared back blankly and just watched her go, the white pills still scattered across the dark tabletop.

I'd never been too young for anything—not for the drugs, or for Ma's graphic stories of teen prostitution—but I was too young for *this*, for AIDS. I absolutely hated myself for proving her right, for doing so little to soothe my mother when she needed me most. I was there for everything else, but when Ma was fighting AIDS, I had put a distance between us. Or, had she taken a distance from me? *Something* happened to us, because after she left University Avenue, after the group home, and now as she was getting sicker, we just weren't close anymore. And now I had Sam, and my days were enlivened with cutting school, dreaming about the future with my friends, and a new vitality

I'd never known before. What it boiled down to was, the more joy I experienced with my friends, the harder it was to come home to Ma and an apartment filled with her sickness. The harder it was to be near her dying. It was so much easier to not come home at all, to be with my group.

"Selfish," I said out loud to myself, harshly wiping tears from my face. On 202nd Street, I looked up at Bobby's living room window, at the warm light glowing from it. I thought of his smile, the way it lit his large eyes, made them so inviting. I headed upstairs.

Paula, his mother, served us pork chops and rice in front of his bedroom TV. It was tuned to wrestling, which made Bobby throw his arms up and cheer every few minutes, in a way that kept revealing his bare stomach and the trail of thin black hair running up to his belly button (I was careful about looking). Back in the hallway, I had wiped my cheeks clean and taken a few deep breaths before knocking, to make sure he didn't have a clue.

"I like your room, Bobby," I said cheerfully. But then I remembered, even as the words escaped my mouth, that I'd told him that already when I'd first walked in.

"Thanks," he said, being gentle with the slipup, gracious as he had been when I'd surprised him at his door. "That's Mankind," he told me, pointing at the screen to a giant, leather-masked guy whose thick flesh glistened with sweat. The guy grunted into the camera, flew off the ropes, and landed squatting on his opponent's back, sending a roar up from the crowd and into the room as Bobby flung his arms in the air again. I had no idea how to participate in the topic; Sam usually kept up the wrestling conversations.

"Yeah? That's cool. . . . Is he, has he been fighting for a long time?"

"Mankind is *nuts*," he answered, stopping for a moment to look into the next room. "Hold on. *Close my door, Chrissy!*" he yelled.

A young girl with softer versions of Bobby's facial features appeared and leaned in to grab his doorknob. Before closing it, she looked me over, spotting the T-shirt Bobby had given me to wear while mine dried off from the rain.

"Shut it and get out," he commanded. She rolled her eyes and slammed it, hard. "Brat," he said. "Yeah, so this guy's completely insane."

"Oh, like that's his gimmick?" I said.

"What do you mean?"

"Nothing, just . . . Um, so he's crazy?"

"Yeah. And then there's Bret Hart, who's known for his precision. See, Liz, they all have something different about them . . ."

Well into the night, I listened to Bobby talk, playing audience as he thumbed through his wrestling magazines. Leaning back on a pile of his soft pillows, with my legs curled under his blanket, we shared his bed and I drifted into sleep, hypnotized by the distant hum from his mother's blow dryer and the sound of Bobby's deep voice.

"Hello, this is Mr. Doumbia from Child Welfare. I am calling regarding Elizabeth Murray, who has been placed in your custody. According to JHS 80, Ms. Murray is not in regular attendance at school and we are concerned about her future in your custody. Please call me at . . ."

I was lucky to catch and erase the answering machine message from Mr. Doumbia before Brick had a chance to hear it. I hadn't been to school in weeks, and I already knew what the message was going to say: I kept up my truancy, I was headed back to St. Anne's. But I didn't want to hear it, so I kept deleting the messages whenever I found them, hoping the problem would just go away.

WARNING!

Apartment 2B is being cleaned and fumigated!

Please take proper precautions for health & safety!

—Management

The bold black-and-white flyers had been strewn about our lobby on University Avenue in surplus, tacked above the rusted mailboxes and slipped under each tenant's door. Daddy hadn't called to tell me that he was losing the apartment; I found out on my own. Sam and I had been discussing keepsakes and family pictures in the diner when I'd realized that almost everything I owned was still at the other apartment.

"I'd at least like to have my pictures with me, and maybe a couple of my books too," I told Sam as we followed the elevated train tracks to University

Avenue. Following the 4 train's route was the only way I knew how to get back to the neighborhood. Every so often a train would rattle by, sparking and screeching overhead. We kicked a can back and forth between us through the weeds growing up out of the sidewalk on Jerome Avenue.

"I have books on sharks and dinosaurs," I told her, raising my voice to be heard over the train. "Do you know who Jacques Cousteau is?" I asked eagerly. She shook her head. "My dad has these books . . . you have to check out his underwater photos. You'd never think some of these things existed."

As we drew closer, I got to what I really wanted to say. "You've never seen a house like this before, Sam, really. When I say it's bad, I mean it, like a hundred times worse than Brick's," I said, hoping to make her realize just how bad the apartment was, so that when she saw for herself she would know that I also realized how bad it was. That way, she wouldn't look at it and think differently of me.

"Liz, shut up," she answered. "You know I love your white ass, don't even sweat it."

Months of sharing with Sam had made me eager to bring her to the apartment on University Avenue, something I'd never done with a friend before, not even Rick and Danny. I'd been too afraid. But after sitting in the diner and talking so much and so often about Daddy and about University, I realized I wanted to show Sam where I came from. More than anyone I knew, I trusted she would understand.

During the ten months since the court removed me, I'd visited Daddy only once, right in the beginning when they let me out. I thought it would feel good to come home again, but it turned out that being a visitor at Daddy's was entirely different from living with him. As a visitor, we had to sit down and face each other, make conversation. We had to fill the time with words. This proved harder than I thought it would be. What were we going to talk about? The group home? Ma's AIDS? His latest high? My new life that didn't include him? Walter O'Brien? So we ended up watching TV together. Daddy fell asleep on the couch while I sat on one of the living room chairs, flipping channels, sitting beneath the fly tape that was still—after all these years—stuck to the ceiling. Garbage bags were open on the floor, and the stench that once seemed tolerable was so rank that I could hardly breathe. The house had become eerie in our absence. My room had been filled with storage boxes and garbage bags Daddy hadn't taken out yet. It was obvious just by looking in my room that he had given up on my ever coming back. So I wrote him a note that said what a great time I'd had, and I slipped out while he was asleep.

I might have gone back to visit Daddy again, except seeing him and our home in that state made me sad in a way that was hard to deal with. Plus, I started having nightmares after that. In them, our family was united and then divided over and over again. Always, we were on the brink of separation in my dreams, the difference hinging on a decision of mine. Always, at the last minute before waking up, I made the wrong call that divided us one more time. The pain was fresh each time it happened. So I stopped coming around altogether.

Now, as Sam and I approached the building, I saw that planks had been nailed over my parents' bedroom window and mine. My first impulse was curiosity, but that was quickly overrun by fear. "Sam, I think there was a fire," I said as we approached the building, our necks craned upward at the boards with black X's spray-painted across them. I played out the worst scenario in my mind as we climbed the stairs. Was my father alive? Had it all burned? I'd gotten in the habit of expecting the worst. We ran up the stairs and reached the apartment door; there was a stainless-steel padlock blocking our entry. An odd sense of relief filled me, accompanied by confusion. It took me moments to make sense of what I saw. Sam's voice drew me back; she was reading something about a marshal and seventy-two hours' notice.

Outside on the fire escape, we pulled futilely at the large boards. For all our tugging, the only effect we could produce was a small wobble in the oversized plank, which wafted out the apartment's musky odor. Soon we slumped onto our butts.

"I just don't understand. I don't know why he wouldn't tell us or where he would even go. I don't know if our stuff's still in there, either. Sam, I'm sorry I brought you all the way here, I didn't—"

"Liz," she said, "come here." I quieted down as we hugged, leaning back on the brick building. Up on the fire escape, placing my head on her shoulder, I breathed in the soft smell of peaches. In that moment I could feel that Sam cared about me as much as I did for her.

"Oh well," was all I said after that.

Sam agreed. "Oh well, Liz. Screw it. What else can you do?"

There was nothing to do, so neither of us said a thing. Not then, and not when I learned that Daddy had fallen behind on the rent and gone to live in a men's shelter. And certainly not when I found out that the entire contents of our apartment had been taken away in dumpsters, way before I ever got there. There was just nothing to say or do, but accept it. So I did, like I had everything else so far.

That spring, I squeaked by, graduating Junior High School 80 with exactly enough attendance to avoid being taken back into the system. After the June ceremony, Ma stood outside on the curb, smoking her Winstons, waiting for me to appear while unknowingly standing right beside a chatting cluster of perfumed, well-dressed parents that happened to include Myers's and Bobby's mothers. The guys stood separately, chucking their caps at one another like Frisbees. Bobby's gown flapped open in the breeze. In his sharp, black suit, he looked like a grown man. His mother looked like the perfect mom; her hair, as brown and thick as her son's, was pinned up in a shiny French twist.

Ma had unearthed a short-sleeved floral, thrift-store dress for the occasion. Her arms bore scars that transformed her skin into something like pale hamburger meat. She'd cut her mullet for the occasion, and the white sandals she wore, with no stockings, emphasized the hair on her legs and provided a blatant view of her yellowed toenails, which curled ever so slightly over the edges of her shoes.

I decided to wait it out in the bushes. As long as I could hide, crouching there, I would avoid the humiliation, preserving any normalcy I enjoyed in my friends' mothers' homes. I was done with being the odd one out; I had reinvented myself. I was normal, generally upbeat, even interesting, and I wasn't giving that back—not now, when I could so easily wait this moment out and avoid the whole ordeal.

Then something happened that I was unprepared for. Mr. Strezou, the man who must have been insane to pass me on to high school, stopped in front of Ma to make conversation. In his suit and tie, with a nonchalant look on his face, Mr. Strezou reached over and clasped Ma's hand and shook it, smiling earnestly at her. His eyes were kind. Though I couldn't hear what they were saying, I saw that Ma had completely come alive with his attention. She was smiling, fidgeting from her medication. I realized I hadn't seen her smile in a long time. And she was keeping him there, asking questions. About me? She shook his hand and held on to his arm with her other hand. I saw her say the words *thank you*. Then, when Mr. Strezou walked away, Ma looked all around for me again. Slowly, her face seemed to fall.

I forced myself to step forward, over the wood chips and out of the bushes. I walked across the sidewalk, straight up to Ma, and hugged her tightly, openly. I loved her so much, and right in the center of my chest I could feel her love for me. I hugged her for the longest time.

"Pumpkin," she said, "I'm so proud of you." I pulled back, still holding on to her arms; there were tears in her eyes. "When they called your name, I clapped so hard, honey. Did you hear me?" I'd received no special distinctions— I'd barely even graduated, but that didn't seem to matter to Ma. I knew that she supported me, trusted my decisions. Maybe too much. I put my arm around her waist and escorted her forward. I was surprised to feel the sharp corner of her hipbone.

"Come here, Ma, I want you to meet some people."

Walking a few feet over, I parted an opening in the circle of women big enough for Ma and me. I clapped my hands together, my heart racing. "Hey, everyone," I said. "I want you all to meet my mother, Jean Murray."

Daddy called one night, a couple weeks after I started high school, as Brick's ceaseless television noise, cigarette fog, and Ma's illness filled the apartment. She'd spent the day vomiting into the toilet and onto the bathroom tiles; even though I'd gone through an entire roll of paper towels, the smell could still be detected, thick and sour. Sam and I passed the time between Ma's bouts by phoning in to radio contests hoping for concert tickets, and by marking up a map of the United States with all the places we would go on our hitchhike cross-country. Although she would never get too close to Ma (I think because the sickness scared her), Sam helped me forget the rough job of cleaning her up by planning our lives on the road together. That evening Lisa had fallen asleep on her homework after a long day at school, a place I hadn't been for days. I marveled at her diligence, wondering how she focused enough to spend hours perfecting essays and lab reports up on the top bunk.

When I lifted the receiver, I didn't initially recognize my father's voice—it was too small and far-away sounding, as though the call had been placed internationally.

"Liz—Liz," he said, "I'm doing okay. Not bad, really. They treat me well here. And I'm eating three squares a day. I've even been getting a stomach, believe it or not." His laugh was tense. I woke Lisa and mouthed the word *Daddy*, but she waved me away, closing her eyes again. He continued, "They always play *Jeopardy!* for me, too; everyone stands there and bets on how many I'll get right."

A scene returned to me of my father fixed on our couch, my child's body curled on the far end, nightgown drawn over my knees as I watched him coach Alex Trebek on the answers. When he paused for a moment to recall a piece of vital information, he'd shut his eyes and rub small circles on his bald head as though to summon it. The living room flickered with the blue light from our old television, and correct answers to each trivia question came in waves of three; first from Daddy, then from the contestant, and lastly from Mr. Trebek. Moments later, Daddy went into the kitchen to shoot up.

"Yeah, you were always good at that," I said.

"It's pretty neat, Lizzy, you should see it."

The trouble was, I *could* see him now, occupying a thin cot in a loft of aging, broken men with wispy beards. *Was he actually one of them?* How had I gone all those years on University Avenue without noticing that there was something broken about my father? He'd once seemed so free, and we had felt so close. I must have been wrong about that. If he lived behind fenced windows, under adult curfew; if he hid an entire life from me; if he didn't even bother to call when we were losing our home and our belongings, then maybe I'd never known Daddy at all.

Or maybe, if he was calling to reach out to me, that meant he hadn't drifted too far away, and maybe his life had only slipped into a temporary rough patch. As he tap-danced his side of the conversation, my mind drew up a checklist of all the things I could do to help him out: work to support him, call the shelter to check in on him more often, find him an apartment somehow, get clothing to him. The ideas spanned the size of my unused hours in the day.

"How's high school?" he asked lightly.

"It's good, real good."

If he was tap-dancing his end of the conversation, so would I. Why tell him I was absent all the time from school? Why confront him? If he couldn't do anything about our problems, then what would be the point in venting at Daddy? It would only stress him more, and I didn't want to do that to him. It felt mean. So I decided to censor my life from my father, and to have him think everything was just great.

"Well, glad to hear it, Lizzy. I was wondering about you. Good to know, good to know." I was doing the right thing; there was no way to tell him that I was afraid of how far I'd fallen behind, that I wasn't sure I could ever find my way back.

"Actually, I should get back to my homework now, Daddy, before it gets too late. I'm sorry. I'm glad you called though." And I was. It had been too long without a phone call to help me paint a picture of what he was doing, knowing whether or not he was safe. We said good night and hung up. Sam looked at me with concern. "What'd he say?" she asked.

"Nothing, he just called to say hi, I guess. He's living in a shelter. I don't know, who knows." Spread across the table, the bright blue map caught my eyes. Sam was hunched over it. In pen, she'd drawn a dotted line to represent the ideal route to travel cross-country. At the base of the line, she'd sketched two stick figure versions of us wearing big brimmed beach hats, our old-lady shades, and purses slung over our forearms. Her character was different only in that it had a Mohawk. Before she could ask more about Daddy, I slipped my finger quickly along the line and stopped, tapping on the West Coast, and asked, "Hey Sam, how long do you think it'll take for us to get *there?*" I pointed to LA.

"Not long," she answered. Then Sam grabbed the map and folded it in half, holding it so that New York directly touched California. "We're practically there already," she said.

We both laughed, more than the joke was worth.

+◆+

High school was a place where Sam and I were registered, but showed up only to receive free train passes. We hung out at Fief's or Bobby's place or on Brick's oversize couch, where I ignored the phone to avoid social services as we watched television throughout the working day. I "accidentally" broke Brick's answering machine, and I learned to remain completely quiet for five minutes whenever the doorbell rang, in case of social worker visits. I was in the clear; I had become a pro at avoiding school, at avoiding Mr. Doumbia, at avoiding everything.

"You can't procrastinate forever," Lisa had scolded me one morning, zipping up her jacket before slamming the front door on her way out to school. By my behavior, you might have guessed that I was trying to prove her wrong.

I felt I'd given school one valid shot, being in strict attendance for two straight weeks before I gave in. But high school was just a different world altogether, one big crowded maze of responsibility that I had no idea how to navigate or care about. And it's not like we intended to mess up so badly; the first cut day was only supposed to be a single Monday. Just one day.

Sam and I took the train downtown, to Greenwich Village in lower Manhattan, a place that was vaguely familiar to me from childhood, when Daddy used to bring me with him to dig through the garbage. From those trips and from Ma's stories, I knew the Village to be where all the interesting people were, identified by their multicolored hair and vintage clothing. We gathered $2.75 in change from all around Brick's house, just enough to buy and split a hot dog and soda while we watched street performers in Washington Square Park. All around us, people were cool. By association, so were we.

We really were only going to cut school that Monday. But then, if I was going to take two days off, it was best to take them back to back. After all, my reason for being out a second day would be more credible if it came right after the first. I mean, who gets sick for just one day, right? And then maybe the third day wasn't so bad if I missed the first two. After all, the reason must have to do with whatever ailment kept me home the first two days. But then if I missed Monday, Tuesday, and Wednesday, then Thursday and Friday were hardly worth salvaging. There was always next week. Besides, we didn't plan on doing this again. That is, until we overslept the following Monday, and the cycle started once more. Eventually, we'd missed so many days that it was hard to keep up in class. Oh well, there was always next semester.

In the meantime, there were other places to focus our energies. For our group of friends, Fief's house was the hub of our neighborhood. With his dad at work all day, and his mom living there only part-time, that's where everyone cut school. It was there I found that when I was willing to sit around and do a whole lot of nothing, lots of other people my age were willing to do the same. We made a routine of it, a carefree weekly schedule of simply being together. I had never been happier.

During these days we leaned on one another heavily, a little family free of judgments or clearly defined roles. Sam's unconventional, indignant style was the focal point. And between Myers's offbeat conversation topics, Bobby's humor, Fief's hospitality, and my affection and adoration for them all, we came together. Bobby, Sam, and I were really the heart of it. The circle expanded outward from there to include a list of names that came and went: Myers, Fief, Jamie, Josh, Diane, Ian, Ray, Felice, and many others. "The group" is what we called ourselves. Collectively, we let one day roll into the next, more or less uneventfully. We sat around barefoot in Fief's graffiti-ridden apartment, taking turns sleeping and talking, but most of all laughing hysterically, together.

Because we were afraid of getting our friends in trouble, it was rare for anyone to do drugs inside the apartments we skipped school in. At most, someone would smoke weed in a back room, or in the hallway. As for myself, I was repulsed by drugs and alcohol and didn't go near either of them. Even the smell of beer on someone's breath made me sick to my stomach. Part of this had to do with everything I saw Ma and Daddy suffer through, but the other part was due to specific things Ma said directly to me. Several times in my childhood when I was with Ma as her high was coming down, she'd turned her attention to me with a grave look in her eyes that was haunting. She cried and pleaded with me, "Lizzy, don't ever get high, baby. It ruined my life. You'd break my heart if you ever got high. Don't ever get high, never, okay, baby?" With dried blood spattered on her arm, her eyes manic with concern, and her voice filled with love, it was probably the most compelling anti-drug message anyone could have given me. So I never got high, not once. And apart from some harmless teasing from my friends that I was the "straight edge," no one pressured me to. Besides, we had other things to keep us entertained.

While other kids developed critical writing skills and picked up arithmetic and science, we conducted experiments of our own. Such as, a spoonful of water, when poured onto a scorching-hot stove burner, breaks into little, audibly bouncing beads. And when you place a lightbulb in the microwave—for the five seconds it's safe to do so—it performs a strobe light show of neon pink, green, and orange. Random experimental mixtures from Fief's cabinet could sometimes yield something edible. Water balloons, when chucked at high speeds from open windows, caused a few minutes of uncontrollable laugher. Every day together was another layer of insulation from the bustling world around us, my experience made richer by my love for Bobby and Sam.

Still, at some point in each day, Ma's illness called me back to reality, back to the stale, inert feeling of Brick's apartment. I could push it away for only a matter of hours before images from previous days came roaring back in. I knew that without my returning to help, Ma could be slumped over in her bedroom doorway, stuck; unable to lift her own weight off the toilet; or crying helplessly for water from her room. So I made regular rounds to check in on her, parting from my friends, to visit what I knew to be her deathbed. I found it hard to admit to myself that it was a trip that I was becoming more and more reluctant to make.

CHAPTER 6

Boys

SAM AND I WEREN'T PREPARED FOR BOYFRIENDS, FOR THE INFLU-
ence that loving a guy can have on your whole life. I can't help but think that
maybe if we had been ready, if someone had told us, things would have turned
out differently.

Carlos came into the picture as a guest of the group, but by the sheer mag-
nitude of his personality, he moved to center stage almost immediately. One
lazy autumn day, as we walked up the stairs to Fief's apartment, we heard the
argumentative banter of male voices echoing through the hall.

"Do you hear that?" I asked Sam.

"Yeah, sounds like someone let a lunatic loose from the nutty bin."

"No, I mean, I think it's coming from Fief's house."

As we approached the door slowly and creaked it open, one voice, with a
rich, news-announcer quality to it, boomed loudly above the rest.

"Son, son. Take this," the voice prompted. "Give it your best shot. Tell me
what you have to lose. . . . Well then, *go on!*"

When we turned the corner into Fief's living room, we came onto a scene:
some familiar and a few unfamiliar faces, around seven people altogether,
crouched over a game of dice. Fief hung back, leaning against the wall. When
I looked his way for an explanation, he shrugged. There, in the center of the
action, I spotted the owner of the voice.

He was a stranger, this tall, slim Puerto Rican guy. His dark, wavy hair
was pulled back in a neat ponytail. His dress was ghetto sharp. Dominating
his face were expressive brown eyes set just above a cluster of freckles sprinkled across his wide cheeks. There was something about the way he moved,
the power in his voice—I couldn't stop watching him. He clapped his hand
hard onto a guy's back, who with the prompt tossed two dice, dense, little red

cubes, roughly against the wall. For a moment, their clicking descent was the only noise in the room. Then people shouted and raised their arms. Someone pointed and laughed into the face of the thrower.

"Whoa," the impressive stranger yelled. "So close, Papa. Give it up now, that's *your* slip." A gangly-looking guy, whom I'd seen around Fief's place only a few times, had suffered the loss. Defeated, he counted money into the stranger's hand.

"Who's up?" the stranger called out.

"Sam, have you seen that guy here before?" I asked her over the noise.

"Nah," she said.

I remained in the doorway of the musty room, my eyes trailing from the graffiti on the wall to the ongoing game, for at least another twenty minutes. Sam lost interest and walked into the kitchen to rummage through Fief's fridge. Finally, after collecting another round of cash from losing participants, the stranger snatched up his dice and called an abrupt end to the game.

"That's it, gentlemen, until next time." Hisses and noises of protest passed through the room. "I would go on," he announced, looking down, running money through his hands, "but I'm busy. I'm taking *her* out to eat. So blame her," he said. Suddenly, without looking up, he pointed a finger from the cash-filled fist straight at me. He resumed counting. I completely froze. A few of the guys looked up for a moment, but lost interest. Until then, I hadn't known he saw me in the room at all. As far as I could tell, he hadn't glanced my way once.

I looked around the crowded room, pointed at myself, and mouthed, "Me?" I was sure he'd seen me then, but he walked into the other room without answering. I saw him clasping hands with various people on his way out. I wondered for a moment whether I might have imagined the whole exchange. When he walked by me and began unsnapping the locks to the front door, my heart fluttered in my chest. I stood still, inhaling the sweet smell of his cologne. Sam stepped out of the kitchen, eating one of Fief's ice cream bars, chocolate smeared on her fingers. The incident would make for a funny story once we got out of there.

The front door creaked open and he paused.

"Well? Are you coming or not?" he said. I looked around for who else he might have been addressing. "Yo, shorty, I don't have all day." He began tapping his foot.

"Do you mean me?" I asked.

He swept his arm forward, dramatically motioning out the door, and winked at me. We shared a smile.

I tried to look casual. "Can my friend come, too?"

His name was Carlos Marcano and he was almost eighteen years old. He grew up in the Bronx, like us. Abandoned by neglectful parents, he was raised on the streets, by street people who lived street lives. He had been stabbed. A scar on his left calf, a small, raised mound of flesh, was given to him by a female gang member who'd stuck him up using a busted bottle. When Carlos spoke, a string of jokes ran through most things he said, no matter how serious the subject matter. He was funny, with a dark sense of humor that appealed to me. Currently, he was crashing on a friend's couch on Bedford Park Boulevard. One day, despite all his hardships, he was going to be a famous comedic actor.

"I've survived out here on my own, God bless. The man was looking out for me," he'd said with his finger pointed skyward, during our first conversation in the diner. "I know you girls know what I mean. It's rough out there, but you gotta keep your head up, don't sleep. *Dream*, but don't sleep. You feel me?"

For hours, he sat across from Sam and me, dazzling us with stories about his life riddled with fights, gang violence, and all kinds of extreme situations he'd found himself in, living on the streets. He was intelligent, resourceful, and most of all he was hilarious in spite of how dark life had been for him. Each story took on enormous dimension, sucking us in. Every so often, when he used a gesture that made him appear particularly handsome, Sam squeezed my leg under the table.

But the information that really endeared Carlos to me, absolutely sealed my fascination with him, didn't surface until further along in the night, near the time we were getting ready to go. In a sense, Carlos explained, he'd really been on his own since his dad died from AIDS when he was nine. After all, his mother was a crackhead who never took care of him.

"She cared about that pipe more than she did me. I know it," he said. "She worshipped the rock. I came up on my own."

Right there, I started a mental checklist of our similarities. He knew about AIDS and drugs, and making it on your own, and he was still bright and forward-moving. He hid from nothing and no one. The outside world was no hurdle for him; it was a platform. I made the decision right there to try to be close to him. Carlos had learned to tap into his own strength in a way I hoped to do for myself. I was afraid that it was too soon to tell him how much we had in common; it would have sounded made up, there were that many similarities.

As he spoke of his loss of family structure, of how he came to be homeless, he stared dramatically out the diner window into the passing crowds.

"Moms took me from one relative to the next until I started going home with friends from school. After a while I didn't know where I was anymore. That's when I realized I had to start looking out for number one, because on the real, that's all you got. But that's a'ight, 'cause I keep it tight. Like a hetero in the prison shower, I don't trust no one, I watch my own ass."

By the time we finished up, Carlos had weaved a tapestry of hard-luck stories, managing to punctuate everything with outrageous humor. He could be talking about someone dying and then suddenly use some elastic facial expression to change the story into a joke, forcing us to laugh. With his lips, he made sound effects, whistles and beeps that startled the other customers. I didn't mind their staring. Just like the attention Sam called to us, it was empowering. I told myself I'd stumbled onto a jackpot in Carlos, an overlooked treasure ignorantly unrecognized by others. Any gawking onlookers could blow it out their asses. That's *their hangup*.

He walked us back to Brick's, stopping every so often to sing and dance, insisting on the utmost amount of foolishness we could stand. He stopped strangers on the street to compliment them on their skills in karate and basket-making, not addressing their confusion as he continued forward. He folded a paper bag over his head in the shape of a hat, crossed his eyes, and stopped more strangers to speak seriously to them about looking both ways when crossing the street. He was fearless, and it seemed magical.

✦✦✦

The next several weeks were an exercise in pursuing Carlos, doing whatever I could to connect without seeming overeager. In Brick's kitchen, twirling the curly phone cord around my finger into figure eights, I spent hours speaking with him, which was nothing next to the amount of time we spent walking the neighborhood some nights, enmeshed in long conversations, during which he would occasionally take my hand. Through the last of summer's warmth, we lingered on the parkway, in nearby Harris Field, under the light of Bronx street lamps, sharing secrets, warming up to each other.

"Liz, I got to thank you." Carlos turned to me one night as we stopped in front of Brick's building, his dark eyes staring intently into mine.

"What for? What'd I do?" I asked hopefully.

"For one, you ain't like any other shorty I ever met. I just got this feeling like I can tell you whatever. I trust you. That's it, Liz, I trust you. And I ain't *never* felt that before. On the real, God bless you." I tried my best to hide the excitement rushing through me. He suggested that we round the block just one more time; there was something he had to tell me. Taking my hand tightly, he made me promise not to tell anyone about a $7,000 inheritance his father left him, that he would receive when he turned eighteen.

"They're all snakes out there, that's why you gotta keep the grass cut low, Shamrock. To see the snakes coming a mile away." He'd nicknamed me Shamrock when he found out I was Irish. "Especially when people know you're loaded. They start thinking, What could that money get me? People are greedy, but I trust you. I want to share everything with you."

"Listen, Carlos," I said, ignoring the part he'd addressed to me. I was too excited at the idea that he was going to finally get off the streets. "This is what you've been waiting for, you could finally get your own apartment." I squeezed his hand and smiled. But he didn't smile back, just stared intently, directly into my eyes.

"Shamrock, maybe you didn't hear me. I want you with me on this. This is the start *we* need." I couldn't hold back my smile; my body tensed with excitement.

"I am not like those people. I just want you to be happy, Carlos."

"*You* make me happy, shorty. Don't doubt it."

When we went to hug each other good night, he suddenly hoisted me over his shoulder with an ease that made me realize his strength, charging forward with my body as a pretend battering ram for the lobby door. I screamed with laughter.

"Boooom!" he bellowed, thrusting the door open ahead of me with his hand. Moments later, with all the force in my body, I had to drag Carlos away from the buzzers to stop him from whistling to Brick over the intercom to make me laugh more. Because boarding the elevator meant saying good-bye for the night, it was a task that we stretched out for half an hour, time filled with eagerly made plans for when we might see each other next.

✦ ✦ ✦

For every third truant day of mine throughout September, notices arrived in the mail from John F. Kennedy High School, informing the parent or guardian of ninth grader Elizabeth Ann Murray to please phone the principal's office. I made a routine out of popping the mailbox to intercept them, so that I could rip the paper into tiny shreds and send them floating down the trash compactor chute like confetti—problem solved. But I hit a snag one day when I discovered an envelope bearing that all-too-familiar emblem from Child Welfare. The notice, presented in boldfaced type, called for a mandatory meeting with Brick to discuss my future in his care, as well as the option of placement back into the system. I couldn't go back in the system; I wouldn't. But I didn't know how to go to school, either. I didn't know what to do.

Outside of my friends, little grabbed my attention. After all, I kept thinking, I could always go to school later. It seemed like things were working out fine without it. With the exception of Bobby, no one in the group was going anyway. And Carlos kept talking about our plans with the money: We would get an apartment somewhere on Bedford Park, and Sam would live with us. Sam and I would go back to high school then, and all three of us would get jobs to keep up with the rent, but first we needed a stable place that was all our own.

So it's not that I wasn't going to go to school at all; it just didn't fit in with my plans at the moment. I would go back soon, just like I would talk to Ma about all the important things I wanted to express to her, soon. Like letting her know that no matter what she might have done, I understood that she loved me; I saw how hard she tried. Most of all, she should know not to worry. I would go back to school. I would be okay, somehow. Just not today, I kept thinking, not right now. Life seemed to be rushing in on me, and all I felt I could do was duck and cover. Not now. Later, I kept telling myself.

Of course, this avoidance was growing increasingly difficult to accomplish. Child Welfare's letter was not the only reminder that I was procrastinating with everything important in my life. Not when my mother's habit of achieving drunkenness before noon each day was wearing on her and on me, while I was there, picking up the pieces.

She'd stumble back to Brick's from Madden's, barely able to stand, covered in vomit, sometimes in blood if she'd fallen down. Once in a while strangers— a chubby crossing guard, a nearby super, an Irish man from the bar—carried her back, bewildered to see my young face answering the door ready to collect her.

Without meaning to, they asked some of the toughest questions. "Where is your father?" some of them would want to know. "Will she be okay from here?" I didn't know how to say, "My father's in a shelter and no, she won't be okay, she's dying. This is the hardest thing I've ever done." All I could do was take her inside and thank them before shutting the door. The rest was for me to work through, alone. I'd take my mother and clean her up; help her, naked and vulnerable, into a warm bath; shampoo her hair as clumps of it came out in my hands. Sometimes she'd vomit in the tub and we had to start all over again.

I became more familiar with the bathroom than any other room in the house. The institutional green paint, the flickering light that bounced that green onto everything in the room, onto my hands as they worked daily to remove the blood, urine, and waste from the tiles. That light that shot green onto my mother's pale skin as her heart still beat, consistently but more slowly now. As she sat, a folded collection of bones in the shallow water, I rubbed a washcloth over her narrow back, ashamed of my own healthy thickness, my fluid movements, and my youth. How unfair that I should flourish while she was steadily reduced, fading; the only successful function remaining within her, the virus that worked diligently in her bloodstream, silently stealing her from us. Yes, her heart still beat, but only to spread the poison, both keeping her alive and killing her more quickly.

It's amazing that when there is just too much to deal with at once, the mind can compartmentalize. If I forgot for a moment that something was terribly wrong with my mother, these confrontations were a stiff reminder of what I had chosen to ignore. Still, after I had her hoisted out of the tub, dressed her in clean clothing, and tucked her in carefully, there was always a way to push it right back out again. I had only to close her door quietly behind me and slip into another world, one that was full of friends who cared about me, places I could go with them, endless adventures with Sam. No one would bother me there. We were all along for the ride together; responsibilities were what other people worried about. Besides, we were a little family. What danger was I in with so many people—Carlos especially—who cared?

The week before my mother began living in hospitals, I found out how much he cared. Before Carlos, I always tended to my mother alone, even with Lisa, Sam, and Bobby nearby. Not that I could blame them. When she came in drunk, my mother was hard to watch, let alone touch, hold, bathe, and dress. I understood. I held no resentment for Sam or Bobby when they looked on from the couch as I underwent the ordeal, repeatedly. But this is also why I was so impressed when Carlos didn't do the same.

"She needs to be talked to more, who talks to her?" he asked me one day as we both lowered her onto the bed. In the living room, music blared over everyone's laughter and conversation. I'd tried to shoo him away, to let Carlos know that I could handle it, but he knew better. When Ma had first come in, he ran to hold on to her arm and back—to support her, not reluctantly, but warmly, as though he saw right past the ugliness of the disease and through to her, the person beneath it all.

"Jean, you seem to need a little help. I'm going to help Liz help you."

"Who are you?" she'd stammered through her crying.

"I'm someone who loves Liz very much, someone who's been wanting to meet you," he told her. If I had known a better way to react, I wouldn't have looked away. *He loves me? Is that what he said?* The whole time I bathed her, he didn't budge from just outside the bathroom door, no matter how much I insisted, "I have it from here Carlos, really." Instead, he spoke clearly through the thin wood, directly to Ma.

"Jean, Liz told me about how you call her pumpkin. I think that's adorable. I call her Shamrock 'cause she's the luckiest thing that's ever come my way. I know you talked to her a lot at night, too, always sitting at the foot of Liz's bed to keep her company." Ma's eyes opened wearily. Tears rolled out of them as she and I listened to Carlos's deep voice vibrate in the bathroom. "My moms had an issue with drugs, too, you know. I wish she could have cared as much as Liz tells me you do. I think it's great that you look out like that. I know Liz loves you, too, and she's proud that you haven't used coke in so long. You've come a long way, Jean. You should be proud of yourself." I reached my hand into the warm, filmy bathwater to hold hers. She closed her eyes again and smiled weakly.

"I love Liz, too. She's my baby," she said softly, speaking to Carlos, but I must have been the only one to hear it. The faintness of her voice made me swallow back tears. I hadn't heard her say that in so long.

Carlos had listened to me; all the details I'd shared, he'd retained. He'd seen my mother as a person, spoken to her, touched her, helped me take care of her.

When I'd tucked my mother in and was ready to leave, Carlos sat on the side of her bed. From the doorway, I watched in amazement as he held my mother's hand and spoke reassuringly to her until she drifted to sleep. Before leaving the room, he knelt down to tighten her quilt. Then, very tenderly, he gripped the blanket's edge and placed a small kiss on her forehead, then stroked the hair from her face.

"Sleep well," he said. "Everything is okay now, sleep well."

Carlos took me by the hand, led me past Sam and Bobby sitting before the noisy TV and into the kitchen, where he sat me down and stood in front of me. Just the two of us. He had said that he loved me and now it was just the two of us.

"Look at me," he said gently. But I couldn't. I was afraid he'd see right through to my hope, my growing attachment to him, and my fear over what was happening to Ma.

"Look at me," he urged, taking my cheeks in his strong hands and staring into my eyes.

"Don't worry, Liz, I'm going to help you through this."

I began to cry.

"I will help you through this, Liz, no doubt. I'm here." He wiped my tears away with his thumbs, kissed my forehead, kissed my cheeks. Then he kissed me on the mouth, tenderly, slowly. I kissed him back and tasted salt, felt the bristly hairs from his goatee, felt his strength, his size, holding on to me.

"I love you, too," I said, pulling back to meet his eyes.

"What did you say, shorty?"

"I love you, too, Carlos. I love you."

His grip grew firmer. "I'm right here," he repeated, pressing my head to his chest, pulling him tighter to feel his warmth and his heartbeat drumming against my ear, consistent and reassuring. I was afraid of how desperately I needed him never to back away.

During the weeks I spent with Carlos, Sam met a boy across the parkway, a guy named Oscar. He was twenty years old; Sam had just turned fourteen a few days after they had their first kiss.

"No big deal. He says I'm mature for my age. He really likes me," she'd said from her spot under the bunk bed one night after Carlos dropped me off. We were splitting a large bag of Oreos and a box of Apple Jacks from Brick's supplies. "Anyway, we're just seeing each other. And besides, he's hot." She smiled. Considering how much Sam had gone through in her life, the things she'd shared with me, I had to agree that she did seem mature for her age.

"Yeah, I can see how you would seem older, I guess. He'd better be good to you, though," I'd threatened playfully.

"Girl, you have no idea," she replied, giving me a small wink.

As we lay in the dark that night, Sam schooled me on all the questions I'd always had about sex.

"Well, Brick and my mother did it, I know that. Sometimes I sleep on the fold-out chair in her room, you know, to be closer to her, and she comes in from the bar and starts asking him for money. 'Brick, can I have five dollars? Just five dollars?' At first he's like, 'No, Jean,' but then I'd hear the springs on the bed squeaking. There would be all these sloshing noises and then I'd hear the crinkle of money. Next thing I know, she's out. I don't know, I guess it gave me the feeling like I didn't want anything to do with sex. Like it's gross."

"Liz, it's nothing like that, I mean *that's* nasty, but sex can really be amazing. Oscar is amazing." I listened closely as Sam described ways she and Oscar shared their bodies, how certain motions, when applied to particular parts of the body, made you rock and sweat and feel a "tingly weakness" that added up to love.

"He loves me, Liz," she said. Lying above her on the bed, I let my body go perfectly limp, trying to mimic the "tingly weakness" she described. The love part was the most confusing.

As she spoke, I shut my eyes to see her experiences more clearly, but the scene was overrun by a picture of Carlos and me lying in the grass in Harris

Field, stars pricking the night sky above us. The tender exchange Sam described didn't seem to fit; it was too difficult to connect my body with any expression of love, even if I strained to. Still, I lingered in the image while she spoke, tried to make Oscar into Carlos, Sam into me, and have it all come together, but I kept losing focus.

✦✦✦

Had I known when I left that there would be no going back, no returning to a roof over my head, I'm not sure I would have done it. After all, isn't that what really draws the line between childhood and adulthood, knowing that you are solely responsible for yourself? If so, then my childhood ended at fifteen.

"What's this? What the hell do you think you're doing? This isn't a shelter. Let's go, get out!"

I will always wonder what tipped Brick off to Sam's hiding spot. Our laughter before bed that night? Lisa? Sam and I were constantly waking her up with our late-night conversations, but we'd refused to do her laundry even one more time in exchange for her silence. Had she done this out of spite? If not, then how did he find out?

"This is *my* house," Brick shouted over us. Lifting the sheet we used to block the bunk bed, a cigarette pinched between his fingers, he exposed Sam's hiding place, his thick body looming like a threat. Spitting as he spoke, he frightened us both. I sat up to create a barrier between them; Sam shifted and curled herself into a ball in the corner. It was near three a.m., and the nighttime shot menacing shadow figures across the wall. Brick was one of them, a cigarette monster menacing us. We said nothing as he stood over the bed, staring down, panting. "Keep it up and you're on your way out, too," he said, looking directly into my eyes. "Let's go, now!" he repeated to Sam, with an angry wave of his arm. Then he walked away and slammed the bedroom door, a trail of Marlboro smoke fading behind him. I could hear him flick on the bedroom lights and begin complaining to Ma, stomping all around the room.

Maybe if not for the letters that had been coming from Child Welfare, I would have given what I was about to do the consideration it deserved. Still, to think that I acted spontaneously is to lie to myself. Truthfully, I had been inching my way onto the streets all along, through my every run-in with premature independence, way before Brick ever caught up with us.

Later, Sam and I would say that at least it wasn't one of the nights we let Carlos stay, the two of them under the L-shaped bunk bed together, their heads poking out to my left. Who knows what a confrontation between Carlos and Brick would have looked like.

Thinking back, it's hard to believe that our setup lasted as long as it did: for well over a year I hid Sam at night, sharing half my meals, covering her with my blanket, and allowing her to come out ten minutes after Brick left for work. Maybe Sam should have slept directly under the bed; that way if he had heard something, he'd come to the living room and assume his ears were playing tricks on him. And I suppose we were pushing it when Carlos started spending nights, too. We hadn't meant to test our luck, but he got thrown out of his friend's place and he'd become too valuable to let out of our sight. Carlos introduced us to a whole new way of life.

"You gotta make moves. I am telling you, once I get my inheritance, we can paint the town green." He'd talk to us of a life in which we could call the shots, and have a place of our very own where no one could yell at us or pull rank. After a few weeks, we had already decided on the color of the carpeting and named our future wolf-dog Katie. The three of us planned to go down to Macy's and take a cheesy family portrait to hang on the wall of the apartment we would get. We couldn't let Carlos sleep outside; he was our future. And it's not like the two of them were under the bed every night. No, we were far more creative than that.

We often made use of the top landing of the staircase in Brick's building. All we had to do was bring quilts and notebooks and peanut butter sandwiches upstairs, and we were set for the night. Spread out across the thin cushioning, we'd use one another for pillows. We spent many nights there, sleeping on one another, like a litter of lazy cubs, breathing in sync and drawing from one another's warmth. If Sam hadn't pulled her pants down one night to pee on the next landing, dissolving a puddle shape into the super's fresh coat of wax, then he might never have known to make us leave the hallway.

Still, we had places to go. Like Bobby's house, where he snuck us in after Paula went to bed. The three of us split his futon, watching movies all night, snacking on Doritos and pound cake. Or Fief's place, where we took one couch cushion each while his ferret, set loose for the night, rummaged in the many garbage bags around us.

For a few brief moments in the dark, after Brick had stormed out, neither Sam nor I spoke.

"Look out," she said toughly, stepping past me. "I'm going to get my stuff." She packed frantically, sniffling, slamming things around.

Lying there, listening to Sam pack and Brick shout from the next room, I thought hard. All my life, I'd looked out for myself. What would be so different if I left with her right now? Why not make my move? Was Brick's place really doing so much for me, or was it a stop among the many that I'd been making lately, drifting? It had never felt like home to begin with. I thought of the boldfaced letter from Child Welfare. A mandatory meeting, the paper had read . . . to discuss the option of placement back into the system. Never again would I go back to the system. That was the thought that put me over the top. If I stayed behind, how much longer before they would just take me back into the system, anyway? That one thought, and the memory of St. Anne's, was all I needed to decide. I'd rather scrape by on my own than go back into the home where people treat you like you're less than a person. I was good at surviving; I could do that.

Besides, what was I going to do, let Sam go out there by herself? Carlos was a survivor; so was Sam. We all were. He could teach us how to get by the way he had for so many years. And, most important, we'd have each other. There was nothing left for either of us here. The answer was simple: *just leave*.

"Sam, wait," I said, running up to her as she zipped her bag shut, a small blue pack containing her journal, underwear, and clothes. "I'm going, too. Wait right there." She looked at me with tears in her eyes.

The closet was a labyrinth of wrong turns. If I left my journal, then I could fit more clothing. If I left my clothing, then I could fit a photo album, a hairbrush, and a change of sneakers. If I didn't carry something, who knew if I'd ever see it again. That's when I cried, too—at my confusion, at yet another change, at the urgency I felt as I heard Brick shouting at Ma. How could I leave her here with him? But how could I stay? I couldn't; not anymore. I cried, frantically tossing clothing, a toothbrush, my journal, and multiple pairs of socks into my bag.

"Let's get out of here before he comes back. I don't want to see him again," Sam said, nervously pointing her thumb at the door to rush me.

"Okay, just one more thing," I told her. "Hold on." I slid a chair over to reach the top shelf of my closet, where I'd hidden Ma's NA coin and that one photo of her, the black-and-white one from when she was a teenager, living on the streets. Opening my journal, I slipped the picture carefully inside and snapped the book shut.

"Now I can go," I said. "Let's just go."

CHAPTER 7

Breaking Night

MOSHOLU PARKWAY, A SEEMINGLY UNENDING STRIP OF TREES AND benches divided by wide streets just off of Bedford Park Boulevard, is supernatural at night. The middle strip, the most wide-open, grassy expanse, is the perfect center from which to draw on its magic. Cuddled into each other for warmth, with our flannel shirts thrown over us as blankets, Sam and I listened to the trees whispering their wind dance, and to the infrequent cars streaking past, so close that our hair fluttered and snapped around us.

"Where do you think they're going at this time of the morning?" Sam wondered aloud.

"I guess the place most people are headed if they're driving around this late . . . home," I said.

Lying there, breathing the rich smell of soil, the parkway's expanse made everything above us seem less real. The stark tenements glowing in the night, park benches, swan-necked light posts, the New York Botanical Garden in the distance; nothing was three-dimensional from the ground. A plane soaring overhead was the last straw.

"Look at it go!" I yelled into the sky, only to have my words swallowed, echoless by the night.

"Whoo!" Sam howled, testing the same effect. The roar of the jet's engine high above us was suddenly hilarious.

"Kind of makes you wonder, who's on the ground, us or them?" I laughed.

"How do you know we won't fall?" she said, biting her bottom lip and faking a frightened face.

"Better buckle down," I shouted, draping my black-and-gray flannel over our heads as we screamed with laughter, high off the risk we'd taken and pumping adrenaline.

When we awoke, tangled together, the sun strained warmly against the seams of my dark shirt. I was the first to peek out. It was barely dawn, and several older Asian women stood nearby, sweeping their arms through the air in sync, slowly, as though under water. Making a visor out of her hand, Sam looked on and asked, "What the hell are they doing?"

"Good morning," I said, plucking leaves from her hair. "I think it's called Tai Chi."

We sat there for a long while, as the sun broke and bled gold over the rooftops and the women did their underwater dance, birds singing and fluttering in the trees.

"We made it," I finally said, taking a whiff of the cool morning air.

"Yup." Sam added, "Maybe this won't be as hard as we thought."

"I have an idea," I said, standing up, brushing myself off and extending my hand down to her.

Just blocks away, in front of Bobby's building, we hunched behind parked cars and waited for Paula to go to work.

"I think she leaves at a little after seven," I told Sam. "Let's just wait it out."

Every so often, the building door swung open and people would emerge into the crisp morning, on their way to work. Women with neat hairdos in button-up pastel blouses, black slacks, and heels clicked away, uphill. Families guided children out the front door, leading them by the hand to school. Men in button-down shirts and ties, wearing thick watches, slung book bags over their shoulders. They were the type of workforce that staffs the receptionist, retail management, and restaurant host jobs of Manhattan. Shaved, shampooed, Walkman-wearing people heading in droves for the subway—different from University Avenue, where those up and out in the morning were few, and they shared the sidewalks with junkies and drunks still lingering from a long night out.

"There she is," Sam whispered, ducking. Paula exited the lobby door looking preoccupied. Checking the time, she made for her car, where she lit a cigarette, pulled out, and drove away, shrinking into the distance. No sooner had she left than we heard Bobby's music, fast-paced punk, blast from his first-floor window.

Once inside, we tore into the refrigerator, feasting on last night's leftovers, pork chops and rice, wrapped in tinfoil. Sam and I passed soda back and forth to wash it down.

"Just be out before my mom gets back at three thirty," Bobby told us on his way out to school. I hugged him goodbye, tightly.

"Thanks, Bobby," I whispered. "We really appreciate it."

Once the front door shut, his apartment became a roadside stop, a fill-up before heading out again.

"Girl, the first thing I need is a shower," Sam said.

"I couldn't agree with you more," I told her, waving the air between us and curling my face in disgust. "You funky." She sucked her teeth and flashed me the finger, smiling playfully.

Over the sound of the water, I flipped through the pages of a notepad Sam had given me weeks ago, past Ma's photograph, past poetry Sam had written in the hallway or under my bunk bed, and turned to a fresh page.

Hey Journal,
Sam and I are free. We're really doing it. Today we're meeting
up with Carlos. He'll be proud we finally made moves.
Too excited to write, for now. —Liz

When we were showered, I took Paula's White Rain deodorant from the shelf and swiped it under my arms, careful to place it back exactly as I'd found it. While I tied my thick hair back with a rubber band from my pocket, Sam stood in front of the mirror, making up her eyes with Paula's eyeliner. When she was done, we paused together. Our pasty reflections stared back at us and our hair dripped. We both looked exhausted.

Sam frowned at the job she'd done on her eyes, and tossed the black pencil into Paula's makeup bag.

"You look better without that crap," I told her.

"I've been thinking about my family," she said in response.

"What do you mean?"

"I don't know," she said, throwing open the cabinet, digging through Paula's knickknacks and retrieving a pair of scissors. I could tell she was irritated; I had seen that look before whenever she spoke of home. Her change in mood was making me uneasy.

"What are you doing?" I asked.

"Do you think I'd look good with a butch cut?" she asked.

"Sam, you sure you want to do that?" I said, reluctant to irritate her further.

"My dad always loved my long hair . . . well, I hope my dad *hates* this." She lifted her thick ponytail above her head, digging four hard cuts into the curls before the whole mass broke loose. "It's hot in California anyway," she said, as she clipped away at what was left. "I've been thinking about doing that for a while. Today seemed like the right time."

I cupped my hands over my mouth and began laughing. "You're crazy!" I yelled. She passed me the huge clumps she'd chopped off.

Holding Sam's silky hair, still moist and fragrant with Bobby's shampoo, the change struck me as funny, but also sad.

"I'm not stopping 'til it shines," she said, smirking.

"You're beautiful either way."

She gave a small grunt in return and stuck out her tongue. I laughed and looped my arm around her tiny waist to hug her.

"It's kind of cool anyway. That takes a lot of guts that I don't have. I'll tell you that much," I said. In Paula's cabinet, I fished for a razor and helped Sam finish the job to her satisfaction. The only hair left on her head were two locks of bangs up front. We spent forever cleaning hairs out of the bathroom, off the sink, out from between tiles, until there was no trace of us left for Paula to find.

Our plan was simple: Stick to the group. One big family, just like we'd said. Maybe this was the only reliable family I'd ever had. Sneak in when their parents went to work, feast, rest, and start again. "Just swing it, baby," Carlos said, promising to stick with us on the streets until his money came through.

"Enjoy the freedom, make it work for you," he said, and we did.

Endless walking. My feet carried me more than any other time in my life, before or since. Downtown, the streets of the Village glowed with nightlife. Freaks, punks, religious fanatics, drag queens, and NYU students crowded the same sidewalks Ma and Daddy must have known in their youth. Street kids littered St. Marks Place, Washington Square Park, Eighth Street; they stared back at us with our own faces. Mohawked, pierced, tattooed versions of ourselves—insane, running, drugged, or just hungry. Hunger: the acidic burn that racked my insides some nights, the visitor from my childhood that did not care whether the rain beat down or if the temperature dropped. It was there to twist and prick and demand, the foremost nuisance in our days.

"You gotta hustle," Carlos said firmly when Sam and I worried where we'd get our next meal. "Yo, there's enough out there for all of us, it's just a matter of getting our hands on it. Keep your head up, 'til we get the cash," he'd insist, his eyebrows arched in urgency. "I been at this for a long time. Do not think, just motivate."

Carlos practiced what he preached. I'd been down the streets of the Bronx and Manhattan many times in my life, frequenting the same few areas, the Village, Eighty-sixth Street, Fordham Road, and Bedford Park. But visiting these places with Carlos was like having never seen them before.

I found that society's guidelines and norms in actuality meant nothing. Carlos showed us that with persuasion—sweet-talking—you could walk into a diner and come out carrying a warm meal and a soft drink, no cash required. Strangers were willing to open their pockets and help out; they just didn't know it yet.

"You see I got a lot of peeps, right? It's all good. They're just people, like you and me. C'mon, if you worked somewhere and someone was hungry, tell me you wouldn't feed them? It's all about the hustle."

Wherever we went, Carlos pressed himself on people. And everywhere we went, he knew someone. Walking with him meant stopping every few minutes for the hot dog guy on Broadway who hugged him and fed us, or the Jamaican man passing out flyers on Broadway, or the tattoo artist at Tommy's who'd etched "Tone," Carlos's DJ alias, into his shoulder for free. But when we stopped for girls, I began to wonder if there was any discretion about how far the hustle went.

Carlos and I had officially become a couple that day in Brick's kitchen, although he formalized it by asking me before the Garibaldi statue in Washington Square Park. We'd been sitting in a diner on West Fourth Street when we heard thunder crack and rain suddenly dropped down in heavy sheets. He grabbed my hand, running and laughing, out to Garibaldi, where he held a large plastic trash bag over our heads. He'd shouted, "Be my girl!" over the pounding downfall in the deserted park. With water sliding off our faces, we'd kissed there, under the plastic bag, his sinewy arms holding me tightly.

But when we ran into the girls, all ages, all body types, and all races, with their cat-claw nails and enormous hoop earrings, they purred their hellos to Carlos, although some called him by other names—Jose or Diego—and he let go of my hand. There was a direct correlation between their beauty and whether or not he chose to introduce us. Sam and I learned to stand off to the side while he greeted them. Every so often, one might shoot me a look, roll her eyes. A few had the nerve to smile and wave at me. Sometimes Carlos took their phone numbers.

"Who was that?" I'd do my best not to sound accusing. Always it was a cousin, a neighbor, or a friend's girlfriend.

"My friend's girl, ain't she a sweetheart," he'd explain. "I might check them for dinner, she just gave me the address." And always, the explanation was a concrete wall that I could not penetrate. The more I persisted, the more I might draw attention to myself. Better to let it slide; he cared about me, I was certain. Besides, there were other things to focus on, like Sam and me learning to navigate our newfound "freedom" for ourselves.

Our tactics were in need of some polishing, Carlos said. We begged for change on a street corner near Washington Square Park, in front of the NYU dorms. Carlos would have come out of the bookstore to help, but he assured us that as females, we'd do better without him. He'd be nearby, observing us.

People streaked past us, more real than we were, an ebb and flow of citizens whose faces surfaced in my dreams like stains. I did all the talking. "Just get them to give you whatever they can and forget them," I'd coach Sam, borrowing from Carlos's confidence, secretly speaking more to myself than to her. "There's nothing to be embarrassed about, they're just people."

They were just people, but what we were must have been something else. If we spoke directly to a person and didn't elicit so much as a sideways glance, we must have been invisible, imaginary. Although some did stop to impart advice, like "Go back to Connecticut" or "Get a job," but wouldn't stick around long enough to let us explain that we didn't know where Connecticut was, and in order to work you needed a reliable address, clean clothes. Then there were the people with kind faces, dropping coins, smiling as they passed. These were the angels who sponsored our meals in diners, where we learned the skill of stretching a dollar as far as it could possibly go.

There were some safe havens along the way.

The public library on Forty-second Street became one of my favorite places, next to Bobby's futon, after a long night—the stone lion guarding the outside, with his twin beside him; mahogany paneling, rows of copper reading lamps, and ceilings intricately carved into abundant floral displays. Nude, Victorian-style characters looked down on us, so real they might have moved. Carlos and Sam took over a table so he could teach her to draw; I lost myself in the stacks.

For hours, I could read through the cellophane-wrapped hardcover books, just like Daddy's books back on University Avenue. "I'm doing fine," I'd insisted just the night before on a pay phone only blocks from his shelter, while the cold blistered my face and fingers. "I'm staying with friends, school is great," I assured him, hoping he would not call Brick's until the next time we spoke. I checked out books that reminded me of Daddy, and kept them with my journal in the front pocket of my book bag, reading them interchangeably every place we stopped to sit: on trains, in hallways, in the quiet corners of friends' apartments.

Friends' apartments were our safe haven for when the journey began to feel less like an adventure and more like a marathon. You could walk only so long before you needed rest. The respite was there for us, with the group. We traveled, schemed, went hungry, laughed, froze, and on the other side of it a group of friends and their friends were willing to help us: Bobby, Fief, Jamie, Diane, Myers, and Josh. *Paula leaves at seven, Jamie's mom is out by eight.* It became so that by morning, we knew just where to go. Deciding was only a matter of whose house we'd hit up too many times that week, whose parents had gone grocery shopping last, making sure that no one parent caught on.

But under the condition of need, friends' apartments and friendships alike warped into something stressful. When 90 percent of the time I visited because I needed something, and 10 percent was just to hang out, even my most valued friendships were tested. Whether Bobby actually wanted company became the smallest component on my list of worries, next to his outright sacrifice of privacy, tension over depleted food supplies for which he was blamed, and the evidence of our sleepovers that Paula might find.

"Shamrock, listen, you can't sweat that. You'd do it for them, wouldn't you?" Carlos reasoned with me. "Come on, it's not like you have other options right now. Your situation is messed up compared to theirs."

But comparison between people was tricky; it seemed an all-purpose rationale that could be wielded in any direction. Yes, compared to Myers and Bobby, who enjoyed sleep in a warm bed and food they had only to open the cabinets to find, you could reason that we weren't asking much of their resources. Still, did we have it all that bad?

It's not like we were those homeless people you saw pushing shopping wagons full of sad things like picture frames, electronic parts, and bags of clothing; such obviously broken people that you could guess, just by looking, what it was that bent and broke to get them there. Compared to them we were lucky, without whole lives that needed pushing in carts or carrying in bags that kept busting open and spilling to remind them just what it was they held on to, and why they refused to stop carrying it.

We were still young. And no matter where we slept, I knew, resting my head to the ceaseless lull of the D train, northbound, or closing my eyes against the unyielding boards of the parkway benches, under stars, I had only to carry with me my family and the notion of home. A bundle easy enough to grip, made light by familiarity, things I'd carried with me all along, far before I ended up in Bedford Park or heard the sound of Sam's warm, sullen voice. In this way, compared to some, I could have explained to Carlos, I had it easy. I'd been practicing all my life for this, carrying things. For others it came as a shock. No matter how exhausted we were or what slant he put on our situation, I was only breaking night, fending off the dark until the sun rose each day, when I'd start over, ready and able to do it again.

I turned sixteen at Fief's house. The group chipped in and bought me a Carvel ice-cream cake. They carried it in, already melting, candlelight illuminating the bare mattress Carlos and Sam and I had been sleeping on, far in the back of the dark apartment. In my slowly waking state, I mistook the dirty mattress for my parents' on University, the one that had been riddled with holes. While everyone sang, I was there, back on University, running my fingers over the coils of the springs, talking to Ma. Someone mashed ice cream on my face and brought me back. There was clapping while Carlos kissed the cream off of me, but everything felt wrong without Ma, Daddy, and Lisa. Shouldn't I be celebrating with them, too? In the bathroom, I turned on Fief's shower, slumped to the filthy floor, and stared at the wall, numb.

By that fall, three or four times a week, Sam and I would wake up to Carlos's absence. If we crashed at a friend's house, he might have left word of where he went, when he'd be back. If we'd slept on the top landing of a stairwell, the most we could hope for was a note. Sam and I might spend a whole morning deciphering it, sitting in the parkway, or while she showered at Bobby's and I sat on the bathroom floor, clutching the paper. This was becoming routine.

Hey Shamrock,
I had to bounce right quick, today's Grandma's birthday. I want to
get her something nice, like some Indian oil and two lampshades.
Be on the roof landing at Brick's or at Bobby's. If you can't, I'll find
you wherever you go.
One Love, Always,
Your Husband,
Carlos Marcano

"You think it's really his grandmother?"

"I don't know, Liz, how can you really ever know with him?" Sam said, leaning out of the shower to shave her legs, her large breasts hanging down as she made careful strokes with Paula's disposable razor. Her arms and legs were sticks, and her head was covered in fuzz too short to look wet.

"Sam, you're losing weight," I said.

"I like food, I just don't catch up with it often. You're no picture of good eating yourself," she said, chuckling.

Lowering Carlos's note, I stood to gaze into the mirror—the same place Sam and I had stood just two months before, after she'd cut her hair off. I kept a single braid of hers taped inside my journal, next to a page of cartoon caricatures Sam had drawn of the two of us, and of Bobby and Fief. Squinting at my reflection, I saw my own weight loss, pale face, and tired green eyes. Momentarily, I was startled to see Ma staring back at me. Sick and weary, she blinked, wondering why I had visited her in the hospital only once this month and when, if ever, I was going back to school.

"I guess if he needs the space, I should just give it to him," I told Sam, pushing Ma's image quickly out of mind. She shut the shower off, leaned on my shoulder to climb out, and began drying herself.

"Yeah, but I know why you worry. You have every reason to; I worry myself. Sometimes I don't know how we would do this without him," she said, looking at me with concern. "I mean, it's one thing to wait it out 'til we get settled, but I couldn't take this crap if I thought it would never end."

"We'll be okay, Sam," I assured her for no good reason.

It was a legitimate fear. Every time Carlos left, we had to wonder whether he was ever coming back. I knew in the same way Sam knew that your life could change in an instant. People caught viruses. Eviction notices were served. You fell in love. Parents just let go of their children. Stability was an illusion. Carlos had similar holes in his life; so did Sam. Without him or her, I wasn't sure I could manage.

The group cared. But they went home at night, kissed their parents, complaining if dinner was burned. I could enjoy them, but only by forgetting portions of myself. And I was done with being lonely. I would grab Carlos and Sam and hold on as tightly as I could.

"I don't know if we can do it without him, either," I finally told Sam. The thought frightened me; saying it out loud made it that much more real.

By Halloween night, the unspoken tension that was bottled up between us snapped. Homelessness was becoming more difficult, and I think we all could feel it, how the strain of not having your most basic needs met can drive you a little crazy. Hunger wears on your nerves; nervousness wears on your energy; malnutrition and stress just plain wear on you. I hadn't realized how uptight it was making me until Halloween, when I decided to join in on Carlos's craziness and to let go of some of the tension myself.

"Happy Halloween . . . *Heepy halawana!*" I screamed behind Carlos as we walked up Bedford Park, loud, surprising myself. Seeing me get into it, Sam jumped in. "Happy Fettuccini!" she yelled. For blocks, I shouted until my throat was sore, screaming into the night sky, kicking up autumn's red and gold leaves in the gutter where I walked. Suddenly, just like Carlos was doing, I began throwing things, smashing bottles on the cold cement, helping him overturn trash cans. We completely lost it together. I was so tired from walking; I felt delirious and angry at people who were sleeping in their homes, rageful even. The more I let loose, the better it felt. Carlos smiled at the sight of it, passed us bottles to toss, egged us on.

The three of us walked for hours, screaming obnoxiously, chucking hard candies in all directions. Perhaps it was out of spite that we'd traveled past most of our friends' windows, in some inadvertent effort to wake them. The closest we'd come was when Bobby, who'd already been up, stuck his head out the window, TV remote in his hand. His hair had grown down to his ears and it shone in the moonlight.

"Waz up?" he asked coolly, looking down at the three of us. What could we say? *"We're tired? This sucks? Can we sleep on your floor tonight again?"*

"Heepy Halawana" was all that came out, from Sam, in one cute yelp that made Bobby laugh. Carlos stood away, aiming hard candy at cars, laughing sickly. A girl's head popped out of the window beside Bobby's. It was Diane, one of the few girls from the group.

"Hiya, guys," she said, so chipper I became irritated. She leaned over and planted a soft kiss on Bobby's cheek. They looked good together, so healthy, rested, and cheerful. I thought of how she probably slept peacefully in his arms, comfortable on his soft pillows. Carlos appeared at my side. I noticed his five o' clock shadow, the way his eyes were pink from lack of sleep. "Let's go, Shamrock," he said, and I followed him up to the Concourse.

Our only other stop was at our friend Jamie's, on whose ground-level window we tacked a note using smashed M&M'S to make it stick. It had a smiley face and read:

Stopped by real quick. Chillin. Heepy Halawana. 10-31-96

Despite our noise, she never woke up. Despite our shouting, the others never knew we'd come by at all.

By sunrise, we had stolen a blanket that had been hanging out of someone's closed window to dry. We camped out with it, leaning against the warmth of the token booth in the Bedford Park D train station. Rush hour brought traffic, people swiping MetroCards that beeped incessantly, rattling us out of any comfort we'd managed. Sam and I cuddled for warmth, tucking the blanket, which was still somewhat damp and smelled soothingly of fabric softener, underneath and over us. Carlos marched in aimless circles around the station and shouted commentary.

"The girl in the green coat knows karate," he announced through his makeshift bullhorn, a poster that he'd stripped off the wall and curled into a funnel. She shot a nasty look his way. Mostly though, he was ignored. "The man in the booth digs disco dancing," he went on and on, fading into a thin, wiry buzz in the distance.

In my dream, Ma was starving to death. Nurses and doctors made a semi-circle around her hospital bed, but could do nothing to help. Nearby, trays of steaming food sat in Tupperware. She smelled the food, cried softly for it, but would eat only if I fed her. While she waited for me, all moisture drained from her body, wrinkling her like a raisin, collapsing her eyes. I walked the halls of the hospital, frantic, lost, and worn, too tired to climb the stairs. When I finally arrived at Ma's room, exhausted from the journey, only red and gold leaves filled her bed.

When I woke up, Sam was nudging my side.

Carlos had vanished.

For the first two nights after Carlos's latest disappearance, Sam and I crashed at Bobby's. In his little room, we tried to stick to the futon and keep as low-key as possible. We washed whatever dishes we used and folded whatever blankets we slept on in hopes of becoming invisible. Though use of the bathroom couldn't be helped, we did our best to do it in runs, together. At least food consumption was a matter of willpower, staved off until absolutely necessary. Bobby was happy to see us, and I could tell that he took little to no notice of our efforts to hide our presence. Good, I thought.

By the light of his television, I thumbed through my journal and studied Carlos's letters.

Your Husband, he always signed them. Curling up beside Sam that second night, I wished I'd never met him.

Our third night without Carlos we spent on one of the rooftops of a very small roof attached to an entrance into Bronx High School of Science. Surrounding us was the large expanse of Clinton High School's football field, deserted and nighttime eerie. The sky was gray and billowy; wind whipped past us in ghostly howls. With our backs pressed to the stark tar landing, Sam and I devoured a bag of salt-and-vinegar chips and slept, cold and still as stones. That night, we were the only two people on earth.

On our fifth night of walking, taking the train all night, and trying to crash at friends' houses, we were worn out. Sam brought up the idea of a group home. It came about when we were so hungry that we couldn't make jokes anymore. As we walked through Tony's diner during the graveyard shift to wash up in the bathroom, the smell and sight of food was just too much. We passed through the club-going crowd typical of predawn hours. Their night magic had visibly worn off, and subtlety was lost: women sat in sequined dresses with their runny makeup, bra straps showing, while men forgot themselves, leaned in close, and put their hands on everything. Together, couples drunkenly occupied the booths, dining on rich breakfasts of hash browns, eggs, and tall glasses of orange juice that made me want to scream.

"I smell like a moose," Sam said in the bathroom. "I don't know, Liz," she continued, looking over her shoulder as she scrubbed her panties in the sink. "I know you say St. Anne's was the worst, but I'm starting to find that hard to believe," she told me, rubbing circles of pink metal-dispenser soap into the cloth.

My period had come. No tampons; I substituted carefully folded toilet paper, again.

"I don't care what happens, Sam, I'm not going to let myself get locked in some prison again."

"Well, all I'm really thinking is food and sleep. You should at least consider coming."

We shoplifted instead.

A few hours later, when the gates of the local C-Town came up, we slipped in, pretending to be customers. With quick sweeps of our hands we made cold, spicy, sweet, and crinkly things disappear into our backpacks. Clanking nervously out the sliding front door, we bolted and made our getaway, pursued by no one, to the nearby P.S. 8 playground. We sat on a jungle gym and tore packages open, stuffing bread and cheese and turkey into our mouths, chewing, coughing, and laughing, drinking orange juice right out of the carton.

That night, I lay in the stairwell of Bobby's building with Sam and considered my options. I thought of returning to Brick's, but quickly decided against it. Mr. Doumbia had promised to put me in a home if I kept up my truancy, and now I hadn't been to school in months. I was *not* going back into the system. But being on the streets was not working out either. I would go pack bags for tips again, but child labor laws had become more strictly enforced over the last few years. Now those packing bags were men in their twenties and thirties, usually immigrants officially employed by the supermarkets. As for the gas station, I was old enough now that I feared doing anything that could get me arrested, so that was out. I really did not know what to do. On a whim, I went to a pay phone and dialed Brick's number, looking for Lisa. I hung up after getting Brick the first time. So I called back a few hours later and got Lisa.

"Hey, what's up?" I said.

"Lizzy? Where the hell are you?" She sounded disgusted and angry; she was too aggressive, and made me regret calling.

"At a pay phone. Lisa—listen, did you tell Brick about Sam? Was that you? I just want to know." I'd decided to confront her with it.

"No, Lizzy."

"Lisa, really, did you?"

"Really, I didn't."

I believed her. "Okay . . . It's been crazy lately."

"You should come home, Lizzy."

No way, I thought.

"Lizzy?"

I stayed quiet, letting Lisa's question hang between us, feeling the weight of her judging me.

"How's Ma?" I asked, finally breaking the silence.

Now it was her turn not to say anything. Lisa was silent for so long that I thought our call had been disconnected. "You should go see her," she answered. "She doesn't have that long. You should really go see her soon."

The following night, I begged Tony to give us a plate of French fries, on the house. We were eagerly waiting for them to arrive when Carlos suddenly walked in. I could feel my body temperature rise when I spotted him. I did not know whether to ask him about where he'd gone and why he'd disappeared, or to just go with it.

"Oh no, he didn't," Sam said, with attitude.

As he approached, I stood to grab him. The days without Carlos had showed me how much I missed his hugs. Relief took the place of resentment. But when I went to reach for him, he held up a hand, indicating I should stand back.

"Ladies," he said smoothly. That's when I saw a thick wad of hundred-dollar bills, rubber-banded together, land with a plop right in the center of the table. Only then did I notice that Carlos had a fresh haircut, and that the green army fatigues he was wearing were new. Sam saw the money and let loose at massive shriek.

"How much is that?" I said, having never seen more than a few hundreds together at a time.

"Just enough to get a burger." He winked. Tony brought us the plate of fries, but before he could set them down, Carlos waved them away with a dainty flick of his fingers. Tony spotted the money and looked at me with a deceived expression.

"*Tienes mucho dinero,*" he gasped.

"That is correct, my good man. So hook it up, will you?" Carlos continued talking to Tony, but looked at us, smiling. "We'll take a dancing chicken, and shrimp that do the shimmy . . . aaaannd a chocolate cake, Shamrock style—no missing slices." Tony took down the order, confused but obedient. As he was walking away, Carlos whistled him back. "That table is on me," he said, motioning to one table of people with his chin but pointing to another with his finger.

"Ju goddit." Tony shrugged.

Drool filled my mouth as I thought, disbelievingly, of all that food. The knot of bills stared back at us from the table. Sam and I sat speechless, smiling, waiting, and alert, our anger as impalpable as the residue of a fleeting dream. At that moment the only things real to me were Sam, Carlos, and the biggest feast I could imagine on its way. Carlos planted a loud kiss on my cheek as I chewed the shrimp.

"I love you, shorty," he whispered.

The taste mingled uncomfortably with his words.

CHAPTER 8

The Motels

WE CHECKED INTO A MOTEL JUST OFF EXIT ELEVEN FROM THE MAJOR Deegan Expressway, where we took the best showers of our lives. I turned the water on hot, scalding, and let it scorch my skin bright pink. R. Kelly sang "I Believe I Can Fly" from Carlos's brand-new portable CD player. My clothes were so gross and textured with dirt that it was difficult to put them back on. I tied a motel towel around my head, turban-style, and entered the room.

It was surprisingly cold. A draft chilled my wet head, sending goose bumps all over my arms and legs.

"Is the heat on?" I asked Sam, who had already bundled herself up in blankets, and was lying, propped up, on one of the queen-size beds.

"No," she replied, "but if you get under the covers, it's a little better." She motioned to the other bed with her eyes.

The carpet was shag, the color of sand, and reassuringly soft under my bare feet. The wood-paneled walls were riddled with scratched-on graffiti left behind by previous renters: *Jason hearts Maria 4-Ever! Rocky and Jessica, together, always 2-20-89*. The residual smell of cigarette smoke gave the air an acrid texture, and anything portable had been bolted down to its neighboring surface. Across the counter, fifties and hundreds were spread about like a scattered deck of cards. The season's first snow tapped lightly against the window.

Right outside the glass, Carlos stood, talking into a cell phone, which was as foreign to me as our new location. Noting the accumulation of snowflakes in his hair, I wondered, with an uneasy feeling, if he might have been talking the whole time I showered. His laughter, muffled from outside, seemed flirty, like it was in those encounters with random girls on the street. Something about it felt deceitful, making everything in the motel feel strange. I looked to Sam, who was chewing on a McDonald's cheeseburger we'd picked up at the drive-through. Despite my anxiety, it felt good seeing her eat, safely tucked under the heavy blankets. We had been walking so much lately; we just needed somewhere to rest.

"Sam."

"I know, girl, don't even say it," she told me. "He came back. It's cool."

"Sam," I said, stepping in front of her. "We need to be careful." I looked over to make sure Carlos was still preoccupied. "We need to start looking into apartments. We need to find a place. After that we can look into jobs and then maybe check out high schools for next year, only *after* we get settled."

"I know," she said. "I would love to get that place."

"Yeah, well, we should get on top of it before anything. You never know. This whole thing feels shaky."

Carlos stepped into the room and swiped the snow off his head, pushing air out through his lips while bulging out his eyes like a cartoon character.

"Brrrr, I was freezing my nipples off out there," he said, shaking his arms clean of snow. We were too quiet to seem amused.

"Waz up, ladies?" he asked, looking around the room in exaggerated confusion. "You look like someone stole your best friend's cat." For a moment I worried that I might have been taking things too seriously, but I spoke up anyway.

"It's nothing. . . . It's just that, now that you have your inheritance, we need to work out the apartment stuff, right? You kind of disappeared for a while, and that was a surprise. We can't really afford any more surprises."

He paused to gather himself in a way that implied restraint. It made me feel I'd overstepped some boundary.

"Like I said, Shamrock, I needed to clear my head. It was wild to pick up Dad's money, so I did it alone. Ain't no way I wasn't coming back. A'ight?"

"Yeah, Carlos, we knew," I lied, too nervous to defy the edge of confrontation in his voice. Plus, I was feeling myself falling into the category of people that just didn't understand him. I was afraid questions about where he'd been, or whether all that money was really an inheritance, would cause me to lose him.

"Well, if you believe me, then act like it and gimme some credit," he snapped.

I didn't move or speak. Sam looked at me as though she were waiting for instruction. Carlos looked from me to Sam and then back again, squinted his eyes, and smiled mischievously. He lifted a pillow off the bed in slow motion and let out a whistle to the theme of an old Western showdown, shifting the mood. Sam smiled and began playfully inching away from him, simultaneously abandoning me in my seriousness. Carlos arched his eyebrows and swung the pillow above his head like a lasso. I took a step backward and chuckled in spite of my frustration. How could I not? He looked ridiculous.

"Hey, we'll get an apartment," he said, whacking my shoulder with the pillow, then quickly dragging Sam clear across the bed by her ankle, swatting her, too. "Stupids," he called out in a pouting child's voice as he halfheartedly swiped the pillow back and forth between us. "Bums. You don't believe me." Sam clawed the mattress for a grip, screaming wildly. I gave in and grabbed a pillow, hitting him on the back using all my force, feeling both the futility of the impact against his strong body, like a mobile boulder, and my own anger come alive with each hit. We fumbled over one another until we became a mass of limbs, sweat, and laughter, collapsed on the smelly motel carpet. Carlos got up first. Gasping for air, Sam and I watched him straighten his shirt and walk to the dresser, where he rolled open the largest drawer.

"Here," he said. "Take a look for yourself."

Wiping sweat off his brow, he tossed a thick newspaper to me. It was *The New York Post*, opened to the classifieds.

"What's this?" I asked.

"Domino's Pizza, ground beef and double pepperoni," he said. "It's the classifieds, Shamrock. What else? I was checking out places for us to get started."

I held the paper up to my eyes and saw the title of the real estate section underlined in black pen. Next to it, there were a couple of phone numbers printed in Carlos's handwriting; one of them was circled.

I was flooded with regret for not believing in him. I saw myself through his eyes and sensed how selfish I must seem. It was his dead father's money, and I gave him grief about it because I was so needy that I couldn't manage without him. I was immediately sorry and determined to make it up to him.

"Carlos," I started, lifting myself up off the ground. But he held a hand up to stop me.

"Listen," he said, smiling, looking from Sam to me, "tonight is . . . tonight is the night. We're gonna paint the town magenta. Forget this. Tonight guys, get on your best T-shirts and jeans, I am taking you out."

We cabbed it downtown, to a mysterious location Carlos said we'd have to see to believe. I had never witnessed anyone pay for a thirty-dollar cab ride before. Carlos sat up front, joking in Spanish with the driver, flipping the radio stations between rock and hip-hop. When he stopped the dial, Foxy Brown's "Gotta Get You Home" blasted. Carlos scratched records on an invisible DJ turntable up front. Sam and I bounced up and down in our seats to the thumping bass of the music, windows down, wind whipping our hair. We laughed, wild with joy. Outside, the sky darkened to a deep blue-purple. I leaned out my window a little and inhaled the cold, late-autumn smell, that fresh moisture that charges the air just before a storm. Families shot by us in their Volvos, babies strapped into their child-safety seats, cars filled with normal teenagers. Their ordinary lives highlighted our own total lack of order.

We were a band of misfits, wild young people carving out our own alternative version of life, together. The adventure struck me as terrifying but thrilling, too, the difference hinging solely on where Carlos was going with all of this, and whether he would keep his promise.

The mysterious location was a small, run-down dim sum restaurant on Mott Street, in Chinatown. Carlos requested that the waitress, with whom he was on a first-name basis, clear a particular booth for us, in the very front. Under his instruction, she brought out no menus; Carlos ordered for the whole table, knowing the list of dishes by heart. He winked rather than explain himself. We laughed rather than ask.

Sitting there, I became enamored with him all over again. The whole night was wonderfully surreal—the way he could walk into a place and change it, make the crazy Chinatown lights brighter; how they shimmered on the wet asphalt outside. The ridiculousness of Carlos going into the kitchen and returning alongside the waitress, helping to serve our food. How he made a beautiful paper rose for me out of a napkin. I couldn't take my eyes off of him, his vibrance, his handsome face; every so often we'd exchange a glance so intimate I was forced to look away.

Sam was smiling wider than I'd ever seen her smile before—she looked completely happy. I was happy, too. The whole night had a dreamlike quality, and I told myself that life should always feel like this, filled with simple happiness. And just maybe, with Carlos around, it could.

✦✦✦

Later, at the motel, Carlos stood in front of me, reasoning with the jammed soda machine for the return of his dollars. The glow of its light against his face turned his freckles auburn and illuminated his eyes. His voice seemed to match the machine's hum. This was the moment I decided to sleep with him; I had finally worked up the courage. He had been persisting for nearly three months, the entire time we'd been together; now I knew that I could go through with it. I told myself that it would show him what he meant to me, and would seal a bond between us that lately had seemed shaky. The sodas clunked down after Carlos gently shook the machine. He made that happen, too.

The cans settled into a bucket of melting ice beside the bed. Sam had disappeared to visit Oscar; it was just the two of us all night, for hours, in this room. I was sure that he sensed my decision, because I started laughing too hard at things, waving my hands around when I talked, like two loose birds. I couldn't initiate it—I didn't have to; I didn't have to move. There was no pain involved, only the weight of his heavy body, the strong smell of latex and of his hot breath. To my surprise, my first thought was that being with him was emptier that I'd expected, more function than joy.

I became distracted by how removed I felt, divided between the physical part of me that I shared with him, and my mind, which drifted. But he didn't notice; he only moved and moved on top of me. For a moment, I resented him for it. In an effort to reverse the bad feeling, I decided to search his eyes, but they were closed. That's when I realized that sex was not necessarily a shared thing. Sex was something you do with someone else, yet you can experience it separately from each other. It didn't necessarily bring you closer. In fact, it could highlight the parts of you that feel most separate. Sex could reveal to you your own isolation. Sam had told me that this act added up to love, but I did not feel loved by Carlos then, nor, in that moment, could I feel my love for him.

When he was done, he rolled off me and cracked open a can of Pepsi. I asked him to pass me the other one and I drank it, letting the icy burn trickle down my throat while my attention sought a focal point in the room—anywhere but him, or us. There was no "tingly weakness" the way Sam had promised.

That afternoon, she had already taped up rip-out magazine posters of dingy rock stars above the other bed. And she had hand-washed and folded shirts and socks and put them in the dresser drawer. This was more stable than we'd been in weeks, and we were appreciative. The rain fell softly outside, collecting on the windowsill, reflecting in its puddle the neon lights of the motel sign. I was miles away from home.

✦·✦·✦

Over the next two weeks in the motel, Carlos rented out three neighboring rooms along with the one we were already living in. He began to act differently, more authoritative. The money was changing him, and with the money, he transformed everything around us. He became good friends with Bobby, Diane, Jamie, Fief, and several other more distant members of the group, all of whom wanted to come over and join in the fun of escaping their parents to sleep in a strange place. Carlos provided it for them, and in doing so, he became their ringleader. Nightly, he called three cabs to collect the bunch of us and take everyone to diners in the Village, for pool on Eighty-sixth Street, or to the movies in Times Square. He tipped his favorite waitress in the West Fourth Street diner fifty dollars, but only after he got her to curtsy, tilt her head, and smile. This, and all of Carlos's jokes lately, made everyone—nearly twelve of his new friends occupying three huge tables—laugh hysterically.

Carlos had become very private about everything. He and Fief or he and Jamie, or whichever other one of my friends was available, routinely took mysterious cab rides to undisclosed places. I was told the purpose was private, and I was asked to stay behind. His cell phone calls, all placed from the balcony outside our room, were extremely private—it was taboo to inquire about them, even when he was talking to my friends. I never knew the details of the calls, or the secret excursions, but they made me think of the way Jamie threw her head back to laugh when Carlos talked; how she, like the other girls, all friends or friends of friends floating in and out of our scene, felt free to enter Carlos's personal space, to touch his arm or pinch his cheeks. "You have the cutest freckles," Diane once said, sitting in his lap. With some of my friends, Carlos shared inside jokes that I didn't get. Sam slipped up and made several censored mentions of private conversations between her and Carlos. This was my first experience in resenting her, and around this time, she and I stopped having our own private conversations. The wedge, at the time, felt permanent.

I couldn't yet speak it out loud, I didn't dare actually say it, but there were two roaring suspicions sitting in my mind. One was that the reason for Carlos's secret trips with my friends was that he was dealing drugs. This occurred to me when I realized how similar he began to look to the drug dealers in my old neighborhood: baggy jeans good for hiding things; a beeper *and* a cell phone for suppliers and customers to reach him; his Latin King beads, which he sometimes wore even in the shower, linking him back to his gang.

The other fear was that he was cheating on me with someone, maybe even with Sam. That suspicion was something I didn't have any evidence of; it was just a feeling that sat in my stomach like a stone.

I was a worrywart, the one who was no fun. I watched Carlos's behavior, kept track of his spending, and reminded him of the hundreds of dollars he wasted every day. I brought up the apartment, told him food was cheaper if we split things, and pointed out, to everyone's great disappointment, that we didn't need cabs—the train was $1.25. He guarded his bank receipts like gold from the mint, and told me he would start saving soon. In the meantime, I should relax, live large—after all, didn't we deserve to live it up after all we'd been through? Why was I so serious all of a sudden? His kisses were rough little pecks that made my skin crawl.

Once in a while, at night while Carlos entertained everyone, I called Brick's from the pay phone downstairs. Sometimes Ma was home, and sometimes Lisa told me she had checked into the hospital, her voice sounding mechanical, resentful. One time when Ma was home, she answered the phone and asked me when I was coming to bring more pillows, and then went on to tell me that the road was wide open; it was only a matter of driving and painting all four walls. Her voice, like some confused child, made my throat feel as if it were splintered with razors. I tried not to cry, but I knew from research I'd done in the Forty-second Street library that dementia was one of the final stages of AIDS. Lisa grabbed the phone.

"Lizzy," she said, "I don't know *what* you're doing, but you might want to think of spending more time with Ma. You may think you have all the time in the world, but you don't." Her voice was furious, but there was no way to communicate my fear of seeing Ma so close to death. I got off the phone as quickly as I could.

Later that night, Carlos was hosting a reggae party, blasting his radio for the crowd and jumping on the bed—which got us kicked out. We moved to another motel, an ancient set of two-story buildings lined with balconies on a desolate road, crowned by a pink fluorescent light that read VAN CORTLANDT MOTEL. Our bathroom window faced the massive expanse of Van Cortlandt Park. Carlos commented that we could make all the noise we wanted to here. He brought the party with us, and I pleaded with him for an extra room so that I could sleep. When we separated, Fief's cousin, a white girl named Denise who wore huge hoop earrings and snapped her gum at me, was holding on to Carlos's arm. I carried some of Sam's, Carlos's, and my things into the next room.

I spotted the paper Carlos had written those real estate phone numbers on protruding from a bag of clothing. I requested an outside line from the front desk so that I could call the one he had circled.

"Hello?" a female voice answered. Her name was Katrina; she was a waitress at some pool hall and had no idea about any apartment for rent. Tears filled my eyes. I hung up on her as she asked again where I got her number.

"Shut up," I said to the ceiling. "Just shut up!"

My sleep was dreamless that night, as I breathed in the stale cigarette smell of my very own empty room while my boyfriend, my best friends, and a bunch of strangers partied, drank, and smoked weed rooms away.

The next morning, Carlos and Sam stood at the foot of my bed. Carlos's voice was what woke me.

"Hey shimmy Shamrock, you want to go get some breakfast?"

"Where is everyone?" I asked. By the bright sun, I could tell it was early morning, and I figured they couldn't have slept yet.

"Gone," he said. "Eighty-sixed about an hour ago."

Sam rubbed her stomach and let out an exaggerated wail.

"Ugh, sooo hungry," she said, casting her thin arm over her forehead. "Fooood."

At that moment I had to make a choice. I could confront Carlos about the phone numbers and take the opportunity to address the way he'd been acting, or I could drop it and go with the moment. I looked at Carlos, and for a second he became as much a stranger as the day I first met him—mysterious, slippery.

But when he smiled, he somehow reversed it and became familiar all over again. My perception of him could change between blinks. How did he truly feel about me? If only he could be wonderful all the time and not send me so deep inside myself for answers that I didn't have.

Sitting there, I decided to drop it. I ignored my anger and went with the flow. Anything else would have been pointless. What would the outcome of a confrontation be? If I got into a fight with Carlos, it's not like I could go home to think about it. This was home; *they* were home. If I just acted like things were fine, maybe eventually they would be.

"Let's go eat," I said, shaking it all off.

Carlos pulled me up out of bed. I layered myself in three sweaters, pulled a knit cap over my head, borrowed a pair of Sam's gloves that had the fingertips cut off, and followed them out. Downstairs, we discovered a tiny little café attached to the motel. It looked as if no one had mopped the floor or cleaned the windows in years, and certainly no one had painted the lime green walls in that long, but the grill shined like new and the air was flavored with the rich smell of bacon and eggs.

"Whatever you girls want," Carlos said. "As usual."

I ordered a toasted bagel with butter, and Sam did the same.

"Lots of butter," she yelled at the grill guy, an ancient man with sparse whiskers. "I want a heart attack, serve it up," she shouted in a deep voice, pounding on the counter. Several of the elderly people who populated the tables stopped their conversation to look her up and down. We took our food and exited. Carlos left a five on the counter and placed a cell phone call outside, standing with his light brown Timberland boots planted in the fresh foot of snow. Looking around, the area seemed familiar, but I couldn't place it. I thought I might have been in either the park or the café before. But when? How? As we walked back toward the stairs with our breakfast, I realized I was right.

"Duck," Sam yelled. "Oh my God." I looked around instead. Then I saw. Grandma, dressed in Ma's old ankle-length bubble coat, clutching her tan purse in the crook of her arm, heading straight for the steps of the little café. Sam knew Grandma from her few visits to Brick's apartment. She yanked me behind the corner of the motel building.

"Sam, oh my God," I said, stumbling. "Her nursing home is right next door! She'll call the cops and report me, I know it." Carlos ran over to us. Without ducking, he threw his hood over his head, gathered the bottom of it with his fist and peeked out the top, exposing only his eyes.

"Who we hiding from?" he asked in a playfully girlish voice. "I'm so scared."

"It's my mother's mother. She'll report me as a runaway. She'll call the cops. They'll take me away to a home. Just be quiet."

We peeked out from behind the wall, watching Grandma make her way through the snow. Her being there was like something from a dream, or an unconvincing scene in a bad movie. Without a thought in my mind, I let out a huge laugh at the ridiculousness of it. Sam placed her hand on my shoulder, squinting in Grandma's direction.

"What's wrong with her?" she asked. "She's walking funny."

Only then did I notice that Grandma wasn't walking so much as inching her way down the street. More than once, she stopped to catch her breath and clutched her chest. As she drew close, I saw that her skin seemed pale, almost white. When she finally made it to the café, it took her several minutes to climb the few steps, while we looked on in silence. Once there, she flopped back onto one of the café's hard plastic seats. None of the other patrons, who I assumed were also from the nursing home, acknowledged Grandma. She sat alone. Promptly, the grill guy brought a cup of tea to her and she passed him a folded bill, which she drew from her bag. It seemed a routine exchange.

Watching the whole thing, I became incredibly sad. It was a glimpse into her isolated world, the one she'd always complained of when I, Ma, or Lisa was stuck on the phone with her. Her words echoed back at me. "I'm lonely at the home. My granddaughters don't come to see me. Even my rosary doesn't cheer me up," she'd always say. Now her loneliness played out in front of me like a somber, silent movie. It made real for me the impact of my neglect throughout the last few years.

"Weird," Sam said. "It's like we're in the Twilight Zone."

"I know," I told her. "It's so strange." I looked behind me; Carlos was already upstairs. We turned to follow him, and made our way up the stairwell together. I wondered whether or not, in Grandma's opinion, I would go to hell for all my sins: driving Ma crazy, abandoning her in her time of need, sleeping with Carlos. If you knew me better, Grandma, you wouldn't want a visit from your granddaughter, at least not this one. I'm not the same little girl who spent Saturdays in the kitchen listening to your scripture. I'm reckless and I neglect everything, especially you.

Sam was speaking a jumble of words at me.

"What did you say?" I asked.

"I said, isn't that crazy, what that guy said to me when I left the store?"

"What?"

"*Happy Thanksgiving.* That's crazy, I didn't even realize. Kind of a downer, I guess, to think today is Thanksgiving," she said.

"Oh," I replied. "Wait, what? It's Thanksgiving? Now? I mean, today?"

"Yeah, ain't that somethin'? Who really cares anyway," she said, pushing the motel room door open to reveal Carlos, who sat flipping channels on the old Zenith TV.

I did. I cared that it was Thanksgiving, and that I was so disconnected from the rest of the world I hadn't even realized. I ate my bagel in a daze and watched the morning news curled up beside Carlos, half listening to him and Sam throw around jokes and conversation. I was busy thinking about how Lisa had begun Lehman College this term. It occurred to me that I never asked her how that was. It always amazed me that she could handle school, our family, and even boyfriends, without ever buckling under the pressure, without missing class. I was suddenly filled with panic at the realization that she was becoming yet another item on my list of growing regrets.

When Sam and Carlos eventually fell asleep, I lifted Carlos's heavy arm up off my side, gathered change out of his army pants, not daring to touch his cell phone, pushed my feet into my boots, and slipped out the door to the pay phone. The cold stung my nose and ears, and the sound of Brick's phone ringing quickened my heartbeat. I prayed for him not to pick up.

"Hello?" It was Lisa.

"Lisa, hi. Did I wake you?" My nervousness made me come off sounding chipper. I held my breath, waiting to see if she noticed.

"Lizzy?"

"Yeah. Hey. Did I wake you?"

"Um, not really. Where are you?" She spoke in a perplexed tone that implied my call was somehow inappropriate.

"Not that far away. I just wanted to see how you are." I wished that I could tell her what had been happening, how unpredictable Carlos had turned out to be, where we were staying, how I had just seen Grandma in all her loneliness. But it wasn't safe. I couldn't trust that she wouldn't tell Brick, who would tell Mr. Doumbia, and then I'd be taken into custody. I wouldn't risk that.

"Oh. How am I?"

"Yeah, how's Lehman?"

"Lehman?"

It was so annoying, the way she kept repeating everything I said in the form of a question and pausing uncomfortably long between her responses. I could feel her suspicion, her mistrust of my good intentions and her anger toward me. It made me aware of every word coming out of my mouth.

"Yes, I, uh, just wanted to call and see how you're doing. I was wondering about school and about you . . . and about Ma."

"Lizzy, Ma's in the hospital. She's sick. She's been there for the last week and a half. She's in the hospital all the time now. She was asking for you before, but I think you blew that. She's been pretty out of it lately."

A lump invaded my throat. Maybe it was the cold or the lack of a good night's sleep that obscured my thinking, but for some reason, I hadn't counted on the confrontation from Lisa. I thought we might talk like sisters, maybe catch up with each other. I fished for something to say.

"Okay. I know . . . do you want to meet up or something?"

"Well . . . why, do *you* want to meet?"

Since as far back as I could remember, I'd felt that Lisa's responses toward me usually bordered on the brink of hostility. Years later, a therapist would explain that growing up with few resources had turned us into competitors—over food, over our parents' love, over everything. At the moment, we were competing for who had the better handle on Ma's illness, and we both knew she was winning.

"I don't know, Lisa. I was thinking maybe we should see Ma." There was another drawn-out pause.

"Well, I can make it around six. Get a pen and paper, I'll give you her room number."

"Lisa?"

"Yeah?"

"Happy Thanksgiving."

"Yeah, Liz, you too. See you at six."

"Hi. I'm looking for my mother, Jean Murray. She was transferred here from North Central last week. My sister told me I could find her on this floor."

The nurse looked at her list.

"Let's see . . . Jean Marie Murray. Okay, you'll have to take a mask."

"A mask? Why?" This was a first.

"All visitors for patients in quarantine need to wear a mask. And how old are you? You can't be here if you're not *at least* fifteen." The nurse looked me over, seeing my confusion. I thought of the reading I'd done on Ma's condition—something struck me as odd.

"Why would I need a mask if AIDS is not airborne?" I asked.

"It protects against TB," she said. "Your mother could cough and expose you. It's for protection."

"What?"

"Tuberculosis, honey. It's a lung infection; people with AIDS are vulnerable to it. Didn't they make you do this before? Don't tell me that someone let you up here without a mask before."

My face went hot. I remembered Leonard and Ma during their weeklong binges in the kitchen on University Avenue. The whole time, he coughed incessantly, his lungs crackling with phlegm until he worked up a sweat that dripped from his face and his skin glowed bright pink. Daddy used to comment, "Boy, you'd think he's ready to keel over and drop dead in there, from the sound of it."

"When was my mother diagnosed with TB?"

"Honey, I'm the charge nurse. I have no idea. You'll have to talk to her doctor about that."

She placed a soft orange mask in my hand. Hesitantly, I slipped it over my head and looked around.

There was a deadness about the ward, and it gave me an eerie sensation. The mute backdrop of the hospital magnified the few noises: the distant ringing of phones and the incessant beeps of numerous machines. The entire area seemed unusually desolate, even for a hospital. It was unlike the last few wards Ma had been in, where nurses bustled around and visiting hours brought all kinds of faces. This place was different. I pushed myself forward, in search of Ma's room.

"Turn left, walk 'til you can't go no more," the nurse called from behind me.

I passed a sign that read INTENSIVE CARE UNIT and another that read ONCOLOGY. I had no idea what oncology was, but figured that it couldn't be any good if it was somewhere between intensive care and quarantine. I passed door after door, within which patients lay unconscious, their heads cocked back to allow for the breathing tubes lodged in their throats.

You need it for protection. I thought of all the times Ma came home from the bar in need of my help. I thought of the vomit that had seeped into her clothing by the time she finally reached me. I recalled the putrid odor of the wet mess mixed with vodka rubbing off on me when I lowered her into the bath; Ma's coughing fits as I washed her body clean and we both pretended not to notice her nakedness and her shame. I thought of her ninety-something-pound body, swathed in clean sheets, lulled to sleep by her own drunkenness, as I breathed in the fresh-out-of-the-box smell of the nurse's mask one more time before deciding it was pointless. I pushed open Ma's door and removed the orange cloth from my face.

"Hi, Ma."

No response came from behind the brown-and-green fishnet curtain surrounding Ma's bed. It took all my courage to pull that curtain aside, and it took that much more to conceal my shock over what I saw behind it.

Ma took up just a fraction of the bed. Her skin was yellowed and tight on her face, cheeks sloped dramatically inward, painstakingly molded by her illness. The hospital sheet was cast off to the side, revealing her emaciated body, curled up like a child's skeleton, barely dimpling the plastic mattress beneath her. Up and down her limbs ran angry, little red scabs, each attached to a raised mound of flesh. Her eyes were wide open, but fixed on nothing, and her mouth was slowly moving, almost spelling out words, sputtering small sounds. That and the machines hooked up to her body were the only noises in the small, airless room.

I was trembling. I opened my mouth almost involuntarily, before I was sure of what would come out.

"Ma? It's Liz . . . Ma?"

Her eyes drifted around the room in response. For a moment they landed on me and I thought I'd captured her attention, but then they kept roaming, her mouth maintaining that same choppy, wordless movement as they went. On the narrow table wheeled to her bedside was the hospital's celebratory Thanksgiving dinner. In teal Tupperware, there sat an untouched serving of sliced meat saturated in congealed gravy that streamed its way through a scoop of mashed potatoes and onto the cranberry sauce. Lying on the tray beside her plate was a smiling cartoon cutout of a turkey decorated in red and gold feathers. The caption above its head read: *A Time to Be Thankful.*

"Ma . . . look." I took a seat. "I'm sorry I didn't come sooner, Ma . . ."

I didn't know how to speak; my throat felt squelched shut, too full to draw breath. I might have been suffocating, drowning on the tears I wasn't allowing to come. I took two deep breaths and reached out for her hand; it was not much warmer than the metal rods upholding her hospital bed. Touching it sent shivers up my arm.

"It's like she's dead already," I mumbled to myself. Then to her I said, "You're not even here right now."

The door clicked open, sucking air outward, floating Ma's curtain into a small breeze. Lisa walked in wearing heels and a black peacoat, her long, dark hair wrapped in a neat bun. She could have been a social worker, a lawyer, or any type of professional grown-up. I felt dingy, dressed in layers of sweaters, thumb holes punctured near the fronts of the sleeves, my long brown hair, tattered and stringy, falling down from under my knitted skull cap. Lisa clicked a few steps forward, looking from Ma to me.

"Hey" was all we said to each other. She avoided eye contact and pulled up a chair to sit down near Ma. My heart raced. Seated there next to her, I judged myself through her perspective: I was a high school dropout who'd abandoned our sick mother to live in a mysterious location with my street boyfriend.

"How long have you been here?" she asked.

"Just a little while."

We spent a few moments sharing an awkward silence, and then Lisa leaned over the side of Ma's hospital bed, tears spilling out of her eyes.

"Ma? Hi, Ma. Sit up. We're here. Lizzy is here. Ma?"

"Lisa, don't bother her. I don't think—"

"She can sit up. Ma?"

Ma's eyes raced all around. Her hand opened and closed, and she began muttering gibberish louder than before.

"Came here . . . came here to give me your soul. Spare me. Spare me . . . that am I all . . . spare it. Mine and yours . . . yours, yours!" She wasn't looking at either of us; there was no sign that she knew who we were.

"Lisa, I just think we should leave her alone. Maybe she'll get up, but she's probably not feeling too good."

"Lizzy, look. She was talking at home last week; I know, *I* was there. She would want to know that we're here."

Her tone was scornful. I quieted down as Lisa moved her chair up, right near Ma's face. She spoke louder than I would have dared.

"Ma, get up. It's Thanksgiving. We came to see you," she said in a softer voice.

More gibberish. But then I was shocked to see Ma start to sit up. Very slowly, she lowered her feet onto the floor and peeled off the monitor as we quietly watched her make an attempt to go to the bathroom, dragging the IV pole behind her. I reached out to support her weight when she wobbled the six-foot distance, steadying herself on the door and the wall. As she turned away from us, Ma's gown floated open in the back, revealing a full view of her upright, naked body. Pictures flashed in my mind of one of Daddy's PBS specials on the Holocaust. If she stood still, I could count her vertebrae; they looked something like the metal links of a bicycle chain with flesh taut over them. Her pelvic bones protruded, and there was absolutely no fat on her bottom or her thighs. In the bathroom, I took a short towel from the chrome towel rack and wet it; I wiped Ma's backside clean with one hand while supporting her frail body with the other. The fluorescent lights flickered on the white walls and on us. I bit down on my lip to keep from crying, and did all I could to stifle my need to cough on the smells of her sickness. "It's okay, Ma, we'll get you all fixed up," I reassured her. "We'll make you nice and comfortable, just relax."

"Okay, Lizzy," she said in the weakest voice.

When we were done, I took her hands in my own and lifted her from the toilet with almost no effort at all; she was so light, it scared me. All of it scared me. I was terrified, and wanted more than anything in this world to make her better. When I tucked her back into bed, I knew I had to get out of there.

"Are you leaving already?" Lisa asked as I hovered in the doorway. I was shaking; I needed to be alone. My heart pounded; I could not take one more moment of being there. And I was not going to lose it in front of Lisa.

"Well, um, it's just that I was here before you, for a while . . . and I just think I should get going soon because I'm kind of tired. I didn't sleep much last night."

"Whatever," she said, rolling her eyes and turning away from me.

"Lisa, it's just not that easy for me, okay?"

"Yeah, I know, Liz. I'm dealing with it, too. I know it's not easy. I figured you wouldn't stay long anyway, so just go ahead and go," she said, sobbing.

"People deal differently, Lisa."

"Yeah, they really do," she snapped.

I hadn't prepared for how scary this would be, for what I'd feel seeing Ma like this and being powerless to help her. I didn't know what to do with the frustration I felt at not being able to change things for Ma; I wished Lisa and I could see each other through this, but she wanted me to sit in it the way she was, and I could not afford to. I felt stuck. If I stayed, I didn't feel I could handle it. If I went, I was a bad daughter and sister.

"I have to go, Lisa. I just have to go. Please understand."

I ignored Lisa rolling her eyes and leaned over to talk to Ma. At the time, I had no idea that it was the last thing I would ever say to her.

"Ma. I have to go, okay? I promise I'll come back later. I promise. I'm okay. I'm staying with friends. I'm going to school, soon. I really am, I promise." I reached down and touched her hand. "I love you," I told her. "I love you, Ma." I did get to tell her that. She said nothing in return, and I slipped out into the hallway, where I rested my back on the wall and inhaled deep breaths; holding in tears, I felt like I was descending, free-falling into nothingness. I wanted to scream. Lisa stepped out into the hall.

She addressed the floor. "You know, Lizzy. You just leave . . . that's fine for you, but it's just so cold."

"This whole thing is hard for both of us in our own way, Lisa; I just can't stay here, sorry. You act like I'm having a blast out there, but it's not like that. Not having a stable place is no fun, okay?"

She turned in disgust and went back into the room; I escaped down the hall away from her, away from Ma, and I left.

✦✧✦

That night, after hearing of my visit to the hospital, Carlos decided I needed cheering up. To get my mind off things, we'd do something absolutely crazy: go out for a good meal at a decent restaurant with good service—dressed in our underwear.

"Let them say something. If I've got the money, they'll serve us," he said, flashing a giant wad of fifties in the cab. "Right, Papa?" he asked the driver, who smiled and nodded blankly, glancing only at the cash. Carlos picked the Land and Sea diner just off of 231st and Broadway, a place where the walls were decorated with plastic fish, plastic lobsters, and plastic ship steering wheels—punctuated by bright pink fluorescent lights that wrapped around the diner walls. We flew down Broadway in the cab, Sam and I screaming as it raced through traffic. We pulled up to the restaurant like cops coming onto a scene, and Carlos peeled off a twenty to pay the driver for what should have been no more than a six-dollar ride. "Cheerio!" Carlos said, applying two hard slaps to the roof of the car to send him on his way.

Carlos led us to the largest table in the front of the restaurant. Customers turned their heads to watch the guy and two girls dressed in men's boxers, boots, and hooded sweaters in the dead of winter. I kept my knitted cap on, hair half tucked in. Sam had found an old tie in one of the motel room drawers; she wore it dangling over her sweatshirt.

"We're all British," Carlos whispered. When the waiter came running up to our table to explain the dress code, Carlos addressed him with a purposefully terrible and unconvincing accent that made Sam and me burst out laughing.

"My good man, where we come from, this *is* appropriate dress. Don't get your knickers in a twist." Carlos took out a wad of money and placed it on the table without ever taking his eyes off the man. Problem solved.

We dined on lobster, T-bone steak, chicken fettuccini Alfredo, and half a dozen appetizers. I ordered using a totally inept British accent, enunciating all the wrong syllables, while Sam and Carlos burst into laughter. It didn't matter; the waiter brought anything we asked for without question. I didn't question it, either. I just watched Carlos pluck twenty after twenty out of his wad to pay for the whole outrageous meal. I didn't care either way anymore; going with the flow was so much easier than pushing against it.

We drove around in cabs all night, stopping wherever, for whatever reason occurred to us, on a whim: Grand Central Station, so we could stretch out on the ground and stare up at the constellations on the massive ceiling; China-town's arcade so Carlos could prove to us that there really was a chicken trapped in a machine who played you in a game of tic-tac-toe. There, we stopped in the black-and-white photo booth and snapped three strips of pictures: all three of us making crazy faces, contemplative faces, and one whole strip of me kissing Carlos, feeling his soft lips pressed to mine, while the heat from the bulb flashed through my closed eyelids onto our profiles.

"He *is* good," I told myself. "He *does* love you, even if it's hard for him to express it. Don't forget the way this feels." And it felt like heaven, the kiss, the whole night spent together—Carlos's magic at work, again.

We took our last cab of the night to the White Castle drive-through on Fordham Road, just as the sky began to show streaks of morning light. We were only going to get milk shakes, but Carlos surprised us, asking for fifty hamburgers. We zipped up and down Webster Avenue, the Grand Concourse, Broadway, chucking the warm burgers out the windows, hitting parked cars, mailboxes, and lowered storefront gates. "Whooo!" Carlos yelled each time he sent another burger flying.

Back at the motel, we stretched out, a sack of greasy burgers on the floor beside us. I fell asleep in Carlos's arms, something I hadn't done since that night we'd first slept together. I wrapped my arms around his chest, where I buried my head in search of his heartbeat. He put soft kisses on my forehead and said, "I told you we'd cheer you up, Shamrock. I want to see a smile on that face again tomorrow, or we'll have to go out there butt-naked next time." Sam giggled hysterically from her bed. I was enchanted with Carlos all over again—with his kisses, his smell, and his ability to make me relax into him, drawing me far away from my growing emptiness.

For the next three weeks, I kept telling myself I was going to visit Ma. I really was, but it became hard not to be distracted by the little things, like how I coaxed Carlos into a real estate office, where we finally filled out forms and made appointments to see places. We wanted a two-bedroom in a quiet building in Bedford Park, just like we had planned, nothing too ghetto. In the meantime, I tried to make our living space as nice as possible. I made our beds, tucking in the corners just the way the maids had when we first moved in. Since we always trashed the rooms so bad, we'd hung "do not disturb" signs on the doors permanently. Sam helped me chase after garbage, several fast food containers per person per day. When we stopped at the corner store, I picked up one of those plug-in fresheners, potpourri scented, for $1.89.

Using gum, I tacked up our Chinatown pictures to the motel mirror, next to all the love notes I'd been writing Carlos. I wrote a fresh one and drew a cartoon frame of hearts around it that I colored in with a red pen. I hung it up beside our pictures.

> Carlos, being with you has made me happier than I've ever felt before. You are my purpose; you have been there for me when it mattered most, a listening ear, a shoulder to cry on, you made me laugh when it all seemed pointless. I love you dearly.
> Liz

I wrote Carlos little love notes like these every day. But over the course of those few weeks in the motel, the theme of the letters turned from gratitude and affection to me expressing that our relationship was worth salvaging, and how glad I was that we were getting past our problems.

✦ ✦ ✦

One day, while Carlos was out visiting an old friend, a big guy they called Mundo on the block, Sam and I used about ten dollars he had left behind to pick up a few things at the store.

We attempted discount makeovers. Sam selected two jars of glitter nail polish and an oversized can of hairspray. Following the advice of a teen magazine, which we propped open on the radiator in the bathroom, we got four packs of imitation Kool-Aid, and tried, unsuccessfully, to dye our hair Quirky Purple and Very Berry Pink.

"Is it working?" I asked Sam, lifting my head out of the bathroom sink.

"Um, I dunno. I guess I can see some purple, but I'm not sure if it's just my imagination. How's my head?"

I laughed out loud at the pinkish streams of water running down her face, between her eyes, dripping off the tip of her nose. Her whole scalp, clearly visible through the inch and a half of hair on her head, was pink.

"You look fab," I said sarcastically.

The only thing we dyed was our skin and our T-shirts, which, splashed on their original white, appeared tie-dyed.

We kicked back, letting our hair and nails dry, and watched *I Love Lucy* reruns, waiting for Carlos to return so we could all go grab dinner. Six o'clock came and went. Eight. One. Four a.m. It occurred to me to call his cell phone, and then I realized he'd never bothered to give me, or Sam, the number. Carlos paid the front desk nightly for the following day, and I was sure he hadn't paid in advance. I wondered what would happen if he didn't come back by noon tomorrow, checkout time. I looked out the window all night, asking Sam over and over if she thought something might have happened to him.

"Yeah, his mother dropped him on the head when he was a baby, that's what happened. Don't worry, he's not in danger. He's just an asshole."

In the morning, I begged the hotelkeeper not to throw us out, using the phone to explain that Carlos would be back to pay any time.

"I'm sick of guys leaving their hookers here. This is not some flophouse."

"We're not prostitutes!" I snapped at him. "He's my fiancé," I lied.

"This is a business, lady, not a drug haven, not a whorehouse. Pay up or go." And he hung up.

We bartered with him, using the only thing of value in sight: a gold watch Carlos had picked up on the day I visited Ma. The cold found its way into every crevice of my clothing as we walked to the front desk clutching our sweaters to our necks for warmth, Sam trailing behind me.

I spotted the person behind the nasty argument, a short, stubby, fifty-something Italian man. He held either side of Carlos's watch, lifting it up to the light. "This will get you until tomorrow," he said.

"But he paid a hundred and fifty for it, it's brand-new," I protested.

"Well," he said, slipping the watch into a backpack on his side of the scratched Plexiglas, "it's not worth the shirt on my back. I'm doing you girls a favor."

By nightfall, we folded. Sam and I got out the trash pail and started digging through it in search of any salvageable leftovers from the last few days. We split rubbery hamburgers, stale strawberry shortcake, and a funky-smelling turkey sandwich. The water from the bathroom tap tasted poisonous. For hours, Sam and I took turns racing to the toilet and checking the window for Carlos. The bad food made bubbles rumble through my midsection; everywhere I walked, I felt sick.

At sunrise, we flopped down on Carlos's and my bed, the one nearest to the door, and lay on our stomachs to look through the window together, out into the bright parking lot. We grew sleepy, watching how the morning sun gleamed gold off the windshields of parked cars and sparrows populated the frosted bare branches of a nearby tree. Neither of us said we were afraid, but under the layers of blankets, Sam grabbed my hand and held on tight. Every so often, when the wind howled on the other side of the thin windowpane and a cold draft kicked up through the crack between the door and the floor, she squeezed my hand harder.

I woke up to her nudging me, less than an hour later. When I opened my eyes, her finger was drawn to her lips, telling me to be quiet. My first instinct told me the hotelkeeper was nearby, ready to evict us. But then Sam motioned to the ground. There, between the foot of the bed and the ancient motel radiator, I saw them: a family of mice, a big one and four little babies, scavenging through the leftovers we'd declared far too rancid to risk eating.

We watched in total silence as the greasy takeout bags shifted and wiggled under the weight of the five mice darting in and out. Their cuteness immobilized us both. They were gray, not much lighter than the motel carpet, with pink noses and glistening black eyes. Remaining totally still, we discovered, as the biggest one carried food back and forth, that their nest was in the radiator, somewhere near the reverse side of the slits that ran along the top row of the vents.

"So that means they can see us from there all the time," I whispered to Sam. She gave a small nod; her eyebrows were bent upward with affection.

"I like the babies," she whispered back.

"Me too," I said, softly, "they're the cutest."

We watched them until the sun was fully up and the motel's overnight visitors vacated their rooms, opening and slamming car doors, starting up their engines.

Dozens of times, the mice zipped in and out of our take-out bags, startling themselves with their own bristly movements, quickly retreating back into their hideout, only to peer through the vents and inevitably venture out again.

I was the first to hear his cab pull up. I felt it had to be Carlos because a hip-hop beat blasted, growing louder as the car approached. The door opened, then slammed. Sam looked at me.

"I don't know whether to be calm or angry," she said.

"Neither do I," I told her. I realized then that I didn't know because I was waiting to see what *he* felt first. I was used to that, sensing my own feelings only in relation to others. If he was content, then so was I. Carlos had been calling the shots all along, because I let him. I caught myself at this moment, ready to do the same, and it sickened me.

We stayed still and waited for his heavy footsteps to come close. Then his keys were jingling in the lock. My heart jackhammered in my chest. Carlos entered whistling.

"Hi," he said casually as he came in. His face appeared worn, eyes drooping, bags underneath them. He looked different somehow. I wondered if he might have been up all night since we last saw him; I wanted to know what he was doing. He sat at the foot of Sam's bed, smelling strongly of cigarettes. "Waz up, shorties," he said, playfully. "I'm ready to pass out." He avoided my eyes and sat, unlacing his boots.

"Where were you, Carlos?" I asked, as though it wasn't in any way controversial to question him.

"I told you, Shamrock. Mundo's house. I ain't seen that fool in years."

"Why didn't you call?" I made sure he sensed the anger in my voice. I was not taking his crap today.

He moved around the room, needlessly arranging things, the TV antenna, his boots under the bed, our hairspray can on the bathroom shelf, ignoring my question.

"Carlos, do you hear me?"

He banged shut a drawer in response, opened another, removed a set of boxers from inside, slammed that one harder.

"The least you could have done was call."

"Where is my watch?" he asked, cool as ice, looking straight into my eyes for the first time since he'd come in. A stab of fear went through my chest. Sam looked at me.

"Where is your watch," I repeated stupidly.

"*Yes*. Where. Is. My. Watch?" His eyes were glassy, no tenderness behind them at all.

"We sold it to the hotelkeeper for a night's stay when you left us here. That's where it is!"

After a pause, Carlos cocked his leg back and kicked the trash pail, sending it sailing across the room, where it crashed against the wall and then onto the ground. Sam and I shot straight up and drew close to each other. I was shaking.

"Why would you sell *my* watch?" he asked through his teeth. I'd never seen him like this; he was possessed.

"You left us here." I hadn't meant to sound so whiny.

"Well, I am not responsible for you!" he screamed.

"Responsible for us? Is that how you feel?" I knew it was true, and I felt both angry and embarrassed when he highlighted it. "We had real estate appointments yesterday. *You* missed them." Now I was crying.

"Don't give me that shit!" he screamed, punching the wall beside the mirror, once, then twice, shaking loose my tacked-up love letters and sending them fluttering to the ground like leaves. Sam clutched one of the pillows, which was stained purple from dye. Together, we watched Carlos storm into the bathroom and slam the door.

He ran the sink and shower full force, and didn't come out for over an hour. For a moment, Sam and I sat in bed together and were totally quiet. I needed something to happen. I got up and turned on the TV for distraction.

"What the hell was that?" I finally said, crying, pointing to the bathroom, my hand shaking. "He's never acted like that."

"I don't know what that was," she whispered. I'm not sure which of us was more afraid. But we didn't leave, we just waited, hoping that when he came out he would be normal again, take us to a diner, crack some jokes, even if it meant ignoring what he had just done.

When Carlos finally came out, his hair wet, his face cleanly shaven, he tugged a blanket from Sam's empty bed and went to sleep on the floor without saying a word to either of us. I was glad he didn't come near me. On the opposite side of the room, it took me forever to relax.

"Sam?"

"Yeah."

"Walk me to the bathroom? I don't want to go alone."

We stepped over Carlos's huge sleeping body. In the bathroom, his things were scattered all over the filthy pink and cream tiles—his army pants heaped into a mound on the floor, that wad of money poking out from them, a disposable razor. Little hairs were peppered all over the sink. Using the mirror, I washed pink dye streaks from behind my ears while Sam peed.

"I got this stuff everywhere," I told her.

"Yeah," she said, swiping her hand over her fuzzy head. "Mine's going to be easier to clean off. Can you pass me some tissue, Liz?"

"Yeah."

I leaned down and lifted one of the two rolls from under the sink, when my eyes caught sight of something shiny. It was a small, silver cut of tinfoil, the exact size of the dime bag packages Ma and Daddy left scattered around our kitchen on University. Without taking my eyes off the foil, I passed Sam the tissue and crouched down.

In the center of the foil, ever so faint and small, I found tiny specks of white powder.

"Sam! Sam."

"Yeah."

"Don't flush. Be quiet and look at this. . . . He's on coke."

The discovery of Carlos's hidden habit transformed him for me from an eccentric, hilariously original person to a junkie with a personality disorder. For the two nights that followed, I stayed away from the parties he started up again in the spare hotel room. All throughout those nights, music blasted from the party and cabs arrived, unloading person after person: Fief and his cousins from Yonkers, people from Bedford Park, Jamie, Mundo, and countless others. Sam passed from one room to the next, doing her best to keep me company. My absence from those parties was a form of protest. I sat by myself, planning the letter I would write to Carlos telling him I knew his secret, and if he kept using drugs, I couldn't be his girlfriend.

I could just see us if he didn't stop using: we'd end up living in a Bronx apartment, a high school dropout and a cokehead. We would be one step away from Ma and Daddy's life. What was the difference? *Hookers*, the hotelkeeper had called us. Maybe you could be a prostitute without knowing it, I thought. Maybe all it took was compromising yourself for the sake of gaining something in return. I was sick of my dependence on Carlos, tired of our sick lifestyle.

I fell asleep drafting different versions of my letter, with my notepad open on my lap.

Dear Carlos,
We've come to a crossroad . . .

✦

The next morning, I woke up to the pounding before Sam and Carlos did, someone's fist slamming against our door, rattling the chain, a man's voice calling on the other side. The two of them were sleeping through it. Still foggy from sleep, I pulled open the door to a guy in his mid-twenties. His fist was lifted, ready to knock again. Sam came up behind me; we'd slept past checkout time.

"If you guys are using the room, I need today's money," he said. "If not, the maid is waiting." He folded his arms across his chest. The cold chilled my bare feet.

"Sure," I said. "Just a second." Carlos sat up and lifted a hand to shield his eyes against the sunlight that poured into our dark room.

I knelt down beside the bed and starting sifting through Carlos's jeans for the money. I counted off three twenties into the man's open hand.

"Next time, you guys come to *us*. Or at least pick up your goddamn phone," he called out, disappearing down the nearby staircase.

"I didn't even hear it ring," I told Sam.

"Me neither." I sat on the bed and examined the phone, realizing that the receiver was not placed directly in its cradle. It could have been that way for days, since we never used it. Carlos and Sam watched me click it back in place.

"Is it about that time?" Carlos asked, pointing down at his stomach. "Yes, I think it is." He was in a good mood.

"What time did you get in, Sam?" I was surprised that I slept through Sam's return, especially since she had lain down next to me in her bed. Carlos got up and unfolded a large Chinese food menu.

"Let's eat, fools," he said, swatting my bare legs with the page.

"What're we ordering?" Sam asked, forgetting my question.

I was too tired and hungry to think about the letter I had written to Carlos. I was too confused. It was easier to just focus on my immediate need: food.

We were sitting in a huddle on his bed, reading over all the selections, when the phone rang. Instantly, we all locked eyes. We never got calls on that phone. I gave Bobby the number to give Lisa only in case of an extreme emergency. Sam got up. Her face tensed when she answered, then she extended the phone toward me.

"Liz, it's for you. It's Lisa."

"Hello?"

"Liz, it's me. Why haven't you been picking up?" But before I could answer, she continued. Her voice was watery, panicked, as she mumbled a blur of horrifying words.

"What?" My knees buckled. I don't remember how I ended up on the bed.

Lisa sobbed, her child's voice returning as she repeated the news again.

"I'll be there in fifteen minutes," I said, setting the phone down on its receiver.

"Liz, what's going on?" Sam asked.

Tears ran down my cheeks. I wiped them away quickly, my eyes still lowered on the phone. "My mother died," I said, sounding as flat and final as it felt.

Carlos's strong arms were suddenly around me.

"I have to go," I said. "I have to see Lisa. I have to call my father."

Sam called us a cab. While I waited for it, I went to the pay phone outside and dialed Daddy's shelter. My stomach lurched when I heard his voice and I knew what I had to tell him.

"Daddy . . . are you sitting down?"

We cried together, him standing in the shelter office being timed and supervised by staff, me standing outside the motel in the cold, at night. Though

I had never actually seen my father cry, we sobbed together then, and I could feel both our hearts breaking.

The cab rushed me to Bedford Park in a haze of tears, my world spinning. Throughout the ride, Carlos kept staring at my face, rubbing my knee repetitively and urging me to speak. I could not have been farther away from him. All I cared about in those moments were Ma, Lisa, and Daddy. The gravity of our loss washed away the pettiness of everything else.

I met Lisa in Tony's diner. She had on an old coat that looked like one of Ma's. She was sitting by herself in front of a cup of coffee, but no food, at one of the tables in back; her eyes were bloodshot. As I approached and we looked at each other, my heart broke all over again.

CHAPTER 9

Pearls

DECEMBER 27, 1996

Dear Ma,

Part of what makes losing you so hard is all the things we will never get to say to each other. That's what death did, Ma—robbed us of the things we still have left to say.

Did you feel it the way I do? The weight of what's unsaid?

Over the last sixteen years, I've learned to swallow my feelings. How to swallow the things I couldn't say because I didn't want to hurt you or push you away.

You and me, Ma, reminds me of how pearls are made. People see pearls as beautiful, perfect gems, but never realize that they actually come from pain—from something hard or dangerous getting trapped inside an oyster where it doesn't belong. The oyster makes a pearl to protect itself.

Behind my own sealed lips, Ma, that's what I have done— oystered our family's pain until pearls were born, thousands of tiny losses to withhold. But you're gone anyway, and I am not sure my silence did us any good.

You died on a Wednesday, around 8:30 in the morning. I was somewhere, sleeping, laughing, or forgetting you.

I will always regret that.

You were alone when you died. No one had visited you for days; I hadn't been there for almost a month. Did you worry that your daughter was never coming back to see you again? Did that make it easier for you to go? I'd always been there, to give you money, to clean you off, to be your diary. Why couldn't I be there when you were dying? When strangers changed your clothing, fed you, put their hands on your naked body, frail as a newly hatched bird?

I know they coldly discussed their private lives with one another over your sick bed, changing your bedpan with their braceleted wrists fragrant with department store perfume. The isolation must have terrified you.

Were you afraid, Ma?

While I made love and ate burgers in diners, and laughed in the sunshine, were you afraid?

I'm not a loner anymore, Ma. I have friends. Some of them came to your funeral. Remember Carlos? He came. He's my boyfriend now. Sam wouldn't get out of bed. "I can't, Liz, those things are depressing," she'd said just before I disappeared into the cab. We paid for the transportation from a pool they took up at Madden's; a friend of yours gathered it for us. I never wrote a thank-you note to her, or to any of them. I'm not sure why.

Lisa, Carlos, Fief, and me pulled up to Gates of Heaven Cemetery just before they were about to bury you. The day was overcast. You had a charity funeral. From the slot they donated, you could hear cars on the highway shooting by. You were put in a pine box that was nailed shut, with your name misspelled on top. Strangers had handled your body.

Were you still wearing your hospital gown inside?

Gene Murry, the box said, underscored by bold letters reading, *Head*, and *Feet*, to note the direction. Carlos knew how much that bothered me. With his black marker, he drew a flowing angel on the front of your box, and filled in all the correct information: *Jean Marie Murray. August 27, 1954–December 18, 1996. Beloved Mother of Lisa and Elizabeth Murray and Wife of Peter Finnerty.*

Mother. You'd nourished us with your body for nine months, given birth to us, and passed us on to the world. Now that body is cold, unmoving, and forever out of reach.

Wife of Peter Finnerty. He didn't make it to the funeral— something about hopping the train and getting ticketed. I was the one to give Daddy the news, over the phone. I asked if he was sitting down, and he knew. Just remembering the horrible moan he let loose, I am filled with love for him and for you. He needed holding then, but you were gone. You are gone.

You didn't know it, but he kissed you on the mouth in the hospital one day and the nurse scolded him. Said you posed a health hazard. I was glad you didn't hear it. People had done that to you all your life, hadn't they? Treated you like something they needed to back away from. Me too.

Did you feel I'd done the same, Ma, backed away? Deserted you? I will always wonder about that.

Can you imagine Daddy's train rides back to the shelter after visiting you alone? I think of them often, how he might have put his head in his hands the way he does when something is really difficult. Passengers surrounding him, reading the day's news while his wife's body failed and his daughters lived their lives elsewhere. How he must have wished for your body to be healthy again so he didn't have to leave you there, in a building smelling of sickness, filled with machines and the dying. Maybe he couldn't accept the fact that you were one of them, dying. I wouldn't.

We buried you the day after Christmas; it had taken almost a week to locate a free funeral service. The night before, Christmas night, I ate a twelve-dollar turkey dinner in the Riverdale Diner, surrounded by friends. Fief, his cousins, Sam, Lisa, Carlos, me—we were all missing our parents. We helped each other forget about you guys, the mothers and fathers who used to tuck us in, sing at our bedsides. The stars of our dreams and the basis of our reasoning. We banished you with the help of one another.

But I saw the diner's Christmas tree blinking red, orange, and yellow onto Lisa's sad face while she picked at her food, everyone laughing and talking around her. She looked so much like you there, with her petite frame and large, amber eyes. Ma, she's beautiful. She's grown into a beautiful woman, just like you. I wish we were closer so that I could have held her then, the way I want so badly to hold her right now and to hold you, and Daddy.

Someone paid for our meals at the counter. Before we slipped out into the winter air again, Carlos dropped two quarters into the table jukebox and played Sade's "Pearls."

Love Always,
Lizzy

CHAPTER 10

The Wall

THE WEEK AFTER WE BURIED MA, I STOPPED SLEEPING. ANY REST that I got was interrupted by cold shivers and my heart, pounding me awake, beating on the walls of my chest frantically like the wings of a caged bird. When I did manage to sleep, guilt tormented me. I had a recurring nightmare that I turned my back on Ma when she needed me most, and because of it, she kept dying all over again—each time I went to sleep. The nightmares gave me insomnia.

New York City was hit with a record-breaking cold front. Motel management finally responded to complaints about the severe cold and turned up the heat. The air became heavy with steam. As I wrestled with sleep, tangled in the motel sheets, I was drenched in Carlos's and my own sweat. My memory of that time is choppy: the fragrance of a dozen roses he carried to my bedside; their day-by-day, sweet-smelling rot, as Carlos's radio fizzed and crackled; slow jams or old school rap, Slick Rick, Grand Master Flash, The Furious Five. Sam, standing in front of the mirror, smearing black makeup over her eyes, glittery gloss over her lips.

When I was awake, my state of mind was fragile. I could not handle my emotions; they just kept spilling out of me, or else I went numb and silent. By the third night, Carlos had had enough of my behavior. He taunted me with flirty cell phone calls to other girls placed right outside our window, within my view. Then he'd invite Sam for long walks alone, and return several unexplained hours later, toting leftovers from fancy restaurants with French or Italian names spelled in curvy script on grease-stained bags; all places he'd never brought me. I knew I was bad company, my sadness sucking all the air out of the room.

Our last night in the motel together was New Year's Eve, into the infant hours of 1997. Spread out over the beds, the three of us split a bag of sunflower seeds and watched the ball drop on TV. At exactly midnight, a million shreds of multicolored paper rained on Times Square. My first one without you, Ma, I thought.

✦·✦·✦

Carlos disappeared for three days. Without anything of real value left to barter, the hotel manager promised Sam and me that we would be out "on our asses" by eleven a.m. and not a minute later. We waited out the long night in silence, neither of us willing to speak what we both knew to be true: he wasn't coming back this time. I don't remember who started packing first, but I do know we helped each other. Sam jammed her belongings into a suitcase she'd found in the trash: comic books, jars of hair dye, her poetry, ripped-up jeans, and old-man sweaters. Everything I owned went into my backpack: my journal, my mother's NA coin, some clothes, underwear, and the one picture of my mother I carried everywhere, the black-and-white one taken in Greenwich Village when she was homeless at seventeen years old. In defiance, we slammed our stuff into our bags, and what didn't belong to us, we threw at the wall, or we kicked, *hard*, across the room.

Sam had been hiding ten dollars in case of emergency. Because the train was too far a walk and our bags were too heavy, when the sun was up, we took a cab—backpacks in our laps and one garbage bag of clothing each—to Bedford Park Boulevard. We had no idea what was next.

We hadn't meant to split up; it just happened. Sam went to visit Oscar to store her bags. Since it was Sunday, I knew my friends would be home, so I went knocking on doors, Bobby's, Jamie's, Josh's, Fief's, anyplace I could think of knocking. Bobby let me leave my garbage bag of stuff in his closet. I showered at Jamie's place while her mom was out. In the middle of drying my hair, Carlos knocked on Jamie's front door. She looked back at me with her hand still on the doorknob, as though to say, "*What do you want to do about him?*" Carlos's eyes were crazy, darting everywhere.

"I got us another room, Shamrock. Let's go," he said.

I needed a place to stay that I could be certain about. But not knowing when Jamie's mom would be home, or if I could even stay at anyone's place for sure, I ignored my gut and went with him. In the cab, my hair still dripping wet, I asked, "Can we stop and get Sam?"

"We'll come back for her," Carlos said, and I knew better than to push him. His army fatigue outfit had become tattered and was in obvious need of cleaning. He was unshaven, and his Timberland boots were mysteriously missing their laces. With one extended knuckle, he knocked on the Plexiglas cab partition. "New England Thruway, exit twelve plus one," he said.

"What?" the driver asked.

"New England Thruway, exit TWELVE PLUS ONE!!" Carlos yelled, frantically rubbing his fingers through his hair in frustration, looking to me. "The devil's all around me, he ain't gonna make me speak his number. He's screwing with me, Shamrock. I know it." My heart jack-hammered.

"Thirteen?" I asked. "You mean Exit Thirteen?" Carlos flinched at the sound of the number and then nodded slowly, his closed fist over his mouth and his eyes winced shut.

"Yes," he said in a way that was both flat and psychotic. Why did I get in the cab in the first place? I thought. I had no idea what Carlos was on, but I knew he was high on something.

Taking a deep breath, I told the driver, "He wants to take the New England Thruway to exit . . . Thirteen," I said, cringing at Carlos's outburst in Spanish. The cab accelerated.

Quietly, I reached into my bag, sifted through my clothing, and began rubbing my fingers along the rough edges of Ma's Narcotics Anonymous coin. All these years I'd kept that coin; holding it made me feel close to her. In the cab with Carlos, I rubbed it over and over as we zigzagged through traffic.

God grant me the serenity to accept the things I cannot change . . .

Our new crash place was a side-of-the-road stop for truckers and people looking for a few hours of pleasure, called the Holiday Motel. It was not unlike the Van Cortlandt Motel, only now I had no clue where we were. I didn't know how to get to any form of transportation that did not depend on Carlos, and I had a sinking feeling we would not be going back for Sam. At this motel there was nothing but highway, seedy-looking people, Carlos, and me.

✦⋮✦⋱

I decided that being agreeable and quiet was my best bet. Whatever Carlos dictated I went with, even if it didn't agree with me. I was too afraid not to, and he played my fear for everything it was worth. What unfolded was like a spiteful game of Simon Says. "Let's go to the room," he barked after he paid the manager. We went. He held the only room key; I waited. Standing in the cold, I watched him move ever so slowly, checking his beeper, then his phone, holding the key in his hand inches from the lock, keeping us in the icy outdoors, just because he could. Several times over the next few days, spontaneously, he called out "Time to eat!" It was—and not a moment earlier or later than he said so. I grabbed my coat and followed. When the cash register rang up, not once but twice, a total of $13.50 for our meal, he pounded the counter and walked out, abandoning our takeout food, impossibly out of reach behind the counter, leaving me hungry. And when he left the motel some evenings with no answer as to whether or not he would be back, I waited then, too.

Those nights come back to me often, the nights I spent alone in the Holiday Motel on exit "12 + 1" on the New England Thruway. Those nights were *my* bottom.

Watching the windows for Carlos, listening to the endless prostitution through the thin wooden walls, no money to use the phone, I had no place to escape to. Daddy told me that he once spent eight weeks in solitary confinement in prison, and all he had to entertain him was a single book. He said he began hallucinating the characters of that book; they began to talk to him, becoming his only companions. I paced the small motel room at night, frantic, heartbroken about Ma, slowly unraveling.

My thoughts fixated on the people in my own life, and how they defined my options. *Where would I go if I left?* To Bobby's? That wouldn't last. To Jamie's? Her mother was a foster care caseworker. She would be just waiting to "help" me go back into a group home, so I couldn't stay there long. After what I'd seen at St. Anne's—the mean girls, the indifferent staff, and the prisonlike environment—I was never going to a place like that again. Back to Brick's apartment? Mr. Doumbia was looking for me there, so that was like choosing the group home. No way.

I was stuck. I tried to numb myself with sleep and television, but thoughts of Ma kept intruding: the damn pine box they buried her in, the coarse nails holding it together. *Was she wearing her hospital gown inside the box? I told her I'd see her "later." I'd really thought I had a later. . . . But if I had her NA coin, if Lisa and Brick still had her clothing hanging in the closet, could she really be dead?* As Carlos's insanity escalated, much like getting caught downstream in a strong current, I felt like I was going right along with him.

Over the next two weeks, whenever Carlos returned from long mysterious hours "out," he emptied his pockets onto the motel table: his black and gold Latin King beads, tubes of antibiotic ointment for his growing number of tattoos, a handgun, Ziploc bags full of pills, block-shaped bricks of weed, and, curiously, two cans of soda. From under the blankets, I would squint in the dim hanging light as he twisted the cap off a fake Coca-Cola can and pulled out a plastic bag of white powder that was undoubtedly cocaine. Standing before a wall lined with mirrors and tacky maroon carpet wallpaper, Carlos turned to me and held the bogus can and the baggie side by side. Counting his reflections, there were three of him. He made an amused gesture with his eyebrows, finding humor in his hiding cocaine in a Coke can.

The one saving grace was that Carlos ceased trying to be physical with me; instead, coming in at dawn those cold January mornings, he kicked off his snow-covered boots and pulled a blanket over himself on the floor. This was both a relief and unnerving for me, because if we didn't speak and we weren't sleeping with each other, what was holding us together at all? And yet my memory stubbornly recalled intense brown eyes gazing at me affectionately and his heartbeat as I slept on his chest. Carlos had once been a source of comfort and of love. He'd cared for Ma, just the way he said he'd cared for his own dad when AIDS took hold. It was hard to be angry at him after all we'd been through, but it wasn't hard to be afraid.

After too many awkward nights of silence and too many disappearances, I risked a couple of questions. One night I used my most timid voice to ask, gingerly, "So where are you headed? Can I come with you? . . . Can we go get Sam?"

I didn't have Oscar's number, and everywhere I called, none of our friends had heard from Sam. I was worried. I was also sick of eating our half-rotten leftovers and watching the window, unsure of whether he'd return. Something had to change. Carlos responded to my questions with a sneer, his jaw slack, a hateful look in his eyes. But we hadn't eaten all day, and unless I pressed him, I might not eat for yet another. I didn't want him to leave without me.

Very gently, I asked again, "Carlos, did you hear me? Can I come with you?" My heart pounded.

Slowly he walked toward me, then he moved very quickly, his arm cocked back. *Wham!* His fist came flying past my head and split the wall's wooden paneling on impact. I screamed. He pulled back his huge fist again, as though readying to punch me in the face. I flinched and raised my arms protectively. Looking me up and down with his fist held high, he laughed. "Stupid," he muttered before walking to the bathroom. I was shaking; I curled up against the headboard and didn't dare say another word. Never before had he threatened violence.

But maybe that wasn't true. Carlos had a silent way of establishing control, ensuring that you just knew not to press him. He was muttering to himself in front of the sink, slamming objects down in the bathroom. I did not dare move or speak. For what felt like forever, I watched Carlos through the mirror as he gelled his hair back, perfected his goatee with a disposable razor, put on his gold rings, and finally stuffed the gun in his belt and his drugs back into the zipper pocket of his army fatigues. He slipped out into the cold, silently.

"*Cops Charge Beau in Stab*," read the January 13 headline in the *New York Daily News*. The write-up was more factual than sentimental. It stated plainly that the woman "had been stabbed about the body and her throat was cut; she was left to die on the motel room floor." It was a single incident of violence against a woman, perpetrated by her boyfriend, in a city where things like this happened all the time. In fact, boyfriend-perpetrated stabbings were not even new at what the paper called this "hot-sheet" motel, at which drug dealing, police raids, and violence against women was the norm.

But I didn't have to wait for the news report to learn about the stabbing; I had only to lift my curtain. At the time, I had been watching the news on television while Carlos was out. At first, it didn't completely sink in: a reporter talking in front of some motel, delivering a story about the gruesome murder of a woman at a dive on the New England Thruway. The motel maid discovered the body, which at that very moment was being wheeled silently into an ambulance behind the wide-eyed reporter. It could have been an episode of Daddy's favorite show, *Law & Order*. Instead, it was a real murder—right outside my window. Rosa Morilla, age thirty-nine, mother of five, had bled out on the floor of her room in the Holiday Motel, just three doors down from my room. I jumped up to look out the window, lifted the curtain, and saw the reporter. It was like having two different TV sets to watch, with two different camera angles. I looked back and forth between the television and out my window to see the same view: Ms. Morilla in a body bag, the ambulance doors slammed, the reporter's blinding portable light shining on her overly made-up face.

I shut everything off, light and TV, and crawled under the blankets. Through the dark, I listened to the police radios crackling, the dozens of footsteps crunching snow, the maids speaking frantically in Spanish. "No," I spoke to the empty room. "Goddamnit." Just a few hours later, you could have never guessed it happened. With the reporter long gone, the police packed up and departed, the whole motel was back to business as usual, as though Rosa Morilla never existed. As though she was not the mother of five children; as if she had not been someone's daughter or sister; as if she didn't even matter.

Turns out people could just vanish. I couldn't help but sit there and think about the woman who'd been murdered a few feet from my room. How had she gotten there, in a seedy motel room with a violent man who claimed he loved her? And was I really any different?

Maybe originally I had loved Carlos, and I wanted the future he said we would have together. I'd wanted him to have his inheritance and a place of his own. I'd wanted to love him the way he'd never been loved. But that future dimmed a long time ago. And now I stayed because I was afraid of him and felt stuck without him. I thought I needed him.

I couldn't help but wonder, What if it had been Carlos and me instead of Rosa and her boyfriend? What if it had been my name the reporter uttered? *Sixteen-year-old Elizabeth Murray allegedly murdered at the hands of her boyfriend, eighteen-year-old drug dealer* . . . I imagined what it would do to Daddy, Lisa, Sam, and Bobby—all the people I loved—if my life ended like that.

The hotel maid took pity and gave me a couple of quarters. I used them to dial Jamie. "I need your help. Can you talk to your mom and see if I can come stay with you? I need to leave, now."

Jamie's apartment was one stop in a series of different friends' homes, patches of refuge as I carved out what was next, this time alone. Jamie had a fierce argument with her mom, and I was granted one week's stay. I'll never forget Jamie's kindness—how she didn't even question me, just helped any way she could, like family. She borrowed cab money from her mom, washed my clothes while I took a steaming hot shower, made us tuna-fish sandwiches with the crusts cut off and hot bowls of chicken soup. On the futon with her at night we fell asleep side by side, clean and warm. Carlos was far away from me, and I felt safe. If it were her choice, I could have stayed longer. But none of my friends had their own places, so it was all about whose place, on which night. And it was all up in the air from here on.

I bounced around aimlessly from one home to another those first few weeks. Sam called to reach me at Bobby's a few times, but I kept missing her. She was safe, in a group home on 241st Street. When I dialed the number she'd left, a girl named Lilah picked up and took a message.

"Naw, Sam ain't here, she out. You wanna leave a message or sumthin'?"

"Tell her it's Liz, and I'm at Bobby's tonight if she wants to call me back. Sam is the Puerto Rican girl with short blue hair. Please make sure she gets the message."

"I *know* who she is," the girl blurted. "I'm her best friend!"

She hung up. Sam had moved on . . . out of nowhere, she was gone, too. It was really going to be just me for now, figuring it out.

Once, in the middle of the night, I had to leave Fief's house when his mom and dad got into an argument. Bobby didn't mind the late-night surprise; he actually seemed very happy to see me. When I popped in on him, he'd already dressed for bed, in shorts made from cut-up jeans and a faded T-shirt bearing the McDonald's logo, only it read MARIJUANA instead, right beneath the golden arches. Seeing the way his warm eyes brightened the moment he opened the door, I realized only then how much I really missed him—missed Bedford Park, the group, and our hangouts. I had stopped a few people outside to ask for money and I brought Chinese food, careful not to come empty-handed.

"Pork fried rice with no vegetables and chicken with broccoli, no broccoli, just the way you like it," I said first thing, lifting the bag up high, in the hallway.

He smiled that half smirk, pressing a finger to his lips, while he led me inside the warm, dimly lit apartment. His mother was getting her last few hours' sleep before her early-morning shift at the hospital. The cat, a gray tiger-striped, was rummaging through the kitchen trash pail. A drawing of his little sister's, a butterfly colored purple and yellow all jagged and outside of the lines, was magnetized to the fridge.

We unwrapped the food in front of his TV. A taped episode of wrestling had just ended. Beside the screen, a picture of Bobby and his girlfriend, Diane, passionately kissing at a wedding was framed, her shiny, black hair falling over her shoulders. Bobby's math homework was spread out over his black futon, shapes and various angles stenciled on the white sheets, his answers penned in beside them. Being in a real home instead of wasting away with Carlos in that motel room was like rejoining the land of the living. Looking at Bobby's papers, his healthy, handsome face, his relationship, it was obvious that the whole thing—society, reality, *life*—had been going on without me, while I had been spacing out in some morbid fantasyland. Next to him, I felt like a ghostly emanation from limbo.

"So, wow. How've you been?" he asked.

"What do you mean?" I said suspiciously. Sitting there, staring at Bobby's stable life, the question felt almost rhetorical. Didn't I look as raggedy as I felt? My clothing was dirty, my hair was greasy and wild.

"Well, I just mean, I dunno, how are you? I know it's been rough, with your mom and everything. And it's been hard, too, Liz . . . not being able to get in touch with you. I wanted to be there for you about everything. So I was just wondering how you're doing." His hair was freshly wet from a shower, combed away from his face, and his eyes were earnest, full of concern. Coming from the motel, it was hard not to be defensive. I had to keep in mind that I wasn't dealing with Carlos; that there were good, sane people in the world.

"Sorry . . . I'm just tired." I kept my eyes on the ground, trying not to show my embarrassment. "A lot's been going on. But I guess you could say that I'm all right."

"All right? That it?" he asked, scooping a spoonful of rice into his mouth. His curiosity was sincere. Looking at him, I relaxed and reminded myself that I actually had friends who really loved me. With Bobby, I was safe.

"Yeah . . . you know right now, that *is* it. I'm all right." And I was. Letting go of Carlos had freed me, jolted me out of some slumber. I felt unusually lighthearted. "Tell me how *you've* been."

We ate while Bobby played back his old wrestling VHS tape, pausing every so often so he could teach me all the correct names to the moves; Razor's Edge, the Tombstone, Elbow Drop. But my eyes kept going back to his math homework spread out on the futon. His penmanship, racy and dark-pressed, seemed confident.

". . . These are the main guys," he said, moving his hands around for emphasis. "But ECW—that's Extreme Championship Wrestling—now *they're* for real. When it comes to actual violence—"

"Bobby," I interrupted. "What's high school like?"

After that night, I finished the rest of the week around the corner, at Fief's. The week after, I jumped from place to place. It was hard to get a full night's rest because I often had to sneak in after parents had gone to bed and be out again before they woke up, but I did manage about four hours a night. At Myers's place, there was this sleeping bag he'd taken camping only once. When he rolled it out for me between his computer table and bed, I took up the only free space in his small, rectangular room.

Jamie's mom made rice and beans, and Jamie split her portions in half with me while we played Nine Inch Nails tapes and gossiped about guys or talked about old movies in her kitchen at night. At Bobby's apartment, I could get the best showers. I savored the fresh smell of his Pantene shampoo, his blue, perfumed bars of Coast soap, and the use of his mom's tampons and deodorant.

My friends fed me, or sometimes I panhandled just enough money to get a plate of fries drenched in mozzarella cheese and gravy at Tony's diner. Tony would let me sit there to eat it, keeping warm for hours. But when there was no one to reach out to, I'd shoplift at C-Town, stealing whatever I could get my hands on. I was bold, fearless, shoving bread, cheese squeeze, and seedless green grapes into my backpack or into the pouch of my hooded sweatshirt. Anything, as long as I could eat enough to make the pains in my stomach go away. This wasn't the hard part. If I needed something, I could figure out how to get it, the same way I had figured out my needs my whole life. No food at home? Go pack bags at the supermarket, go pump gas. Ma and Daddy too chaotic? Leave. School sucks? Don't go. Simple. I had always been able to meet my needs. No, the hard part about being on my own turned out to be something else altogether.

With Sam and Carlos by my side, knocking on doors and living off the help of my friends had been manageable. If I ever felt self-conscious asking for help, I could always tell myself that we were all just being "social," the three of us were coming over to "visit." But being homeless alone turned everything upside down. It revealed just how needy I was, and I hated that.

Yes, sometimes I could stay over, but not without a cost. It was the little things that got to me. The way I'd hear the smallest whispers over the stove around dinnertime at Bobby's place; Bobby and his mom, in hushed voices, would debate if there was enough food that particular night to split with me. Or how from the hallway of Jamie's building, I could hear her arguments with her mom, the knock-down, drag-out battles to get me to stay one more night. Even Fief's apartment could get tricky, when he disappeared to Yonkers for weeks to see his cousins, and his dad answered the door to tell me he didn't know when Fief was coming back. They were my friends, but I was something else . . . I was "Need a place to stay, can you spare a plate of food? Do you have another blanket? Mind if I use the shower? Do you have any extra . . . ?" That's what I was, and I couldn't stand being that.

Not only was this not who I wanted to be, but it was also terrifying, because as much as my friends, my new family, were helping me, I had to wonder: When would they stop? At what point would I become too much? When would they start saying no? This couldn't go on forever. And just the thought of being in dire need and having to, one day, hear my friends flat-out say no to my hunger and my need for shelter—and to turn away from my desperation—well, the thought of that rejection was just too much to deal with. I dreaded that moment of "no" that I sensed was coming. What does it feel like, the moment someone you love turns you down? I didn't want to find out. So I decided it was better to stop needing so much. It wouldn't be instant, and it would take some time, but I resolved to never be so needy again.

And then, this back-against-the-wall situation gave me another piece of clarity: Friends don't pay your rent. It was a simple and powerful thought. It hit me as I was trying to sleep on Bobby's futon one night. But as simple as that thought was, it caused a huge shift in my thinking. Friends are great. They are loving, they are supportive, they are fun—but friends don't pay your rent. I never really had to worry about rent before, but now that I absolutely had to worry, I was trying to grasp the concept of actually *getting an apartment* and *gathering the money for rent* when it hit me: everything I had been obsessing about (Carlos, friends, hanging out, thinking about my past)—none of it paid my rent. Paying rent would require something new to focus on.

After a few weeks of being so dependent on people, I began sleeping a few nights a week on the subway, alone. Into the far corner of the subway car, I appeared just like any other traveler taking public transportation, rocked to sleep by the train's rhythm, well on my way home. No one had to know. But this wasn't safe. Sometimes thugs boarded the train, teenage guys in hoods, their pants sagging, barking loud words to one another, dominating the subway car. I'd awoken a few times to their stares, but never anything more. It was luck. So I chose hallways as my main refuge; they were a better bet.

The top landing of any Bedford Park building's stairwell felt so much safer. Lying there, flat on a bed of marble, using my backpack for a pillow, whole lives played out beneath me: the smell of food cooking; lovers' arguments; dishes clanking; TVs blasting at top volume; my old shows, *The Simpsons* and *Jeopardy!*; rap music—all carrying me back to University Avenue. Mostly, though, I heard families: children calling out for mothers, husbands speaking their wives' names, sending me reminders of the way love stretched between a handful of people fills a space, transforms it into a home. I wondered how Lisa was doing at Brick's. How was she dealing with school when we had just lost Ma? I didn't have the strength to call her; I knew I just couldn't handle the questions I was sure she'd ask: *"What are you doing out there, Liz? What are you going to do with your life? Are you going back to school?"* It was too much to deal with, so I stayed away.

Many nights, I longed for home. But it occurred to me as I struggled for a feeling of comfort and safety: I have no idea where home is.

Sometimes, waking up, I didn't initially recognize where I was. For those first few seconds, it could be University Avenue, the footsteps nearby, Ma and Daddy getting ready to binge for the night. Or Brick's place, Sam somewhere right within my reach. But when my eyes adjusted, it was always someone else's personal touches, their family's noises surrounding me, and their scents in the air. I was at Bobby's, Fief's, or one of a few other random places I'd sometimes go, the apartments of friends' friends.

I spent almost a week in this one girl's place. The guys were all crashing there a lot, hanging out with Danny, a friend of Bobby's who had always come and gone through our group of friends over the years and had become someone I counted as a friend, someone in my tribe. He was a tall, light-skinned Puerto Rican guy with large hazel eyes, handsome. Like Bobby, Danny loved video games and hanging out with our group. He always had a different girlfriend, and several other girls who thought they were his girlfriend. Paige was his latest. He had just moved in with her, and brought the group of us along with him to hang out.

Paige was twenty-two years old, a former runaway, grown up. Danny told me she'd done really well for herself, had a steady job and her own apartment, which she could pay for without a roommate. It was a tiny, one-bedroom apartment above a Chinese restaurant, so small that you could roll right out of the living room and into the kitchen because they were actually the same tiny room. But it was all hers. She made it happen herself.

When Paige cooked chicken and rice for all of us, the smell and the heat filled the small space like a sauna. That was when her curly hair moistened to her temples, making it cling. She wiped it back before speaking.

"Are you sure you're not looking for a GED?" she asked me while lowering a steaming dinner plate onto my lap.

"No. I've been thinking I want to get my high school diploma," I told her. "I'm really not interested in a GED. I've heard they're great, but it's not what I'm looking for. . . . But it's hard for me to be in school, ya know? It's crowded, and I feel really behind."

"Well, my old high school might be the perfect place for you then," Paige said as she filled a dinner plate for Danny.

From Paige I learned what an alternative high school in New York City was like. "It's a place like a private school, but for anyone who is really motivated to go, even if they don't have the money. The teachers really care about you," she told me.

I scrawled the name and address of her school down in my journal while she went on, speaking about her experiences in high school, trailing off into a story about an ex-boyfriend. As she spoke, I took my pen and darkened in the phone number to her school, until I gave the digits dimension, a life of their own that soared up from the page.

Later, when the apartment was dark and everyone was sleeping, I took over her loveseat and wrote by the nightstand light.

On one page, I made a list:

Things to Look Forward to When I Eventually Get a Place:
1. Privacy
2. Being warm all the time
3. Food, any time I want
4. A big bed!!!
5. Clean clothes, socks especially!
6. Sleeping and no one wakes me up
7. Warm baths

I turned to the next blank page and tapped my pen down a few times. The hall clock was ticking. All over the walls were Paige's abstract paintings from her high school art class, vivid reds, yellows, and greens splashed across big, beige canvases. I studied a photograph tacked up beside the paintings; a woman who looked like an older version of Paige with curlier hair was wearing her Sunday best, standing beside a stout man with a salt-and-pepper beard and a tie. Paige was sandwiched between them. "That was at my graduation," Paige had told me earlier. "We took a million shots that day. Yeah, my art teacher cried, sad to see me go," she'd said.

I tapped on my journal's empty page again, and wrote:

Number of credits required for graduation from high school
40? . . . 42? (find this out)

My age when the next school year will begin
17

My current address
Wherever I am staying at the moment

My current total of high school credits
1

It would have been zero credits, except that every now and then I used to swing by John F. Kennedy High School with Sam. She didn't even officially go to my high school, but with more than six thousand students enrolled, who would notice one extra? Together, Sam and I sat in the back of Ms. Nedgrin's overcrowded social studies class and performed an act you could call "I'm totally weird, look at me." Sam's hair back then was fire-engine red, held in a bun with large chopsticks, and her black makeup was caked around her eyes like a raccoon. I was Goth and wore all black, as I had almost every day since I got out of the group home. For a matching accessory to my outfit, I shoplifted and proudly wore a black leather dog collar, crowned with silver studs. Our clothing was torn up in holes that were "cool." It just so happened that on one of the days when I sauntered into Ms. Nedgrin's classroom, I took a social studies test and passed. This is the reason I was given the one high school credit. Well, that and the pity Ms. Nedgrin took on me.

With no in-class preparation, I had scored an 81 out of 100 on an exam, and this got her curious enough to pull me out in the hall one day to plead with me to come to school. "You're a smart girl," she said. "I read your file. . . . Your mother is sick, isn't she? You've been in placement before?" Her eyes were watery and sympathetic.

"Yeah," was all I said, avoiding eye contact.

My whole life teachers had acted that way, like they felt sorry for me. The Westchester-living, string-of-pearls-wearing ladies took one look at my life and it always made them sad. And anyway, if she thought I was so smart, she was mistaken. The only reason I passed the test was because I read one of Daddy's books that was on the same subject, the Civil War. And the questions on her test were super basic. Really, what I did wasn't as impressive as she thought it was. And why was she crying? She stood there with her crisp, royal blue dry-clean-only dress and her eyes filled with worry, wiping away tears. She hugged me and said something, words that I held on to for years: "I understand why you don't come to school, and it's not your fault. You are a *victim* of these things, I understand, sweetheart. It's okay."

For all of Ms. Nedgrin's good intentions, I'd heard only one thing she said, and that was that I didn't have to do my schoolwork, for reasons that were not my fault. I was a "victim." She understood. Well, I didn't want to do my work anyway, so, great.

That was the last time I showed up to school at Kennedy, and when my report card arrived in the mail at Brick's place, there it was, a row of F's and a single D, just one passing grade from Ms. Nedgrin's class. I was the same age as someone getting ready to enter college and this was my entire high school education so far—one pity credit.

Under the light of Paige's end table lamp, I used my pen to continue darkening in the phone number and address in my journal, and along with it some new words, *alternative high school*.

When I woke up in the morning, Paige was stepping around everyone sprawled out, sleeping and snoring across the floor. She had on a BLOCKBUSTER VIDEO shirt, tucked neatly into khaki pants; her hair was pulled into a tight bun. She was searching for her keys. I watched her silently for a moment, walking beside all these sleeping people, being the only productive one. In that moment, I looked up to her, for the way she just made things happen. Out of the corner of my eye, I spotted her bright orange Garfield key chain, partially concealed under a magazine.

I sat up and grabbed her keys. "Hold on, Paige," I whispered. "I'll leave with you."

After she nodded permission, I swiped two quarters off the fridge, pulled my jeans over a pair of Carlos's boxers that I'd worn to sleep, and hurried to follow Paige out the door. My eyes ached in the morning sun. By then, months had passed since I left the motel, and the weather was warming up, the trees beginning to bud little green leaves, and birds were out. I threw my jacket over my shoulder. Paige wore her headphones, humming to something, and she smelled strongly of a fruity lotion when I hugged her good-bye.

We separated on her corner. Stores were just opening, workers rattling their gates open for business. An old man swept the sidewalk in front of the Chinese restaurant beneath Paige's windows. As she faded into the distance, I took out my journal and flipped it open to the page where I'd written the number. I dropped the quarters into the phone, hesitated, and hung up. Picking the receiver back up, I began dialing slowly. I started over twice more before I got all the way through, and took a deep breath.

2-1-2-5-7-0 . . .

"Hello. H-how are you? My name is Liz Murray. I'd like to make an appointment. . . . Yes, um to come in for an interview . . . for the upcoming semester."

In the coming weeks I located, researched, and interviewed with as many alternative high schools as I could find. Something in my gut told me to focus on Manhattan, probably because Daddy always held up Manhattan as the place where people go to get things done. I liked the feel of taking the number 4 train or the D train to various stops on the east and west sides of the city; I'd wear my black jeans and black T-shirt, my book bag with all my belongings on my lap. I'd ride the train beside business types with their newspapers and appointments to travel to. My ears were pierced up and down on both sides and I wore my greasy hair waist-length, the front of which I used to cover my eyes. Reading the addresses I'd scribbled into my journal, I'd walk through side streets to huge Manhattan buildings, moving along sidewalks that were teeming with people, until I found the actual location of the schools that I'd been dialing from pay phones in the Bronx. Sometimes I'd pace outside the building for a little while, taking deep breaths, mustering the courage to enter.

It took everything I had to walk into those buildings. I did not want to enter them. For years, maybe for my whole life, it felt as though there was a brick wall down the middle of everything. Standing outside those buildings, I could almost picture it. On one side of the wall there was society, and on the other side there was me, us, the people in the place I came from. Separate. We were separate. The feeling in my heart was of the world being divided into an "us" versus "them," and everyone on the other side of the wall felt like "those people." The everyday working people on the train, the smart students who raised their hands in class and got everything right, the functional families, the people who went away to college—they all felt like "those people" to me. And then there were people like us: the dropouts, welfare cases, truants, and discipline problems. Different. And there were specific things that made us different.

For one thing, in my family and for the people in our neighborhood, the pace of life was frantic, determined solely by immediate needs: hunger, rent, heat, the electric bill. A standard of "for right now" was applied to every dilemma. Welfare wasn't a solid life plan, but for right now bills were due and the check must be cashed. Ma and Daddy shouldn't be getting high, but for right now Ma had the shakes and needed her fix. I should go to school, but for right now I had no clean clothes and I'd already fallen too far behind. Thirty-five dollars of groceries wouldn't feed all four of us for a month, but for right now we could sure try. On our side of the wall, priority was given to whatever thing might solve the most immediate problem. This is why the lives of those on the other side of the wall held so much mystery for me.

How was it that anyone ended up possessing oddities such as a savings account, a car, or a house that they actually owned? How exactly did anyone go about getting and maintaining a job? And what was the thinking that got people to take four extra years of school after they'd already earned a high school diploma? Why would anyone go to school for four extra years? For people on our side of the wall, talking about the future always meant our near future, and our greatest concern was the immediate solution to our most urgent needs. We did not set our sights on anything as lofty as long-term planning. Sure, for us, there was always a chance that we might make a better life one day, but for right now, there were more pressing things to worry about.

Walking into those schools was like visiting the other side of the wall, and interviewing with teachers meant talking to "those people." This entire process was my first-ever attempt at having life be about something broader than the needs right in front of me, and it felt risky and forbidden. My lack of familiarity with these massive, official-looking buildings made them feel unwelcoming, and their promise for advancement seem untouchable to me. The schools might as well have been any stockbroker building on Wall Street or a high-end jewelry store on Fifth Avenue, or even the White House; walking into those schools was as ridiculous as walking into any one of those places, because it meant walking onto "their" side. It took all the courage I had to enter those buildings, my heart pounding the whole time.

The interviews were a big disappointment. There is a distinct look someone gives when they are not really listening. It's a blank kind of a stare that involves lots of unnecessary nodding. It comes with the "toothless grin," as Daddy often called that fake, thin smile people put on when they are placating you. I knew by the way some teachers looked at me that the answer was "no" before the interview even started. I'd get the once-over, the head-to-toe scan of someone taking me in superficially and labeling me: Goth, truant, trouble. And then came the toothless grin and the BS: "Our spots are limited, thank you for applying," and "If something opens up, we will contact you at home."

Well, they would contact me at Bobby's house, whose address I'd given them. But when they did, it was only to say, "*No*, sorry, we are all full this semester. . . . We'd like to take you, but given your limited amount of credits, we need to say *no* and give someone else a chance. . . . *No*, sorry, we don't think it would be a good fit." Who wanted to take someone old enough to be graduating, with an F average and almost no credits, so I could *begin* my education at their school? Particularly when I did not make eye contact and looked like, well, me? Across the board, the answer was a straight "no."

Being told "no" wasn't so bad the first few times, but after several rejections, I could feel my resolve slipping. Exiting from yet another "no" one sunny afternoon, I stomped down a crowded city block angry, ready to drop the whole thing. It would have been easy. Danny, Fief, Bobby, or Jamie—*somebody*—would house me until I figured out something. And maybe I could even go back to the block and look for Carlos. I could always go back to him. I sat down to think.

The corner of Lexington and Sixty-fifth Street was bustling with people—Hunter College students, office types breaking for their power lunches, the long line at the hot dog stand. The day was unusually hot for an early May afternoon in Manhattan. I counted my options. I had enough money in my pocket to do one of two things. One, I could afford the subway fare to the next interview, someplace called Humanities Preparatory Academy. Or I could take the train back to the Bronx, about an hour's ride, and still afford some pizza.

But I could not do both. Weighing my options, I sat on the stone partition in front of the college, and I did some people-watching.

Pizza or interview?

I was so tired—tired of interviews, tired of getting rejected, tired of hearing no. And if I was going to be told no anyway, what was the point? At least if I left now, I could still afford some pizza. If I was being realistic, there was a high probability I was wasting my time.

But sitting there, I started thinking, Well, what if? Yes, it was likely that this school would be like all the others, but what if the answer just this one time wasn't no? The thought had struck me out of nowhere, and I found it as compelling as it was simple. "What if? What if, despite all the evidence I had that said it wouldn't work out, what if this very next time, just this once, it turned out to be the school that let me in?"

The thought made my heart swell with a rush of emotion that suddenly made me miss Ma. I became lonely on that sidewalk by myself, surrounded by all those people. My mind was racing. One minute I had a home, a family, a roof over my head, and loved ones to orient me in the world. And now I was on Sixty-fifth Street and Ma was dead, Daddy was gone, Lisa and I were separated. Everything was different.

Life has a way of doing that; one minute everything makes sense, the next, things change. People get sick. Families break apart, your friends could close the door on you. The rapid changes I had experienced were hitting me hard as I sat there, and yet sadness wasn't what came up in my gut. Out of nowhere, for whatever reason, a different feeling snuck up in its place, hope. If life could change for the worst, I thought, then maybe life could change for the better.

It was *possible* that I could get into the next school, and it was even *possible* I could get straight A's. Yes, based on all the things that happened before, it wasn't necessarily realistic, but it was possible that I could change everything.

I ditched the idea of pizza and went for the interview.

In the mid-1990s, the Bayard Rustin High School for the Humanities was in trouble. They faced a problem of severe overcrowding, with 2,400 students enrolled in a school meant to hold no more than 1,500. In the overpacked classrooms there were lots of kids who were failing. Morale among the teaching staff was low and cynicism high. A handful of teachers who sat on a governing committee called School Based Management (SBM) within the school proposed a desperate solution: segregate the failing kids from everyone else, give them only basic classes and their teachers the benefit of fewer classes to teach, and get them out of the building by noon. Behind the scenes, a small group of teachers nicknamed the project Failure Academy.

Failure Academy would be a small thing, a separate school lodged in the back bottom corner of the building within the much larger High School for the Humanities on Eighteenth Street, between Eighth and Ninth avenues in Chelsea. The plan was for it to be populated by the hundred-plus students who were screwing up their education so badly that they were seen as a detraction within the mainstream school. The thinking was, with the help of this program, the larger school could focus on educating those kids who were actually performing, while the students of Failure Academy could be segregated, parked in the annex for those from whom no one expected too much. And this is exactly what the school would have been, if not for Perry Weiner.

The chairman of the board of SBM and a passionate English teacher for many years, Perry was absolutely indignant about the idea of segregation, and he challenged the committee to instead start a real alternative high school that met the needs of these struggling students. Several people supported Perry, including the chairman of the teachers' union, Vincent Brevetti, another man who dedicated his life to empowering young people through the betterment of education. Together, Perry and Vince spent months meeting to design a school that would serve, rather than "park," this at-risk population of kids who had failed within the structure of mainstream education. The two men became a team.

Every morning at seven a.m., Perry and Vince would arrive at school for an hour or more of planning. The school they were building would be so much more than a dropout prevention program. Rather than base the model of their alternative school on what was *not* working with the troubled students, they decided to seek out an educational model that *did* work, one that had already proven to be highly successful. They visited and observed other high schools, ones that catered to more elite and privileged populations of kids. What they found in the design of those schools deeply inspired them, and they returned to Chelsea determined.

The students of so-called Failure Academy would instead become the students of Humanities Preparatory Academy. "Prep," as Perry and Vince began calling it, would become a mini-school that provided at-risk students the opportunities and privileges of a personalized education traditionally reserved only for those who could afford elite private schooling. The design of Prep would be radically different from typical mainstream education.

Prep would cap the number of students at 180, so that pupils could benefit from one-on-one attention from teachers. High-stakes tests would not be the measure of a student's success at Prep, for the feeling was that it narrowed the curriculum and the students' ability to demonstrate their real knowledge. Instead, something called Performance-Based Assessment Tasks took their place. PBATs were a rigorous and personalized means of testing students by allowing them to respond to test questions in depth, as opposed to the traditional fill-in-the-blank style of high-stakes New York State Regents exams, which in so many cases were the catalyst for students failing. Instead, PBATs would require students to produce thorough, in-depth work that demonstrated real world knowledge and application of their semester-long classes. This could be done a number of ways, via portfolios, extended writing projects, or even through classroom presentations wherein a student was given the opportunity to teach the class the lessons they learned throughout a semester. In doing this, PBATs would open the space for an alternative curriculum, and with it, a way for teachers to teach students differently.

So courses at Prep expanded beyond standard names and themes such as Global 1,2,3, and Literature 2, trading them in for dynamic classes like Facing History & Ourselves, in which students studied the implications of genocide, and Themes in Humanity, in which these formerly failing students would read Dante's *Inferno* or Kafka. English 1 would become Shakespeare on Stage, and students would comprehend and perform *Hamlet* to earn their English credit.

Far more than mere name changes, the courses themselves were meant to cultivate an environment of authenticity and encourage depth of thought. To do this, classrooms were capped at around fifteen students per class. This way, student and teacher alike sat in a circle of chairs, looking one another in the eyes for an active, heavily participatory discussion-based lesson. There would be no place for a student to hide out at Prep, no place for them to get lost, and no place where they might be forgotten.

For Perry, Prep was a labor of love; he was dedicated to seeing his second-chance students win. His belief was that if the mainstream school system had failed, then it would require something different for these students to succeed. Prep would be that difference. In this way, the students were not looked at as dysfunctional; the system was dysfunctional. The concept of "failure" incorporated within the system's very design was not in any stage of the planning of Humanities Prep. By design, Prep was made to facilitate for its students what was possible.

I flew through the double doors fifteen minutes late, my forehead broken into beads of sweat, the bun I'd attempted curling with flyaways. Humanities Preparatory Academy. I read and reread my journal page to ensure that I was in the right building. The place looked so small, like the back office of an actual school.

The main office, Prep's only office, contained a set of four sectioned-off cubicles with walls that didn't quite touch the ceiling. Filing cabinets had been rolled into the short partitions that made up each room; one had a shipment sticker still stuck to the side of it, with the school's address penned onto the boxes from their delivery. A fan whirred from on top of a bookcase that was filled with random, secondhand books. Above it, a faded poster read, LIFE REWARDS ACTION, in bold, purple script. The secretary, April, an African American woman with pretty eyes, instructed me to have a seat in the waiting area, which was a row of classroom chairs strung along the wall across from her desk.

"You're late. They started without you," she said, tilting her head, gold jewelry dangling from her neck, wrists, and ears. "Don't worry, Perry will be out real soon and you can talk to him."

Looking down at the last cubicle, to the far left, through a thin glass window in a door, I saw a chalkboard with a sentence written and underlined on top:

Pick one of the following topics and write an essay on its meaning.
Diversity
Community
Leadership

A middle-aged white man with a goatee and glasses led a discussion that was mostly muted behind the partition. He was dressed in dark corduroys and a maroon tie. The first thing I noticed about him was that he seemed to laugh and smile easily. He looked friendly. Five or so young people sat in a semi-circle around him, listening and answering questions at length. I pulled out my pen and got to work on the essay. I didn't know what I could write about community or leadership, so I chose diversity because my mind went to the discrimination I faced in my old schools.

For three pages, I detailed the way people assumed things about me based on appearance, my race, or my being unkempt. They'd called me *blanquita*, little white girl, for so many years on University Avenue. "You must be rich, white girl, snotty, too," they'd hiss as I went through the halls of Junior High School 141. I also went on about the way I was often stared at for my Goth clothing in my previous high school interviews. In detail I described the anger I felt when I knew a teacher had rejected me before really listening. Written with sloppy blue penmanship, my paragraphs were fat and long. Reading them over, I felt they made a coherent point about diversity and discrimination. It was the first writing assignment I'd completed in years. I chewed on my pen. The meeting I should have been in suddenly let out.

I had to stop the teacher. He was on his way out, dashing past me.

"S-sir," I said. "Sir." He turned and smiled warmly.

"Hello," he said, his open hand extended. "Perry." He finished his sentence laughing, looking directly into my eyes. I looked away. He was one of "those people" on the other side of the wall. The intensity of his eye contact caught me off guard and made my heart pound; I flinched when he put out his hand, stared at it too long, and grabbed hold to shake it only at the last possible moment.

"Hi, I had an appointment to be in there, too."

"Elizabeth—" he held up a notepad—". . . Murray. What happened?" he asked, raising his eyes from reading, looking at me through his glasses. His to-tally focused attention made me uneasy, but it also made him interesting. He seemed different. If there were a photograph of the day I met Perry, it would be a perfect study in opposites: Goth mess meets jovial man who, based on his glasses and desk of Shakespeare books, appeared to live in the library.

"Well, Liz, actually. Call me Liz. Please, I just need a chance to sit and talk to you. I'm really sorry about being late."

I was so nervous my palms were sweating. I was not good at this sort of thing; I'd never felt the permission to just *talk to* authority figures, ever. The other teachers interviewing me must have noticed it. I worried what this guy would do when he noticed it. I mean, what must I look like to him? A ratty street person. Lice girl, dirty, truant, thief, late, irresponsible.

"Look, Liz," he said, without taking his eyes off me, "I would love to take you inside to talk, but I've got a class in ten and there's an essay component to the interview. It's going to take too long. I'm afraid you'll have to reschedule."

I held up my completed essay for Perry to see. "Done," I told him. "I did it already." He looked surprised, squinting at the papers, taking them from my hand to skim over, quickly. "Now can I have those ten minutes?" I pushed.

He laughed that lighthearted laugh again, took a few steps back into the office, and swung open his door. *They're just people*, I reminded myself as I took a seat.

"Look," I started, "my record is bad, I know that . . ."

I wanted to control that conversation, direct it, defend myself before he could judge me. Only, as I spoke, I quickly saw by his facial expressions—empathetic and interested—that he didn't seem to judge me at all. Perry just listened. He watched me and took in everything I said. He was genuinely connected; I could see it on his face. A feeling of trust opened in me as we spoke, and spontaneously, because of it, I told him everything. Everything except that I was homeless. I did not want to go back into the system, and I knew it would be Perry's job to report me if he knew I had nowhere to live. So I withheld that one detail, and shared with him everything else.

"And I have this friend Sam who I cut school with a lot, so I could, I don't know, cut loose. Well, I always meant to graduate. I really did. But then years passed and it got out of hand."

It was all flooding out of me, and I became more emotional in front of him than any of the teachers who had interviewed and rejected me in the last few weeks, more emotional than I wanted to be. I couldn't help it. It was just an alien feeling, having a teacher really connect the way he did, and not at all with pity. Instead he listened actively, asking clarifying questions, offering insight, even relating to me, sighing audibly at the details of my mother's funeral, but never once indicating pity, only understanding and interest. But listening to the sound of my own voice as I opened up to him, I began to judge myself. When I heard myself explaining my life to someone else, particularly to a professional type like him, I sounded so dysfunctional—and he looked so normal. My eyes traveled around the room, from the computer in back to Perry's clean brown leather shoes, then to my own rotten, ten-dollar boots.

"Liz," he stepped in, a grim expression on his face. He was suddenly very serious. "That's . . . *horrendous*. It sounds like you've been through a lot, and I do want to help. But I also want to make sure I'm helping in the right way, do you understand?" I don't know why I thought he meant calling social services. My eyes found the quickest exits. I could outrun this guy; the train back to Bedford was just five blocks away. "What I mean, Liz, is that I see from your appointment slip that you'll soon be seventeen, with no high school history whatsoever. Is that right?"

"I have one credit," I said. Coming out of his mouth, seventeen sounded so old. Of all the kids who interviewed before me, none of them could have been older than fifteen.

"Well, I admire your effort to come here today. I just want to say, if this is the right place for you, then that's one thing. But that depends on what you're looking for. Four years of high school might be a lot for a seventeen-year-old. I would be remiss if I did not inform you that there is an excellent, six-month GED program offered at night on the other side of this building. . . . Before we talk more, I just want to make you aware of your options."

Options. He'd struck a nerve. All those times I'd watched Ma humble herself to Brick, accepting his demands, his rough shoves, his shouting, opening her legs to him out of need—all because she lacked options. Daddy with his sharp mind and his rich life experiences, his education, living in a shelter, without options.

"I'm an ex-con, who would hire me?" he often said. "My options are limited." Being in the motels, eating from the trash Carlos left behind, no options. I'd heard GEDs turned out great for many people. But after all that Ma and Daddy had gone through, something in my gut told me graduating high school meant I'd have more options.

"I see where you're coming from, Perry, and I really appreciate your help . . . but I want to graduate high school. It's just something I have to do."

Hearing myself say it out loud made it real. Speaking what I wanted was totally different from just thinking it. Speaking it made me connect; I could feel it. I was shaking. Perry's eyes were still on me. I tried to guess what he was thinking about what I said, what he thought of me: *Failure. Dirty. Train wreck.* Or he was trying to decide how to tell me no in the most polite way possible. With that tie and those glasses, those shiny shoes, he looked like the polite type. He probably grew up in Westchester, I thought. He probably told people like me "no" all the time, just like the rest of them did.

Perry leaned back heavily in his chair and let out a small sigh. But he didn't look stressed; he looked emotional. I waited.

"Liz," he started, sitting up again, sending my heart racing. *Here it comes,* I thought. His voice was much lower, his face completely serious. "Can you get here on time?"

A smile pushed itself across my face and my eyes welled up. "Absolutely," I answered. "Yes."

The only catch was that I had to bring in a guardian to officially register me in school, as soon as possible.

Daddy and I met on Nineteenth Street and Seventh Avenue later that week. By then, I'd started to sketch out a plan. I would register for school, spend the summer working, save money, and attend Prep while living off my savings. It seemed solid. But the whole thing hinged on Daddy's help—I needed him to get me past these registration papers. From there, everything else I could handle on my own.

When I showed up for our meeting that muggy Thursday morning, I found Daddy leaning on a lamppost, engrossed in a book. I paced myself as I approached him, taking time to ready myself and take deep, relaxing breaths. The last thing I wanted was for Daddy to see me emotional; I don't think either of us knew how to deal with each other's emotions. That's probably why we had a silent agreement to pretend we didn't have any. But seeing him there, I was emotional. For months, I'd grown so accustomed to seeing strange faces and moving endlessly to new locations that the familiarity of Daddy's face, standing out from a sea of faces, hit me hard. No matter how much time or hurt had passed between us, I simply missed my father. Now here he was again, resurfaced, a thinner, unshaved version of himself, tattered-looking, made offbeat by the busy Manhattan life that surrounded him. He looked as fragile as Ma had that day on Mosholu Parkway when we blew our wishes into the sky on dandelion puffs. Rarely had I experienced my parents outside of our home, or away from University Avenue, but every time I did, the world around us kept reminding me of their limitations, how society made them look vagrant.

The night before, I'd called his shelter and was patched through to him by a woman who called out his name sharply, which made me feel sorry for him, protective. The way he'd spoken, so faintly into the phone, I might have woken him from a nap, I thought.

"Daddy. I'm going back to school. I need you to register me. Uh, I was hoping you could register me." I got right to the point because time on the shelter phone is limited. He'd asked twice for clarification. "No, not a program, Daddy, a real high school, yes. I kind of need you there." Everything in my body resisted using the word *need* with him. "Do you think you can make it?" If his answer had been "no" for any reason, I'm not sure what I would have done. But it wasn't. He agreed to meet me, without the hesitation I'd expected. Though I hadn't explained to him about the lying part. That I would save for later.

For the school's administration, I designed an airtight story that in no way indicated I was homeless. I would use a friend's address and a fake phone number as my cover. Because I knew the school would never be able to reach Daddy, I'd tell them he was a long-haul truck driver who was on the road for weeks at a time. I decided the story was believable enough to work, so long as I could get Daddy to go along with it.

He smiled as I walked up to greet him, a huge smile at me from under his newsboy cap. I smiled back, and my hesitation gave way to the simple joy I felt from seeing him again. We hugged, and after he rubbed a single page from his thick book carefully between his fingers, and took a moment to dog-ear it, tucking it into his shoulder bag, we began walking. I was nervous about talking to him about anything too serious—our current lives, Lisa, *Ma*—so I got right into the details about Prep, as though we saw each other every day and could afford to be casual. I coached him on all the little, important parts.

"Two hundred sixty-four East 202nd Street." I recited a phone number. "Zip code 10458. Can you remember all that, Daddy?"

His face was all twisted up, and I could tell he was wondering what he'd gotten himself into. "You want me to say *what?*" he yelled. "Lizzy, they think I'm a *truck driver?*"

"Yes, but that doesn't matter. They're not going to quiz you about the industry, ya know?" He seemed more panicked than he was angry; I noticed his hands shaking a little.

Maybe my own uneasiness about entering meetings like these was inherited.

"And I live *where?*" he asked.

Vince, the co-director of Prep, Perry's partner in running the school, met us. Also a middle-aged man with glasses, Vince seemed a little more serious than Perry, with a harder edge to him. Still, he smiled just as much and he turned out to be equally as warm and kind. When we walked into his office, he presented Daddy with a set of papers, spreading them out on the table between the two of them. The parts where Daddy needed to sign were already X'd.

"Good to meet you, Mr. Murray," he said, shaking Daddy's hand. Daddy smiled a complacent smile, obviously uncomfortable.

"Finnerty, actually," Daddy corrected. "Liz's mother and I were never married. It was the seventies, you know. She was spirited and all—actually she was completely crazy." He laughed. I cringed. Vince didn't bat an eye; he only smiled at Daddy. "Call me Peter," Daddy said.

He was so nervous, it was making me nervous. What would I do if we couldn't pull this off? Where would I go if we blew my one chance? I stared at Vince in search of any sign of suspicion. "Okay," I intervened, clapping my hands together. "Let's get this moving, then. I don't mean to rush, it's just that I don't want to hold up my dad or anything. You know, with work and all."

Even though his hands were trembling, Daddy managed to sign the same neat, jagged signature I'd seen him apply to absent notes and welfare documents my whole life. He muttered to himself and kept pushing his tongue around in his cheek.

"Hmmm, okay. Good, great. Perfect," he kept saying. "Good, got it."

My eyes were fixed on Vince, my heart pounding. I tried to look calm and cheerful. "Address?" Vince asked, with his fingertips perched onto a computer keyboard.

I looked over at Daddy. His eyes were trained on the ceiling and he was rubbing his hand on his forehead to jog his memory. "Nine thirty three—" he began, butchering Bobby's address.

"Two six four! Two six four, Daddy!" I quickly interrupted. "See what happens when you don't get enough sleep!" I patted Daddy's hand, my smile nervous. "He works too much," I said to Vince, shaking my head to fake light-hearted disapproval. "Two hundred sixty-four East 202nd Street," I finished for him. I gave Vince the phone number, too. Now I was shaking. We almost blew it. But I finally relaxed as I saw the meeting come to an end when Vince stood and reached out for Daddy to shake his hand again. Daddy gave Vince a smile familiar to me from our meetings with social workers.

"Well, okay then. Welcome to Prep, Liz," Vince said, suddenly turning to me. I shifted my weight from foot to foot, hoping Daddy wouldn't say another word. "Next thing you should do is see April for another appointment to come back and get your schedule drawn up for the fall."

I smiled and thanked Vince. The moment he retreated into his office, I ushered Daddy toward the door. On our way out of Prep I had to talk Daddy out of stealing a copy of *Time* magazine from the office.

✦✦✦

Back on Nineteenth Street, I walked Daddy to the train. We'd visited for less than forty-five minutes. Standing in front of the station entrance, I watched Daddy fidget, strapping and unstrapping a Velcro flap that tightened his closed umbrella. He didn't make eye contact with me, but kept looking past me, from the umbrella and then into the train station.

"Well, I hope that did it, Liz. Sorry if I messed up in there. I think it worked out anyway. . . . Do you think you'll actually go to school this time?" His question stabbed doubt at me, mocked my assurance.

"Yes. I know I will," I said, with more certainty than I expected from my-self. I'd borrowed some of Bobby's clothing for the day, baggy, but still clean. I had designed a cover story about my life for Daddy, too. On our few recent phone calls, I'd told him I lived at Bobby's house permanently now, and that I was fine. He didn't ask questions, and I hoped it would stay that way. What I was avoiding, in every way possible, was for him to know what I was really going through. Because if he found out, I knew it would hurt him. Then he'd be living in a shelter *and* worrying about me, too. Then I'd worry about him worrying about me, and what good would that do either of us? Better to have him believe I was okay.

"Well, that's good you're really going this time," he said. "Good to know. I think you might actually do that then. That's good. . . . Yeah, Lizzy, maybe you'll go all the way now." Coming from Daddy, it was a real compliment.

"That's the idea," I said, smiling at him.

He took out a napkin to blow his nose and I saw by its insignia that he'd taken it from McDonald's. Daddy had been doing that since I was a kid, dipping into fast food places, raiding their supplies.

"So things, are they all right at the shelter, going good and all?" I asked, leading him in my question. Maybe I didn't want all the information about his life either; maybe I was protecting myself from worrying about him, too.

"Oh, yeah," he said. "I, uh, get my three squares there. It's air-conditioned. They treat me well. Can't complain. Hey, Lizzy, do you have any money? Maybe for tokens or lunch?" I'd borrowed ten dollars from Bobby that morning. I had eight left. I removed what I needed to take the subway back to the Bronx and gave the rest to him.

"Hey thanks," Daddy said. It felt good to be helpful to him again.

"No problem. I have some money saved, it's no big deal," I lied.

I walked him downstairs into the train station and we hugged good-bye, exchanging promises to talk and meet up more often. He didn't stay at the turnstiles and wait for the train with me. Instead, he said good-bye and walked away far down the platform to wait. When he passed a pay phone, he stuck his fingers inside to search for loose change.

I was scheduled to begin high school in September; it was May now. I would use the months ahead to prepare; I had four years to make up. The next thing I had to do, in order to complete my registration in Prep, was return to JFK, my old high school, and get my official transcript.

Having seen Prep, JFK looked absolutely massive in comparison. I passed through metal detectors to enter the building. No one looked at me. Students were everywhere, thousands of them. It felt like a bus station. Taking the number 1 train back to Prep later that day, I sat down and ripped open the manila envelope. Columns of failing grades—45, 60, 50—were everywhere. It was unnerving, reading row after row of flunking marks. I felt like a mess, a big walking train wreck. The experience of talking about my grades (having been lectured by adults so many times) versus actually *seeing* my transcripts was night and day. Transcripts were a real thing, a tangible expression of what I had and had not done with my life, and a road map of what still had to be done. Looking at my academic disaster, I could see that I had a mountain ahead of me to climb.

Then, very suddenly, sitting on the train gazing at the JFK stationery, it dawned on me—my Prep transcripts were still completely blank. I literally had nothing, no grades, zip on my Prep transcripts yet. I could start fresh.

The thought of a clean slate was thrilling, especially after looking at the mess I had created. With all the things that had been difficult, it was one blessing to count on, the knowledge that what I did from this moment on didn't have to depend on what I had done before. Back on Nineteenth Street, I asked April to give me a copy of my blank Prep transcripts, which was a simple printout of my name on Prep stationery and rows of blank columns waiting to be filled by my future grades. The JFK ones I handed in to April and never looked at again. The blank ones I kept with me at all times. They were a reminder that I was, day by day, writing my future. Sleeping in a hallway around Bedford Park later that week, I took out my blank transcripts and filled in the grades I wanted, making neat little columns of A's. If I could picture it—if I could take out these transcripts and look at them—then it was almost as if the A's had already happened. Day by day, I was just catching up with what was already real. My future A's, in my heart, had already occurred. Now I just had to get to them.

A memory of Ma helped me decide this. The only papers I'd ever seen that were as "official" looking as transcripts were Ma's short stack of documents to verify qualification for welfare. Ma's caseworkers were always so difficult, so technical with us. And the walls of those depressing welfare offices, for some reason, were always painted puke green, a color made uglier by the harsh fluorescent lights and the iron bars on the large windows. There were so many people waiting in those offices—dozens, hundreds. When the hard little seats filled up, people sat on windowsills or on the floor; they stood or they paced.

Ma, Lisa, and I would wait for hours, too, one of dozens of other families all nervously checking and rechecking their own short stack of vital documents. When it was finally our turn, what I can remember most about being hoisted onto Ma's lap is the bizarre interaction between Ma and her caseworker. It did not matter what Ma was saying. All that the caseworker focused on were Ma's documents. Birth certificates, notarized letters, doctors' notes to verify mental illness, our lease. Ma's actual words, and particularly Ma herself, were invisible to this woman, a woman who had the power to give or take away our food, rent, and safety. All that it boiled down to was this: either we had the exact documents required for approval, or we did not. There was no in between. And even if we were missing only something small, like a second set of copies or one of Ma's doctors' notes, a single error could make all of our effort—the document gathering, the travel, and the hours of waiting—irrelevant. One missing or invalid document and our file was shut, tossed. They called "next," and we had to come back another day to start from scratch. All because the documents were either correct or they weren't, period.

How was this different from my high school transcripts? It wasn't. I thought, if one day, maybe just maybe I wanted to go to college, some person in a suit in a very different kind of office would open *my* file, read my documents, and either I would have the qualifications, or I wouldn't. Yes or no, and nothing in between. And if I didn't, my file would be shut and they would call "next." I would be out of luck. Some things in life, I'd learned, were nonnegotiable. Documents as official as these transcripts were big, they were my yes or no, they were my options. They were my ticket. Now I was going to think of everything I did at Prep inside the framework of my transcripts—and that turned out to mean everything.

Later, there would be times when I did not want to go to school. I wanted to sleep on Fief's floor and not get up. Bobby and Jamie were hanging out, walking around the Village. People were cutting school, and I was missing all the fun. There would be times I did not want to sit in a chair all day long while the fresh air was outside and I was missing out. But all I had to do was think of my transcripts, and I would go to school, on time, every day, for the first time in my life. Either I would have the qualifications or I wouldn't—and besides, my friends weren't going to pay my rent.

CHAPTER 11

The Visit(or)

WAITRESS-MIDTOWN
Part-time server wanted for busy midtown coffee &
sandwich shop, "can-do attitude" a must, long hours
required.

BABYSITTER & HOUSEKEEPER
Upper East Side family seeking female-only applicants,
good with house chores and patient with children,
must be flexible, and <u>must</u> speak English!

PEN IN HAND, I COMBED THROUGH THE CLASSIFIED ADS AS I SAT IN
the health clinic waiting room of a local youth organization called The Door.
I'd been thumbing through *The Village Voice* for days. My focus was on
finding food, work, health services, and tutoring. My limits were being un-
derage (I wouldn't turn seventeen until September), with the status of runaway. My fear was that I'd attract the attention of Child Welfare and get sent
back to the group home, so I did everything I could *not* to call attention to myself, as I mined the city for resources. Through word of mouth, mostly, I found
some good leads. The Door was one of the best things that could have happened
to me.

On Broome Street in lower Manhattan, The Door is in a three-story
building and is dedicated completely to meeting young people's needs. You
just had to be under twenty-one, which was perfect—no questions asked.
Frequently, I left The Door with pantry packs bursting with food: Cheerios,

peanut butter, raisins, and bread. I'd slip these supplies into my backpack and walk around Manhattan collecting applications for employment in convenience stores, gas stations, and retail outlets. Five days a week at 5:30 p.m., The Door served free hot meals on the second floor. After long tiresome days spent in search of work, I made it a regular thing to stop by The Door for dinner. This way I didn't have to steal from C-Town as much. Instead, I'd sit down, anonymous in the crowd of young people at the cafeteria-style tables, eat my chicken and mashed potatoes, and review my job options.

On a weekday afternoon, I sat in The Door's waiting area, thumbing through the classifieds. The paper offered all kinds of positions, but mostly ones for people with experience and education—I had neither. So I searched for ads that emphasized words like *ambitious*, *hard-working*, and *flexible*. The ad for a non-profit environmental agency called New York Public Interest Research Group (NYPIRG) stood out:

> "Do you care about the environment? Do you like working with people? Are you passionate about making a difference? Then NYPIRG may be the right place for you. Call to schedule your interview to canvass for a cause today. . . . Remember, if you're not part of the solution, you're part of the problem!"
> Earn from $350-$500* a week making the world a better place!
> No prior experience required.
>
> *salary commission-based.

I didn't know what the word *commission* meant, but I could really use $350 to $500 a week. I ripped the ad from *The Village Voice* and shoved it into my back pocket.

NYPIRG became my summer job, and the job of dozens of students on summer break from college. As the youngest and worst-dressed person in the room, I was worried that I wouldn't get hired, but everyone got hired. Apparently your organization can do that if the only pay that employees receive is a percentage of the money they raise. So I learned the meaning of *commission*. Your salary was a percentage of what you earned. If you didn't raise anything, you didn't make anything. If you raised a lot, you made a lot. I had to wonder, how hard was it to raise money?

It *was* possible to make a living at this job, a woman named Nicole, a veteran of NYPIRG, assured us during orientation. The small downtown conference room was packed with college students who looked like they were making identical hobo-chic fashion statements: white people experimenting with dreadlocks, hemp jewelry, and T-shirts emblazoned with a variety of social causes. Bleeding-heart private school students dressed like casual slobs, with holes in their expensive clothing—their efforts to look hobo-poor were painfully obvious to me. That worked out fine on my end, being that I was probably the closest thing in the room to a real hobo. Most of them had money; I could tell by their Urban Outfitters bags, expensive jewelry, and high-end mountain shoes and Birkenstocks. But if they liked to project their interpretation of poverty in their personal style, that was okay with me.

Nicole explained how the job would work. Five days a week, following an afternoon briefing on their latest environmental campaign progress, NYPIRG would pack all of us canvassers (as we were called) eight at a time into vans, and drive us to key fund-raising areas in New York State. Our job was to knock on doors and engage everyday citizens in NYPIRG's fight against cancer, which was linked to indiscriminate spraying of pesticides in residential neighborhoods, according to a research study that Nicole waved around throughout her spiel. NYPIRG was busy lobbying to pass something called the Neighborhood Notification Bill. As canvassers, we would stand on people's doorsteps and hold their attention while we repeated what we'd learned at each afternoon briefing. Then we'd invite them to join us in the fight against cancer with "membership," which meant we asked them for money. Our paycheck was a percentage of what we raised. We were given copies of the key research study on our way out the door, along with individual clipboards and temporary IDs.

In the van, northbound on the Henry Hudson Parkway, I was sure I'd made a mistake in being there. We each practiced what was called our "rap"; I was by far the worst.

"Hi, um, my name is Liz, um . . . I'm from the New York Public Institute of Research. I mean, Research of Public Interest . . . I'm here to fight cancer with you . . . um?"

The others were so much better than me. The girl next to me, Anna from Scarsdale, was polished on her very first run: "I want to invite you to join our campaign to combat the effects of these toxic chemicals. Together, we have to stand up as a community."

I was struck by how perfect and put-together she looked with her expensive pearl earrings and canvas bag, and by the way she strung words together, compared to my fumbling speech. It was intimidating. And what was that word? *Combat?* Wasn't that the brand name of the stuff we used to kill roaches on University? Obviously, from the way she used it, it must have another meaning. I took out my journal and began keeping a list of words I overheard from my coworkers.

Each of them spoke eloquently, expressing themselves using confident body language and rich vocabulary. I couldn't take my eyes off of them, especially this one guy named Ken.

I both liked and felt incredibly uncomfortable around Ken. He was nothing like the guys from my neighborhood, and he made me nervous. Ken was clean-cut and wholesome. He was also gorgeous. He had shaggy, sandy-blond hair and mint-colored eyes, like green ice with flecks of gold in them. He was tall, and his skin was a golden olive that contrasted with the bright white Human Equality T-shirt he wore. On summer break from Brown University, Ken was recently single, out of a long-term relationship, I'd overheard him telling Anna.

Somehow, we ended up seated next to each other in the van and were told by our field manager, Shen, to practice our "rap" together. Underneath my black Korn T-shirt and thick black jeans, I was sweating heavily, pulling my hair back into a ponytail so I had something to do with my hands. Ken went right after I did, and he stumbled on his words, too, but managed to be compelling anyway. "Good job," I said with more enthusiasm than I had intended. My face flushed red with embarrassment. "Thanks," Ken said, smiling sincerely. He also blushed a bit when he fumbled his words, and laughed at himself. I tried, but could not stop looking his way.

Shen "cut turf" (assigned us designated areas), depending on his assessment of our earning potential. Less skilled canvassers spent their evenings on "dry" blocks, those areas with dilapidated houses and sparse amounts of annual renewals. Those more skilled were given larger houses that looked like castles, whose fat lawns were golf-course green, punctuated by things like fountains and lawn jockey statues. It took no less than five minutes to walk from driveway to doorbell in those places.

That very first day, I was slated for dry turf, my earning potential apparently assessed as low. They gave me a street that was falling to pieces, with chain-link fences rusting around ratty front yards. The quota was $120 for the day—good luck! But to Shen's surprise, when the van came back to pick me up at nine p.m., I had collected $240; a neat little row of checks were pinched to the top of my clipboard, their watermark background making a rainbow of pastel along the chrome clip.

"Is this good enough?" I asked Shen, holding my clipboard up to the orange glow of the van's brake lights, the summer sky falling dark blue as we stood, canopied under heavy treetops. He read my total once, then twice, and said, "Yeah, it's great." After that day, I was assigned to the wealthier houses, where my daily amounts continued to rise, often topping several hundred dollars for the night.

I was pegged as highly unlikely for this kind of success at NYPIRG, since even the most polished and gregarious types faltered after one too many doors slammed in their faces. No one said the job was easy. Interpretations of my success flew around the office: "Liz is passionate about the environment." "She had the most training." "She probably had experience before coming here."

None of that was true, nor did my success have much to do with skill. The reason behind my success was simple. I was hungry, and for me, this was no summer vacation. Unlike my coworkers, who looked forward to weekend outings and happy hour, I was stocking up on supplies before the winter, saving every penny, sink or swim, packing for the long haul. I needed this. My intention was to save every dollar so that I could get through the months ahead of me when my school schedule might prohibit me from working. For the first time, I was making my daily life fit into a bigger purpose: climbing out of the place I'd been born into. That was my edge.

There was also another kind of hunger I felt, one that was harder to put my finger on. It had something to do with the newness of all of this, the rush I got from experiencing these new places. Never before had I seen big houses with cars parked in endless gravel driveways, children looping bikes down tree-lined streets in the sun. The way housewives would open their front doors to me, all put-together looking, their children clinging waist-high, steadying themselves on the sturdiness of their mothers' hips. I relished the *whoosh* of air-conditioning seeping from their homes, cooling my cheeks and forearms as I held the clipboard, book bag on my back with all my belongings inside, as I stole glimpses into their lives. It was thrilling, to see how people built a life so different from what I'd known. It filled me with a longing to build the same; it was inspiring to me. There was a sense of adventure in it, an exhilaration in every door opened, every conversation, each new encounter. I went up and down the sidewalks of those suburban neighborhoods captivated, curious to see what could possibly be next.

But the best days, by far, were the ones when Ken and I had our turf right near each other. I lived for those days. As soon as Shen pulled the van away, Ken and I would secretly catch up with each other to share turf, sometimes hitting doors together as a team. We did not plan who would do the talking; instead, a sense of partnership just flowed. We were good together. Fund-raising, that is. We could knock out a day's quota, and then some. If we finished early enough, we'd go find someplace just to hang out, to sit in the shade and talk—though I was deeply unsure of what I could possibly talk to Ken about. Would I tell him about Ma? University Avenue? How I left the motel just in time to save myself from Carlos? That I'd slept on the D train that week? All of that didn't seem to have a place in our conversations. Not when the sun was shining and you could smell fresh soil from the park and hear the cicadas buzzing in the treetops. Not when Ken was smiling like that. If talking about my life would be a downer, then why talk about it? So I let Ken do the talking—about his family, his ex-girlfriend, and lots about Brown University. I soaked it all in, took in his joy and his kindness. We'd do impersonations of Nicole or Shen and crack each other up, laugh at the job, laugh at life—just laugh until we couldn't laugh anymore.

It was easy to laugh around Ken. Easy to believe that a life surrounded by these storybook houses, perfect lawns, and sunny days was just as possible as the life I'd already known.

One day in August, I was taking the A train to fill out some paperwork at Prep and I saw Sam. She was on the C; we spotted each other the very moment the subway doors closed; our cars were directly across the platform that separated us. Like two horses running side by side on a racetrack, the subway cars pulled out and began to run parallel through the dark tunnels, dipping in and out of sync. I planted my open hands flat on the glass window of the door, and Sam did the same. The ridiculousness of the encounter made us both laugh. Sam smiled and stuck her middle finger up at me; her hair was green, tied up in two buns on top of her head, and she was wearing a long skirt and a lacy maroon camisole. She looked well groomed and was a much healthier weight than when I'd last seen her. I motioned with my hands for her to get out at the next stop, but the pillars in the subway tunnels kept blocking our view. We got out at Fourteenth Street and ran to hug each other, tight. She smelled of soap and baby powder. I was shaking.

"Where you been?" she yelled, smacking my shoulder. Back at the motel, our friendship had been strained by the stress of Carlos. But in the subway on a cool August afternoon months later, our friendship was new again. I loved her like she was my sister.

"Around," I told her. "I'm getting myself together, actually, that's where. I got a job and all. Wanna take a walk with me somewhere?"

We walked through Chelsea, toting our book bags. I was taken aback when she pulled out a pack of cigarettes and began smoking, but I didn't say anything about it. With all the time that had passed since I'd seen her, I couldn't gauge if we were still close enough to give our opinions about anything too personal. We walked and she caught me up on her life. Group home living wasn't all that bad; the girls had become her family. She was going to marry Oscar for sure. Not that they had official plans just yet, but she could just feel it. Lilah, a group home girl from Staten Island, would be maid of honor, after all they had been through together.

"Lilah's my partner in crime. GHFL, that means Group Home for Life," she said. "I might get it tattooed. All of us might."

I kicked a small stone around in front of us while we walked, my eyes downcast.

"Sounds great," I told her. Had I imagined our closeness? Did she miss me at all? I missed her. "You wanna check out this school thing I'm going to?" I asked.

"Sure," she said casually, shrugging her shoulders as though, since she had free time on that particular afternoon, she might as well enroll in high school.

Sam came with me and filled out an application to Prep. April told her she would get a call at her listed number soon. Perry wasn't around to meet Sam, so we slipped out the side door and walked back to the train, where we went in separate directions. Sam wrote her group home phone number on my hand in blue, curly script. Her hug good-bye was big, and the gesture felt deeply loving. *There* she is, I thought. We made promises to see each other soon and she would let me know, for sure, when Prep got back to her. Or, if she and Oscar picked a date before then, she'd definitely call me for that, too.

It was raining when Ken's mother pulled up in the family minivan. She turned out to be blond like her son, with a haircut just as short as his, except hers was darker and had flecks of gray that offset her tiny pearl earrings. She drove all five of us, Ken's coworkers, from the A train to their beachside home in Far Rockaway, through a light drizzle that made the nighttime asphalt shimmer under the streetlights of the quiet Queens suburb. Her arms were muscular and tanned in a way that suggested exercise and healthy diet. Her clothes—cargo shorts and an impossibly white V-neck T-shirt—were so clean they might have been fresh off a wooden hanger at Banana Republic. She kept up a cheerful conversation, inquiring about our schools and what we did for fun. I stayed as quiet as possible, afraid I might draw attention to myself and have to give up my cover: a normal high school senior readying myself for college applications.

At a traffic stop, I saw her reach over and stroke Ken's forehead and hair, smiling at him, their matching faces made pink under the red traffic light. I could tell she was a kind woman. You could see it in the way she reached for her son and in the way he softened to her. Watching them, I felt like I did when watching a movie I'd snuck into at Loews Paradise; like at any moment I might get caught and asked to leave, my presence discovered as fraudulent.

The basement in the family's home was set up like an apartment. It had been Ken's until he left for Brown; since then, his little sister Erica (who I was mortified to find out was exactly my age) had taken it over as her own, mixing Ken's old philosophy books with her posters of environmental causes like "Save the Whales," "Save the Trees," and "Save the Children." Erica and her mom had prepared refreshments and set them on a small table: a foot-long sandwich cut diagonally into slices and a selection of juice boxes.

I changed into my sleep clothes in the upstairs bathroom while the group began a game of cards. My plan was to accidentally end up sitting as close to Ken as possible during the game. We would brush up against each other ever so slightly, by mistake, several times during the evening. I would pretend to be oblivious. When I could identify where he was sleeping, I would coincidentally fall asleep near his spot, prompting him to act upon the "vibe" we'd built all night. His lips would be soft as the inside of my cheek, silky. Looking in the mirror, I rubbed vanilla-scented shampoo into my dry hands and carefully spread bits of it throughout my hair with my fingertips: preparation for when we'd spoon together later.

My reflection looked back at me: my brown/purple hair was waist length and wavy. I hoped Ken liked it. I wore no makeup, and I hated the way my face gave away how little I'd been sleeping—a few hours here and there on friends' couches and in hallways. Four small silver hoop earrings ran up each of my ears, and my eyebrows were thicker than I wanted them to be. My sleep pants were jogger's sweats decorated by a cartoon skull embroidered on the thigh. Underneath, I had on a pair of Carlos's old boxers. Ken's mother had loaned me a T-shirt of Ken's for the night, three sizes too big.

The night played out in front of me like a first evening in some foreign country whose language I could not understand. We sat on sleeping bags along the basement floor, in a circle made for storytelling. Kat, Anna, Steven, Jeremy, and Ken talked about things totally unfamiliar to me. "Rich people," Daddy would have called them. I didn't know if they were rich, but it quickly became clear that they were different from me. After all, in the ghetto, by no means do we talk about things like different types of cheese.

No, sir, we do not go on about the distinctions between Brie, Havarti, and Gorgonzola. In the ghetto, we buy *one* kind of cheese, and that is American. We get it when we ask the bodega man for "a dollar ham and a dollar cheese" wrapped in thick waxed paper and handed to us on the day the government check is cashed. And in the ghetto, we do not talk about backpacking through Europe (wherever Europe is).

However, in the ghetto, we do talk about the block that we live on and the blocks surrounding the block we live on: "Did you hear about the shootout on Grand Avenue? They got Milkshake! *He dead!*" "Yo, on Andrews Avenue Mrs. Olga's selling piraguas out of 1C again? They a dollar cheaper than Mrs.

Lulu's! She got coconut!" Other countries and cultures were never discussed at home. In fact, anything farther than our own block, and the blocks surrounding it, was just a vague concept. So when Ken shared with us that he had managed to find a way to travel to Cuba last summer with a youth group, I asked, "Why, is it hard to get to Cuba?"

"Well, given the embargo and all . . . yes," he said. I nodded stupidly, as though I'd somehow misheard him. My heart jackhammered. Embargo? This was probably something they teach you about in high school. I hated feeling like I should know something that I didn't. Sometimes it was easier just to be quiet.

And then there was the topic of college. All of them compared campuses, dorms, professors, and plans for graduate school, using words like *fellowship*, *thesis*, and *registrar*. What was graduate school, exactly? Was that different from college? Because if I *graduate* from high school, then I can go to college, so maybe college *was* graduate school? But that couldn't be it, because they were already in college. I made the most casual face I could make, a face that said: "I know what you're talking about, why wouldn't I?" And while I didn't get it at all, this idea of college did begin to interest me.

Their excitement was part of it, but above all, it was their belonging with one another that really got me interested. It was the way that college seemed to make you fit in with people whom you had never even met before, gave you things to talk about. And then the question struck me: Could *I* go to college? Even if I didn't know where Europe was, or the difference between Brie and Havarti, could I have what they had? Ma left school after the eighth grade, and Daddy dropped out too. But could I go to college?

"Anything else to drink?" Ken asked me, touching my forearm unnecessarily. My heart raced again, my cheeks flushed hot. "No thanks, I'm good."

"Okay then," he said, smiling.

Ken tossed a pillow onto a particular sleeping bag and leaned back. Anna declared that "her song" was playing and raised the radio volume, flipping her ginger-colored hair. Four Non Blondes' "What's Up" blared through the basement. "Wicked!" she yelled. Anna and Kat became a chorus, singing along. Ken laughed and looked around. Had he just looked at me, or did I imagine it? I was pretty sure that he gave me a look. I found his eyes and smiled back.

Using a bathroom break as an excuse to get up, I returned a few minutes later and ever-so-casually changed my seat to the sleeping bag beside Ken's, rejoining our circle. Two hours later, chips and bits of sandwich were strewn about the floor and tabletops throughout the darkened basement. Everyone was falling asleep on their sleeping bags across the wide floor. Ken was closest to me, just like I'd planned. Our communication in the dark, silent room would now take place in code.

In the silence, a cough would signal: *I'm still awake, Ken; in case you're worried I fell asleep.* Getting up for water was like saying, *Go ahead and move nearer to my spot while I'm gone.* "Accidentally" brushing my foot against Ken's foot was erotic. I waited out the silence for his advance. Nothing. The basement was filled with dry heat from the hissing steam pipes. Moonlight streamed in from the tiny windows and illuminated his little sister's pictures: two teenage girls holding up a turtle on the sunny beach of some faraway place, matching friendship bracelets on their wrists. I waited. Nothing. Then suddenly, something!

A noise, a signal, some kind of movement! . . . Ken's snoring sounded over the hissing pipes. He was completely, without a doubt, 100 percent asleep.

The next morning, Ken's mother set the breakfast table with knives and forks wrapped in napkins, like they did at Tony's diner. His father came in from a jog, sweat under the armpits of his Martha's Vineyard T-shirt. "Hey, kiddo!" he said, ruffling Erica's blond hair as she sat curled up on the large living room sofa in her cotton pajamas. Jeremy, Steven, and Kat grabbed seats at the table. I sat in the chair farthest from everyone and pretended to be busy toasting my bread, avoiding eye contact all around. The front door opened, and Ken and Anna came bounding in dressed in sweats, laughing.

"So," Anna's voice boomed like an announcement, "told ya we . . . could do another lap," she said, playfully poking Ken in the ribs, her blue eyes bright, her breathing labored from running. Ken was bent down with his palms on his knees, catching his breath. Anna rested her hand on Ken's back with an ease I hadn't realized existed in their friendship. How could I have ever thought this guy was interested in me? All along he was being friendly, and here I was thinking something else entirely. I felt like an idiot.

Ken's mom lowered a huge wicker basket brimming with pastries onto the breakfast table: muffins with sugar drizzled over their golden tops, mouthwatering Danishes, bagels studded with raisins and poppy seeds. It was commercial-perfect, and the sight of it stunned me. I stared disbelievingly; I'd never had access to an entire basket of pastries before. On the stove behind us, Ken's dad cracked an egg on the edge of the frying pan. A full pitcher of orange juice sat untouched on the table. Steven and Kat began to spread cream cheese on bagels. Ken reached over and set down a plate.

"You, *here*," he said, gesturing to Anna. "I believe I lost that bet and I owe you breakfast." She beamed at him, took a seat, and played with her hair while he poured her juice from the heavy glass pitcher. This was a *Saturday Night Live* skit, and the theme of the comedy was "How perfect this guy and his wonderful family that you will never have, Liz." Suddenly, it struck me as over-the-top funny.

Before I could stop myself, I blurted out a laugh. Heads turned my way; there was nothing obviously funny happening. I knew it was weird of me, but I caught the giggles then and cupped my hand over my mouth, quaking with laughter that I could not control. It was the ridiculousness of it all: the conversations about cheese, the beautiful home, Ken's too-good-to-be-true looks and kindness, Ken and Anna as a pair, his parents . . . but it was that damn bread basket that put me over the top. Sam would have laughed with me if she were there, at that wonderful, inaccessible life of theirs, like a gorgeous Christmas display in the windows at Macy's, enticing to the eyes, glorious in every detail, and locked behind glass. You let the sparkle dazzle you from the sidewalk, and you kept things moving.

My giggles drew looks from everyone. Hey, I know what crazy looks like, and how disconcerting it can be when someone is acting off. So I tried to explain why I was laughing, to put them at ease, but it only made things worse. It drew more confused faces.

"It's just that, you have a whole basket, full of . . . *pastries*," I snorted. "Well, ahem, no, you know . . . I just mean, there's *a whole basket* and the pitcher of juice is *huge*, ya know?!" I waited through a painfully awkward silence. "I mean, do you have breakfast like this *every day*?" I asked. "I mean . . . it's great, I'm just saying." Mercifully, my giggling finally let up then. "Never mind, I just really like these pastries," I told them. "They're *great*."

Ken's mother spoke first, rescuing me.

"It is great, isn't it?" she responded, as though what I said had made any sense. "The bakery makes everything right there on the premises, so it's fresh. That's why it's so yummy."

I bit into a blueberry muffin and straightened up in my seat. Steven, Jeremy, and Kat began discussing plans to hit a jazz club in the Village later that night. The apprehensive vibe that filled the room was not lost on me, nor was the fact that they did not invite me to come along with them.

Soon everyone finished their breakfasts and began to shuffle around, pack up their bags. The doorbell rang; Anna's mom had come to pick her up. From my seat, alone at the kitchen table, I watched the two mothers greet each other at the front door; Anna and Ken joined them, forming a circle of conversation and laughter. Momentarily, I ached for Ma. A flash of tears welled up in me and subsided. Watching the four of them, hearing the others downstairs packing, and Ken's sister in her room, something occurred to me.

Nothing here was mine to keep.

Everything I enjoyed here was temporary, a visit. My NYPIRG coworkers would soon be back at their respective colleges, and we would lose touch. The warm feel of this home and these interesting people were not mine. This group was no more my own than was the family's house itself. Nor did I have an actual connection with Ken. He, like the entire situation, was not mine to keep; none of it was. Their lives enjoyed a social symmetry that held the possibility of connection, and with it, membership in a club I comprehended only enough to understand that I was a poor fit. Soon, I'd be back in the Bronx sleeping wherever, and this—*they*—would all be past tense.

I looked down at the basket full of muffins and bagels. I looked up at the circle of them standing, sharing one another, Ken's smiling face, his warmth and casual wonderfulness. Covertly, I zipped open my book bag—full of dingy clothes and the wad of rubber-banded hundred-dollar bills I'd saved up over the summer—and I began stuffing muffins, bagels, bananas, and oranges into my bag. I threw in a whole loaf of bread, too. Why not? These things would be mine to keep.

I would have emptied the juice into my bag, if I could have.

Possibility

THE TWO YEARS I SPENT AT HUMANITIES PREP UNFOLDED LIKE AN urban-academic-survival-study marathon, and it took everything I had to get through it.

I learned that there is a distinct difference between saying something and doing something, just as there is a distinct difference between setting a goal and actually living the reality of that goal. I wanted to catch up as quickly as possible, so I set a target: I would graduate with an A average, nothing less. And I would do it in two years, while homeless. This sounded like a great plan to help me get on with my life. It was very inspiring to read about in my journal, too. But then I actually had to go do it, and that was a whole different story altogether.

It started out fine, with that first hopeful week in school, when I went around gathering as many classes as possible, stacking work on top of work and responsibilities on top of more responsibilities. I didn't exactly announce to the teachers at Prep what I was doing; it's more that I went around on my own collecting classes à la carte, adding them onto my plate wherever I could find them. There were the standard five courses; I took those. Then there was an extra early-morning math class for those needing to catch up on their math credits, so I took that, too. Also, according to flyers tacked up in the office, nearby Washington Irving High School provided night classes twice a week. I took those. Then there was the Seward Park High School on the Lower East Side that offered a Saturday history course for another credit. I took that. I also found out that I could approach teachers individually for off-hours independent studies, which I did. I had a lot of catching up to do. So my goal at Prep became to complete one year of high school per semester, which is exactly what I set out to do, starting that September.

I was inspired by a question that kept repeating itself in my mind: Could I really change my life? I'd spent so many days, weeks, months, and years thinking about doing things with my life, and now I wanted to know, if I committed to a goal and woke up every single day working hard at it, could I change my life?

Those first few weeks it seemed especially possible, back when teachers were still lecturing on their course introductions and handing us assignments that wouldn't be due for a while. I gleefully took notes, arrived on time, or even early, for class and I accepted my work happily, collecting assignment handouts in optimistic little piles that grew thick in my backpack. This was fine at first. But soon, deadlines were looming and reports and presentations were actually due. That was when my optimistic attitude of the first few weeks was replaced by a sense of dread and a deep feeling of uncertainty, a rubber-meets-the-road reality check of what it would take to actually figure this out. Indeed, thinking about my goal or even stating it was so much different from actually living it.

Figuring out high school while homeless meant handling details that never would have occurred to me until I was actually living in the situation. For one, who knew schoolbooks were so heavy? By itself, that's already something. But when I carried the heavy things around while also navigating several different living situations with no predictability whatsoever of where I could stay on a given night, while also trying to follow an assignment schedule that dictated exactly which books I would need and when, I kept slipping up.

If I didn't time things correctly, I'd end up crashing at Bobby's or Fief's or Jamie's with the wrong book for a particular assignment on a given night. The consequence of a miscalculation like this could mean having the wrong material with me to study for a deadline, which could mean the difference between an A and a B or, in the case of test preparation, a grade drop even more severe than that. Between my numerous classes, numerous places to stay, and numerous assignments, there were just too many variables for me to keep track of to get it right 100 percent of the time. So to solve the problem, I began carrying almost all my books with me, along with my clothing, my journal, Ma's NA coin and her picture, my toothbrush and toiletries; I stuffed everything all in one huge bag. But it was very heavy, and it made moving around the city difficult, with the straps pressed into my shoulders, pinching at my skin. My back hurt every single day.

Then there was the sleep factor. Sometimes my friends' parents would let me stay over outright; sometimes not. On the occasions when I had to sneak into a friend's place, I would need to wait until their parents went to bed, which meant doing homework or napping in the hallway until the late-night hours when the coast was clear. I'd enter their apartments ever so quietly and sleep on someone's futon, or behind the futon on the floor hidden from sight under blankets, just in case. A couple of times I napped in a friend's large closet. Then, in most cases I would need to be out again in the morning before their parents woke up. For this, I carried a small vibrating alarm clock in my pocket, so that I could be alerted silently when it was time to get up. When it went off, wherever I was, I quietly sat up, slipped my feet into my black boots, tiptoed over to slide my book bag—with great effort—onto my back, and I went out the door again. Sometimes I'd spend the remaining couple of hours between five and six thirty or seven a.m. in a hallway, up on the top landing of a stairwell, napping. Sometimes I'd head straight to school while the sun was just coming up and the air was still nighttime cold and the gates to stores were still lowered, not yet open for business.

Then there was actually getting my assignments done. That was a whole other thing, too. It turned out I needed a certain amount of sleep in order to be clear-minded enough to turn in a well-written paper, a paper worthy of an A. Without enough sleep, it was like trying to think straight with a fog in my brain, and that wouldn't get me the A's I needed. But I could not always get enough sleep when keeping the schedules of my friends. Getting the sleep I needed was sometimes easier if I simply climbed the staircase in a building and slept at the top landing, alone. At least there I had some privacy and, so long as I picked a reasonably clean and safe building, probably no one would bother me. I could work by the hallway light, sleep on the marble floor, use my sweater as a blanket and my remaining clothing as a pillow. When I really needed some rest, the hallway landings worked best.

With all of these details figured out, I could mostly manage, especially with the help of my NYPIRG savings, the hot meals and pantry packs from The Door, and especially with such a supportive group of friends. But there were other moments much more difficult to deal with, moments when I came dangerously close to saying, "Forget it." There was one recurring situation that particularly threatened to break me.

It happened on days when my alarm clock went off at 6:20 a.m. and I'd wake up in Fief's apartment, or some other place where parents were absent, rules were not enforced, and there was no limit to how long I could sleep. I'd wake to the sight of more than ten people sleeping on random tattered cushions and mattresses across the floor; the sun was barely up, graffiti along the apartment walls, beer bottles everywhere. Everyone had partied all night and gone to sleep not too long ago. Most nights I had done my homework in the stairwell—using my transcripts to get me focused—and separating myself to avoid the awful smell of cigarette smoke and the noisy distraction of everyone's partying. When things died down at night, I'd slip back into my friends' apartments and get some sleep in whatever little spot I could find. A few hours later, my little alarm clock would go off and I'd wake up and lie there, perfectly still, staring up at the ceiling. In this moment, I was *so tempted* to just pull the blanket over my head and go back to sleep. That temptation, in that moment, is exactly when I almost lost my resolve and gave up.

Warm blanket, or walk through the door?

These were the moments when I was most tested, when comfort was an option. Not when I was sleeping in the hallway, not when I had to exit my friends' apartments forcibly at odd hours, and not even when I had to ride the subway all night long and sleep there. Instead, lying around in my friends' apartments when I had the option to sleep was the most difficult of all these situations for me. This was because, without being forced outdoors, I somehow had to find a reason to choose school, a reason from inside myself.

In this way I didn't have to choose to go to high school just once, I had to choose it over and over again, every single time I was tempted not to go. During these mornings that were full of rare and precious quiet, soft pillows and warmth, I was tempted more than any other time to just pull the blanket back over me. It took everything I had to choose to walk through the door to go to school instead. In these moments, *I* was my biggest obstacle. Warm blanket or walk through the door?

Making these choices, as it turned out, wasn't about willpower. I always admired people who "willed" themselves to do something, because I have never felt I was one of them. If sheer will were enough by itself, it would have been enough a long time ago, back on University Avenue, I figured. It wasn't, not for me anyway. Instead, I needed something to motivate me. I needed a few things that I could think about in my moments of weakness that would cause me to throw off the blanket and walk through the front door. More than will, I needed something to inspire me.

One thing that helped was a picture I kept in mind, this image that I used over and over whenever I was faced with these daily choices. I pictured a runner running on a racetrack. The image was set in the summertime and the race-track was a reddish orange, divided in white racing stripes to flag the runners' columns. Only, the runner in my mental image did not run alongside others; she ran solo, with no one watching her. And she did not run a free and clear track, she ran one that required her to jump numerous hurdles, which made her break into a heavy sweat under the sun. I used this image every time I thought of things that frustrated me: the heavy books, my crazy sleep schedule, the question of where I would sleep and what I would eat. To overcome these issues I pictured my runner bolting down the track, jumping hurdles toward the finish line.

Hunger, hurdle. Finding sleep, hurdle, schoolwork, hurdle. If I closed my eyes I could see the runner's back, the movement of her sinewy muscles, glis-tening with sweat, bounding over the hurdles, one by one. On mornings when I did not want to get out of bed, I saw another hurdle to leap over. This way, obstacles became a natural part of the course, an indication that I was right where I needed to be, running the track, which was entirely different from let-ting obstacles make me believe I was off it. On a racing track, why wouldn't there be hurdles? With this picture in mind—using the hurdles to leap forward toward my diploma—I shrugged the blanket off, went through the door, and got myself to school.

That was at least half of my motivation on those tough mornings, and the other half was thinking about my teachers. In my weaker moments of blanket versus door, I knew Perry was waiting for me at school, and so were the other teachers that, much to my surprise, I came to love during my time at Prep.

Susan taught early-morning math classes. A heavyset woman who wore floral dresses and penny loafers to work every day, Susan loved literature. Sometimes we talked more about books than we did math. Susan always had a unique take on the love stories that were my favorite. She offered me insights I would have missed on my own; she always encouraged me to go deeper. Susan arrived extra early to be one of the first teachers turning on the lights, greeting our tiny seven-person class with high energy and a huge smile. "Great to see you today," she sang every morning, and she seemed to really mean it. With Susan teaching my first class of the day, I never wanted to be late, and just thinking of her could get me going.

Then there were Caleb, Doug, and Elijah, who were all in their twenties. Each of them had recently graduated from schools like Cornell and Princeton, school names familiar to me from conversations at NYPIRG. Collectively, they were dedicated to teaching, generous with their time, lighthearted, and friendly. Elijah had a way of challenging his students not with statements, but with questions. Being around Elijah made me become much more deliberate in my choice of words, something I'd never considered much before. And like Perry, Elijah made eye contact with me, searched my face when I spoke in class—he connected. He inspired me to want to connect, too.

Doug was inclusive and humble. One day I asked a question in class, and when he fumbled in answering, he interrupted himself to say, "Liz, I don't know, and I was trying to seem like I did. But really I don't, sorry. If you're interested in the answer, I can find out for you." I was stunned. Never had teachers been so human with me. From Doug I learned the importance of authenticity.

And I had never met anyone like Caleb. Perry once joked that the teachers at Prep put in so many hours, they must have thought they were investment bankers. I think he was talking about Caleb. Prep already had a culture different from mainstream schools, in that there wasn't a mass exodus at three p.m. when the bell rang. People actually stayed around after school, lounging in our one large public area, which was called Prep Central. Or students stayed for tutoring or extracurricular activities with the Prep staff until well into the late afternoon. The teachers did this without additional pay, and even with the extra hours they put in, Caleb stayed later. Long after school let out, and even after everyone meeting for extracurricular activities went home, you could still find Caleb by himself in one of the small, cramped staff offices, hunched over the phone, calling late and absent students, one by one.

"Hi, this is Caleb Perkins. Sorry we missed you today. Do you mind sharing why you were late or absent? Can we help you get here on time from now on?" One by one, Caleb reached out to students, asked them questions, listened carefully to their answers, and offered them help. He kept track of their promises, and he held students accountable. "Say what you mean and mean what you say" seemed to be his motto. I'd never seen anything like it. From Caleb I learned what it meant when a teacher was both compassionate *and* held a student to a higher standard. I also learned, from Caleb, what it meant to be committed to something and to put in hours upon hours of work to attain it.

I knew Caleb worked so hard because I often stayed late at Prep myself. In the space of a narrow corner office with high ceilings, one wall made up of painted-over cinder blocks and massive bookshelves, I hunched over a desk and taught myself how to use a computer to get my work done. These heavy square things with dim, flickering monitors and chunky keyboards were completely foreign to me. I realized that my task was twofold: I had to study while also learning how to study at the same time. It felt as if I were climbing a mountain with bricks in my pocket. I wrote an essay about *The Catcher in the Rye* while learning about essay writing, and while learning how to type, all at once. I did so by tapping a single button at a time, frustrating myself with countless mistakes, messing up and starting again and again and again. It was exhausting; I had never been one of those students who learned things quickly. Instead, I always had to read and reread a textbook to understand it, and it often took me two or three times as long as my classmates to complete my assignments. It got so late most evenings that Prep's empty classrooms sat in the dark, their chairs motionless in the setting sun. The janitor would ask me to lift my feet while he mopped the tile floor around me, Caleb within earshot calling students in the next room, one by one, while I created endless pages of work, a single letter at a time.

This was the environment in which I finally came to my education, the environment in which I knew I could no longer lie in bed and give up. How could I pull the blanket back over my head when I knew my teachers were waiting for me? When they were willing to work so hard, how could I not do the same?

With the Prep staff, my negative feelings about school began to dissolve, replaced by an actual love for learning, and with it, at last, a tangible hope for my life.

My feelings about the teachers *were* my feelings about the school. If they were wonderful, school was wonderful. It had always been that way for me.

And if the teachers believed in me, that was at least the first step in a long journey of believing in myself. This was especially true during my more vulnerable moments, back when I was labeled "truant" and "discipline problem." I was always seeing myself through the eyes of adults, my parents, caseworkers, psychiatrists, and teachers. If I saw a failure in their eyes, then I was one. And if I saw someone capable, then I was capable. Professional adults had credibility and were my standard for deciding what was legitimate or not, including myself. Previously, when teachers like Ms. Nedgrin saw me as a victim— despite her good intentions—that's what I believed about myself, too. Now I had teachers at Prep who held me to a higher standard, and that helped me rise to the occasion. If I kept at it, slowly, I could do this. The deeply personal relationships with my teachers in this intimate school setting made me believe it.

I learned a lot in the years I spent at Prep. I was engrossed in Shakespeare (I played Hamlet and Macbeth in school plays); I participated in student government, and traveled with student groups on buses north of the city to represent Prep in regional conferences. I began wearing colorful clothing, taking my hair out of my face and, slowly, looking people in the eyes. I learned that my voice mattered. But I think that it was the teachers themselves who were my biggest lesson at Prep. My teachers, my role models, became my compass in an otherwise dark and confusing world.

Eva and I became friends in our after-school peer education science class, which met every Monday and Wednesday. Enrolled in the class were fifteen students, fourteen girls and one boy, Jonathan, who assured us all that he was very much "one of the girls." The class was an add-on to my already full schedule and it counted for one solid credit, one more toward the forty I needed to meet my goal of graduating in two years.

Our group sat in guidance counselor Jessie Klein's rectangular office, some of us curling up on a futon and the rest of us on metal chairs we'd dragged in from a nearby classroom for the occasion. A woman named Kate Barnhart sat before us. She was plump with large, circular glasses and long, Halloween-wig-frizzy red hair. Her jacket was a patchwork quilt of mix-matched colors,

like an old rug that someone had stitched sleeves into. She smiled often, revealing her small, perfectly white teeth; she seemed happy to see us, happy to teach
us. Kate came from a program named CASES, which trained kids in the court
system to be peer educators in the subject of HIV/AIDS. Jessie gave her the
floor.

Kate introduced the topic by asking, "Ever had a guy try to tell you he's
too big to wear a condom?" The room erupted into nervous giggles.

Jonathan called out, *"Yes!"*

"Thank you, Jonathan," Kate said, "because that's how this is gonna work,
we are gonna get real in here. Now, who else? Please raise your hand." Several
girls obliged.

"Great," Kate said. "We're just getting started. Now raise your hand if a
guy ever caught an attitude with you about putting on a condom."

The majority of hands went up, including my own. I had sometimes had to
argue with Carlos to put one on, but I assumed it was a problem specific to him.

"Thanks, hands down ladies, and Jonathan."

"Yes *ma'am*," he said, in a Southern woman's voice, snapping his fingers.
The girls laughed and someone high-fived him.

"Great. Now I want you to watch *this*," Kate said. She produced a red condom from a bag, ripped it open, and began stretching it out with all the exper-
tise of a pizza maker maneuvering warm dough. As she stretched out the latex,
she spoke.

"What you're going to do in this course is empower yourself to teach your
peers all about HIV/AIDS and STD prevention." Tug, pull, tug, stretch. "But
first, *you* have to learn all about HIV/AIDS and STD prevention, and to do
that, we are going to get a little outrageous."

With her ten fingers protruding out in a cat's cradle, Kate stretched the
bottom of the condom to a cartoonishly broad width. To the classes' collective
shock, she began to pull it over her head, Halloween hair and all. She spared
the glasses, which sat on her lap. Tugging and stretching, to the sound of our
laughter, Kate pulled until the latex condom hugged her face firmly and
cupped her nose. With her nostrils, she blew air into the condom. It filled like
one of those clowns whose mouths you shoot water into at a street fair, until
the balloon pops and you get a prize. When the thing had inflated to a reasonable

size over her head, she reached up with a hairpin—like she'd done it a million times before—and pierced it with a small *pop*. Then she yanked the broken pieces away one by one.

It felt right to clap; we all did. "So, who's too big for a condom?" she said defiantly, refluffing her hair and reapplying her saucer-shaped glasses. "The first step to taking control of your health is to know you are worthwhile. You are important, and you get to ask for things you need. Your rights and needs, safety and comfort, are important. And *you* can steer the ship with your guy. Remember, you have something he wants. You have more power than you realize." From her desk, Jessie smiled at all of us.

I looked at Jessie, then back at Kate, and I was flooded with a sense of pride. I loved the feel of these two grown women pulling us aside for what felt like girl talk. It made me feel special, as if they were sharing secrets.

"Your well-being has a direct relationship with your self-esteem, mentally, physically, spiritually. Your body is a temple, and you have to protect yourself from abuse and misuse of your temple. You must be your own guardian! You get to say what happens to you," Kate said.

Her enthusiasm became my enthusiasm. I could feel a glimmer of what Kate was talking about . . . like maybe there could be something beautiful about me. I wondered why I'd let Carlos treat me the way he had; how I came so close to letting him break me. I didn't stand up to Carlos, and it wasn't me who got us out of the bathtub with Ron that day—it was Lisa. *"You must be your own guardian. You get to say what happens to you."*

We spent the rest of the session with Kate going over a list of what she called Didjaknows, which were a series of facts introduced by the question, "Didjaknow?"

"Didjaknow Cool Whip can trigger yeast infections? And so can anything else heavy in sugar, when applied to your labia majora. Do we all know what a labia majora is?"

"It can trigger what?" asked a concerned voice across the room. The owner of the voice was a thick, pretty white girl with big green eyes wearing a sparkling stud of a nose ring and tall leather boots. Her name was Eva; I'd seen her in two of my classes. Her style was hip-hop with a club girl twist. Her pink lipstick was outlined in deep red lip liner, and her long brown hair was highlighted blond and pulled into a sleek ponytail.

"Does it *always* cause an infection, really?" she asked. Everyone laughed.

"Whatchoo been up to?" Jonathan quipped, laughing and taking more high fives.

Kate smiled. "Not always, dear, it's just something to watch out for."

"Oh," Eva said, still showing obvious concern but slowly beginning to smile. "Well . . . I'm just asking," she said, her hands raised in mock defense. "'Cause it doesn't say all that on the label, and a girl needs to know," and then she laughed, too; we all did.

Eva lived on Twenty-eighth Street and Eighth Avenue, close to Prep. Other than a visit to one of Daddy's friend's apartments growing up, I'd never been inside a home in Manhattan before. I expected it to be "rich" like Daddy said, but instead Eva and her father, Yurick, a Holocaust survivor, lived in Chelsea's version of the projects, in one of a cluster of tall redbrick buildings that primarily housed elderly and low-income families. Yurick was a painter. His mother, Eva's grandmother, had smuggled him out of the Warsaw ghetto when he was an infant, saving his life. There were abstract paintings of the Holocaust all over the walls of their large, sun-filled, two-bedroom apartment.

"They make me feel guilty for having food," Eva half joked, gesturing over the microwave, toward a painting of a gaunt and horrified cluster of people lost in the woods.

"You're hilarious," I told her as she served us a late dinner, two plates of creamy bowtie pasta with peas and carrots. Eva was always making me laugh, and she was deeply insightful, easy to talk to. The moment I met her in Jessie's class, I decided I liked her instantly.

Eva became my first real friend at Prep. Our short talks after class had grown into lunches on the stoops of Chelsea brownstones, which grew into visits to her apartment, and eventually into sleepovers. We were quickly becoming close. I told Eva an edited version of my situation, withholding the full extent for when I felt more trusting. Without ever really stating explicitly that she wanted to help me, she did. We had dozens of sleepovers and hangouts on Twenty-eighth Street. Eva would always cook something, loan me clothing, let me take hot showers upstairs. Often, she split her extra snacks with me during lunchtime at Prep, and she never once showed a sign of being inconvenienced.

"Does your dad remember much about the war?" I asked, dressed in my pajamas in her kitchen, ready for bed. I always felt it was easier keeping the conversation about other people. And after taking "Facing History and Ourselves" with Caleb, I'd learned all about genocide and the Holocaust. It felt good to be able to engage Eva in conversation with some confidence.

"Parts. He was really little, but his dad was the head of an important Jewish organization, so mostly his memories are of after the war, when my grandfather counseled survivors in their living room. My dad overheard all of it, which had to be tough for a small kid," she said.

Eva loved psychology, and she had a way of seeing deeply into people, always listening to someone's sharing from the angle of discovering their motivations, struggles, and needs. "I think his paintings are cathartic for him," she said. "After you experience trauma that deep, you need to do something to heal. Something to make meaning out of all the loss."

I ate everything Eva gave me, and then a second plate, too.

"There're clean sheets on the couch for you, Liz. For whenever you get tired and are ready to sleep."

With Eva, I felt totally understood and cared for. She was safe, loving, and funny. I looked forward to seeing her every day, and I wanted her to be a part of my life always.

Sometimes, another new friend from Prep joined us at Eva's house. His name was James, and he took history class with us. James was over six feet tall, half-black and half-white, with beautiful caramel skin, a toned, muscular build, and a very messy and very large Afro. He loved all things Japanese, and often wore T-shirts with Japanese characters across the chest, or old martial arts shirts from his kung fu class. His clothes were always disheveled, and he had an innocence about him that made me want to be his friend. We connected one day when our teacher unknowingly repeated a nervous tic throughout his lecture, saying the word *mmkay* dozens of times in a single class session. It was so frequent and so funny that I looked for witnesses and saw James beside me, holding back laughter. I slid him a note marked, "Matt says mmkay," with tallies underneath, tallied to well over a hundred. He erupted into laughter in the tiny classroom and we were asked to move seats, both of us still smirking and sharing the joke silently, making eye contact from across the room. Later at lunch, I saw him eating alone, and I used a memory of Sam to summon the courage to approach him. I promptly walked over and stuck my fingers, *splat*, into his mashed potatoes.

"This lunch sucks," I said. "You wanna come eat with me at the deli, my treat?"

With a disbelieving smile on his face, he looked up at me, then back down at my fingers in his food, then back up at me, and said, "Sure."

We split a sandwich in a park off the West Side Highway, facing the crashing waves of the Hudson. I devoured a bag of chips and watched James rollerblade in lazy circles around the pier in the brisk afternoon air. We started having lunch together every day after that, and soon the three of us, Eva, James, and me, began hanging out all the time. Some nights I slept over at Eva's, other nights I crashed at James's. James lived with his mother in a one-bedroom in Washington Heights, uptown near the Bronx. At first I slept on the top bunk of his bunk bed. We'd sit up talking into all hours of the night, posters of Mount Fuji across the walls and a beautiful oak tree outside his window. Eventually, I started lying down next to James to talk. Some nights, we'd fall asleep telling each other stories, wrapped together like pretzels. Other times, things would go further. James was gentle and protective. Our sex was affectionate and it happened naturally, like our friendship.

I slept so well on those nights with James, knowing that I was completely safe.

I had lost my family, but I was building another one. Between Eva, Bobby, Sam, Fief, Danny, Josh, James, and Jamie, I had a collection of people in my life bound together by love. These were the people I leaned on to get through.

Not that Lisa and Daddy weren't my family, but after Ma passed, we'd drifted from one another. Lisa stayed with Brick, and Daddy was in the shelter system. I think a lot of hurt went unspoken between us. I felt that Lisa blamed me for leaving her alone with Ma at the worst possible time. And Daddy and I hadn't been the same since I was taken into St. Anne's. Something essential had broken between us, and it felt as though with time, he was just getting further and further away. I felt as if I had failed him by not going to school and by getting taken into a group home. However irrational, I felt that I'd left him. And then, when he'd lost the apartment on University and hadn't even told me, it was so painful for me because I knew it was proof that we weren't close any-more. I wasn't his little tomboy who played with trucks and helped him sneak past Lisa late at night. I was lost to him.

Without a shared living situation to connect us, Daddy, Lisa, and I spun out of one another's orbits and made independent lives of our own that barely even touched. By the time I finished my first year of high school, the truth was, we barely knew one another.

Painfully, we made the most awkward attempts to be together. We sat through holidays and forced birthday celebrations at a favorite dessert place of Daddy's in the Village. I worked at NYPIRG a second summer, and with my savings, I paid for the cake. These celebrations would always play out the same way. Daddy and I would arrive early, Lisa shortly after. Daddy and I would chit-chat, but provide no real details about what was going on in our lives. When Lisa arrived, we would be seated. Being seated was the worst part because there is no such thing as a table for three. There would always be one empty seat at our table, as if to announce clearly Ma's absence. And because it was often one of our birthdays, a waitress would carry out a cake glowing with candles and the three of us, who no longer really knew one another, would sing in celebration of each other's lives.

Lisa's birthdays were the hardest, for the way I could see Daddy's nervous-ness peak then. He was always so anxious with her, even more so than he was with me. The only other time I could recall seeing him that anxious was in my faded memories of our brief encounters with our older sister Meredith. He seemed fraught with guilt and eager for escape. I couldn't take my eyes off Daddy then, clasping and unclasping his hands, fidgeting through birthday songs with his forced smile, and the absurdity of his reluctant singing. It knot-ted my stomach to watch. I hoped Lisa didn't see it. And I was grateful she didn't know that I had to call Daddy to orchestrate the whole event to begin with. How he would send me to the drugstore to pick out a card for Lisa, from him. "I'm bad at that stuff, Lizzy, and kinda low on cash right now. Pick out something nice, okay," he'd ask. "Thanks, Lizzy, you're the best."

But it was no easy task to pick out a birthday card from Daddy to Lisa. What could I possibly pick? They were all designed for men who had lived up to their responsibilities as father, cards decorated with shimmering monikers of Dad, Daddy, sayings like, "This card is from your loving Father." *"Through all the years watching you grow, it's been my joy to raise you."* But he hadn't, not really. *"To my Daughter on her birthday, the light of my life."* I didn't want to insult Lisa, or to embarrass him. So I came up with my own solution. Neither of them knew it, but more than once I found the perfect card from Daddy to Lisa in the sympathy section of the card store: *"Been Thinking About You,"* or *"On This Day and Always, I Remain by Your Side,"* cards that expressed love but left room for the implication of tragedy and distance. These were the only greeting cards that captured Daddy's role as a father. My role, as Daddy engaged me and as I accepted, was to minimize the awkwardness of these moments, to facilitate the experience of a holiday gone smoothly for all of us.

For the same reason, when Lisa would look away or go to the bathroom, I always slipped Daddy the money to pay for our "celebrations." The waitress would come with the check and Daddy would reach up to grab the black leather fold, inserting cash. "I got it," he'd say. "Happy birthday, Lisa."

It's not that we didn't love one another—we did. I just think we didn't know how to be with one another anymore. No one had prepared us for this, for what to do when tragedy breaks up your family. We had no idea what to do when disease took hold, mental illness struck, when Ma died. And we weren't prepared for what happens when proximity no longer brings you together, and instead connecting became a matter of making an effort toward one another. We were doing the best we could with what we had.

A few days after my eighteenth birthday, we met up at our regular place to celebrate. I arrived on East Eleventh Street first and Daddy showed up a few minutes later. Together, we waited for Lisa.

"How's school?" he asked, picking our safest topic.

It was going well. He knew it was going well. That was probably about the only thing Daddy knew about my life. He fumbled for more small talk, and surprisingly came up with something he'd read in the paper: "You know, Lizzy, they are doing remarkable research on AIDS and AIDS medication these days. They think they're close to finding a cure."

Normally we avoided any topic that could lead to one of us mentioning Ma. The confusion must have read on my face, because when I looked at Daddy again, he turned his head away, pretending to look for Lisa. But he did not change the subject. "With the medication they have now, the quality of life for someone who's got it. . . . It's so much better than it used to be. You really can live for a long time."

I was trying to figure out how to respectfully tell him to talk about something else when he let it out. "I've got it, sweetheart. I'm HIV positive. I was diagnosed in April."

April? It was almost October. All that time, and he hadn't told me? Even with the distance between us, how could he keep this to himself? It felt like someone had punched me in the chest—my heart started pounding and my face grew flush. I looked up at him, my only living parent, and was struck by the idea of losing him, too; the idea of even more loss. Standing on the sidewalk beside him, my world drained of color.

Out of the throng of people making their way up the sidewalk, Lisa emerged. Before she came close, Daddy leaned over and quickly whispered, "Please, Lizzy, do me a favor. Don't tell Lisa."

We sat down to cake on Eleventh Street and I listened to Daddy and Lisa strain through conversation. My head was spinning. I tried to look normal. Get Lisa's birthday cards, make reservations, call and remind him of the holidays, "I'm HIV positive, Lizzy, don't tell Lisa." That night, he joked and laughed harder than I had seen in a while, harder than he really meant it, I suspect. When the cake arrived, glowing with eighteen candles, they both sang me happy birthday and Daddy gently squeezed my hand below the tabletop—one awkward touch with his own shaky hand. The physical contact was out of place coming from him, and I know it took a lot for Daddy. In his gesture, I could feel him reaching out to me across our distance, assuring me silently, "*I know, Lizzy, and I'm with you.*" I couldn't take my eyes off him. I was captured by this image: my father clapping his hands before the smoke of my extinguished birthday candles, so vulnerable and still full of life right in front of me, for now. I wanted to grab on to him, to protect him from AIDS. I wanted to make this stop happening to our family, to keep him safe and to make him healthy again.

God grant me the serenity to accept the things I cannot change, the courage to change the things I can, and the wisdom to know the difference . . .

I did not make a wish over my candles. Instead, I chose to forgive my father, and made a quiet promise to work on healing our relationship. I wouldn't make the same mistake that I'd made with Ma, I would be there for him through this. We would be in each other's lives again. No, he hadn't been the best father, but he was my father, and we loved each other. We needed each other. Though he'd disappointed me countless times through the years, life had already proven too short for me to hold on to that. So I let go of my hurt. I let go years of frustration between us. Most of all, I let go of any desire to change my father and I accepted him for who he was. I took all of my anguish and released it like a fistful of helium balloons to the sky, and I chose to forgive him.

The irony is, despite all the years I spent avoiding it, school became my refuge. For my remaining two semesters at Prep, I squeezed into my schedule as many classes as I could possibly take, and I fell in love with the process of using my education to rebuild my life. I began to relish the sense of achievement I took from completing long hours of course readings, and I savored the creative process of ever so carefully constructing essays on authors like Shakespeare and Salinger. Deciding exactly how to fit which words into which sentences felt like a puzzle to solve, a challenge made compelling by Perry's enthusiastic class discussions on character motivation, syntax, and even his bold assertion one afternoon that "grammar saves lives!" "Punctuation changes everything," he proclaimed in white chalk across our blackboard. "Let's eat, Grandpa!— versus—Let's eat Grandpa! To Grandpa, these are *very* different sentences," he teased, making the class erupt into chuckles and groans. I smiled widely at Perry then, filled with joy by his exuberance.

But I know I didn't love school for school's sake. I had never really been what people call an "academic" person, nor did I see myself becoming one. Instead, I took pleasure in the fact that my work existed in a social setting, one that was based on the promise of a brighter future. I knew that what I adored about school was that each of my assignments—readings, essays, or in-class presentations—was inseparable from my relationships, both with my teachers and with my new friends at Prep. If I loved school at all, I loved it for what it provided me access to: bonds with people I grew to cherish. And nothing was better than working toward my dreams alongside people I loved who were doing the same.

Like those study nights at Eva's place, when she, James, and I would work sprawled out across her living room, our books and papers littering the table-tops, couches, and floor. We'd study side by side, passing the hours together. I'd curl up on the couch, my head resting on James's lap while he ran his fin-gers through my hair. Sometimes we'd make faces at each other, or laugh at one another's stupid jokes while I read for class, and James flipped through his book on Japanese Kanji. Diligently, he'd practice writing neat rows of charac-ters on dozens of fresh notebook pages. Eva cooked for us, typically making pasta with chicken, peas, and carrots in creamy sauce. And on days when we could afford it, she'd cook with extras like portabella mushrooms or scoops of avocado on the side. For my part, I always liked to show up at Eva's apartment bringing food to share, making sure that I had something to contribute. De-spite my full schedule, it wasn't difficult to make time to stop and get a few things; the grocery store was close enough—on Twenty-sixth Street, just off of Eighth Avenue, two blocks from Eva's place.

On one particular evening after night school, when I was on my way to Eva's place from Union Square, I devised a small plan. As I had on many other occasions, I would stop in the supermarket, slip groceries into my book bag to steal them, and then exit discreetly through the sliding doors. This way, Eva, James, and I could pig out while we watched a movie on Eva's couch later that night. The three of us would be well fed and cozy in our pajamas, and it would be perfect. Eva had already gone shopping and because I had no intention of showing up empty-handed, from a pay phone on Fourteenth Street I'd prom-ised Eva a pack of chicken cutlets and a jar of Parmesan cheese (both items I knew I could slip into my bag in mere seconds). It's not that I didn't have money to purchase the food. In fact, I carried with me everywhere I went my savings from my second summer working at NYPIRG. But money equaled survival, and I did everything I could to conserve it. So that night, just as I had done many nights, I entered the supermarket with absolutely no intention of paying.

At first, the plan was going smoothly. I had both items in hand and was searching for a place to hide them in my bag when, to my surprise, I stopped myself. It was the sight of the manager that triggered me. He was a short, thick, Latin guy wearing a tie, with a pen tucked behind his ear. I saw him reading papers off a clipboard in the distance, checking a shipment, managing several employees. He was sweating. I looked over at the cashiers ringing up groceries, and then over at an older woman filling her cart with bags to bring home. I stood and watched each of them and realized, I didn't want to take anything from this store; something about it felt wrong. Here was this manager working hard to make this business work, and for the first time, I could actually see that. Standing there, I didn't know how I hadn't seen it before. Holding that jar of powdered cheese and those chicken cutlets in my hand, ready to steal, I suddenly felt off, creepy.

Earlier into my current semester at Prep, there had been an incident of someone taking a student's wallet. A town meeting was called, and Perry led the discussion. "It's not the wallet that is our biggest loss," Perry said. "A trust has been broken in our community. This creates a question of whether or not we are safe with one another. It's going to take a while before we can build back that trust. It's a hurt to our community."

The cause and effect of one person's actions onto a larger group of people, at that moment in Prep, was clear. But as far as out in the world was concerned, the idea had remained abstract to me. Until, that is, I found myself standing in that supermarket, considering yet another theft in a long line of thefts, and my eyes found that store manager. Before Prep, I had never been a part of what everyone kept calling a "community," and the idea that what I did impacted anyone other than myself, than my small circle, had not been real to me. I felt like an island.

But standing in that supermarket, recalling our Town Hall meeting, I was beginning to identify more clearly the connection between my own cause and effect. At best, the impact of people stealing from this store would cause prices to go up. Families would have to pay more for their groceries to compensate, if they could afford to pay more. At worst, the store could go out of business and the cashiers and this manager would lose their jobs. People's trust in people would be tarnished, I imagined. I looked at the manager again and thought of Perry's words. Then I approached the register with the chicken cutlets and the jar of cheese.

It was not that I never stole again, because truthfully, I did. But that day was the *beginning* of my never stealing again, and it was the start of a long process of me understanding that I was not, in fact, an island unto myself.

I walked over to the register with my groceries and dug out some loose bills from the bottom of my book bag. The cashier smiled and gave me some change. I stopped to watch the man at the end of the counter pack my bag, filling it in two quick swipes. It felt like ages ago that I was packing bags in the supermarket myself. On my way out, I gave the guy my change. "Gracias," he said, and I went on my way.

✦ ✦ ✦

The poster boards were bloody with red ink, wet with blues and yellows that lit up the white page, bringing the biology lesson to life: *"The B-cells tell the T-cells to fight illness and disease."*

As part of a student team of three, Eva and I selected an original design for our presentation depicting the roles of cells at work in the immune system's fight against HIV/AIDS. Together, we stood back to take in the image our team had chosen: boxers in a boxing ring, red gloves raised chin-high. On the outskirts of the ring a coach with a towel wrapped around his neck, water bottle in hand, was the B-cell, the communicator. The smaller boxer represented the T-cell, the hopeful fighter. The largest contender represented HIV itself, and it stood tall and menacing in opposition.

Crouched down low, lifting her long hair over her ears, hoop earrings dangling, Eva puffed out her cheeks and blew on the ink. Sam, now in her second semester at Prep, passed her a Sharpie to deepen the bold headline: *"Empower Yourself, Fight the Spread of HIV."*

"Shoulda made 'em the Crips and the Bloods fighting. Like, *'I'll cut choo!* Ya feel me?'" Sam said, motioning a knife-swing through the air. All three of us laughed. Living in the group home, Sam was full of gang and prison references, and her slang now had a deeper street twist to it. Having her at Prep was like having a piece of my family back together again. Sam didn't come to school every day, but she came in often enough to enjoy the experience of our little community; she made friends and was well loved by our teachers. I was so happy to have her there. That afternoon was a big day for us, and Sam had dressed for the occasion: her long skirt was tattered, and she wore a man's blue button-down shirt with a pinstriped tie and combat boots.

"The boxer thing is cool, though," Sam conceded, shrugging her shoulders and snapping her gum. She leaned down and spontaneously penciled a black eye onto HIV's face. "Forget this guy," she said, etching it in deeper. "He should get knocked out."

"Word," I said to Sam, smirking. "Good idea." Suddenly, I was on my knees, too, pencil in hand, giving HIV a busted lip. "Let's ugly him up," I told her. Side by side, we vigorously scratched our pencils to the page.

We had a presentation to make; a small crowd of students waited for us in Prep Central. Our job was to use these characters to engage our classmates in HIV/AIDS awareness, to have the cellular struggle between HIV/AIDS and the immune system jump out from the page to create prevention in the lives of others. Bobby, Josh, and Fief were also in the waiting crowd, sitting among the other Prep students. It was their second semester at Prep, too. It had taken me only a few weeks at Prep to understand how welcoming the environment was, for me to feel and trust the safety that these teachers were. But as soon as I knew what Prep could be like, what high school could be like, I went back to my friends and encouraged them to interview. They got in, and now several of us were enrolled. Sam, Bobby, and I even had a few of the same classes together.

At times, having my friends at Prep could be rocky. More than once, a couple of them wanted to skip class and they urged me to come with them. It was so tempting, seeing them huddled by the exit door, slipping out into the bustling streets of Manhattan. I wanted to hang out, like the old days. And it could feel so stale in the classroom compared to the fun I knew they would have walking all around Greenwich Village and Chelsea, sneaking into a movie or sitting in the park. Plus, I didn't want to be the uptight one in our group, serious and obedient of school regulations. There were moments when it was hard not to cut class too. But I kept thinking about my transcripts, the neat little columns of A's that I'd written in blue pen sitting in the stairwell that night, and that woman running track, jumping hurdles, checking off one A at a time. They were adding up, and I was writing my ticket; no one could get me into college, but me.

Still, my group at Prep was my family, and meant everything to me; it made the school feel like a kind of home. It reminded me of those late-night episodes of the TV show *Cheers* that Daddy and I used to watch sitting on the couch together, how whenever the character Norm walked in, everyone would call out his name in unison. As a child I didn't understand the show much, but I understood the sense of belonging shared by the characters, and I longed to have it for myself, a place where I could belong. Before Prep, and especially before my friends came to Prep, I'd never had a place where everyone knew everyone's name, a place where everyone was welcome and working on their goals together. And now here we were working to make our lives better, side by side. It meant everything to me.

"Let's go, guys, I think they're ready for us," Eva said, lifting a poster board up high. The characters she'd drawn were a worried couple seated bedside, troubled because neither could remember whether or not they had used a condom during a night of drinking and irresponsible sex. Eva had given the girl bee-stung lips, a nose ring, and eyebrows arched in concern. Their thought bubbles were decorated in glitter, highlighting words like *trust, choice,* and *consequences.* Armed with our materials, the three of us, Eva, Sam, and I, stepped through the doors of the meeting room.

"No one ever expects to contract HIV," I said, opening our discussion to the room of students. I wore a green sweater and blue jeans for the occasion, one of many articles of colorful clothing that I'd begun to trade in place of my standard black uniform.

"But it happens anyway, and it breaks up families and it takes lives. We're here today to keep it from happening to you. That's what this is about."

For a half hour, Sam, Eva, and I used our posters and the information we learned with CASES for our presentation. When it came to the part about exactly how HIV spreads through the human body, I saw Ma. But not the sick version of Ma in the hospital—instead I saw a smiling one, full of life and love. I saw her laughing with me, clasping my hand on Mosholu Parkway, blowing dandelion fluff into the sky and making wishes, the HIV virus already multiplying in her body. Her wish for me to stay in school, her wish for me to build a life of options, her wish for me to be okay.

The Xerox machine spit out ten clean copies of my transcripts. Sitting in Jessie's empty guidance counselor office, I ran my fingertip down the columns of grades: 92, 94, 100, 100, 100, 98—more than ten classes per semester in total, many of which were high A's. As I'd planned, I was moving at a pace of one full school year per semester. That morning, the rest of the school was in an assembly in Prep Central, just on the other side of the wall from Jessie's office. My task that Friday, I decided, was to finally deal with scholarship applications. I wouldn't fill out college apps until later in the year, but my plan was to have the funds gathered ahead of time.

Jessie Klein, my guidance counselor, helped me decide this. Throughout the last few months, we'd sat in her small office during lunch or after school and talked about college.

"With your grades, Liz, you have so many schools to pick from. You're in great shape," she'd said. "But you want to think about how you plan to pay your tuition, and sooner rather than later."

On one of those afternoons, Jessie had handed me a manila envelope packed with scholarship applications that she had personally taken the time to select as well suited for me. State schools, Jessie explained, would probably give someone with my grades full funding, no problem. I just had to fill out something called a FASFA form, Free Application for Federal Student Aid. But, Jessie explained, tuition for other types of schools could be much more expensive, so the best thing to do would be to fill out lots of scholarship applications so that I could secure all the funding possible and keep my options open, which sounded great to me.

"Um . . . so if tuition at top colleges is really high," I said, taking the envelope in my hand, and opening it to thumb through the stack, "like more than thirty thousand a year . . . are these scholarships about that much? Enough to cover tuition?" I asked Jessie.

Her look told me I had no idea what I was in for.

Weeks later, as I set out to spend the afternoon by myself working on my scholarship application process, I quickly found out why Jessie had given me that look. In her empty office, I flipped the fluorescent light off and worked only by sunlight, which shone in through the crisscross window guards. For nearly an hour, I sorted through leaflets and brochures decorated with glossy photos of students from racially diverse backgrounds, all smiling, giving their thumbs-up endorsement of company-sponsored loans, scholarships, and grants. Every other moment or so, on the other side of the wall that separated us, the whole student body broke into applause, cheering on a series of teacher's announcements that I couldn't quite hear. I'd decided to skip the gathering because I knew deadlines were approaching, fast, and I had to get this taken care of. With so much information to sort through on the application forms, I began flipping past everything in search of only the most pertinent info, the amount of funding they were offering.

These people had to be kidding! What a disappointment! The applications requested far too much time-consuming work for far too little money. And the whole thing was confusing. A financial products company offered $500 to the winner of an essay contest about "free trade in the free market." Another round of applause sounded next door. Someone whistled loudly. I set that application aside for later; it would require time at the library. Another company gave $250 to the student with the best politically based short story about any prominent politician who had held office in the last one hundred years. Another scholarship was for $400, and another for $1,000. These scholarships would barely cover food at top colleges, I thought. I began to wonder how it was that poor people managed to get a great education without thirty scholarships per year. Finally, I turned a page and found the one I'd been hoping for, one that Jessie had flagged with a Post-it marked *"PERFECT FOR YOU,"* in deep blue pen strokes. This application was issued from *The New York Times* College Scholarship Program, and it offered "$12,000, per year, every year of college." Clearly, they had some idea of how much top colleges cost. On the form, apart from questions of GPA and after-school activities, it simply asked for an essay in which I was to describe any obstacles that I may have had to overcome in my life in order to thrive academically.

My eyes widened. Seriously? I mean, really? It was so ridiculously perfect that I laughed. With a sweep of my arm, I pushed everything to one side of the table and set down a blank sheet of notebook paper to begin outlining my essay. My hand raced across the page, making bullet points to work from. I laid down a paragraph in only a few short minutes. This was it, I thought. I decided to take a break and step out of the office for some water. Just as I did, the meeting broke; students were swarming out of the large room, talking to one another. Bessim, one of the seniors, came up to me and patted me on the shoulder. "Good job," he said. Holding my cup I looked at him, totally baffled.

"Mm, okay," I said, confused.

"Congratulations," he told me.

I continued to stare blankly at his face, until I finally asked, "For what?"

"For all the awards," he said. "They called your name for everything. So, congratulations."

I walked away in a daze. I hadn't even realized that it was an awards ceremony.

I ran to see Perry in his office. He was on the phone, but paused and said, "We missed you in there," before handing me a folder with my name on it.

Back in Jessie's office, I opened the front of the folder and lifted my awards out. They were made of decorative white paper framed in an intricate blue design with "Liz Murray" spelled out in calligraphy. There were almost a dozen awards inside, including ones for best onstage performance for my role as Hamlet in the school talent show, commitment to community service for the HIV/AIDS peer education program, and outstanding achievement in various academic areas.

I immediately picked up the *Times* scholarship application again. Outside the first-floor window, I saw students mingling, smoking cigarettes, snapping bubble gum, and talking. Class had let out for the day.

I held my pen to the paper, trembling. I worked in some kind of trance, pouring everything I had onto that page. My frustrations, my sadness, *all* of my grief, they pushed the pen across that page; they wrote the essay, or the essay wrote itself. Whatever it was, it wasn't me writing because I wasn't there. I was floating above looking down on myself, watching my hand move feverishly across the page, watching everything in my life that had ever held me back, breaking.

When my typed essay emerged from the office printer that evening, I stapled it to my transcripts. All I had to do now was apply to college.

It was only supposed to be a group picture for our yearbook, that's all. I had no idea I'd apply to Harvard because of it. It happened when the top ten students in a school-wide course called Urban Explorations were chosen for a field trip to Boston. Perry wanted to reward us for all the hard work. Along with another teacher, Christina, he packed the group of us onto Amtrak for the weekend trip. Our "hotel" would be dorm rooms at Boston College. Eva and I both qualified for the trip, and we sat next to each other on the huge commuter train, talking nonstop for the whole four-hour ride. I kept interrupting, pointing at things out the window, yelling, "Look!" to Eva at the scenery whipping past us, streaks of houses, sparkling bodies of water, open sky. She'd been to Paris with her dad and grandmother before, so Amtrak was nothing big. But she indulged me anyway, turning every time and searching for the source of my delight in everyday things.

First-time travel on this regional train felt like an adventure. The thrill made me giddy, talkative. We'd moved to the food car for privacy, and I interrupted Eva again, this time in the middle of a story about her boyfriend, Adrian. Abruptly, I got up from the seat across from Eva and slid in right beside her. "I have nowhere to live," I confessed, very much out of nowhere. "Don't tell anyone, okay?" We had been sharing pretzels in the food car, talking about James and Adrian. I worried that my sudden announcement was too heavy for the conversation.

"I won't," she said, and in no way did she look surprised. With all my nights at her apartment, it probably wasn't news. "Promise," she added, smiling at me. She extended the open bag of pretzels. For the rest of the train ride, we were each other's diaries. We talked about our boyfriends, about music, and about our dreams.

Eva wanted to go to college, too, "someplace I can just go and shut the door to my room, lock it, and read all day. Someplace with a really good education. Oh! And someplace in nature, out of the city. Someplace beautiful, with trees," she said. "And I want Adrian to come with me, too." She asked about my plans.

"I don't know where I want to go . . . maybe Brown? I heard Brown is good. Maybe someplace in California," I said. "Sam and I used to say we were going to live there together. . . . I want to go someplace beautiful, too."

The dorms of Boston College were a world unto themselves. Eva and I shared a room. I tossed my things onto my single bed and joined my classmates in a game of tag. I was enlivened in the halls of this strange and exciting place. We ran after one another, sliding up and down the halls in our socks, shrieking with laughter as we flew past the soda machine, triangle sports flags, and pegboard flyers tacked up high on the hallway walls. Monique, a tall girl with yellow hair and hoop earrings, chased after Eva and me, and we all ended up crashing onto the floor, holding our sides with laughter. Out the window was a massive track field and in the distance, the busy city of Boston. This is what Ken and the others had been so excited about when they mentioned "dorms," a wide-open space to just be. Before heading out to explore, I hung my T-shirts in the closet, folded my spare jeans in one of the drawers, touched the picture of

Ma with my fingertips, and put her coin in my front jeans pocket to take with me for the day. It was the first space in years over which I could claim some ownership, even if it was only for two nights. It gave me a small sense of pride to know that I'd earned it. I could live someplace like this, I thought.

Boston was beautiful. Perry led us down tree-lined streets with town houses and brownstones through an area called Beacon Hill. You could see right into the windows on the ground floor of the old houses, and you'd get a perfect view of their living rooms: crystal chandeliers and old bookcases built into the wooden walls, antique furniture, rooms warmed by the glow of fireplaces. I could not get enough of looking into these windows. They made me feel hopeful. There was just something enchanting about the buildings with their gray shuttered windows set against the lush green trees sprinkled with white flowers, their petals drizzled along the cobblestone streets. The neighborhood was otherworldly, magical even.

Perry indulged my every question. "How much do these houses cost? What do these people do for a living? . . . What's college like?"

We built up a hunger walking all afternoon. Lunch was scheduled at a Chinese restaurant named Yenching, in Harvard Square. But first, Perry said, we needed just one group picture—in front of the John Harvard statue in Harvard Yard. I'd heard of Harvard on TV, but I'd never seen Harvard before, not even a picture of it, and I was curious.

I don't know that I can ever really put into words the experience of walking through that yard on that afternoon, at a time when everything I owned fit into my book bag and I was dressed in ratty clothing, still buzzing from the novelty of an Amtrak train ride, which at that point was the highlight of my worldly experience.

As I said earlier, for years, maybe for my whole life, it felt as though there was a brick wall down the middle of everything. Standing outside those buildings, I could almost picture it. On one side of the wall there was society, and on the other side there was me, us, the people in the place I come from. Separate.

Standing in Harvard Yard was like touching the wall, running my hands along its rough edges, questioning its authority.

Students walked alongside the rich green grass, carrying books or pushing bikes, wearing crimson sweaters with HARVARD across them. The statue was crowded by a group of Japanese tourists posing for pictures. Our class lined up behind them to take our picture next. Harvard students laid out across the open lawn on sheets, reading. The redbrick buildings looked like they were made by the same architects who made Beacon Hill, old and important-looking structures, as ancient as they were inaccessible. But also beautiful—and the sight of the buildings filled me with a deep longing for something I could not explain. The feeling must have shown on my face because, right then and there without a word between us, Perry leaned over and said to me, "Hey Liz, it would be a reach, but it's not impossible . . . Ever think about applying to Harvard?"

I stopped everything to absorb Perry's words. No, I most certainly had not ever thought of applying to Harvard before. But standing there, touching the wall, I considered that while I most likely would not get in, it was, at the very least, possible that I could.

On a rainy February afternoon, I shut my umbrella and walked through the rotating doors of *The New York Times* building on Forty-third Street, right off Times Square, for my scholarship interview. Sam and I had gone thrift store shopping on Fordham Road to locate the pair of khaki pants I was wearing, the button-down shirt that almost fit me, and the used pair of black boots that sort of looked like dress shoes when my pants covered them. Lisa loaned me her peacoat, with one button missing, but the coat still looked professional, I thought. Three thousand high school students had applied for the six scholarships, and twenty-one finalists had been picked. I was chosen as one of them and on that brutally cold afternoon, the day of my interview, I was ready. Also, I was tired; I'd already had a long day.

It had begun with a trip that Lisa and I took to welfare. The reason we were in welfare was because we were fighting to get rent. We needed rent because we'd gotten an apartment.

With money I'd saved from my second summer working at NYPIRG, Lisa and I made a deal. Soon after I turned eighteen and was old enough to legally sign a lease and old enough to no longer worry about being taken to a group home, I would spend my entire savings, every dollar of it, to get us into a one-bedroom on Bedford Park. Between real estate fees, first month's rent, and a security deposit, a mattress, several pots and pans, and a kitchen table with two chairs, I was flat broke when we were done. And I was busy around the clock with eleven classes and college applications, too busy to get a job. In return for my contribution, Lisa, who was employed at the Gap, would pay all of our bills while I finished my classes, until I could work again. This would also leave her flat broke. On this tight budget, we could keep the lights on, buy some food sometimes, have very basic telephone service, and just barely pay the rent. A reliable source of food would come from local soup kitchens and especially from the pantry packs they gave me at The Door, which were a life-saver. As part of the deal, Sam could share my room with me; she moved in the same day that Lisa and I did.

On a Saturday in December, on a day of heavy snowfall, Lisa, Fief, Sam, Eva, Bobby, James, and I helped carry Lisa's belongings from Brick's apartment to our new place, which was a short distance. We carried lamps and bags. We slipped, running and sliding through the slush at two a.m., watching the chunky white snowflakes shine by the light of street lamps; we were laughing hysterically. James pulled me into a snowbank, collapsing us into a clumsy pile; he kissed me and hit me in the face with a heaping fistful of cold snow and I screamed, chasing him. Brick was out of town for the upcoming holiday, so Sam and I had the opportunity to find old bags of stuff we didn't even know we had left behind there so long ago. Toward the end of the night, Fief and Bobby carried Lisa's bed into Fief's dad's work van, wearing their big bubble North Face coats, slipping on the wet metal of the vehicle in their thick mountain boots.

From that day on, Lisa, Sam, and I were supposed to be okay. But two days after we moved in, Lisa lost her job. We hadn't even paid a single bill yet. We were depending on Lisa's paycheck for everything. When her last check came, it ended up going to food and we really didn't have anything left.

That last semester, I had a full year of high school to complete and college interviews. I couldn't work. For weeks I'd been spending an average of ten hours a day at school, coming home at night to work on college applications, which I fanned out on the kitchen table, and I rationed food with Lisa and Sam from the pantry packs we got from The Door. It was terrifying to have spent my NYPIRG money while having no time to work, while being committed to so many classes and college applications all at once. It was every bit a gamble, and it seemed it was the wrong one. At least on my own, I could be cautious and spend as little money as possible, using my savings to survive. That savings was my security blanket. But having invested it all in an apartment, I was as broke as the day I left the Holiday Motel. Every day I'd exit the house to go to school and Lisa would be poring over the classifieds, with no luck. Then the cut-off notices started arriving in the mail, bills in white envelopes with thick red lines down the middle, stamped with end-of-service dates for us to count down to. And the pressure was mounting.

Welfare seemed like the reasonable solution. They had to help us. Public assistance was nothing new to Lisa and me. We had gone with Ma to many of her appointments, so I knew what to expect. Still, nothing prepared me for the way the surly, rude woman in charge of our case treated us. We had been sent away time after time for supposedly not having one document or another, no proof that Ma had passed away, or that Daddy wasn't taking care of us. How do you prove something that isn't happening? And what if we couldn't find a copy of Ma's death certificate? But then, on the day of my scholarship interview, I was certain we had done everything right and that I was only going to the office that morning to finalize our case, get approved, have our rent paid, and get some food stamps.

"You are not eligible for public assistance," the caseworker said matter-of-factly, closing the file in her hand and tossing it on her desk.

"What do you mean?" I asked when it was obvious she wasn't going to elaborate.

There was a sharp intake of breath, a sucking noise through her teeth, and then she rolled her eyes. "I *mean* exactly what I said, Princess. You are not eligible."

Princess? Her name-calling took me back to the group home, and back to motels with Carlos. Life was holding up a truth for me: There were just as many people deciding my life *for* me as there was neediness in my life, and never more than that. The more needy I kept myself, the more it would always be up to other people what happened to me. I decided I would make my life so full of things that empowered me, people like this woman would shrink away, until they disappeared from my sight.

"I understand what you said, ma'am. I am just asking you why I am not eligible." She came back with a lot of words, more eye-rolling, but no real answer. Like many of the other people I saw being "helped" that morning, I found myself yelling at an indifferent caseworker, another brick in that wall that stood between me and things I wanted and needed.

I could feel my anger growing. She became, for that moment, all the people who ever told me no, all the caseworkers who ever frustrated me, and the teachers at those first high schools who turned me down. I became livid. Finally, I raised my hand in a "stop" motion, closer to her face than I knew was okay. I said, "You know what? I am going to be late for my interview for Harvard if I keep wasting time with you." My intention was to lash out at her, to let her know that even though she had power over me in this moment, I was going somewhere bigger than the welfare office, bigger than her.

She laughed in my face. "Yeah? Well, I got Ms. Yale coming in here next. So why don't you get on to your meetin' with Haaar-vud!"

Blood rushed to my cheeks, and I stormed out. That's okay, I thought, pushing open the double doors and exiting that miserable office. That's okay, because despite my caseworker's disbelief, I did have an interview with a Harvard alumnus that afternoon. In fact, my schedule that day was packed; I had what I thought would have been a routine appointment to have my welfare approved, a college interview in midtown Manhattan, and then my *New York Times* interview. Because I was trying to minimize any absences from school, I packed all of these appointments into the same long day, which I hoped would go smoothly—a one-two-three day: welfare, Harvard, *New York Times*. Welfare, as it turned out, would be the only thing that did not go well that day.

I met the alumnus in his office at a law firm in the East Fifties. Even now, the interview is a blur of politeness and standard questions about school, what I wanted to do with my life, and my education and career goals. I just remember riding down the elevator after the interview believing that it had gone well, opening my journal, and double-checking my next stop, 229 West Forty-third Street.

After coming in out of the freezing rain, I made my way through security, found the elevators, and was directed to a tiny room where the scholarship finalists were gathered. I found a seat and immediately took in my surroundings. Two very nervous-looking high school students sat with their parents on the couch in the airless room. Someone paced; a mother kept rubbing her daughter's shoulders. Copies of *The New York Times* were stacked on a small table.

I understood the importance of winning a scholarship, but not the importance of winning *this* scholarship, not really. I knew that without, at least, a partial scholarship, I would not be able to go to a top college. Top colleges provided the most options, which is what I was seeking. Harvard tuition was incredible and I could not afford a turkey sandwich at the moment, so I understood that I needed college funding. But what I did not get was the significance that came with being awarded a scholarship from the *Times*. Never, not once, had I seen anyone I knew personally reading *The New York Times*. I simply had no frame of reference for how influential a newspaper it was. In my neighborhood, if people read the paper at all, they read the *New York Post* or the *New York Daily News*. The only people I'd ever seen read the thicker, larger *New York Times* were professional people, people who looked highly functional, usually on the train. Certainly I had never read it before. So the pacing, obvious anxiety, and near hyperventilating one guy was doing was all lost on me. My ignorance left me blessedly unaware of just how important this was. And by now, with my experience at Prep and with how it was becoming easier to talk to people, I wasn't too nervous. In fact, after the long day it felt good to be somewhere warm, and I even relaxed into my chair.

Sitting in this small, windowless waiting area, for what I thought of as my third meeting of the day, my eyes landed on a table of refreshments. Bottles of water were lined up in factorylike perfect rows, alongside a tray of croissants, bagels, and muffins. A cheerful woman with a pretty smile and thin dreadlocks named Sheila was our host, checking in finalists to get us ready for the big interview. She encouraged me to help myself. "Please, sweetie, no one's touched a thing, we'll end up throwing them out. Please, the whole tray is up for grabs."

That was all I needed to hear. When they called my name and she turned around to walk out ahead of me, I quickly stuffed doughnuts and muffins into my bag. She said I could help myself; besides, they were throwing them out anyway.

I walked into a conference room with a long oak table in the center, around which sat twelve or so women and men dressed in business attire. There was an empty seat at the end of the table clearly meant for me. I approached it.

My hands still had sugar on them from the doughnuts. "Sorry, give me one second," I said as I took a tissue from a box that was sitting on the table. I sat as I wiped my hands. Twelve sets of eyes stared at me, taking me in.

I knew the interview would be about my essay. They'd asked: Describe an obstacle you have overcome. Since I was eighteen by then and couldn't be forced into the custody of Child Welfare, I had written my *New York Times* essay about being homeless. I held nothing back.

In the interview, I shared even more than what I'd written. I told them— these writers, editors, people in business suits, with expensive-looking brace- lets and bow ties—about Ma and Daddy; about University Avenue; Ma selling the Thanksgiving turkey. I told them about surviving on the generosity of friends and sleeping in stairwells. I told them about not eating every day and getting meals at places like The Door. The room fell quiet. One man with a red tie and glasses leaned forward on the large conference room table and broke the silence.

"Liz . . . is there anything else you'd like to tell us?" he asked.

I was stumped. Obviously I was supposed to say something impressive, a thoughtful something that would have them believe I deserved this.

"Well, I need the scholarship" was the first thing that came to mind. "I just really need it." Everyone laughed. Had I thought of something more complex and impressive sounding, I would have said that instead, but it was the one simple truth that came to mind.

Someone said it was nice to meet me. Several people shook my hand.

A reporter named Randy took me upstairs to a cafeteria where *Times* em- ployees ate their lunch every day. Everyone was walking around in business clothing, ID cards dangling from their waists or key chains. He sat across from me, a white man in his thirties, in a blue button-down shirt and a tie. He was friendly enough, and he bought me lunch.

"Sorry, I wasn't in the official interview, Liz," he said, clicking his pen. "Can you tell me how you became homeless? And why your parents couldn't take care of you?"

Sitting there with him, I jammed warm macaroni and cheese and chicken into my mouth and gulped down delicious sweet apple juice. My head was buzzing with excitement at the warm meal and the attention of this reporter. I was thrilled to be inside a real office building full of professional people, like the ones I'd seen on TV. After everything I'd been through in the last few years and everything I'd been through on that day alone, it was surprisingly easy to talk to this guy. I told him everything, too. I told him about growing up watching my parents get high, about losing Ma, about the motels, and even about my morning in the welfare office.

Years later, I've often reflected on how blessed I was to have no real understanding of how difficult that day was supposed to be. Had I known how difficult it was supposed to be to interview with Harvard or *The New York Times*; had anyone told me that those were hard, nearly impossible, things to do, then I may have never done them. But I didn't know enough about the world to analyze the likelihood of my success; I had only the commitment to actually show up and do it. In the years ahead of me, I learned that the world is actually filled with people ready to tell you how likely something is, and what it means to be realistic. But what I have also learned is that no one, *no one* truly knows what is possible until they go and do it.

When we were done talking, for the second time that day, I got into an elevator feeling that I had taken a step forward. I saw my track runner bounding top speed, one more hurdle behind her.

The following Friday, the phone in our apartment rang. I was actually startled to hear it, because I expected it to be cut off by then. For weeks we'd been getting these disconnection notices for the phone and the lights. In fact, I was certain we had only a couple more weeks left before we would lose everything, including the apartment. I had already planned out the bag I would pack.

"May I speak to Elizabeth Murray, please?" a very professional-sounding voice said when I picked up.

"This is Liz."

"I am Roger Lehecka from the *New York Times* Scholarship Program. . . . I am just calling to tell you that you are one of the six students chosen to be awarded the *New York Times* Scholarship!"

Whirlwind. That's the word that comes to mind when I think of how to describe my life after winning the scholarship. A floodgate had opened, and I had no way of knowing that my life would simply never be the same. If I had no real understanding of it before, I very quickly learned about the influence of *The New York Times*.

The six scholarship winners were called back to the *Times* to be photographed the week after we had been notified. Lisa came along with me. We were seated with the other winners and their parents back in that tiny airless room. Lisa was adorable, with the way she kept looking at everything around the office, holding in laughter.

"Where are we?" she said, giggling. "This is so funny."

"I know," I said, giggling too. We both played it cool and sat there quietly amazed.

I was photographed once with the group, and then once alone. For that second picture, I was taken up the elevator to a high floor in *The New York Times* building, to one of the libraries. Being among those stacks of books reminded me of all the times Daddy had taken me to the library when we lived on University Avenue. The photographer had me sit on a large windowsill, the sun illuminating the room from behind me. As his camera clicked away, I wondered what Daddy would say when he saw it. I wondered if somehow Ma could see me, too.

It really did not dawn on me until the day that the article hit newsstands, featuring the six winners on the cover of the Metro Section (next to an article about Bill and Hillary Clinton), that the entire world would see it. Everyone, including my teachers at Prep, was going to know my whole situation. Part of me was worried that they would think differently about me. The truth turned out to be quite the opposite. Perry was proud, all my teachers were. But everyone expressed concern over how I was going to pay my rent and remain stable. And my teachers weren't the only ones.

I'd mentioned my high school in the *Times* interview. That created something I never anticipated, what I eventually came to call the Angel Brigade. People I did not know began showing up at Prep to meet me, to hug me, to give me encouraging words, clothing, food, and care packages. They came to help me, and they asked for nothing in return.

Mail came flooding in. People sent cards with smiling pictures of their families, invitations to visit them in their homes across America. They sent books. One man, learning about my situation, got his friends together and reached out to several people in our community, and they paid what Lisa, Sam, and I owed in back rent. People we did not know paid our back rent, they kept on our lights, and they filled up our fridge.

I never slept another night on the streets, ever again.

What was most moving about all of this unexpected generosity was the spirit in which people helped. It was something in their moods and in their general being when they showed up at my school, how they were smiling, looking me right in the eyes, asking in every way what I needed. One lady in her late forties, wearing a yellow dress, showed up in front of my school around the time we finished. April got me from the back office and when I came out front, this woman looked nervous, clutching her necklace and fidgeting; she stepped forward to introduce herself.

"I'm Teressa. Terry . . . First of all, I want to apologize to you," she said, standing on the sidewalk on Nineteenth Street. I was confused; I had never laid eyes on her before. She continued, "I've had the article about you on my fridge for weeks. Since I didn't have any money to help you out, I thought I couldn't do anything for you at all. And then last night, I was doing my daughter's laundry, and I thought, how silly of me, maybe you had laundry I could do for you. I mean, your parents, someone, should be helping you with these things while you're busy with school." I stared at her in disbelief. She asked again, "Well, do you? Do you have some laundry?"

Once a week, every week, she stopped by the school in her silver minivan and picked up and dropped off my clean, folded clothing, true to her word. She even added a bag of cookies most weeks. "I can't do much, Liz, but I know I can do that," she said. So while I was studying for my eleven classes, Teressa— Terry—did my laundry.

There are countless ways in which people appeared out of nowhere and supported me. When it first started happening, I didn't trust it. I didn't believe that anyone who wasn't my family or my close tribe of friends would be willing to help just because they'd read about me in the paper. I most certainly did not think that "those people," the people I had judged as "separate" from myself, would want to help someone like me. But they did. They just gave and asked for nothing back. And in doing this, they knocked every brick out of my wall. For the first time I could really see there was no difference between myself and others; we were all just people. Just as there was no real difference between people who accomplished their goals and me, as long as I was willing to do the work and able to have some help along the way.

My favorite thing that I received was a hand-stitched quilt from a lady named Debbie Fike. Attached to the beautiful quilt was a small note that read, "It gets cold in those dorms. May you warm yourself knowing that people care about you."

I wanted Harvard. Badly. When I received a letter, not accepting me but telling me that I had been wait-listed, I put on a brave front and looked on the bright side. It wasn't a rejection, so there was still a chance that I could get in. So many things in my life had changed just because I had been given a chance—I had done great at Prep, had won the *New York Times* Scholarship, and had my Angel Brigade. Going to Harvard could still be another thing on that list. But underneath the positive face I wore, part of me wondered if, after all I had come through, my luck had just run out. Was this dream simply too much to ask for?

The uncertainty frightened me. I refused to leave anything to chance, so I decided not to take this wait-listed thing lying down. Phone calls were made and letters were written on my behalf. I even managed to land a second interview and everyone pitched in to help me get ready. The staff at Prep called on New Visions, a New York–based group that helps alternative high schools like ours; they sent over a representative to take me shopping at Banana Republic so that I would have something professional to wear. Lisa and I were like two little kids in the store, laughing, tearing things off of racks, holding up clothing high for each other to see. She helped me pick out a long black skirt and dainty long-sleeved sweater. They bought me some real dress shoes too.

The second interview, like my first, went well, and things felt promising. But afterward, I still wasn't sure what would happen. I was told to expect a letter to arrive, telling me my fate. So, I waited.

Those last few weeks of high school became all about the mailman and what size envelope he would bring me. According to my teachers, a large envelope meant good news, an acceptance letter or packet stuffed with pages of orientation material and calendar dates transporting me back to those stately redbrick buildings in New England. But a small envelope, that would mean bad news, a single sheet of paper whose formal statement of rejection would appear on letterhead stamped by the crimson crest that is Harvard University's logo. That crest had appeared everywhere for me in the last few months, in my countless Internet searches, on the application materials that I labored over in empty offices of my high school, in my dreams.

Over the past several months, Harvard had become my mind's single focus. It had started out reasonably enough, with research on admission statistics, course offerings, and campus life. These inquiries, I decided, were understandable, given my status as a hopeful applicant. But being on the wait-list, the standard four-month window of time between application and answer had dragged out into six agonizing months, and that's when my fascination deteriorated into admittedly pointless and obsessive fact-finding.

For instance, who knew that during the Revolutionary War, cannonballs had been dropped right out of dormitory windows, causing huge dents in the Harvard Yard sidewalk? Also, occurring inside Harvard Yard twice a year is an event called the "Primal Scream," which is a ritual that takes place at exactly midnight on the night before final exams. Students gather in the yard to relieve their exam stress by running at least one lap around the yard, completely naked—even in the winter. The most compelling moment in my research was the day I used the Internet to map out the miles—almost two hundred exactly—between Harvard Yard and my doorstep.

Those days I spent scouring the Internet for needless information felt like progress to me. I couldn't just wait it out; I had to feel like I was doing something. It felt better reading the same information over and over than it did just sitting there.

For this very same reason, I absolutely lived for my trips to the mailbox. Each day I walked briskly from the D train on Bedford Park to my apartment building, where I jammed my key into the mailbox, eager for news. But for weeks I found nothing. During those moments, I couldn't help but feel like Ma on check day, impatient, unable to put myself at ease, pacing my apartment, as though pacing would bring the mail any sooner. As though anything I was doing in New York City would have an impact on the decision of a committee all the way in Cambridge, Massachusetts.

This pressure I put on myself was familiar to me. My whole life felt as though it had been packed with situations shaped just like this: Something crucial was at stake, the outcome could go either way, and it was up to me to change it—like those nights on University Avenue when Ma and Daddy placed themselves in danger, leaving the house at all hours of the night, while I waited by the window ready to dial 911. *Would my one emergency phone call be the difference between my parents' injury and well-being?* And when I was starving as a kid, what would have happened if I hadn't gotten a job? *Who would have fed me if I hadn't fed myself?* And now, wait-listed at Harvard, faced with agonizing uncertainty, the same questions persisted: *What would I do about it?*

From Prep, I called the office of admissions every Friday like clockwork to ask whether or not a decision had been reached and if so, had my letter been mailed, and every Friday I got the same response: "The committee has not yet rendered its final decision," but, I was "welcome to call again," and of course I should expect an answer by mail, soon.

Then one Friday, at last, something different. While she could not give out specific admission information over the phone, a secretary informed me that a decision had in fact been reached and a response had been mailed. I should receive it any day now, if it wasn't in my mailbox already. I hung up the phone and all but danced around the office at Prep; I went looking for my teachers.

For months I had hounded them incessantly with my school-related questions, and they had shown me the patience of saints. Caleb's father was a professor at Harvard, so he'd gotten the worst of it. On more than one occasion, I'd cornered Caleb after hours, in that tiny office of his, interrupting his work and mining him for information. *Does your dad know how the committee decides? Do people from the wait-list ever really get in?* Perry was another frequent recipient of my pestering. His tendency to listen carefully to others and to take time to be decisive and sincere left Perry totally vulnerable to my relentless need to talk about it. Looking back on that time now, I don't know how my teachers put up with me, when no amount of talking was enough to have me cease my worrying.

That afternoon, I scoured the office for someone I could share the news with. Luckily for them, most of the teachers were in a meeting. Only Perry was available, in his office, the same office where he'd interviewed me almost two years ago, back when I'd judged him to be one of "those people," back when I couldn't look him, or anyone, directly in the eyes. I found Perry at his desk. He looked up at me with friendly curiosity. "Well hello," he said, putting down his pen to turn toward me.

"Good news, Perry, they mailed the letter. I'm going to find out . . . It could be in my mailbox right now."

"Oh . . . Well, good," Perry responded, and he leaned back in his chair and began smiling widely at me, an amused expression across his face. "Great," he added. And then he didn't say a word, nothing else. I had expected just a little more enthusiasm than that.

"It's exciting," I said. "Isn't it?"

"Yes, Liz, it is exciting," he said, laughing a bit. His expression was more of a smirk than a smile.

"I mean, *this is it*," I said, as though to force my excitement onto him. "It's the moment . . . Soon I'll know."

Perry's expression, familiar to me from two years of being his student, told me I was about to get some advice.

"What?" I asked, smiling nervously at him. "You have this *look*." I respected Perry's opinion, and if he had some private joke in his head, I wanted to know what it was. He leaned forward and with a shrug of his shoulders he said something that will stick with me always.

"It's exciting, Liz . . . But I hope you understand that no matter where you go to school, you'll always be you. Wherever you go, college, job interviews, relationships, all of it . . . the answer from Harvard really is only incidental to who you are. So cut yourself a break . . . You really will be fine either way."

If I didn't love and trust Perry, I might have thought he was undermining something very important to me. Or, at the very least, that he was simply too privileged to understand why Harvard mattered so much for someone like me, because unlike him, I could not afford to be so casual. But I did love and respect Perry, and my trust in him told me to take his words into consideration. I nodded and said, "Okay, Perry," but I was obviously unsettled.

"Look, Liz, all I mean is, wherever you go, you'll make the best of things. Look at your life, you already have . . . That's why I know you'll be all right. . . . Try and relax, have some compassion for yourself."

Those words stopped me. The idea that I deserved or could even afford to relax, and the notion of compassion—for myself . . .

On the train ride home and in bed that night (after I returned to find nothing in my mailbox), I lay awake and mulled over Perry's words, let them echo in my head as I considered their implications. In my ceaseless fight for survival, I had simply not taken even a single moment to consider the enormity of all that had happened to me, and how I might have been impacted by it. But how could I take a moment? There had been too much to do. Every day there had been some pressing need to handle, some schoolwork to complete, some urgent problem that needed solving.

But lying in bed that night, Perry's words slowed my life's frantic pace and gave me permission to take time, not to do anything, just to think and to feel. In my darkened bedroom, alone, what surfaced was not easy. Underneath all the achievement and bustle of my life was a heartbreaking catalog of losses: Daddy surrendering me to the state with absolutely no protest; Ma in the hospital room that day, her mouth moving noiselessly over words; nights spent alone in a staircase, wondering how long it would take anyone to notice if I disappeared. Under the blankets, I lay there and allowed my feelings to take me over. I tasted the salt of my tears, let them flow, felt the places in my heart that were the most broken, and I finally allowed myself the space to mourn. I cried until I no longer had to.

When I let myself experience my sorrow and I did not resist it or cover it with any distraction, another experience surfaced. Willing to face my pain, I began to see its inverse. The invisible victories of my life came into focus: the countless acts of love toward my parents; getting myself out of bed those mornings at friends' houses to go to school; earning a paycheck that I used to take care of myself; taking the hair out of my face to risk eye contact; my loving friendships; and every single day that I kept on going, when I would so much rather not have. Accepting my sorrow, I then was able to accept my strength in the face of so much loss.

More than anything, though, I took into my heart the knowledge that I was in fact all right, as Perry had said. Terrible things had happened, but they were not happening now. I was no longer sleeping outside, but safe in my bed. And then for the first night in months, I focused on something other than my admission letter, and I let the knowledge that I was finally safe relax me to sleep.

The next day, on a sweltering Saturday in June, I took a book out to the front stoop and had a seat, where I waited for the mailman. Hours passed. The ice cream truck circled the block. I saw mothers wearing spandex pants and plastic flip-flops, clutching thick key chains, perched on stoops, eyes trained on their children. Latin music blasted from someone's speakers high up on a floor above. I tapped my foot relentlessly, sweating under the sun, ticking away at the pages of my book. I kept my eye on the corner, searching for any sight of him.

Finally, some time in the early afternoon, I looked up to find the mailman standing just four buildings away from me. I shut my book. Someone stopped him to make conversation, holding him there.

Will the envelope be big or small?

The ice cream truck pulled over and children clamored to the window ahead of their parents. Someone had opened the fire hydrant for relief from the intense heat. Nearby, teenagers bounced a basketball. I watched the mailman drawing closer, slowly. I knew that very likely in that bag he was carrying the letter. But in this moment of anticipation, I soothed myself using Perry's words, *"You'll be fine either way."*

With months of angst and worry, fret and fuss, here was the answer I'd been waiting for, and yet I did not feel the distress I expected to feel as I waited. A simple realization took its place: The letter already stated whatever it stated, and there was nothing I could do now to change that. In this moment it was clear to me that I had already done everything I could do.

God grant me the serenity to accept the things I cannot change, the courage to change the things I can, and the wisdom to know the difference . . .

Things turning around for me had been the result of my focusing on the few areas in life I could change, and surrendering to the knowledge that there were many more things that I just couldn't make different.

I could not rescue Sam from her family life, but I could be her friend. I could never change Carlos, but I could leave that relationship and take care of myself. I couldn't heal my parents, as much as I wanted to, but I could forgive and love them.

I could also choose to carve out a life for myself that was in no way limited by what had already occurred in my past.

Watching the mailman approach, I realized that the letter from Harvard, whatever it would reveal, would not make or break my life. Instead, what I was beginning to understand was that however things unfolded from here on, whatever the next chapter was, my life could never be the sum of one circumstance. It would be determined, as it had always been, by my willingness to put one foot in front of the other, moving forward, come what may.

Epilogue

I WAS SEATED IN THE MAIN EXHIBIT HALL OF A CONFERENCE CENTER in Buenos Aires, Argentina, one person in a crowd of people waiting for the Dalai Lama to take the stage. It was the thick of summer and the air conditioning was weak, so my skirt suit got itchy, causing me to shift in my seat, which was near the front, stage-side. I had to strain to find a good view over the heads of the people in front of me, an audience of top-performing CEOs from different countries around the world. Seven hundred of them had gathered for their annual conference of networking and inspiration; the Dalai Lama was their keynote address. After him, I would take the stage as the next presenter.

As the Dalai Lama spoke, a handful of CEOs had the rare opportunity to ask him questions. Most of the inquiries were complex—political or philosophical in nature—and in response, the Dalai Lama gave generously of his time. With the help of a translator, his Holiness took nearly ten to fifteen minutes to answer each question in painstaking detail. When his time finally drew to a close, a point person searched the room to choose who would get to ask the final question. As a fellow presenter that day, that person happened to be me. I was allowed to ask the Dali Lama a single question. But what would I ask? All eyes fell on me in the hushed exhibit hall; hundreds of CEOs and his Holiness himself stared and waited. What happened next would turn out to reveal one of the greatest life lessons I have ever learned. But I will get back to that lesson later.

First, a little explanation of how that day came to be. That day with the Dalai Lama became yet another occurrence in my life that caused my friends in the Bronx to tease me with my nickname: "Forrest Gump." Over the years, they have grown used to me traveling to various countries, working with thousands of people to deliver workshops and speeches to inspire others. In New York City I founded and currently direct Manifest Living, a company that empowers adults to create lives that are most meaningful to them. In doing this work, it just so happened, I found a path that has become most meaningful to me.

I had no idea things would turn out this way. It started after the *New York Times* article; other media followed. There were magazine articles, awards, a half-hour *20/20* special, and even a Lifetime Television movie, *Homeless to Harvard: The Liz Murray Story*. What unfolded from there was a series of events so rich and detailed that they cannot be told in this short space—they are another story altogether. What I can say here is that my years at Harvard up until my graduation in 2009 were packed with experiences that taught me lessons about the strength of the human spirit; the truth that people from all walks of life face adversity and must learn to overcome it. Ultimately these experiences inspired me to develop workshops designed to empower people to change their own lives, which is my passion, and the work that I dedicate my life to today.

Over the years, I traveled, took part-time study, full-time study, and even year-long breaks in my education, and I kept my home base in New York City, where the biggest grounding force in my life became my relationships with friends and the time I spent caring for my father.

Daddy quit drugs after he was diagnosed HIV positive. His shelter played a vital role in connecting him to the right medical resources for each one of his illnesses. When all was said and done, after more than thirty years of hardcore drug abuse, Daddy was HIV positive, his heart needed massive repair requiring open-heart surgery, he had hepatitis C, and over three quarters of his liver was cirrhotic, gnarled as a calcified sponge.

One afternoon, in the middle of one of my early semesters at college, I was walking through Harvard Yard when I received a phone call about Daddy from a doctor who spoke in a hushed voice that told me it was serious. As Peter Finnerty's medical proxy, I'd "better hurry to New York before it was too late," he said. Daddy had had a heart attack and was on life support. I rushed for a bus to get to him (a trip that had become routine) and, shortly after I arrived, the priest stood over Daddy's bed, reading him his last rites. I held Daddy's hand and searched his face for signs of life, but his eyes were shut tight and the tubes through which he was breathing just pushed his chest up and down, his forehead crinkled as though frozen in worry.

Somehow, Daddy survived this and other brushes with death, and so my friends—who helped care for him and who also liked to tease Daddy to keep him in high spirits—gave him a nickname, something that made Daddy chuckle after they removed the intubation tube: "Peter Infinity," for his ability to survive a mountain of life-threatening medical conditions. He found the name so funny that when the nurse signed his discharge papers he repeated it to her, trying (unsuccessfully) to get her to laugh, insisting out loud that he had "more lives than a cat." I wheeled Daddy out the sliding doors of Mt. Sinai Hospital onto the sunny streets of New York City, and from that moment on I took full responsibility for his care.

Once it became clear that death was a constant possibility for Daddy, I asked him to move in with me in my New York apartment. He required a firm regimen of medical care to keep him alive, which included rotations to the key doctors, ongoing blood work, constant (often painful) medical exams, chemotherapy for his Hep C, and, to help contain the viral load of his HIV, antiretroviral meds as well. Or the "cocktail," as his doctors called it—medication made available to HIV patients only after Ma had died. Getting Daddy's needs met, staying on track in college, and traveling internationally to deliver my workshops and speeches shaped the next few years of my life. There were many ups and downs during this period, and I could not have gotten through it without the love of my friends.

The support that sprang up around me was nothing short of a miracle. Through every twist and turn in our lives, my friends and I were there for one another and in the process, we truly became a family. There were my longtime friends like Bobby, Eva, James, Jamie, Sam, and Josh, and also new ones who came to stay, like Ruben and Edwin. We celebrated birthdays and holidays together, and even lent a hand with one another's families when it was needed. On any given day I could come in from Boston to find Daddy at home watching the latest episode of *Law & Order* in the living room with Edwin sitting beside him; they would be splitting a bag of cookies and laughing together.

Whenever I had to travel or be away at school, Edwin (Ed), whom I met through Eva, faithfully took Daddy to all of his medical appointments, bought and carried Daddy's groceries, and made sure he had clean clothing and hot meals. More than that, he became Daddy's friend. Ed and I purposefully kept apartments within walking distance of one another in New York and whenever I could be home, we spent our days taking trips to the local diner with Daddy, or to the movies, where we helped Daddy sneak his contraband Snickers bars and water bottle into the theater. Ed and I shared a smile each time Daddy unwrapped the candy bars before the flickering movie screen with a pleased little smirk across his face. In those moments I do believe Ed and I witnessed in Daddy a glimmer of pride for outsmarting "the man" just one more time in his life.

Lisa and Sam ultimately landed on their feet. Today, Sam is happily married and lives in Madison, Wisconsin, with her husband. After years of struggle and her own ups and downs, Lisa successfully graduated from Purchase College in New York State. Today, she is a schoolteacher for autistic children. Jamie has two children and is married, living in Nevada. Bobby is in school studying to be a nurse, and he is happily married with two children. We remain essential parts of each other's lives.

In the last few years of Daddy's life, after I had spent some time away from school to live in New York and see him through heart surgery, I returned to Cambridge to complete college, and Daddy came with me. We rented a five-bedroom house near Harvard, one bedroom for each of us: Ed, Ruben, Ed's little cousin whom he took care of, Daddy, and me. Just a month before Daddy died, Ed and I took him on a long-awaited trip to San Francisco. Daddy insisted on showing us areas he said were meaningful to him in his youth. We never asked for details, and he didn't offer any. Ed and I just followed Daddy to his favorite spots: Haight-Ashbury, Alcatraz, and his beloved City Lights Bookstore. Together, we stood before old wooden shelves where Daddy skimmed the pages of Allen Ginsberg's and Jack Kerouac's books, privately smiling at familiar passages. When we flew back to Boston at the end of that week, and I was alone in my room, I found a card that Daddy secretly put inside my suitcase. It read:

"Lizzy, I left my dreams behind a long time ago, but I know now that they are safe with you. Thank you for making us a family again."

I taped the card high up above my desk, right where I did all my papers and school assignments, so that I could look at it while I worked. Each time I saw Daddy's familiar bold script, it filled me with love for my father and a certain peace, knowing that he was nearby, warm and safe.

Just three weeks later, Daddy went to sleep upstairs, and he did not wake up. His heart gave out in his sleep. Daddy was eight years sober and sixty-four years old when he died. For much of those eight years, he led a weekly "relapse prevention group" for recovering addicts, and he kept a tight circle of friends from the group whom he loved dearly. The night he died in my apartment, I found myself in my bedroom surrounded by friends. Eva, Ruben, Ed, and a couple more friends dragged two extra mattresses into my bedroom so that we could huddle near one another under blankets and talk. We shut the door tight so that Ed and I would not have to hear the crackle of policemen's walkie-talkies and the medical examiner carrying Daddy out of our home.

By Daddy's request, he was cremated. On Father's Day, Lisa, Edwin, Ruben, Eva, and I spread his ashes throughout Greenwich Village, stopping to place small handfuls of ash at each of his favorite spots: the doorstep of a friend's building, in front of his methadone clinic, and on the block where he first lived with Ma back before they ever had children. Then we took the rest of his ashes and mixed them with rose petals, and sent them out to the sea off the boardwalk in Battery Park. The pink petals floated away in the receding sunlight that evening, and Lisa, my friends, and I sat on a bench leaning on one another, sharing stories of our favorite memories of Daddy. Quietly, Ed reached down and squeezed my hand, tight, and I knew we were both heartbroken but also proud that Daddy died happy, surrounded by people who love him.

When I graduated from college, my friends Dick and Patty threw me a party at their home in Newton, Massachusetts, and Lisa and all my friends came out to celebrate. When they brought out the cake I looked up to see a ring of support surrounding me, the faces of loved ones old and new, everywhere: Lisa, Ruben, Anthony, Ed, Eva, Shari, Bobby, Su, Felice, Dick and Patty, Mary and Eddie, all singing in celebration. I stood there and took them in, my patchwork family, and I loved each of them. In that moment, I could feel my heart opened by the love I first knew from Ma and Daddy, the same love I felt staring at my friends; the love I feel for all of my family still.

On the day that I had just one question to ask the Dalai Lama, here's what I asked. I wanted to know: "Your Holiness, you inspire so many people, but what inspires you?" He paused and leaned over for a moment to talk with his translator. Then His Holiness turned to me and with a lighthearted laugh he said, "I don't know, I am just a simple monk." The enormous conference hall erupted into giggles and whispers. It was by far the shortest time he'd spent answering any question that day, and it did not go unnoticed. With that, the Dalai Lama's speech ended abruptly, he was whisked backstage, and the CEOs and I dispersed for a break into the crowded lobby. And that's when the real lesson from that morning hit me, through the reactions I experienced from others.

Walking in the massive marble lobby among the crowd of executives, I was trying to sort out what had just happened when all of a sudden, one by one, the CEOs approached to tell me what they *knew* His Holiness had actually meant by his answer. First, a gruff man in his forties approached me and said, "I'll tell you, it was very Zen of the Dalai Lama, the way he talked to you, very Zen. His answer was all about *simplicity*." A tall woman in a power suit was next. "It's deep," she said, "the *not-knowingness* of it all. As a monk, he is okay with the ignorance inherent in the human condition." And next, a tall man with a furrowed brow, obviously angry, said, "Liz, he didn't answer you about what inspires him because he didn't want to lower himself to our level. It's arrogance!"

Nearly a dozen executives came to me during the short break and interpreted, with certainty, the *meaning* of the Dalai Lama's answer. Until finally, later on, backstage, when I was being miked for my own speech, one of the Dalai Lama's stagehands found me to apologize. "Sorry, Liz," he said, "the interpreter fumbled your question and His Holiness wasn't able to understand you, because, well . . . *we goofed*. Oops."

It turns out there was actually *no* meaning whatsoever to the Dalai Lama's answer. Or rather, there was no meaning beyond the one each person had assigned it. What's more, each person had witnessed the very same exchange, and not one of them came away with the same interpretation.

Standing there ready for my speech, I peeked out onto the crowd, and I smiled inside. Much more than the differences between people, what was so clear to me in that moment, instead, were our similarities: the tendency for people to make meaning of their experiences. Like my certainty of my love for Ma and Daddy; or the moment I finally trusted that I could, in fact, change my life. The executives were certain of their interpretations of the Dalai Lama, just as my homeless friends were once certain that there was simply "no way out." Not unlike the belief I once held that "a wall" blocked me from my dreams, the same walls I watch tumble down when participants in my workshops finally decide that the only time to embrace life fully is now.

As I stepped out into the bright lights before the room of executives crowding the enormous exhibit hall, I took them in, marveling at one thing I know for sure: homeless person or business person, doctor or teacher, whatever your background may be, the same holds true for each of us: life takes on the meaning that you give it.

ACKNOWLEDGMENTS

THE DEEPEST GRATITUDE GOES OUT TO A POWERHOUSE TEAM OF people at Hyperion, whose patience and faith saw this book through to fruition. In particular, I am grateful to my editor, Leslie Wells, for her diligent work and heartfelt vision, which she poured onto these pages. I am equally grateful to Ellen Archer and Elisabeth Dyssegaard for their support and commitment to this book. Thank you for hanging in there with me, for your backing and belief in my story. You ladies have the patience of saints.

Thank you to my agent, Alan Nevins at Renaissance, who was there with me from the beginning. What can I say, Alan? From the start, you believed in what was possible with my story and then you went and made it happen. I am so grateful to you.

I am proud to acknowledge and thank author Travis Montez for his invaluable insight, edits, and hard work that were key to making *Breaking Night* possible. Travis, thanks for the many late nights, for being count-on-able, for lending your time and exceptional talent for poetry to the details of this project. This book would not be the same without you.

Thanks to my dear friend and sister, Eva Bitter, for helping lay the foundation of this book. Eva, your insights and edits were key in shaping the expression of my story, and your support and love throughout the years have given me the courage to tell it. I love you.

Much love and gratitude to my dear friend and brother, Robert Bender, who has been nothing less than completely supportive of my dreams from day one, including this book. Bobby, thank you for your unwavering love all these years, and for being my family. Here's to many more years to come.

A very special thank you to my dear friend Ruben, my "FP." Ruben, this book and so much of the person I am today is because of you. I am forever grateful for your tireless support and unconditional love, for you opening your heart and your family to me. There are no proper words to express what you mean to me, Ruben. I love you, *siempre*.

Love and appreciation to my sister, Lisa Murray, whose life also appears in the pages of this book. Lisa, thank you for your support throughout all these years. It was your love of writing that first inspired me to pick up my own pen, and I am grateful to you. I love you.

Thank you to "Sam," whose life also appears in the pages of this book and whose friendship got me through some of my darkest moments. Sam, I love you.

The utmost appreciation to Alan Goldberg from *20/20*, whose commitment and vision took my story from a handful of newspaper articles into the homes of millions of people, where it could make a difference in the lives of others. Alan, during that whirlwind of an experience, I want to thank you for your kindness. Your compassionate response to my family left an impression on my heart that I will never forget.

Absolute gratitude to Christine Farrell, president of Washington Speakers Bureau, for her love and unconditional support in helping me share my message over the years to thousands of people throughout the world. Christine, when it was time to take care of my father and follow my dreams at the same time, your tireless work and solid friendship lifted me up and made it all possible. There is no way to measure or express the difference you have been in my life. Thank you.

I want to thank my high school teacher, Perry, who appears in this book, for dedicating so much of his life to teaching. Perry, what greater gift could you have given us students than your passion? Thank you for your part in making Humanities Preparatory Academy a place where anyone can come in earnest to enrich their mind and soul, and belong to a community that accepts and uplifts them.

Equally heartfelt gratitude goes out to my teachers at Prep. This book and much of my life simply would not be the same without your care and commitment to your students. The deepest thank you to Vincent Brevetti, Jessie Klein, Douglas Knecht, Caleb Perkins, Elijah Hawkes, Maria Hantzopoulos, Jorge Cordero, Susan Petrey, Christina Kemp, and Matt Holzer.

Thank you to Elizabeth Garrison, and her sons, my Puerto Rican brothers, Rick, Danny, John, and Sean, whose names appear in these pages and who fed, housed, and loved me like one of their own. I love each of you and want you to know that I am forever grateful for the difference you have made in my life. We will always be family.

There are a handful of people who opened their homes to me when I had nowhere else to go, and who fed me, in some cases, with the very last of their food. I am so grateful to you: Elizabeth Garrison, Paula Smajlaj, Julia Brignoni, Maria "Cookie" Porras, Martha Haddock, Margaret S., Jerzy Bitter, Daniel Lachica, and Michelle Brown.

Special thanks to my friend and fellow speaker Tony Litster for his generous advice and time spent laboring over these pages into the wee hours of the morning. Thank you, Tony.

Thank you to the *New York Times* Scholarship Program for their commitment to supporting students who are working hard to better their lives. Though I know this list will fall short of all the folks at the *Times* who made a difference in my life, I would like to give special thanks to: Arthur Gelb, Jack Rosenthal, Nancy Sharkey, Jan Sidorowicz, Dana Canedy, Cory Dean, the late Gerald Boyd, Chip McGrath, Bob Harris, Sheila Rule, Bill Schmidt, and Roger Lehecka. One way or another, I have witnessed and been moved by your dedication to seeing young people break through boundaries of poverty and move onto lives wide open with possibility. Thank you for the difference you have made.

I would like to particularly thank some of my friends and family for their support year after year, through thick and thin, as I worked on this book. Whether directly or indirectly, your love and encouragement has held me up in a way that made this book possible. I love you guys: Bobby, Ruben, Edwin, Eva, Dave Santana, Chris, James, Shari Moy, Lisa, Arthur, Jamie, Josh, Ramiro, Felice, Fief, Ray, Melvin Miller, Dick and Patty Simon, Jaci Lebherz, Mary Gauthier, Ed Romanoff, Travis Montez, Robin Diane Lynn, Robinson Lynn, Dick Silberman, Lisa Layne, and Lawrence Field.

Last but not least, thank you to Stan Curtis and Blessings in a Backpack, for allowing me to be a spokesperson and dedicated advocate for your cause of feeding hungry children across America. If only I'd had access to a program like Blessings in a Backpack when I was an undernourished child in New York City, I may not have gone to bed hungry all those nights. Thankfully, with your continued commitment, thousands of children across America won't have to.

Dear Reader,

Today, it is my life's purpose and passion to deliver workshops and speeches that empower others to lead their best lives. Nothing brings me more joy than seeing people overcome obstacles to succeed. For this reason, I've created a free video series for my readers where I share stories, ideas, and tools designed to inspire you. These videos are available on my website. To join in the conversation about reclaiming your vitality and achieving your dreams, I'd like to personally invite you to: www.homelesstoharvard.com

I look forward to connecting with you there.

In the meantime, I wish you every blessing.

Joy & Love to You,

Liz Murray